On Adam Smith's *Wealth of Nations*

On Adam Smith's
Wealth of Nations

A Philosophical Companion

Samuel Fleischacker

PRINCETON UNIVERSITY PRESS
Princeton and Oxford

Copyright © 2004 by Princeton University Press
Published by Princeton University Press, 41 William Street, Princeton, New Jersey 08540
In the United Kingdom: Princeton University Press, 3 Market Place,
Woodstock, Oxfordshire OX20 1SY

Third printing, and first paperback printing, 2005
Paperback ISBN-13: 978-0-691-12390-5
Paperback ISBN-10: 0-691-12390-X

The Library of Congress has cataloged the cloth edition of this book as follows

Fleischacker, Samuel.
 On Adam Smith's Wealth of nations : a philosophical companion / Samuel Fleischacker.
  p. cm.
 Includes bibliographical references and index.
 ISBN-13: 978-0-691-11502-3 (cl : alk. paper)
 ISBN-10: 0-691-11502-8 (cl : alk. paper)
  1. Smith, Adam, 1723–1790. 2. Economics—Philosophy. 3. Ethics. I. Title.

 HB103.S6F59 2004
 330.15′3—dc21   2003042889

British Library Cataloging-in-Publication Data is available

This book has been composed in Berkeley Book

Printed on acid-free paper. ∞

pup.princeton.edu

Printed in the United States of America

10 9 8 7 6 5 4 3

In memory of my parents

CONTENTS

PART V
Politics

Epilogue

ACKNOWLEDGMENTS

This book was begun during a year's leave underwritten by the University Center for Human Values at Princeton and the John M. Olin Foundation. More recently, a year at the Institute for the Humanities at the University of Illinois, Chicago provided me with the time and support to complete the book. I would also like to thank Kate Abramson, Thomas Brockelman, Lauren Brubaker, Lisa Downing, Charles Griswold, Ryan Hanley, David Hilbert, Rachana Kamtekar, Deirdre McCloskey, Jerry Muller, Amy Reichert, Ian Ross, Eric Schliesser, and Jeff Weintraub for helpful comments and criticism. Lori Watson provided both useful comments and extremely efficient research assistance. In addition to her editorial help, my wife, Amy Reichert, has borne the irritations attendant on writing a book with wonderful patience and understanding.

ABBREVIATIONS

When citing Smith, I will use page numbers, rather than the subdivisions provided in the standard Glasgow edition. I also include in the text references to all the works listed below by abbreviation and page number. If I cite a text several times in a row, in a single paragraph, I provide its abbreviation the first time and include only a page number for subsequent citations.

Works by Adam Smith

Corr   *Correspondence of Adam Smith*, ed. E. C. Mossner, Ian Simpson Ross (New York: Oxford University Press, second edition, 1987).

ED   "Early Draft" of the *Wealth of Nations*, included in LJ.

EPS   *Essays on Philosophical Subjects*, ed. W.P.D. Wightman, J. C. Bryce (Oxford: Oxford University Press, 1980); first published (posthumously) in 1795.

LJ   *Lectures on Jurisprudence*, ed. R. L. Meek, D. D. Raphael, P. G. Stein (Oxford: Oxford University Press, 1978). Unpublished in the author's lifetime.

LRBL   *Lectures on Rhetoric and Belles-Lettres,* ed. J. C. Bryce (Oxford: Oxford University Press, 1983). Unpublished in the author's lifetime.

TMS   *Theory of Moral Sentiments*, ed. D. D. Raphael, A. L. Macfie (Oxford: Oxford University Press, 1976); first published in 1759.

WN   *An Inquiry into the Nature and Causes of the Wealth of Nations*, ed. R. H. Campbell, A. S. Skinner, W. B. Todd (Oxford: Oxford University Press, 1976); first published in 1776.

Other Works

ASD   Vivienne Brown, *Adam Smith's Discourse* (London: Routledge, 1994).

ASP   Donald Winch, *Adam Smith's Politics* (Cambridge: Cambridge University Press, 1978).

AVE   Charles Griswold, *Adam Smith and the Virtues of Enlightenment* (Cambridge: Cambridge University Press, 1999).

E   David Hume, *Enquiries*, ed. L. A. Selby-Bigge, P. H. Nidditch, third edition (Oxford: Clarendon, 1975).

ES   Emma Rothschild, *Economic Sentiments* (Cambridge: Harvard University Press, 2001).

LNN   Samuel Pufendorf, *The Law of Nature and Nations*, trans. C. H. and W. A. Oldfather (Oxford: Clarendon Press, 1934).

LWP   Hugo Grotius, *The Law of War and Peace*, trans. F. W. Kelsey (Indianapolis: Bobbs-Merrill, 1925).

NE   Aristotle, *Nicomachean Ethics,* as translated in Jonathan Barnes (ed.), *The Complete Works of Aristotle* (Princeton: Princeton University Press, 1984).

NJ   Istvan Hont and Michael Ignatieff, "Needs and Justice in the *Wealth of Nations*," in *Wealth and Virtue*, Hont and Ignatieff (eds.) (Cambridge: Cambridge University Press, 1983).

NL   Knud Haakonssen, *Natural Law and Moral Philosophy* (Cambridge: Cambridge University Press, 1996).

OB,   Francis Hutcheson, *Inquiry into the Original of Our Ideas of Beauty and*
OV   *Virtue* (London: J. Darby, 1726); OB for the treatise on beauty, OV for the treatise on virtue.

PE   Joseph Cropsey, *Polity and Economy*, second edition (South Bend: St. Augustine's Press, 2001).

RP   Donald Winch, *Riches and Poverty* (Cambridge: Cambridge University Press, 1996).

SI   Frances Hutcheson, *A Short Introduction to Moral Philosophy* (Glasgow: R. Foulis, 1747).

SL   Knud Haakonssen, *The Science of the Legislator* (Cambridge: Cambridge University Press, 1981).

SMP   Frances Hutcheson, *A System of Moral Philosophy* (London: A. Millar, 1755).

ST   John Locke, *Second Treatise of Government* (any edition will do: references are by chapter and section number).

T   David Hume, *Treatise of Human Nature*, eds. L. A. Selby-Bigge and P. H. Nidditch, second edition (Oxford: Clarendon, 1978).

INTRODUCTION

Adam Smith was a philosopher before he was a social scientist, yet it remains unclear to this day what relationship his philosophical writings bear to his treatise on economics. There is little indication in the *Inquiry into the Nature and Causes of the Wealth of Nations* (WN) that the book was written by a person who had rich views on subjects ranging from scientific method to the foundation of moral judgment, and there is no explicit mention at all of Smith's earlier published work, the much-acclaimed *Theory of Moral Sentiments* (TMS). The apparent absence of moral concerns, in particular, from WN has puzzled many commentators. Perhaps we should view the writing of WN as a triumph of self-command, Smith's favorite virtue: Smith contributes to the founding of social science precisely by *refraining* from direct moral commentary most of the time in WN, by laying out the facts of political economy mostly in an impartial tone, free of his own attitudes toward those facts. But, if so, he seems to have achieved this impartial voice too well, leading people, wrongly, to suppose that he left his moral beliefs behind when he came to write WN. It is part of my purpose to help correct this supposition, to help bring us back to the virtues that lie within and just beyond the frame of WN. Social science today often requires that one refrain from talking about virtues, but Smith does not fully carry out this suspension of moral discourse, and where he does I think we can give moral reasons for the suspension. In any case, one thing that will concern us throughout this book is the tension between moral philosophy and social science.

There are several other running themes. Among them: that Smith is best regarded as a "common sense" philosopher, anticipating elements in the thought of his academic successor, Thomas Reid, and certain trends in twentieth-century philosophy; that Smith has an unusually strong belief in human equality, which has important implications for both his moral philosophy and his political economy; and that Smith played a role very different from the one usually assigned to him in the history of distributive justice. But my goal in this book is not to explicate or defend any overarching thesis about Smith; it is, rather, to provide a guide to the many philosophical questions that inform WN or are raised by its conclusions. (The book is indeed meant to be readable in separate sections, such that someone interested in Smith's views of justice, for instance, could read that section without the rest.) I hope that such a guide will be useful not just to experts, but to people coming to WN for the first time, or who have studied its political economy but never considered it from a philosophical angle.

Although Smith was a philosopher, no book of this sort has appeared before. Charles Griswold has given us a beautiful study of Smith's entire corpus from a philosophical perspective, and there is a careful and thorough examination of Smith's views on justice by Knud Haakonssen.[1] There are also one or two short philosophical surveys of all of Smith's work.[2] But the overwhelming bulk of commentary on WN has come from economists and intellectual historians, and thus far there has been no book devoted to that work by a philosopher.[3]

Economists tend to argue with Smith on matters of fact rather than of principle, whereas intellectual historians tend to be more interested in the sources of an idea, or its impact, than in its justification or its implications for future times. When I call the present study a "philosophical" companion, I mean both that I take up issues in WN that are likely to concern philosophers and that I have tried to address those issues in the *way* that philosophers do. That means that my interests are above all in the arguments Smith gives for his views, and that I sometimes reconstruct his arguments in modern terms, and argue with him when it seems to me that he holds a problematic view. I hope to stimulate questions about Smith as much as to answer such questions. Many of the difficulties in Smith's views and arguments arise from the fact that he was dealing with questions that remain difficult for us today. One model for my writing on Smith is his own account of other philosophers in Book VII of TMS. Smith respects his predecessors and reports their views faithfully, yet at the same time he translates those views into the terms of his own moral system and criticizes them where, by his lights, they fail. This is an excellent example of the philosophical history of philosophy. Philosophers tend to bring all ideas into the present tense, to look at each other's work as if the author were alive right now and trying to persuade us of his or her ideas. They are rightly accused, sometimes, of being too uninterested in historical context when they do this, but on the other hand, it is hard to see why reasoning is worthwhile at all if ideas are merely determined by their context—if we cannot, by way of argument, rise on occasion above the prejudices and concerns of our time. That this is possible is an essential part of a philosopher's faith, perhaps even part of the definition of "philosophy," as that term has been understood since Socrates.

I do not mean by these remarks to dismiss the importance of a historical perspective on Smith, and I have tried throughout to place his ideas in the context of those who influenced him, especially his teacher Francis Hutcheson and friend David Hume. I agree very much with Quentin Skinner that one cannot discern a writer's meaning unless one places his or her writings in the polemical context to which they responded. Yet those who follow Skinner on this have obscured the degree to which philosophers, unlike, say, political pamphleteers, see themselves as belonging not *just* to the polemical context of their day but also to a polemical context that spans millennia. Smith sees himself as arguing with Plato as well as James Steuart, Aristotle as well as Quesnay. He lives in two contexts: the immediate one of the eighteenth-century policies and institutions around him, and a larger one of questions that concern human beings in every age. What he says as an inhabitant of the second context we can and must bring into conversation with what we ourselves say in that capacity.

What he says as an inhabitant of eighteenth-century Europe can be brought into our own world only with considerably more caution. I try to strike a balance between these two aspects of his writing, between what he said to his contemporaries and what he might say to us. We can learn from Adam Smith today, but to do so, we need to distinguish carefully between his local and his universal teachings.

PART I

Methodology

CHAPTER ONE

Literary Method

I begin with Smith's writing style, since I will contend throughout this book that scholars have persistently misread the *Wealth of Nations* (WN), and I'd like to show right off why it is easy to do that. WN tends to appear, in both scholarly and popular literature, by way of striking snippets. One can properly grasp its teachings, however, only by engaging in the painstaking exercise of reading the long, elaborate arguments from which the snippets get snipped. So I begin with some warnings about how not to read Smith and some suggestions about what can be gained by submitting to the discipline of reading Smith slowly, of treating him as the refined eighteenth-century belles-lettrist that he set out to be.

By comparison with most philosophers, Adam Smith is easy to read. There is no abstract jargon, as in Kant or Hegel, no stilted syntax, as in Locke, and there are few passages with the subtle argumentation to be found in Descartes or Hume. Smith the economist is also easier to read than many other social scientists, abjuring technical coinages and mathematical algorithms in favor of historical narrative and explanations, laced with vivid examples drawn from ordinary life. Smith also organizes his material very clearly, announcing in the beginning of a chapter or section which two or three items he will be discussing and then proceeding to take up those items one by one, in the order in which he listed them. I suspect that many scholars are drawn to working on Smith by the ease and pleasure of reading him, and he has certainly thereby lent himself to quotation, by everyone from teachers of elementary economics to public intellectuals.

The clarity of these quotations can be misleading, however. This is partly because Smith is, even on the surface, a more complex writer than might appear from such famous lines as the one about appealing to the self-interest of butchers and bakers. In addition, Smith was well aware of the uses of rhetoric, and his seeming straightforwardness does not preclude him from making use of a variety of literary devices, either for polemical purposes or to add levels of suggested meaning to his literal one. Finally, the very project of writing philosophy and political economy in appealing, everyday language flows from a sophisticated theory about how human knowledge works, which itself needs to be grasped in order to make clear the full import of Smith's teachings. Let us take up each of these factors in turn.

1. Obstacles to Reading Smith

When I say that Smith's writing is more complex than it seems even on a surface level, I mean above all to draw attention to his irony and his prolixity, two features of his style that are not uncommon in eighteenth-century writers, but that are rather more pronounced, and carry more weight, in Smith than in many of his peers. Smith's conception of morality made the way one expresses one's emotions central to virtue, and he believed strongly that modes of literary expression could reflect character. In his lectures on rhetoric he told his students, "When the characters of a plain and a simple man are so different we may naturally expect that the stile they express themselves in will be far from being the same" (LRBL 38).[1] Cicero's elegance and propriety make evident, he says, "that the author conceive[d] himself to be of importance, and dignity" (LRBL 159). Xenophon's style expresses his "simplicity and innocence of manners" (LRBL 169). We may, accordingly, expect the ironic and prolix features of Smith's style to express something about his character, or at least about the character he wished to present to his readers. And in any case we must be careful, as many readers have not been, to recognize Smith's irony when we see it, and to unpack his unhurried way of getting to a point, or we will misunderstand even the literal level of his meaning.

The irony is sometimes obvious: "The fortunate and the proud wonder at the insolence of human wretchedness, that it should dare to present itself before them, and with the loathsome aspect of its misery presume to disturb the serenity of their happiness" (TMS 51).

But on other occasions it can be hard to tell whether Smith is being ironic or not. About love, he says that "[t]he passion appears to every body, but the man who feels it, entirely disproportioned to the value of the object," and that "though a lover may be good company to his mistress, he is so to nobody else" (TMS 31). Is this simply supposed to describe a fact about love, or does it include some gentle mockery of that passion?

In pondering this question, we should bear in mind two points. First, Smith was a great admirer of Jonathan Swift, who was supremely gifted at stating the most outrageous of propositions in the most moderate of tones. Often, Smith emulates this tight-lipped way of conveying moral outrage. It fits well with his theory of how to express emotions, and especially anger, in *The Theory of Moral Sentiments* (TMS): to win the sympathy of our audience, he says, we must "lower [. . . our] passion to that pitch, in which the spectators are capable of going along with [us]" (TMS 22; on anger specifically, see 37–8). But Smith also differs from Swift in an important respect, and that brings us to a second reason for his understated tone. Swift, in part perhaps out of a gloomy disposition and in part, certainly, out of deep Pauline convictions, is willing to condemn human nature entirely. Smith's strongly naturalistic orientation, his belief that moral standards—the very standards we might use to condemn human nature—arise out of human nature itself, leads him instead to try to understand what good purposes even bad features of human nature might serve. The difficulty of this commitment is something he worries about explicitly. He says, for instance, about our reaction to the consistently sorrowful person: "we . . . despise him; unjustly, perhaps, if any sentiment could be regarded as unjust, to which we are by nature irresistibly determined" (TMS 49). Knud Haakonssen nicely describes a passage in Smith on one of our natural tendencies as a "piece of teasing, double-edged scepticism" (SL 81), and that description captures Smith's stance toward natural human impulses throughout his work. On the one hand, he sees some of them as foolish or dangerous, as leading us away from virtue and happiness. On the other hand, *as* something natural, they cannot simply be rejected. An ironic distance may enable us to moderate their force, or to see ways of acting against them, and he gently urges us to achieve such a distance. But he also wants us to recognize that our natural tendencies will not go away, even when we do achieve ironic distance from them, that we are "irresistibly determined" to be drawn by them. We need to reconcile ourselves to that fact even while trying to avoid the pitfalls to which they lead us. A Socratic irony— or, better, what Kierkegaard would later call "humor" as opposed to irony[2]—can encourage this wry acceptance of what we cannot change. Rather than railing against human nature, Smith would have us adopt a humorous, unanxious attitude toward our own failings, a resolution to work against them where possible conjoined with a clear-eyed acceptance of the fact that they will never fully disappear, hence the odd ambiguity in passages like the remarks on love quoted above.

This ironic stance and tone pervade TMS, but show up to a significant extent in WN as well. There are some obviously ironic moments. "The laudable motive" of a series of mercantile regulations, Smith says, "is to extend our own manufactures, not by their own improvement, but by the depression of those of all our neighbours, and by putting an end, as much as possible, to the troublesome competition of such odious and disagreeable rivals" (WN 660; see also 555). Sometimes, as in this example, the irony is tinged with anger; at other times, it shades toward simple humor: "After all that has been said of the levity and inconstancy of human nature, it appears evidently from experience that a man is of all sorts of luggage the most difficult to be transported" (WN 92). There are also moments that partake of the ambiguity between irony and plain description entailed by Smith's general outlook on the world. To mention three examples that will be important to us later on: First, to what degree should we hear an acid note in the word "wisest," given what else Smith has to say about the foolishness of commercial regulations, when he tells us that the act of navigation "is, perhaps, the wisest of all the commercial regulations of England" (WN 465)? Second, given that TMS regards "tranquillity" as essential to happiness, what is Smith telling us about the restless desire to better our condition when he says that it "comes with us from the womb, and never leaves us till we go into the grave" (WN 341)? And third, is the entire "invisible hand" account of social phenomena just a literal description of how things work, or is it also an ironic commentary on the corruption and foolishness involved in attempts to control society with a visible hand?

By Smith's prolixity I mean first the fact that Smith is given to long, complexly structured sentences. Here is a delightful example, which also exhibits the dry wit that Smith shared with Swift. Smith has just announced that "small vexations excite no sympathy":

> The man who is made uneasy by every little disagreeable incident, who is hurt if either the cook or the butler have failed in the least article of their duty, who feels every defect in the highest ceremonial of politeness, whether it be shewn to himself or to any other person, who takes it amiss that his intimate friend did not bid him good-morrow when they met in the forenoon, and that his brother hummed a tune all the time he himself was telling a story; who is put out of humour by the badness of the weather when in the country, by the badness of the roads when upon a journey, and by the want of company, and dulness of all the public diversions when in town; such a person, I say, though he should have some reason, will seldom meet with much sympathy. (TMS 42)

It is helpful to read this passage aloud. One then realizes just how much Smith is fond not merely of detailed visual images but of elaborate rhythmic patterns, with parallel clauses ("who is . . . ," "who feels . . . ," "who takes . . .") interspersed with an occasional clause that has another clause nested within it, and with longish clauses at first yielding to shorter ones at the end, the whole being drawn together, and relieved of the tension built up by the long wait for the main verb, by the brief summary after the semicolon. Anglophone writing in the eighteenth century prized this kind of complex composition as the height of elegance. Today, clipped, ascetic prose is favored instead, and scholars tend to cut many of the subsidiary clauses and phrases when quoting Smith. I do this myself; I worry about my editors growling if I leave the original quotations intact. But the many clauses in Smith's sentences are sometimes all needed for his philosophical purposes, and we may do him an injustice when we make these cuts. Take another example:

> As ignorant and groundless praise can give no solid joy, no satisfaction that will bear any serious examination, so, on the contrary, it often gives real comfort to reflect, that though no praise should actually be bestowed upon us, our conduct, however, has been such as to deserve it, and has been in every respect suitable to those measures and rules by which praise and approbation are naturally and commonly bestowed. (TMS 115)

The length of this sentence can be explained in part by considerations of elegance. The second clause—"no satisfaction that will bear any serious examination"—is there mostly to balance "no solid joy," or to emphasize it, to allow us to dwell longer upon it, and "on the contrary" and "however" are there simply to give the sentence a relaxed tempo. Yet "no satisfaction that will bear any serious examination" does not *merely* add a rhythmic element; it also does something to clarify the word "solid" in "solid joy." Even the apparent redundancy in the pairs that conclude the sentence—"measures and rules," "praise and approbation," "naturally and commonly"—is not there solely for rhythmic effect. By giving us two words, Smith encourages us to think about the difference between "measures" and "rules" and the similarity between what is "natural" and what is done "commonly." Especially in TMS, we must always bear in mind the musical function of Smith's mode of expression—most of the book is drawn from a lecture course, and Smith needed rhetorical virtuosity to keep his fourteen- to sixteen-year old students alert—but these concerns do not exhaust his reasons for writing as he does. If nothing else, the qualifying phrases in a sentence like the one above teach us to regard moral thought as something highly nuanced, something not easily reduced to simple categories or rules. It is clear, from many passages, that Smith did think of good moral judgment in precisely that way.

In addition, the length and complexity of Smith's sentences teach patience to the reader, and patience, the self-command by which one withholds quick, passionate judgment, is again a high virtue for Smith. The point of many of Smith's longer sentences does not come out at all until one has read through every clause carefully and then gone back to bring the whole thing together. Smith tends to help his readers through this process by introducing the more complex sentences with one or two short ones that give the long one's gist. Here are two examples from WN:

> The trade of Holland, it has been pretended by some people, is decaying, and it may perhaps be true that some particular branches of it are so. But . . . there is no general decay. . . . The great property which [the Dutch] possess both in the French and English funds, about forty millions, it is said, in the latter (in which I suspect, however, there is a considerable exaggeration); the great sums which they lend to private people in countries where the rate of interest is higher than in their own, are circumstances which no doubt demonstrate the redundancy of their own stock, or that it has increased beyond what they can employ with tolerable profit in the proper business of their own country: but they do not demonstrate that that business has decreased. (WN 108–9)

> Entails are the natural consequences of the law of primogeniture. They were introduced to preserve a certain lineal succession, of which the law of primogeniture first gave the idea, and to hinder any part of the original estate from being carried out of the proposed line either by gift, or devise, or alienation; either by the folly, or by the misfortune of any of its successive owners. (WN 384)

In the first case, Smith incorporates a number of qualifications to his main point within the evidence he is giving for that point. His main point requires him to show that the Dutch have a large share of English funds, but he throws in some parenthetical skepticism about his evidence for the size of that share. He also gestures vaguely and intriguingly toward the end of the sentence at a notion of "redundancy" of stock and a related notion of a country's "proper business," although neither of these notions is necessary for his overall argument. In the second case, Smith manages to pack both a survey of the legal terms to which entail is related and a theory of the psychological genealogy of entail within the confines of a single sentence. Without its introductory summary—"Entails are the natural consequences of the law of primogeniture"—the sentence would be practically impossible to follow.

By demanding patience and close attention of his reader in both TMS and WN, Smith teaches us that ethics and political economy are nuanced matters, in which one needs to qualify one's evidence carefully and be willing to draw fine analytic, legal, and historical distinctions. But his complicated style also reflects another teaching: that in both philosophy and social science we need to enter fully into the arguments, or mental network, of our opponents in order to respond to them properly. The most recently cited passage from TMS implicitly does that, by elaborating the phrase "solid joy" so as to grant to a hypothetical objector that "ignorant and groundless praise" can indeed be *momentarily* satisfying. The first passage above from WN explicitly grants something to an imagined objector—the people who "pretend" that Dutch trade is decaying—and the second one lays out some of the logic behind an institution that Smith despises. As I have noted, the TMS and first WN passages also incorporate qualifications to Smith's own position within his statement of that position. The complexity of Smith's sentences thus reflects a deeper complexity: the feature of his thought that Vivienne Brown has nicely called "dialogic," the fact that Smith often presents his views by way of an implicit or explicit dialogue with views he opposes.

This feature of Smith's writing shapes more than just his sentences. As we move to larger and larger blocks of text—to paragraphs, chapters, and indeed whole works—we find Smith at each level setting forth a position in cursory form, then introducing an objection to it at some length, then responding to that objection, and finally re-instating his original position, sometimes with qualifications that reflect his treatment of the objection. Herein lies, I think, a major source of common misunderstandings of Smith. Instead of seeing the way each piece of Smith's texts fits into a larger whole, readers get lost in the middle of an objection Smith has been presenting and assume that the objection represents Smith's own view.

Take, for example, the account of justice in Book II, part ii, chapter 3 of TMS. The chapter begins by acknowledging that the maintenance of justice is essential for society to exist, and elaborating that point vividly: "if this principle did not stand up within [most human beings] in [every individual's] defence, . . . they would, like wild beasts, be at all times ready to fly upon him; and a man would enter an assembly of men as he enters a den of lions" (TMS 86). Then comes a paragraph warning us that the fact that systems of justice are useful does not necessarily mean that they came about because people found them useful; we must be beware of "imagin[ing] that to be the wisdom of man, which in reality is the wisdom of God" (TMS 87). With that warning in place, Smith says "it has been thought" that justice comes about because people find it useful, and devotes a paragraph to the utilitarian account of why justice is considered a virtue, which he calls the account "commonly given" of that virtue (TMS 88).[3] In the next two paragraphs (TMS 88–9), he gives two ways in which "this account is undoubtedly true": it describes accurately how we think about justice when we need to steel ourselves to punish a criminal who has now "cease[d] to be an object of fear" and become instead an object of pity, and how we defend justice to "the young and licentious" when they come up with clever arguments by which to sneer at the rules that seem sacred to us. Finally, after granting so much to the utilitarian account, Smith begins the next paragraph with a "But" and proceeds to make clear that he rejects the utilitarian view: "it is not a regard to the preservation of society, which originally interests us in the punishment of crimes committed against individuals" (TMS 89). Yet even here, in the midst of his refutation, he throws in another concession, granting that the execution of soldiers for dereliction of duty is carried out for utilitarian reasons, although he quickly adds evidence to show that our approval of this policy "is far from being founded upon the same principles" on which we normally think about justice (TMS 90–91). So the chapter as a whole argues that our regard for justice is based primarily on a regard for individuals, taken on their own; that justice in fact serves the good of whole societies, but that our regard for it does not arise out of a concern for this social utility; yet it qualifies that argument with a sympathetic consideration of the opposing view and a series of concessions to the partial truth contained in that view. The result, one would like to think, is that readers come away with a great respect both for Smith's own thoughtfulness and impartiality and for the thoughtfulness of the moral philosophers with whom he disagrees—come away themselves prepared to sift, thoughtfully and impartially, for nuggets of truth in their opponents' views even as they affirm their own moral beliefs. The result *in fact* has often been that readers suppose Smith himself to hold the utilitarian views he so carefully delineates before rejecting.

Similarly, in the very beginning of TMS, Smith lays out an account of sympathetic feelings as arising when we place ourselves imaginatively in the situation of others, but then goes on to address an alternative account by which emotions are passed along infectiously when we observe that emotion in others. In this connection, he grants that there are occasions on which "sympathy *may seem* to arise merely from the view of a certain emotion in another person" (TMS 11, my emphasis).[4] Again, he concedes that the "sympathy-as-infection" theory accounts well for certain cases of sympathy. But the next few paragraphs go on to criticize the infection view, arguing, first, that it does not hold at all for many passions—the behavior of a furious person does not inspire us to join him in his fury—and, second, that even when an emotion does seem to be passed along infectiously, the best explanation of what is going on is that the other person's expressions of grief or joy suggest to us that they have met with good or bad fortune, and we feel grief or joy because we imagine ourselves meeting with similar fortune. Even in these cases, therefore, we are really projecting ourselves into other people's situations, rather than merely adopting the emotion they seem to be experiencing. The pericope concludes with a paragraph whose topic sentence is: "Sympathy, therefore, does not arise so much from the view of the passion, as from that of the situation which excites it." We could not have a clearer indication that Smith's consideration of the sympathy-as-infection theory is merely part of his case for his opposing sympathy-as-imaginative-projection theory. Yet readers frequently take Smith himself to hold the sympathy-as-infection view.[5]

The same roundabout, qualified way of making points runs through WN and has often led to the same sorts of mistakes in interpretation. Book II, chapter iii devotes three pages to showing that prodigality and misconduct can take away from the public wealth—concluding with the declaration that "every prodigal appears to be a publick enemy"—before going on to argue that on the whole a nation can never be "much affected either by the prodigality or misconduct of individuals" (WN 340–41). But the initial warning against prodigality tends to get quoted without the wider context.[6] Part V, chapter i has a section on the military which criticizes the effectiveness of militias vis-à-vis standing armies, but a later section of that chapter concedes that militias serve some useful purposes. It also has a section on education that criticizes public universities but recommends that the public should help support educational institutions for the poor, and a section on religion that first defends complete separation of church and state, and then, conceding that establishment is inevitable, shows how some forms of establishment are better than others. Right from WN's initial publication, Smith's readers have tended to see one part of these complex views without the other, complaining that he gives no role to militias because they read the initial section on the military and overlooked the later discussion, or focusing on the good things he says about churches while ignoring the fact that his ideal is disestablishment.[7]

Something similar happens with other important passages. Book IV, chapter ii moves from the well-known argument for relying on the "invisible hand" rather than government intervention to a series of cases that may constitute exceptions to this general rule. One of these possible exceptions arises when an industry is needed for a country's defense and Smith uses this as an excuse to discuss Britain's Navigation Laws, which were justified in part on a defense basis. The discussion consists primarily of an attack on the economic value of these laws, but Smith concludes by conceding that "as defence is much more important than opulence," the Navigation Acts represent the most acceptable kind of interventionism (WN 465). The paragraph that ends with this line begins with the sentence, "The act of navigation is not favourable to foreign commerce, or to the growth of that opulence which can arise from it." To people who thought the Navigation Acts enhanced commerce—and they had been justified for economic reasons as much as military ones—Smith's defense of those laws will not be at all satisfying. It is as though one said to a spouse who proposes a vacation on the grounds that it will be both delightful and healthy, "Well, actually it will make us miserable. But since health is more important than happiness, let's go anyway." Rhetorically, this response functions as a way of discouraging the proposal, not supporting it. But from the fame of the little tag about defence being more important than opulence, one would never guess that it occurs within a context in which Smith is concerned mostly to *criticize* measures taken in the name of defense.[8]

From the fame of the "pin factory" example in the beginning of WN, one might also never guess that Smith says very little about factories. Smith illustrates the importance of the division of labor with an account of a pin factory, but describes this example—four times! (three times in ¶2 and once in ¶4)—as a "trifling" one, before going on to explain its point in detail. At the end of the chapter, he turns to what he clearly considers a better paradigm of the division of labor: the many independent trades that are needed to make a laborer's coat. Why is the initial example there at all? Because it was the standard example for writers before Smith, and because it enables Smith to make his point clearly; Smith concedes that the division is especially "obvious" in this case (¶2). Here, as in TMS, Smith grants something to a view he rejects before turning to his own view. The effect of his concession, however, has been to lead many readers to suppose that Smith considers factory work to be paradigmatic of an advanced division of labor. His real point is precisely the opposite: that advanced economies are marked by a plethora of small, independent trades that fit into one another without deliberate organization (22–4).

Finally, Smith follows a winding route to his conclusions in his works taken as a whole. Not only does TMS raise and respond to possible objections all along the way, but it concludes with an entire division on the prior history of moral philosophy, in which Smith takes the opportunity to incorporate everything useful he can find in his predecessors, while rejecting those aspects of their systems that are incompatible with his views. WN has a similar section— part IV—devoted to opposing views, although it finds little to like about them. More importantly, the structure of WN as a whole proceeds from a general view about how human beings "naturally" increase their production of goods (parts I and II) to an explanation of why European history has not followed this natural course (part III), to a diagnosis and refutation of other views about how production works (part IV), and only then, when the opposing views have been thoroughly dismantled, does Smith say that "the obvious and simple system of natural liberty establishes itself of its own accord" (WN 687). Thus a view is set up, obstacles to that view are surveyed and overcome, and the original view returns as if "of its own accord" once the obstacles are cleared away. The method here, perhaps not accidentally, recalls that of Aristotle, who also tended to raise common objections to his own proposed view, incorporate some truth from them while on the whole criticizing them, and then take the somewhat altered view that resulted from this passage via objections to be justified primarily because it had survived that passage. For both Smith and Aristotle, argument for one's own view consists in taking up and responding to objections; the view is defended indirectly, by way of showing that alternatives to it will not work. But it is crucial, if this method is to work, that the reader not confuse the view being defended with its alternatives.

2. Rhetoric

I have spent so long on Smith's winding route to his conclusions because it has been little discussed. I can be briefer with Smith's more sophisticated rhetorical techniques, since they are now the subject of a considerable literature.

Smith taught rhetoric and belles-lettres before he taught moral philosophy; he has indeed been called the first professor of English.[9] Recent scholars have tried to apply several distinctions that Smith draws in those lectures to his own writings, with mixed results. Jerry Muller has usefully brought out ways in which Smith's presentation of certain policy proposals in WN may be informed by his remark to his rhetoric students that people who urgently want to persuade someone of something need to "magnif[y] all the arguments on . . . one side," and "diminish" or "conceal" those on the other. For example, when Smith says that "unless government takes some pains to prevent it," the laboring poor in every advanced society become "as stupid and ignorant as it is possible for a human being to become," Muller suggests that Smith is painting a particularly gloomy picture of the poor's condition in order to inspire political agents to alleviate that condition.[10] On the other hand, Vivienne Brown has persuasively argued that a crucial distinction drawn by Smith between "didactic" and "rhetorical" discourse, between the objective narration of facts and the attempt to persuade, does little or nothing to illuminate Smith's own work (ASD 16–19, 24).

Better results have come from attending, not to Smith's analysis of literary style, but to the way he himself writes. Brown has provided a brilliant and exhaustive study of the "dialogic" quality of Smith's moral writings, of the way in which Smith not only sees moral judgment as reached by a process of dialogue but includes such dialogues himself in TMS, and of the contrasting, "monologic" style of WN (ASD 23–54). She argues that the sharply different styles represent sharply different notions of the way morality and economics ought to be conducted. As I indicated in the preceding section, I endorse the general mode of analysis here but I see more dialogue in WN than Brown does, albeit, in this case, a dialogue in which Smith treats his opponents with less respect than he did in TMS.

Charles Griswold and David Marshall have drawn attention to Smith's declared fondness for the theater and suggested that TMS itself ought to be seen as in some measure a theatrical performance.[11] Setting the theater, specifically, aside for the moment, it is clear that Smith gives literature a remarkably prominent role in his moral philosophy. TMS frequently brings in examples from poetry and drama to explain or give evidence for its points (e.g., TMS 30, 32–3, 34, 177, 227), and recommends "Racine and Voltaire; Richardson, Maurivaux, and Riccoboni" as "instructors" in the nature of love and friendship (TMS 143). There are deep philosophical reasons for this merging of moral philosophy with literature. Since moral judgment is rooted in sympathy, for Smith, and since he understands sympathy as an act of the imagination, rather than of the senses alone, imaginative writing can quite directly enliven or enrich our capacity for moral judgment. Indeed Smith seems to see moral philosophy itself as something of a work of the imagination, a project that needs to draw on imaginative resources and that aims at extending the moral imaginations of its readers. In addition to drawing on literary resources, he fashions his own examples into vivid little stories (e.g., TMS 84, 149–50, 177–8). WN is also filled with memorable little stories, and, as we will see later on, it also aims to expand our moral imaginations in important respects.

Let us return now to Griswold's and Marshall's suggestion that we treat Smith's writings like works of theater, specifically. Smith explicitly says that we should issue moral judgments from the standpoint of an "impartial spectator," and he implicitly urges us to be "spectators" as we go through his study of moral judgments. Marshall says that "for Adam Smith, moral philosophy has entered the theater," and notes, rightly, that Smith understands both our relation to others and our relation to ourselves in a thoroughly theatrical way: we are "constantly imagining ourselves appearing before the eyes of other people."[12] Griswold stresses more the theatrical nature of Smith's books. In the beginning of TMS, "the curtain goes up," Griswold says, "and the play begins" (AVE 44). Griswold notes "the strong sense of audience . . . throughout TMS" (49, 51), Smith's presentation of human life as a "spectacle" to be observed (62, 65, 68–70), Smith's suggestion that the proper model for doing ethics is the literary critic, perhaps specifically the theater critic (65), and the fact that one meaning of the Greek word *theoria*, of which the "theory" of moral sentiments is an instance, is a "viewing," like the viewing by which audiences and critics watch a play (69–70). Citing Marshall, Griswold also finds a "theatrical" conception of the self within TMS, in that it seems from Smith's account that we constantly adopt one or another type of mask, and thereby distance ourselves both from ourselves and from other people (AVE 110 and n37). Griswold indicates that his points about theatricality can be extended to WN (67, 70), and he notes that in the "History of Astronomy" Smith describes *all* "philosophical systems"—which here includes systems of natural philosophy or what today we call "science"—as "inventions of the imagination." Smith also, in that essay, and in a brief passage at the beginning of WN, characterizes speculative or philosophical thought as a matter of "observ[ing] every thing" and then "combining together the powers of the most distant and dissimilar objects" (WN 21). The philosopher sits in the audience, putting the whole together while others participate in this or that piece of the whole. The philosopher is a spectator of a drama—only this time of the *theatrum mundi,* the drama of the entire universe, if he is a natural philosopher like Newton, or at least of the entire social universe, if he is a social philosopher like Adam Smith.

Griswold's interpretation gives us a useful way of looking at WN. WN presents us with the spectacle that is political economy, calling out explicitly "Observe" at the end of its first chapter, ending that same chapter, and many others, with dramatic flourishes that look like the exit lines of heroic theatrical characters, and surveying the entirety of economic life, and its roots in and effects on society and politics, in a way that no participant will normally do. It is even structured as something of a drama, in which the noble, free "system of natural liberty" gets introduced to us in Acts I and II, grapples with a variety of obstacles and opponents in Acts III and IV, and triumphs over them gloriously—or shows us what it would look like *if* it triumphed gloriously—in the fifth and final act. As is proper for tragedy, the climax comes at the end of the fourth act, when "all systems, either of preference or of restraint" are "completely taken away," and our hero is thereby released to "establish itself of its own accord" (WN 687).

The considerations in this section should encourage at least the presumption that a passage in WN need not mean only what it might in a work of social science today. To the extent that Smith engages in political persuasion, uses a dialogic style or represses dialogue with a monologic voice, or employs dramatic and other forms from fictional literature to illustrate or structure his writings on political economy, we need to read him more carefully than we might read Milton Friedman or Kenneth Arrow.[13] I will not dwell on these concerns very much, but they lie in the background of much that I will say. In Smith's case, the recent scholarly attention to literary effects is not just a reflection of a faddish preoccupation with finding such effects everywhere. Smith described himself in a late letter as "a slow a very slow workman, who do and undo everything I write at least half a dozen of times before I can be tolerably pleased with it" (Corr 311). And a glance at the footnotes to the Glasgow edition of TMS shows that much of what Smith "did and redid," when revising his major moral work for new editions, was to change a word here or a bit of phrasing there. One thing we know he "did and redid" many times was the opening chapter of WN (see LJ 338–49, 489–92 and ED 562–70)—yet all that really changed, over thirteen years, was the *presentation* of his argument and evidence, the rhetorical structure with which he put together the pin factory, the three reasons for the usefulness of the division of labor, the different tasks that go into the worker's coat, and the comparison between a poor laborer and an Amerindian or African king. Even aside from his early interest in rhetoric, therefore, we have good reason to think that Smith himself considered the proper literary presentation of his arguments to be essential to what he was doing.

A brief word, now, on esotericism. A number of scholars see Smith as in some way disguising his true beliefs throughout his work: presenting himself disingenuously as a believer in natural benevolence, or suppressing his true atheism or deep moral skepticism. Although I endorse the notion that Smith sometimes shades his views in one direction or another for political effect, and that he leaves out of WN discussions that he thought might irritate or lose the interest of the merchants, aristocrats, and politicians whom he hoped would read the book, I am disinclined to accept the more thoroughgoing hunts for an "esoteric" teaching in Smith that conflicts with what he says on the surface. To those— Straussian and others—who see Smith as suppressing atheist convictions, in particular, out of a fear of persecution, I would respond simply that (1) Smith in fact expresses enough heresy in both TMS and WN, and publicly showed enough fondness for heretics like Hume and Voltaire, to bring on himself the wrath of the religious establishment, and that he indeed was disliked by much of that establishment; (2) Smith had little reason to fear punishment for expressing such views after he resigned his chair in Glasgow in 1764; and (3) there is no avowal of atheism, or of Hobbesian egoism, or of moral skepticism, anywhere in Smith's published *or unpublished* writings, or in any report of his private remarks. The last of these points is particularly important. Smith is reputed to have privately expressed highly unorthodox opinions on certain subjects—he is reported to have said "Bravo!" about John Wilkes, claimed that "the Christian Religion debased the human mind," and called sodomy "a thing in itself indifferent"[14]—but there is no report of his ever avowing atheism, egoism, or moral skepticism. Nor does Smith ever suggest in his writings that there might be a difference between "common life" beliefs and the views of philosophers, as his friend David Hume had done. So I regard the hunt for Smith's esoteric doctrines, or the dismissal of what he says about, for instance, the importance and irreducibility of benevolence, as simply a projection of certain scholars' own preoccupations, an attempt to pull Smith into a framework that these scholars feel *must* fit him, whether it in fact does or not.

3. Genre

A literary issue that raises particularly acute problems for WN is the question of what *genre* Smith takes himself to be employing. An uneasy hybrid of polemical tract and historical survey, WN also contains a bundle of political recommendations, some striking observations about human nature, and, of course, a set of foundational principles for economic science. How are these various pieces supposed to fit together? How, in the light of its appearance within such a mixture, are we to understand Smith's conception of economic analysis? How might his political recommendations be colored by their historical and polemical context? And why did a moral philosopher, famous at the time for his treatise on moral sentiments, write a book in which moral considerations are given such oblique and cursory treatment? WN presents what literary scholars call a "genre" problem, of which its political and moral ambiguities are but symptoms.

Some of these issues will haunt us throughout this book. Right now I shall focus on just one: the tension between Smith's scientific and polemical purposes. WN is on the one hand a massive analysis of how economies work in general, supposed to hold good across historical time periods and capable of serving as a textbook, for many generations, on economic analysis. On the other hand, it is a work directed to the making of a historically specific, polemical point: that mercantilist and Physiocratic attempts to have the state control or guide economic production are misguided. We might say: The book is simultaneously a "treatise" and a "tract," an heir both to Montesquieu's *Spirit of the Laws* or Hutcheson's *System* and to the many little pamphlets on corn or money by now-forgotten writers like John Law or Thomas Mun, which it often has occasion to quote. Compare WN with John Locke's *Second Treatise on Government*. A. J. Simmons has pointed out that Locke took his *Treatise* to be not merely "an occasional tract in favor of the Glorious Revolution," but a general theory of politics comparable in scope to Aristotle's *Politics* or the jurisprudential systems of Grotius and Pufendorf.[15] Nevertheless, Locke's little book has often been read as *either* a tract *or* a treatise; it is hard to hold the two things together. The fact that Locke is trying to justify a particular event raises some suspicions, after all, about just how general his political principles can possibly be, whereas if his principles really are so general, one wonders how they could be as helpful as they were for justifying the positions of one side in a particular political struggle. The common scholarly verdict at the moment seems to be that Locke's work is supremely successful as a tract, and somewhat less so as a treatise. With Smith, the judgment tends to be reversed. The mere length and comprehensiveness of WN makes it read most obviously as a treatise, and it has been set aside summarily as too "theoretical," by many politicians, whenever its conclusions do not fit their current projects. Nevertheless, the enormous WN is as much a polemical tract as Locke's little book is a treatise. They are, indeed, quite similar in this respect (as in the fact that they look back to Aristotle, Grotius, and Pufendorf); they both try, uneasily, to straddle the gap between polemics and philosophy.

I have argued elsewhere that this feature of WN is one of its great attractions—that political philosophers cannot afford to stay above the actual political fray if they want to say something significant.[16] Politics always deals with specific situations, and political principles must be applied to specific cases if they are to serve as an exemplar for further political decision-making. Thus we can say that when Smith refused to listen to admonitions that his remarks on the American controversy at the end of WN made the book too "topical," it was really he rather than his critics who understood the proper nature of political philosophy, who understood that commentary on a specific issue gave his principles clearer, more specific meaning.[17] But we can also say precisely the opposite: that including such specific political issues takes away from his book's ability to speak across generations. Moreover, WN does not merely engage in polemics here and there about issues like the American crisis. At almost every point, it can be read either as tract or as treatise, and the "tract" reading is often easier to make out than the "treatise" one. A full fifth of the book (Book IV) is given over explicitly to polemics—and that is really an underestimate, since polemics against various mercantilist measures and attitudes also pervade much of Books I and V—while the seemingly "neutral," purely theoretical opening two books can easily be seen as merely paving the way for the polemical payoff to come.

Let me elaborate this last suggestion a little. Smith's main polemical target in WN is the mercantilists. The mercantilist system rested, he believed, on an exaggerated emphasis on the importance of money—of the precious metals "for which every thing is readily given in exchange" (WN 438). Often mercantilists would write as if these metals *were* wealth; although they themselves were aware that wealth and money are not the same thing, they appealed to a popular confusion between the two to help make their position plausible.[18] But in any case they believed that governments needed large stocks of precious metals on hand, and that nations could gain an advantage in foreign trade if such currency was readily available. Now since the supply of precious metals was limited, on this view nations would forever be locked in a zero-sum competition for them, and each nation would need constantly to take measures ensuring that its own stock of money, or command over sources of money, was superior to that of its neighbors. The mercantilists recommended several such measures, above all (1) sending out national expeditions to secure gold and silver mines, and (2) encouraging manufacturing over agriculture, and giving local industries as much of an edge as possible over the industries of other countries. They promoted the second because they believed that foreign coin could be more readily obtained in exchange for manufactured goods than for agricultural goods. They promoted the first because they believed that the value of silver and gold was bound to decline over time, as the amount of silver and gold increased in wealthy nations, hence that each nation would need more and more silver and gold to retain the same level of purchasing power. Both types of measure meant that nations had to be always prepared for war and often engaged in it. To control gold and silver mines, one needs to conquer lands where such mines are plentiful. To get an advantage in trade over one's neighbors, one needs to expand one's own markets and restrict theirs; it helps enormously, in doing that, if one can protect one's shipping militarily. The mercantilist economic program went, therefore, with colonialism, nationalism, and a strong belief in the value of military adventures.

Smith takes on every part of this program in WN. His own views are opposed to colonialism, to the hunt for national glory, and to military adventures (see § 60 in chapter 12), and he does not think that international relations, in either the economic or the political realm, need be a zero-sum game. The system of free trade that he sets in opposition to mercantilism is supposed to result in a lessening of international tensions and a reduction in the use of war to further national interests (WN 493); free trade will replace conquest as the primary mode by which one nation relates to another. But these subjects appear explicitly only in Books IV and V, so one might suppose that WN, to the extent that it is a tract, becomes one after it has first laid out a neutral portrait of the facts about how economies work. It is unclear that this is true, however. The supposedly neutral discussions of Book I seem directed throughout to the polemic that Smith will be making against the mercantilists later on. Smith devotes a long and astute chapter in Book I to debunking the mercantilist myth that precious metals will inevitably slide in price (I.xi).[19] Earlier in Book I, one chapter directly attacks restrictions on trade promoted by "the clamour and sophistry of merchants and manufacturers" (WN 144), and another ends with a complaint about the way "merchants and master manufacturers" dishonestly represent economic facts (WN 115)—here, not coincidentally, facts about what makes a nation's goods competitive on the world market. The polemic against mercantilists is only slightly less obvious when chapters I.viii, I.ix, and I.xi address themselves to the relationship between wages, profit, or rent and the overall wealth of a national economy. Given the way that chapters I.i–I.vii slowly develop the elements of economic analysis, one would have expected that I.viii–I.xi would treat the components of price on their own, leaving the matter of how to assess an entire economy until a later chapter. Instead, each component of price is considered *in relation to* the wealth of the entire society, as if to say that the economic analysis in this book is all directed toward the single question of what furthers and what hinders "the wealth of nations."

Indeed, this question can really be traced back to the very beginning of the book. The first chapter of Book I sets up the division of labor, as opposed to any sort of natural resource, as the basis of wealth, and the second chapter shows, against the mercantilist conception of trade as a zero-sum game, that human beings mutually gain in trade. Chapter iii explains how the spread of trade naturally makes possible increases in the division of labor, and therefore in total wealth, and chapters iv and v provide Smith with a crucial tool—the distinction between "real" and "nominal" prices—for his later analysis of how the price of precious metals tends to rise rather than fall (consider the use of "real price" at WN 205–9, 219, 236, or 253–5). And chapter vii lays out the basic argument that Smith will use many times later on for the claim that free markets need no government help to find the "natural price" that enables as much of a commodity to be produced as there is demand for. So the whole of Book I is implicitly directed against mercantilist arguments (and, to a lesser extent, Physiocratic ones) even where it is not explicitly so directed. The same goes for the succeeding two books. Book II continues the polemic against exaggerating the importance of money, making clear that an increase in stock, not in money, is what leads to national wealth and greatness, and Book III shows in detail how economies were diverted for centuries from their natural course, and thereby from the wealth they could have achieved, by misguided laws.

It is thus no surprise that the explicit critique of mercantilism and Physiocracy, in Book IV, flows directly out of the earlier theoretical analysis. This provokes a difficult question: Are Smith's polemics but the logical consequence of his theoretical commitments, or did he construct his theory to fit his polemical purposes? After studying Smith for more than a decade, I still feel incapable of answering that question. What I can say with confidence is that there are good reasons why people generally separate "theory" from "polemic"—recent critiques of this distinction notwithstanding—and that the time-bound, context-dependent nature of a polemic will normally stand in some tension with the broad, transhistorical concerns that a philosophical or scientific theory is supposed to address. This tension pervades WN, and I do not believe that Smith ever resolves it, leaving us without a clear indication whether, or to what extent, the theory of WN is supposed to apply in historical periods other than his own, the extent to which it should remain relevant once Physiocracy and mercantilism have been defeated. To take an important example of why this matters: Physiocracy and mercantilism are systems prescribing how governments can improve the *production* of goods, and Smith's concern throughout the book is almost exclusively with production. Beginning almost immediately after Smith died, however, and continuing through to the present day, political economy turned much of its attention to *distribution* rather than production. What can we infer, from Smith's teaching that governments should not try to direct production (the overall size of a nation's "pie"), about how he might have regarded government attempts to control distribution (how that pie is to be cut up)? Not much, as I shall argue later in this book. Smith's general views can be and have been used to support both "left" and "right" views of government programs that redistribute wealth. Both uses of Smith are plausible, and both require considerable extrapolation from what he actually said. A more abstract organization of the topics to be covered by WN might perhaps have led Smith to address this issue explicitly, and thereby given him a clearer, stronger voice in the debates of the generations to come.

4. Style and Philosophical Method

Let us now turn away from the complexities, subtle literary effects, and questions of genre in Smith's writing, and return to the clarity, the seeming transparency, for which he has been most praised. Even this clarity, this simplicity, has a philosophical justification, and philosophical implications, that are not at all simple.

Take up WN and reread its first three paragraphs or so. What do you find? The first thing that appears is one of the most important claims of the entire book—that the division of labor, far more than natural resources, is primarily responsible for increases in economic production. How is this important claim defended? We are given an example, supposedly drawn from life, of what happens in a pin factory. The paragraph containing that example begins by describing how many pins a worker "not educated to" pin-making is likely to make in a day, thereby inviting the reader, who most likely belongs among those not educated to this business, to imagine how many pins he himself might make. Smith guesses, I think rightly, what most readers will say: that, even if we put our "utmost industry" into it, we could scarcely make "one pin in a day, and certainly could not make twenty." Then he details the many different processes that go into the making of pins once it becomes "a peculiar trade," and this list—drawing out the wire, straightening it, cutting it, grinding it at the top to receive the head: in all about "eighteen distinct operations"—serves to reinforce our original impression that pin-making is a difficult business and that we could make few pins on our own. Next Smith tells us that he has himself seen a pin factory in which only ten people worked, so the division of labor was not carried as far as it can be. Now comes the punch line: *Even* in this poor case, where the division of labor was divided among ten people rather than the eighteen or so that would be optimal, the factory produced "upwards of forty-eight thousand pins in a day"—thus over *four thousand eight hundred* pins per person. The number is staggering. The difference between the number of pins we thought we could make by ourselves and the number we could make if we were part of even a ten-person team is so overwhelming that we would not believe Smith had he not assured us that he had seen this himself. As it is, we are instantly brought over to his view of the importance of the division of labor. Nothing more needs to be said on the subject. Although he does go on to say a little more, he has already won his point. Three paragraphs in, and one of the main argumentative battles of the book is over.

But what has happened here? We have been given *one* piece of evidence, one datum, for a major point—far from enough to establish it in the eyes of any self-respecting empiricist. We might have expected a flurry of cases, drawn from history or from Smith's own observations, or perhaps a derivation of the power of the division of labor from more fundamental psychological or biological or physical laws. Instead a brilliant rhetorical presentation transforms a single example into the complete case for a theoretical principle. Smith draws on our imaginations, which he considers essential both to good science and to good moral philosophy, rather than giving us a substantial body of evidence or deriving his conclusion from general laws or principles. He will proceed to do some of both in the ensuing paragraphs, pointing us, in paragraph 4, to the difference between the degree of divided labor in "rude" and "improved" countries, and their proportional differences in productivity, and sketching, in paragraphs 6 to 8, a few reasons why the division of labor might improve productivity. But these remarks—which themselves are persuasive because they appeal to common-sense observation ("A man commonly saunters a little in turning his hand from one sort of employment to another"), not because they reflect an exhaustive survey of history—come after the main work of getting us to see the importance of the division of labor has already been done. The pin factory is one of the most famous passages in WN, and understandably so: It is a rhetorical masterpiece, which Smith carefully honed, pruning and reshaping the paragraph from its first appearance in his lecture courses in the 1760s to the 1776 version in the book. And the central purpose Smith's rhetoric serves here is *clarity*: He sets up the point of his example with an imaginative exercise drawing on the reader's own experience, strips the example down to the one feature he most needs in it, emphasizes the contrast between what the example shows and what we expected as a result of the imaginative exercise, and then drives the conclusion home. The brief compass within which all this takes place, moreover, ensures that the reader can hold the whole thing together easily in his or her imagination. This simplification and concentration of a point, and this way of connecting it to the reader's own experiences, will run through the book, making abstruse economic phenomena appear familiar and easy to understand.

WN has always been praised for its clarity. When it first appeared, Edward Gibbon said that WN expressed "the most profound ideas . . . in the most perspicuous language," and Hugh Blair said that all other writers on political economy had only puzzled him, while Smith's style was "clear and distinct to the last degree."[20] Lord Shelburne remarked that he owed to a conversation on political economy with Smith, on a journey from Edinburgh to London, "the difference between light and darkness through the best part of my life."[21] In the twentieth century, Joseph Schumpeter, who accused WN of not containing a single original idea, also acknowledged the clarity and systematicity with which Smith presented his material.[22] Recently, Jerry Muller has written that the impact of WN "lay in its synthesis of ideas clearly articulated, conceptually linked, and forcefully impressed on the minds of its readers."[23]

This praise is unquestionably merited. For all his use of theatrical tropes, and for all the ambiguity one might find in his tone, Smith conducts his analyses of economic systems with great precision and masterly organization. The precision is particularly striking. Much of the book looks as if it had been written on a word processor, with certain phrases programmed into the function keys, or block-copied from place to place, so that similar ideas are given similar wording across vast stretches of the text.[24] Although inelegant, this precision is perhaps Smith's most philosophical characteristic, ensuring that his abstract modes of classification are carried along consistently, so that one can see at a glance how one point or piece of evidence fits together with the others. He also lays out the main thesis of many chapters in a short introductory paragraph at the head of the chapter (see, for example, 13, 25, 105), offers brief recapitulations of long arguments whenever he fears the reader might have gotten lost (e.g., 288, ¶11) or forgotten them (e.g., 286, ¶1), numbers his points whenever he has several of them ("First, . . . ," "Secondly, . . ."), and follows up every implied or explicit statement that a particular argument comprises two or three points with two or three paragraphs making exactly those points, in the order in which they were introduced (e.g., 17–20 or 294). The clarity of presentation he achieves in all these ways is very important to him. "I am always willing to run some hazard of being tedious in order to be sure that I am perspicuous," he says, avowing that he "tak[es] the utmost pains to be perspicuous" (WN 46; see also 309, 354, 449).

Now of course most writers aim to be perspicuous, but I suggest that for Smith perspicuity is the overriding object of his work, especially in WN. He does not claim to have discovered any new economic facts or forces—nor did he do so, if Schumpeter is right—nor to have found, like an economic Newton, fundamental mathematical laws for all economic systems. Rather, he arranges fairly familiar ideas about society and economics, ideas that are latent in our ordinary understandings, and by so arranging them, tries to clarify them and their relations to one another—tries to put them into a system. In the "History of Astronomy," he makes clear what a system is: "all philosophical systems [are] inventions of the imagination, to connect together the otherwise disjointed and discordant phaenomena of nature" (EPS 105).

Behind this emphasis on perspicuity and concomitant conception of systems lies, I believe, a sophisticated epistemological theory. Smith's work belongs chronologically just after that of the sceptical philosopher Hume and just before that of the common-sense philosopher Thomas Reid (Smith's successor at Glasgow), and I think it belongs between them philosophically as well. Hume and Reid are themselves not so far apart. Hume is typically represented as a sceptic who undermined our ordinary beliefs in personal identity, causation, and independent reality, while Reid is supposed to have responded to Hume by insisting that common sense undermines Hume's philosophical method. But this characterization of the two underestimates Hume's regard for what he called "common life" beliefs and exaggerates Reid's success in restoring those beliefs. As the nineteenth-century Edinburgh philosopher Thomas Brown remarked:

> "Yes," Reid bawled out, "We must believe in an external world"; but added in a whisper, "We can give no reason for our belief." Hume cries out, "We can give no reason for such a notion"; but whispers, "I own we cannot get rid of it."[25]

Of course, Hume and Reid do differ in many ways. Reid buttressed his rejection of Hume's scepticism with a diagnosis of the "way of ideas" that he considered, rightly, to underlie the Humean position. And Hume believed, contra Reid, that we can at least momentarily suspend the beliefs of common life, that philosophy, therefore, need not be entirely "root[ed in] the principles of Common Sense," as Reid would have had it,[26] and that our common beliefs do not in any case form a coherent, systematic body. For Hume, we can take up a philosophical perspective somewhat independent of our common-life beliefs, even if we cannot and should not try to carry out our lives from that perspective. For Reid, any philosophical perspective itself is and must be rooted in common sense. These are important philosophical differences, even if they issue in similar practical conclusions. But the fact remains that both Hume and Reid call upon us to return from philosophy to common sense. Smith, who goes along with this call, does not make clear where he stands on the issues that divided Reid from Hume. We do have one passage in which Smith, in an apparently Reidian vein, describes moral philosophy as the science that "pretends to investigate and explain [the] connecting principles" by which the "maxims of common life" can be brought together in a "methodical order" (WN 769). But on the whole Smith simply finesses the differences between Hume and Reid. Hume at one point defines philosophy as "the reflections of common life, methodized and corrected" (E 162), and we may see Smith as following this definition more strictly than Hume himself did. Hume's endorsement of common life comes generally with something of a wink and a nod, and with a scepticism in reserve that pops up periodically to remind us of the hollowness of our common beliefs. Some recent scholars read Smith as similarly sceptical, but there is no good evidence for this.[27] Smith never endorses Hume's sceptical arguments, nor constructs any such arguments of his own, and he rarely peeks above or beyond common-life beliefs to remind us of their ultimate insubstantiality from a philosophical perspective. Unlike Reid, on the other hand, Smith never declares a proud faith in common sense vis-à-vis philosophy.[28] Smith neither affirms nor denies the ultimate truth of common-sense beliefs; he merely works within them.

Now one could read this silence on the question that divides Hume from Reid as a sign that Smith was ignorant of or insensitive to the issues that might lead one to question the reliability of common sense, or one can read it, as seems more reasonable given Smith's thorough knowledge of the history of philosophy, and of Hume's work in particular, as a sophisticated realization that *the very attempt to defend common sense suggests, wrongly, that common sense needs defense*. One can, that is, read Smith as an anticipator of Wittgenstein, who, in *On Certainty*, pointed out that his colleague G. E. Moore's Reidian attempts to provide a philosophical defense for common sense simply raised issues that need not be raised at all, but that, once raised, cannot be resolved with common sense's own tools. If common sense is truly self-sufficient, can truly provide the proper foundation for all our beliefs, then it should just be allowed to do that, to bring forward its claims and arguments in its own way. One who truly understands and trusts the workings of common sense will neither criticize nor praise it in the light of some "further" philosophical perspective—a perspective that, ex hypothesi, cannot really be "further," must be either unintelligible or yet another product of common sense itself.

Smith never lays out any such argument for how to regard common sense. Of course, on my account of what he is doing, he really *should* not lay out any such argument, should not defend even his unwillingness to defend common-sense. But I don't want to rest my case for Smith's common sense methodology on such a tricky "argument from silence." Rather, I ascribe to Smith a proto-Wittgensteinian attitude toward common sense for three reasons: (1) because nearly all his arguments, both in TMS and in WN, begin from common-sense observations and draw on examples from ordinary life for evidence; (2) because he often either talks of "real philosophy" as some sort of wisdom about what to expect from life, implying that the sort of philosophy that Descartes or Hume did is somehow "unreal" ("language on holiday," as Wittgenstein would say) or contrasts the "refinement[s] of philosophy" unfavorably with the views we come to "by nature" (TMS 287; see also 299); and, above all, (3) because it fits well with a central commitment, running through all his work, to vindicating ordinary people's judgments, and fending off attempts by philosophers and policymakers to replace those judgments with the supposedly better "systems" invented by intellectuals. In one of Smith's earliest writings, he is concerned to refute the notion that the ordinary person objectifies secondary qualities (EPS 141–2); in the "History of Astronomy," he characterizes philosophy as a discipline that attempts to connect and regularize the data of everyday experience (EPS 44–7); in TMS, he criticizes several philosophical theories of morality for not attending properly to the way moral sentiments are actually experienced (TMS 89, 291–3, 303) and condemns those entranced by "the love of system" (185, 232–4); and in WN he directs a central polemic against the notion that governments must guide the economic decisions of ordinary people. He also remarks several times that one need turn only to "plain," "simple," or "obvious" observations for evidence of his points, rather than to "tedious or doubtful calculation[s]" (WN 91, 142, 374).[29] Similarly, he often clarifies complex points about the workings of large national economies by way of a comparison with the workings of ordinary household economies. For instance:

> The capital of all the individuals of a nation, has its limits in the same manner as that of a single individual, and is capable of executing only certain purposes. The capital of all the individuals of a nation is increased in the same manner as that of a single individual, by their continually accumulating and adding to it whatever they save out of their revenue. (WN 366)

Or:

> It is the maxim of every prudent master of a family, never to attempt to make at home what it will cost him more to make than to buy. The taylor does not attempt to make his own shoes, but buys them of the shoemaker. . . . What is prudence in the conduct of every private family, can scarce be folly in that of a great kingdom. If a foreign country can supply us with a commodity cheaper than we ourselves can make it, better buy it of them. (WN 456–7)[30]

Smith wants economics to make ready sense to us; he wants to show how its fundamental principles are but extrapolations of what we already ordinarily believe. It seems methodologically important to him that the reader be able to verify his arguments without going beyond common sense, as it is politically important to him that the three duties he attributes to the sovereign are "plain and intelligible to common understandings" (WN 449, 687). In the light of all this, it seems reasonable to see Smith as a forerunner of "common-sense philosophy," and, relatedly, as one of the first modern philosophers to be suspicious of philosophy itself—at least of philosophy as conducted from a foundationalist standpoint, a position outside the modes of thought and practice it examines.

This is not to say that Smith is uncritical of ordinary modes of thought and practice. But it is important that he almost always calls the notions he opposes "absurdities," "follies," "delusions," or "prejudices" and not mere errors.[31] It is the nature of an absurdity or folly to require, not so much refutation, as clarification: When brought out into the clear light of day, its absurdity should become apparent, and it should simply dissolve. Absurdities and follies are not just falsehoods but falsehoods so glaring that, once they are pointed out, no reasonable person can go on believing them. Delusions are diseased perceptions, fancies or fantasies that ought simply to vanish if one's senses can be cured. And prejudices are unconscious commitments that block or pre-empt judgment. All these are the sort of problems that characteristically plague common sense, not the sort of cognitive error characteristic of philosophers or scientific experts, such as a mistake in argumentation or ignorance of a crucial piece of empirical evidence. (If you are at the point where you can appreciate arguments and evidence, you are beyond the point at which you can be fooled by cognitive illusions.) Now the way one would expect to dispose of obstacles to common sense is simply to point them out, and to clarify the context that produced them. And this is exactly what Smith does. He repeatedly shows, for instance, that "the real wealth and revenue of a country" consist in the produce of land and labor rather than in the quantity of precious metals in the country, and he describes the first view as what "plain reason seems to dictate" and the second as what "vulgar prejudices suppose" (WN 340). Later, he calls the latter a "popular notion" enshrined by "common language," which if properly thought through reveals itself as an "absurdity"(WN 449). Thoughts couched in common language can, here, correct the mistakes of common language. Smith shows the foolishness of protectionism by way of an amusing example:

> By means of glasses, hotbeds, and hotwalls, very good grapes can be raised in Scotland, and very good wine too can be made of them at about thirty times the expence for which at least equally good can be brought from foreign countries. Would it be a reasonable law to prohibit the importation of all foreign wines, merely to encourage the making of claret and burgundy in Scotland? (WN 458)

But the "manifest absurdity" of this example, Smith says, should just bring out the equal, if more hidden, absurdity of all protectionist measures. This pericope displays Smith's general method very well. By way of an example drawn on our ordinary experience, he shows that a principle we are ordinarily attached to is absurd.

To say that Smith gives common sense, or ordinary experience, priority over philosophical principles is therefore not to say that Smith merely lists common-sense beliefs, or arranges them in an attractive order. An important objection to any sort of common-sense philosophy is that it may leave us with no room for criticizing our ordinary views, that it can collapse into uncritical faith in whatever dogmas happen to be abroad in our society. No such objection holds good of Smith, who criticizes many aspects of our ordinary moral attitudes in TMS and who devotes WN to a thoroughgoing critique of the standard views of political economy in his day (and of many contemporary institutions, from the laws of settlement to primogeniture and slavery).[32] But Smith locates his critical stance *within* the common-sense beliefs and attitudes that he criticizes. Stanley Cavell has described the task he sets for himself in philosophy as "a convening of my culture's criteria, in order to confront them with my words and life as I pursue them and as I may imagine them." Smith shares this conception of philosophy, I believe, and shares in particular what Cavell declares as his goal: "to confront my culture with itself, along the lines in which it meets in me."[33] Laying out the common sense of one's culture can be a critical project, insofar as it provokes the culture to face contradictions in its beliefs, or half-buried prejudices or follies that it does not like to acknowledge. And indeed common sense, viewed as Cavell and Smith view it, is itself a critical mode of thinking, not a collection of dogmas. Our common way of looking at things is fluid and self-corrective—criticizing our own and each other's beliefs is a large part of what we do in ordinary life—and Smith will use one aspect of our common views against other common views that he thinks represent superstitions or fanaticism. Alternatively, he will bring the comprehensive picture he has constructed out of ordinary beliefs to bear on a particular belief here or there, showing how it does not fit into the whole, how our beliefs taken as a whole tend to undermine it. This is what philosophers are supposed to do, according to both the "History of Astronomy" and WN (WN 21–2): help our thinking by providing us with a view of the whole, by connecting many different beliefs in a clear "system" or "theory." Thus the comprehensive picture in TMS of how religious principles grow out of our moral sentiments is supposed to help make clear the absurdity in believing that God prefers the fulfillment of rituals to the performance of moral duties, and thus Smith's lucid explanation, in the light of WN's general economic system, of how "engrossing and forestalling" helps prevent famines is supposed to dispel common prejudices against corn merchants.[34]

In the latter case, Smith explicitly compares the "popular fear of engrossing and forestalling . . . to the popular terrors and suspicions of witchcraft" (534), and claims that government policy is capable of either supporting or eliminating such fears. Elsewhere, he claims that the advantages of free trade are "so manifest" that no-one would ever have questioned that policy "had not the interested sophistry of merchants and manufacturers confounded the common sense of mankind" (494). These claims suggest a theory of how common life beliefs, the beliefs of ordinary people, can go wrong: powerful figures—politicians and merchants, in these cases, and religious leaders elsewhere (TMS 133–4, 177–8)—prop up what might otherwise have been a passing fancy with the authority of law or religious sanction, give credibility to abstract and unnatural "systems" that justify this fancy, and thereby insert into the self-correcting flow of common sense a clog, something that blocks judgment rather than being informed by and yielding to it, a "prejudice" in the literal sense of that word. And the proper response to this clog is to dissolve it with other, more freely flowing thought, to bring our daily observations and modes of reasoning to bear on it. Smith is aware of the ability of a few well-spoken people to "lead and direct," and sometimes to mislead and misdirect, the common sense of many other people (TMS 336, LJ 202, 211–12, WN 651); he tries by his own work to provide facts and clear explanations that will correct for that influence. What Smith does *not* do, in response to prejudices or other errors, is construct a mathematical model to show that ordinary people's intuitions are wrong, nor does he develop abstract moral principles on which to base proofs of counterintuitive moral conclusions, as Benthamites and Kantians would do over the ensuing two centuries. Smith is a critic of our ordinary beliefs, but he is an *immanent* critic, not a transcendental one, bringing out the rationality already inherent in ordinary life, mapping it from within and correcting it, where necessary, with its own tools, rather than trying either to justify or to criticize it from a "higher" standpoint. This intellectual aim is not unconnected with, and no less important than, his political interest in guaranteeing to ordinary individuals the "natural liberty" of thought and action that he believes they rightly possess.

Even if we set aside the ways in which Smith's writing is more complex than it seems, therefore, its very simplicity reflects a sophisticated view of how human knowledge is grounded and how it may be corrected—and, consequently, of the proper task of the philosopher. We turn in the next chapter to a more detailed investigation of how Smith understood this task.

CHAPTER TWO
_____

Epistemology and Philosophy of Science

5. Epistemology

Smith has surprisingly little to say, directly, about epistemology. Unlike Hume, he wrote practically nothing about the nature of or justification for claims to knowledge, devoting even his "Of the External Senses" primarily to how our senses work rather than to strictly philosophical questions. Similarly, in his essay on "Ancient Logics and Metaphysics," although he gives us an extensive and largely accurate account of Platonic, Aristotelian, Stoic, and medieval views of universals and essences, he says almost nothing to indicate his own views on these subjects.[1] Nor does he, in these essays or elsewhere, expressly declare any position for or against Hume's sceptical views about causation, objecthood, and personal identity. The one passage in which some recent scholars have found hints of scepticism[2] concerns, not meta-scientific issues like the reality of matter or the justification for causality, but the finality of any *scientific* theory. Even "the most sceptical" among us, says Smith, is likely to be so impressed by Newtonian science as to imagine that it, unlike all its predecessors in the history of astrophysics, has "a degree of solidity and firmness that we should in vain look for in any other system" (EPS 105). Still, he reminds the reader, every scientific system is but a creation of the imagination, an attempt, in imagination, to connect the things we perceive with the senses; no system is ever identical with the things it describes. But this caution about the distance of scientific theories from the objects they describe, and their consequent fallibility, does not entail any doubt about the reality or materiality of those objects themselves, or about the epistemic principles guiding the theories. It does not amount, that is, to any sort of metaphysical or epistemological scepticism. Whether Smith held the proto-Wittgensteinian attitude toward scepticism that I attributed to him above (§4), or whether he was simply not much interested in the issues Hume had raised, he avoided taking a stand on them, avoided engaging in the major metaphysical and epistemological controversy of his day.

For all that, Smith seems well acquainted with the history of epistemology, as the two essays I have mentioned will attest, and makes clear his allegiance to empiricist rather than rationalist views of thought. Thus he calls Malebranche an "ingenious and sublime philosopher" in the "History of Ancient Logics and Metaphysics" but nevertheless rejects the latter's hypothesis on universals as overly fanciful, while he paraphrases and accepts Hume's account of the "association of ideas" in the beginning of the "History of Astronomy." He also adopts Hume's term "impressions" for immediate sense-data, in the beginning of TMS,[3] and shortly afterward drops an intriguing but undeveloped hint that he shares Hume's view of belief as "more properly a matter of the sensitive, than of the cogitative part of our nature."[4] Smith's very interest in psychology over epistemology is also but part of his general fascination with scientific observations and experiments, and his fondness for appealing to facts, about the mind or society or history, rather than a priori principles, to back up claims in his moral theory and political economy. He values the (empirical) "imagination" over the (a priori) "understanding," like Hume and unlike Descartes, which is probably a good part of the reason why he avoids mathematical models in political economy.

This commitment to empiricism is therefore important to Smith's social scientific methodology, and it is important also to the view of common sense I attributed to Smith at the end of the last section. Common sense is fluidly self-corrective, if it is, *because it responds quickly and precisely to empirical data.* Ordinary people, even without education, are constantly engaged in adjusting their beliefs to accord with what they see and hear around them, and this is sufficient, Smith believes, for them to work out most of what they need to know about their fellow human beings, especially those they observe often. Hence "every individual can, in his local situation, judge much better than any statesman or lawgiver can do for him" (WN 456). We come here to what Knud Haakonssen calls Smith's notion of "contextual knowledge": "the kind of concrete knowledge which arises from specific situations and which gives rise to common-sense ideas of behaviour wherever people live together" (SL 79). As Haakonssen points out, what Smith calls "system knowledge"—scientific knowledge—of human societies must always begin from, and account for, the contextual knowledge "people have of themselves and others" (SL 81; cf. WN 768–9). Smith's version of empiricism is highly particularist; he maintains that what we know most firmly are particular cases, and that generalizations are more or less unfirm to the degree to which they abstract from the detail of these cases.[5] In TMS, Smith tells us that general moral rules are "founded upon experience of what, in particular instances, our moral faculties . . . approve, or disapprove of" (TMS 159), and that "it is in particular instances only" that the propriety or impropriety of actions is clear (188). In WN, he tells us again and again that economic agents succeed only when they pay "exact attention to small savings and gains" (385), when they lavish care on "particular portions" of stock (928), when, like the corn merchant, their interest "makes [them] study" to carry out a particular task "as exactly as [they] can" (534). Interest and exact attention are linked in this last passage in the way that perception and the sentiments moving one to act are linked in Aristotle's theory of motion: I perceive details *insofar as* I am worried about achieving a certain end to which they are relevant.[6] And, in general, judgment requires "exact" and "vigilant" attention (385, 530, 755), and judgment is Smith's term for the kind of knowledge we need most in our ordinary lives.[7] We shall see the importance of this for social science in due course.

We can make one other point about Smith's epistemological commitments. Smith seems to have accepted important parts of Hume's account of causality, while keeping his distance from its sceptical implications. In the "History of Astronomy," Smith endorses the notion that the imagination creates connections between commonly associated impressions, using language very similar to Hume's: "[w]hen two objects, however unlike, have often been observed to follow each other, . . . they come to be so connected together in the fancy, that the idea of the one seems, of its own accord, to call up and introduce that of the other" (EPS 40). Smith never mentions Hume's scepticism about induction, however, and it is unclear whether he agreed with Hume that the psychological propensity to associate conjoined impressions is all there is to causality.[8] In WN, he often seems to want a rather stronger notion of causality than one could get from Hume. At one point in his argument, he needs to distinguish between a coincidence and a causal sequence (WN 255–6); at another, it is important to him that people have confused cause and effect in looking at a particular sequence of economic events (WN 373). These passages, which contain some of Smith's central arguments against mercantilism, depend on the distinction between an accidental and a law-governed conjunction of events: precisely the distinction that Hume's reduction of causality to constant conjunction had threatened to erode.[9] Still, Hume himself seems to have believed that the distinction could be revived within his epistemology by proper attention to the difference between commonly and uncommonly conjoined events,[10] and Smith may have accepted that claim. In any case, he clearly did share Hume's view that causality applies to human events in the same way that it applies to nonhuman ones. Hume argued that rejecting a "necessary connexion" between causes and effects, a causal glue binding the one to the other, makes it easy to see that there is just one *kind* of cause in the universe, that human and other natural events display the same causal regularities. He notes that a condemned man, imagining his forthcoming execution, will run the natural factors and the human factors preventing his escape together, seeing the "obstinacy of the gaoler" as no less an obstacle than the hardness of the prison bars (E 90). The very recognition that we need not seek any mysterious glue between physical causes and physical effects, says Hume, puts their relationship exactly on a level with the relationship between our motivations and our actions.[11] This insight provides a deep ground for the naturalistic study of history, society, politics, and economics. If causality in general is nothing more than a "conjunction" of events—and a conjunction that may vary, in its frequency, from the exceptionless regularities of physics through a whole spectrum of lesser regularities[12]— then science, which looks for causes, can carry out its work as happily among human events as anywhere else. A somewhat looser set of generalizations than we might otherwise have insisted upon can now count as "science," and we may expect to be presented with a set of regularities with many exceptions, rather than a set of universal laws describing universal forces, from someone who purports to describe for us "the nature and causes" of the wealth of nations.

There is a corresponding looseness, or spectrum of strengths, in that word "nature," which accompanies "causes" in WN's title. "Nature" is one of the most frequently used words in WN.[13] At one point, it appears in two successive paragraphs that describe (1) "the natural course of things," according to which "the greater part of the capital of every growing society is, first, directed to agriculture, afterwards to manufactures, and last of all to foreign commerce," and (2) the fact that this natural order has been "entirely inverted" in all the modern states of Europe (WN 380). The question that this juxtaposition immediately prompts is why an order should be called "natural" if it can be so entirely inverted, and if it is in fact so inverted in all the cases with which the author is immediately acquainted. The first answer to this question is that Smith does say, between the two sentences I have quoted, that the supposedly "natural" order "has . . . been in some degree observed" in every society that had land. He doesn't give any evidence for this, but clearly he is aware that to call something "natural" suggests that it actually occurs in most cases. A second answer to the question is that Smith here means by "natural" what would happen if human activity did not deliberately and forcibly interfere with the course of events, and he will go on to give us detailed evidence that laws enforced by "the modern states of Europe" reversed the natural order of economic development. But the third and deepest answer to our question, which underpins the second one as well, is that by "nature" Smith does not mean what happens necessarily and uniformly, as a Newtonian physicist might, but merely what happens ordinarily, normally, according to some fairly predictable pattern. The nature of a thing need not be its unvarying underlying structure, just something that characterizes how it behaves for the most part. Nature, for Smith, like cause, goes flexible and not fully predictable after Hume's treatment of it.

"Nature" also depends as much on what goes in human minds as on what is out there in the world, for both Hume and Smith. The things of the world are not themselves in our minds, of course, but the patterns we see in their activities, the regularities we discern among them, consist in what Hume, and Smith after him, calls "associations of ideas." Smith adds to Hume that what counts as "natural" may legitimately vary from one group of people to another: "The same orders of succession, which to one set of men seem quite according to the natural course of things, and such as require no intermediate events to join them, shall to another appear altogether incoherent and disjointed" (EPS 44). The *usualness* of a particular order of succession is what defines it as "natural," for Smith, and he realizes that usualness varies with the different courses of experience people have undergone. People with different flows of experience will find different things natural, and the philosopher merely tries, by acquainting him- or herself with as much experience as possible, to find orders that are likely to appear natural to practically anyone, with practically any flow of experience. What seems natural to the philosopher will be so in a fuller sense than what seems natural to anyone else if and only if the philosopher has done the work of incorporating into his own experience as many other people's types of experience as possible: The philosopher goes to work "after the *largest* experience that common observation can acquire" (EPS 45, my emphasis). His advantage over ordinary people consists neither in that he somehow reaches *beyond* experience nor in that he gains access to an unusual, specially veridical *type* of experience, only in that, when he does his job properly, he surveys and brings together all the various experiences that different groups of people ordinarily have. Things thus seem natural to him still only in proportion to the degree to which they flow commonly for him, but if he has done his job well, they will flow in a similar way for most or even all human beings, and not just for this or that idiosyncratic group. Smith, then, calls a particular order of economic development "natural," in the paragraphs from WN discussed above, because, from his wide survey of economic experience, he thinks it conforms with the way most human beings would experience the economic world, if they got beyond some peculiarities of their histories.

6. Philosophy of Science

I distinguish philosophy of science from epistemology. Epistemology is concerned with the basic principles of all knowledge, and investigates questions like whether our thought ever represents reality, what aspect of it does so, and whether the general principles it relies on, like causality, can be justified, while philosophy of science tends to take these questions for granted while asking what methodology yields the best theories of empirical reality. The distinction is not a sharp one, but it does make clear why epistemology but not philosophy of science will investigate whether we can know anything about God, while philosophy of science but not epistemology will ask why some scientific programs are more successful than others. Epistemology operates on a more abstract level than philosophy of science; they stand more or less in the relation that political philosophy has to jurisprudence.

With this distinction in mind, we can say that while Smith does not have much of an epistemology, he does have a philosophy of science. In WN, Smith characterizes "philosophers or men of speculation" as people "whose trade it is, not to do any thing, but to observe every thing" (WN 21); parallel passages in ED and LJ make clear that physicists, astronomers, chemists, and analysts of politics and commerce are to be included under "philosopher," along with moral philosophers and metaphysicians. There is a paradox in this description. Smith is in the middle of his account of the division of labor, of how occupations become more and more differentiated, and in that context it is a bit odd to say that the specific occupation of a philosopher is to be a generalist, to observe "every thing." What matters about this paradox for our purposes is that the job of the philosopher or scientist seems *not* primarily to be the observation of *new* things, the discovery of something no one else has experienced, but the gathering of what everyone else experiences in pieces. Smith does say that this very gathering of observations makes one "capable of combining together the powers of the most distant and dissimilar objects," and thereby of discovering ways of inventing new machines. But, for Smith, the fact that scientists might invent new technology seems to be a side effect of their work, not its primary goal or criterion for success. Smith seems not to share Francis Bacon's famous understanding of science as directed primarily toward greater control over the universe.

Instead, for Smith science is an attempt by the imagination to solve problems it faces in coming to grips with large numbers of "distant and dissimilar" observations. Scientific systems consist in constructions by which the imagination soothes the discomfort it feels when it encounters disruptions in experience. In his *History of Astronomy*, Smith says that "philosophy," which he here again uses to describe physics, astronomy, and chemistry, is "the science of the connecting principles of nature." Nature "seems to abound with events which appear solitary and incoherent with all that go before them" and "which therefore disturb the easy movement of the imagination." The natural philosopher tries to alleviate these disturbances: "Philosophy, by representing the invisible chains which bind together all these disjointed objects, endeavours to introduce order into this chaos of jarring and discordant appearances, to allay this tumult of the imagination" (EPS 45–6). Smith stresses that natural philosophy therefore "may be regarded as one of those arts which address themselves to the imagination," and he proceeds to show how the history of astronomy consists in one attempt after another to "sooth the imagination" by "render[ing] the theatre of nature a more coherent, and therefore a more magnificent spectacle, than otherwise it would have appeared to be" (EPS 46). Scientists come up with "systems," which are "imaginary machine[s] invented to connect in the fancy" the events that are already taking place in reality (EPS 66). These systems—theories—are like machines in their ability to hold complex parts together in a functioning whole: They are complex enough to represent a variety of phenomena, yet unified enough to show our minds how those phenomena may relate to one another. Their purpose is to assist the functioning of our imaginations, and we judge them for their novelty and for their "beauty and simplicity" (EPS 75). The advantage of Newton over Descartes, Descartes over Copernicus, and Copernicus over Ptolemy lies in each case in the fact that the newer system satisfies the imagination more than the one that went before it, that it provides a beautiful and simple explanation for phenomena that were "disturbances" under the older system.

As Andrew Skinner has pointed out, there are startlingly close anticipations of Thomas Kuhn in this account of science,[14] and it is certainly not the picture of the scientist one might have expected in the mid-eighteenth century. Smith's scientist does not primarily go around making precise observations, nor does he mostly carry out carefully designed experiments, nor need he find mathematical laws that explain the observed phenomena. A good scientist *may* come up with such mathematical laws, as Newton did, but the general description of what scientists do, for Smith, is to come up with explanations that "sooth" the imagination, whether by way of mathematical formulae or not. Furthermore, the good scientist addresses himself as much to the systems by which his predecessors arranged the relevant empirical facts as to those facts themselves; his work is defined in large part by its relation to the history of his discipline, not merely by an ahistorical relationship to empirical phenomena. Scientific explanation for Smith soothes the disturbances caused in the imagination by (1) a lack of clarity or coherence in earlier explanations, or (2) a perceived incoherence or tension between earlier explanations and what we currently observe. Thus the validity of each explanation is always relative to its success in overcoming the problems in earlier explanations; there is no absolute and timeless standard by which an explanation might be measured against observations and judged true or false without reference to earlier modes of explanation. As we have seen, Smith ends the history of astronomy by expressing some reservations about the firmness and solidity even of Newton's system, despite the fact that it had thus far "prevail[ed] over all opposition, and . . . advanced to the acquisition of the most universal empire that was ever established in philosophy" (EPS 104). It is not that Smith has doubts about any of Newton's actual principles. He just has shown, in the course of his history of astronomical systems, that it is the way of scientific systems to triumph over past ones and be triumphed over in turn. The effect of this system *of* scientific systems—this system of the philosophy of science—is to put in doubt the possibility that any scientific system, on any subject, will ever provide the final word on that subject, the invincible explanation of the problems with which it is concerned.

This system of scientific systems raises interesting questions about the status of Smith's enterprise in WN. In accordance with his own teachings, Smith presents his "system of natural liberty" in WN in relation to the systems of political economy that preceded him, arguing that its merits are demonstrated by the fact that it can explain what is wrong with mercantilism and Physiocracy (see §3, above). But this means that Smith's system "soothes the imagination," in relation to economic facts, better than the other systems available to people *in his time*. It does not suggest that Smith's system is the final word on political economy, that its principles will hold, that its author even *expects* them to hold, timelessly, in relation to the economic facts available to every generation. Those who make it their business to show how Smith's principles can explain every economic phenomenon today may thus not be using Smith's work as Smith himself hoped future readers would. They may be betraying their master's methodological legacy, rather than preserving it.

Smith's system of systems also has implications for WN in that it presents science as primarily a *backward-looking* rather than a forward-looking enterprise. A common characterization of science today holds, as Bacon did, that it is oriented toward "explanation, prediction, and control,"[15] where the test of a good explanation is that it yields successful predictions that would not have been made otherwise, and enables useful extensions of our technological control over our environment. Smith does not entirely ignore either the role of prediction in evaluating a scientific system (EPS 103) or the possibility that such systems will lend themselves to technological improvements (WN 21), but he plays down these factors in favor of the beauty and simplicity with which a proposed new explanation solves problems in earlier systems.[16] The main job of

Smith's scientist is to put together what has thus far been learned about the world, rather than to go out and learn new facts. Scientific explanation for Smith primarily looks backward, to the ability of the explanation to resolve tensions between past systems and observed facts, rather than forward, to the prediction of future observations or the creation of new tools. Of course, the clarity gained by a backward-looking explanation may lead to good predictions and useful inventions, but that is not the explanation's main goal, nor its main test for validity.[17]

7. Philosophy of Social Science

From the time of Wilhelm Dilthey onward, and in part as a result of Kant's separation of free-willed humanity from the rest of nature, much has been made of the differences between the "sciences of man" (*Geisteswissenschaften*) and the "sciences of nature" (*Naturwissenschaften*). Smith never explicitly separated the science of man from the science of nature, and on the whole I think we can read off his views on what today we call "social science" fairly well from what he says about science in general. Still, there is reason to believe that the imagination, and a backward-looking orientation, play a rather greater role for him in social science than in natural science, and that some of his views anticipate the distinction between the two.

A backward-looking orientation helps account for what would otherwise be a mystery about why Smith engages in building a system of social science at all. Smith's most famous doctrine about political economy, after all, is the doctrine of unanticipated consequences. Social and political policies have a strong tendency to veer from what they were intended to do, according to Smith, to have effects of which their inventors never dreamt. Smith's cognitive particularism, his emphasis on "contextual knowledge," comes into play here: What we grasp best about human life are the detailed facts of our immediate circumstances, and we often err when we try to extrapolate general principles of human behavior from those circumstances and project them into the future. Institutions and policies that are supposed to be around for a long time must necessarily be designed with some such general principles in mind, however, and they often come to grief because their designers failed to anticipate details that eventually undermine their workings.

This effect is intensified by a point that Smith stresses in a very famous passage of TMS: that social facts, unlike facts about inanimate objects, concern an entity—society—every piece of which "has a principle of motion of its own," altogether different from the one a social planner "might chuse to impress upon it" (TMS 234). Smith uses this point to argue against politicians filled with the "spirit of system," politicians who want to impose a grand plan on society. But the point should spell an equally great difficulty for social scientists. If it is impossible to foresee the consequences of human actions in any detail, what can a social science amount to? One can certainly not expect of it the predictive and technological payoff that one might hope for from the work of a James Watt or Joseph Priestley. If we construe "science" as an enterprise whose validity depends on its ability to yield predictive and technological success, then the doctrine of unanticipated consequences would seem to entail that there can be no social science. But, as we have already seen, Smith does not conceive science as directed primarily towards prediction and control. When we bear in mind that Smith, who knew and admired Watt and Priestley, took technological innovations to be a secondary effect, not the primary object, even of systems in natural science, that he saw even systems of natural science as having to have a backward-looking orientation, toward solving the problems of earlier systems, then it becomes clear that there is really no difficulty, for him, about the possibility of a science of man. Social science should be perfectly possible—as long as it has a backward-looking rather than a forward-looking orientation.

And when we look at WN, backward-looking explanation is what we find throughout. After laying out some general principles explaining the nature of markets and prices, Smith proceeds to account for such things as the development of money, the relationship between growth and profit, and the role of banks by drawing patterns out of and applying his general principles to a vast number of historical facts. He then moves on to an historical account of economic development in Europe, explaining away the "unnatural" lack of interest in agriculture prevalent in Europe since the fall of the Roman Empire on the basis of errors made by people in power. These historical reflections lead naturally to a vast attack on the major systems—mercantilism and Physiocracy—that recommended political management of the economy in Smith's day, and the book concludes with modest suggestions for what sorts of things political powers can spend money on, and how they can raise money, without interfering too much with the workings of the economy. So WN moves toward a warning against the hubris of thinking one can predict and control the economy—against the notion that the science of economics might properly yield anything like an economic technology—and it does so by way of an approach that proceeds for the most part by considering historical facts, not general, atemporal principles. Throughout, one is urged to accept the picture in WN largely because it improves upon—clarifies and soothes the tensions in—the analyses of Smith's predecessors. With this backward-looking orientation, it is of course possible to explain consequences of past actions that were unanticipated when the actions were taken, but there is no implication that Smith's system will adequately predict consequences of actions taken now. Nor is there any reason to expect much of a "technological" payoff from the picture. Smith does offer a few proposals for improving his local politico-economic scene, and he may well think of these as parallel to the inventions that scientists, like Watt, can derive from their exhaustive understanding of natural phenomena (see §58 below). But these proposals are small-scale and indexed to British history and tradition; famously, he abjures revolutionary programs for radically remaking society.

The tone in which Smith offers these proposals is, moreover, a modest, even tentative one—they are rarely offered as conclusions from research that he, as an expert on political economy, is uniquely positioned to understand. This makes excellent sense, given the warnings against the spirit of system discussed above. If society, unlike a chessboard, consists of "pieces" each of which "has a principle of motion of its own," then the social scientist, like the politician, should expect his or her proposals to be taken up as at most a *suggestion*, by each of those "pieces," rather than as a statement of what they must do if they are to have any hope of accomplishing their own purposes. The social scientist who recognizes the freedom of other people—it is freedom, of course, that Smith's "principle of motion" obliquely describes—will also recognize that, qua social scientist, he can speak but as one free being to another, not as though his expertise enables him to know his readers better than they know themselves. The social scientist, unlike the natural scientist, describes a system composed of free parts, and he describes it *to* readers who themselves constitute those parts: he must therefore woo his subjects' assent to his account of how they work. To the extent that his work issues in guides to action, his lay readers may reasonably object to his proposals, however well-informed they may be, on the grounds that they run up against what the readers truly want. So if he wants to draw practical proposals out of his work, he will be well-advised to write as an informed layperson, or rather to work against any sharp distinction between "experts" and "laypeople" in this area: to write as an equal partner in the practical conversations of his readership, superior to them only in that he has extended their own mode of thought to a wider range of facts than they know, and to a wider view of how the facts might hold together.

This humane and humanistic conception of social science, with its downplaying of the distinction between expert and layperson, gives us a moral reason for Smith's common-sense style of writing. It also helps bridge the supposed gap between facts and values, between science and moral thinking. For a free person addressing other free people, in ordinary conversation, normally will not siphon off descriptions of the "facts" from his or her moral judgment of those facts. Trying to achieve a "pure objectivity" in which moral standards have no place requires a weird *break* from our ordinary way of looking at things,[18] an affectation that would, if successful, sharply differentiate the author from the ordinary people being addressed. If Smith is trying to conduct social science as an extension of ordinary conversation, of the way free and equal people normally talk to one another, then he should eschew the sharp distinction between facts and values that Hume had urged, and mingle normative comments in with description throughout his work. As we will see below, this is just what he does.

8. Types of Evidence

I noted in section 5 that Smith emphasizes the role of judgment in assessing human affairs, and endorsed Haakonssen's claim that he gives "contextual knowledge," the often inexplicit grasp of complex particulars, priority over theoretical or "system knowledge." One consequence of this emphasis on judgment, and respect for the complexity of particular cases, is that Smith is happy to make use of anecdotal evidence in constructing his economic theory, and suspicious of statistics. He will tell us something about ancient Roman interest rates by way of an inference from a passage in Cicero, while avoiding direct attempts to give precise numerical expression to economic phenomena in his own time. His method, that is, resembles more what we would today consider the method of a historian than the method of an economist. That may be in part because he did not have access to the plethora of economic statistics available to us, but I think it also reflects fundamental methodological commitments. Smith's economics is more like what we would call "history" than what in his own day was called "political arithmetick."[19] We will better understand Smith's version of empiricism if we spend a few moments on the types of evidence found in WN.[20]

First, Smith eschews what he calls "tedious or doubtful calculation[s]" in favor of evidence from very general features of every reader's experience. Thus, in the passage from which this phrase comes (WN 91–3), Smith endeavors to prove that workers' wages are normally above subsistence in Britain by way of (a) the uncontroversial assumption that subsistence is the lowest possible wage level (else workers would die off), together with (b) the facts that wages tend to be higher in the summer than the winter, and that they vary, from year to year and place to place, independently of the price of provisions. If workers can survive on their winter wages, or on the lowest wages available for a given price of provisions, they must do more than survive on the higher wages they earn in the summer and at better-paid places and times. Smith prefers this indirect way of proving his point to the political arithmetic that tries to calculate the wages of working families directly, because he thinks the latter information "cannot be ascertained very accurately . . . , different prices being often paid at the same place and for the same sort of labour, not only according to the different abilities of the workmen, but according to the easiness or hardness of the masters" (WN 95). For similar reasons, he prefers to approximate average profits of stock by way of a country's interest rate than try to calculate those profits directly (105), and he abjures using "very nice computations" to support his claim that industry is more advantageous than agriculture in favor of the "very simple and obvious observation" that all over Europe far more people make great fortunes in trade and manufactures than in agriculture (142; see also 374). In each of these cases, as in Smith's declaration that he has "no great faith in political arithmetick" (534), we see a preference for what everyone knows over what experts know, and a related preference for observation over calculation.

That said, Smith relies a great deal on such experts as Quesnay, Cantillon, Montesquieu, Charles Smith, and Thomas Mun. He constantly alerts us to the fallibility of these experts, however, at one point devoting several pages to the circumstances, including the "slovenly" transcription of ancient statutes of assize by "lazy copiers" (WN 201), that have misled previous writers on the history of the price of silver. He will cite a writer while remarking that the writer may have been "ill informed" (WN 175), acknowledges a mistake in his own research (201), or engages in a "fallacious" type of comparison (170). On the other hand, he assures us that a Monsieur Poivre is "a very careful observer" (173), that a M. Messance is "an author of great knowledge and ingenuity" (102), and that Richard Burn is "very intelligent" (156).[21] Both the criticisms and the assurances put us on our guard. Smith wants us always to be able to evaluate his sources, not just to believe them. Even when he invokes experts, he discourages us from putting too much trust in them.[22]

In addition to relying on other political economists, Smith gleans information from travelogues and works of history. He relies on travelers' accounts particularly often,[23] sometimes noting that a particular traveler was "respectable and well-informed" (187) or "less disposed to the marvellous" than others of his ilk (730).[24] He delights in drawing economic information from historical works not particularly devoted to economic matters, as when he gets an estimate of the early seventeenth century price of butcher's meat from a biography of a prince of Wales (167). Similarly, he treats literary works as opening windows on economic practice in the world of their composition. A conversation in Homer between Agamemnon and Achilles gives evidence for how sovereigns were remunerated in ancient Greece (717–18); another Homeric passage demonstrates the use of oxen for money (38). The fact that Abraham's shekels are said to be "current money with the merchant," yet that he still must weigh them out when he pays Ephron, is offered as proof that coin at that time was marked to indicate fineness but not weight (41). From Cicero's letters, Smith deduces the interest rate in ancient Cyprus (111), and he determines the economic status of teachers in the ancient world with the help of Plutarch and Pliny (149–50).[25]

This use of histories and classical texts is wonderful, but a far more important written source of information to Smith is the law. Over and over again, Smith will use statutes to clinch a point. Of course WN is a book devoted above all to the ways in which governments try to shape and interfere with economies, mostly to ill effect, so law is often its subject matter. But Smith also uses laws to give evidence of ordinary economic practice. He infers market interest rates in sixteenth- and early seventeenth-century Britain from legally imposed interest rates, on the assumption that legal rates need to track the market rate to be effective: "All these different statutory regulations seem . . . to have followed and not to have gone before the market rate of interest" (106; cf. 356–7). Elsewhere, he uses a statute attempting to prevent corruption among parish officers as evidence of such corruption before the statute was passed (153), or says that a sumptuary law prohibiting common people from wearing clothes worth more than 2 shillings per yard is evidence that people had often worn more expensive clothes before that (262). All of these are good inferences, and of types that are still used by historians today. But laws, especially as they appear on the books, are not entirely reliable indicators of actual practice. Legislators may be ignorant of actual practice and try to prohibit something that is either not occurring at all or occurring so often that it cannot be effectively prohibited. Alternatively, some laws are not much enforced, and may even not be intended to be enforced. For reasons like these, Smith has been widely faulted for his heavy reliance on statutes in his account of the laws of settle-ment.[26] Less attention has been paid to the remarkable fact simply *that* Smith, the arch-opponent of legislative involvement in economic matters, should ex-amine economic practice by way of statutes. Smith was of course a great scholar of jurisprudence, giving an influential set of lectures on law a decade before Blackstone, and it is out of those lectures that WN grew. But it is striking that a political economist so strongly identified with the project of getting legislators out of the workings of commerce should perceive those workings so heavily through the lens of the law. That he did so buttresses the case of those, like Nathan Rosenberg, who argue that for Smith economic transactions are never mere "natural" events, spontaneously occurring in the midst of human relation-ships, but practices shaped by their institutional context.[27] On the other hand, perhaps the legal lens through which Smith saw the economy is precisely what persuaded him that law generally does more economic harm than good.

By no means does all of Smith's information come from secondary sources or by drawing inferences from laws. Occasionally Smith tells us things he deter-mined by his own study of public accounts (WN 102, 204, 211), and often he reports bits of information derived either from his own observation or from conversation with people who personally observed the facts in question. He relies particularly often on this sort of information when he describes the prac-tices and circumstances of the poor:

> A common smith, . . . will scarce, I am assured, be able to make above two or three hundred nails in a day, and those too very bad ones. (18)

> [T]here is at this day a village in Scotland where it is not uncommon, I am told, for a workman to carry nails instead of money to the baker's shop or the alehouse. (38)

> In some parts of Lancashire it is pretended, I have been told, that bread of oatmeal is a heartier food for labouring people than wheaten bread, and I have frequently heard the same doctrine held in Scotland. (177)[28]

On other occasions, Smith reports information about labouring people that he does not say he has gathered from personal experience or conversations but that it is hard to imagine he could have come across otherwise; a particularly good example is his detailed description of the lives of the Scottish "Cotters or Cot-tagers" (133). He also tells us, in the opening chapter of WN, that he has personally "seen a small [pin] manufactory" made up of ten workers too poor to afford the appropriate machinery for their work (15), and later in the same chapter that he has observed "several boys under twenty years of age who had never exercised any other trade but that of making nails" (18). These two re-marks suggest that Smith is speaking of himself when he talks, two pages later, of people who are "much accustomed to visit such manufactures" (20). And the wording of this sentence, together with the experiences Smith describes in the first chapter, in turn suggest that Smith is speaking of himself when he refers, in a later chapter, to those "whom either business or curiosity has led to converse much with" the lower ranks of people in both the country and the town. It thus appears that Smith sought out information on the lives of the poor, either by conversations with their employers or by conversations with, and visits to, poor people themselves.[29] To an extent that is surprising in a philosopher, Smith seems to have engaged in what today we would call "field research" on the poor.

But often the experience on which Smith relies cannot be characterized with as lofty a term as "field research." Rather he uses facts available to him casually, as a participant in the common life of his day. Since Smith so often reports his own experience or conversations in support of points about the world around him, I think it is reasonable to presume that whenever he gives no other source for a claim about England or Scotland, and perhaps also for some of his claims about France, he is drawing on this type of evidence. Thus when he tells us that a London carpenter "is not supposed to last in his utmost vigour above eight years" (100) or that 18 pence is "the common price of labor" in and around London while 10 pence is its price in and around Edinburgh (92), it makes sense that his own "contextual knowledge" of these places—two of his own homes for extended periods—is the source of his information. Similarly, Smith is presumably drawing on his own experience, with the experience of his readers as an external check, when he reports on what people "commonly" say or believe: when he talks of the "common complaint that luxury extends itself even to the lowest ranks of the people" (96), of "the popular notion" that the price of silver tends to diminish over time (200), or of the typical complaints of "merchants and master-manufacturers" (108, 115).

If this easy use of the author's everyday experience seems unremarkable, consider how unusual it would be for a social scientist today to rely to any significant degree on what he sees or hears in everyday life. Works of social science today footnote practically every factual claim, no matter how obvious, with references to studies and writings by experts. We wouldn't expect anything quite like that in Smith, to be sure. Still, he seems remarkably unworried about whether his own sense of what is "commonly" felt or opined might be tainted by bias or limited information. Sometimes he seems, indeed, to defy any worry we might have on this score. Thus he tells us that the boys put out to apprenticeships from public charities "generally turn out very idle and worthless" (139). Or, as evidence for the wholesomeness of potatoes, he cites the fact that London streetporters and prostitutes, whom he believes tend to be Irish and therefore raised on potatoes, are "the strongest men and the most beautiful women perhaps in the British dominions" (177). Here he openly uses as evidence, not only his own observation of "neutral" facts, but his own assessment of idleness, strength, and beauty, laden with values as such assessments must be. A reliance on experience is, for him, a reliance on the facts of ordinary or common experience *as they ordinarily or commonly appear*, not stripped of all value-judgments or sifted through some other philosophical sieve for separating objective sense-data from subjective chaff. It is as if he were saying to us, "The participation of the social scientist in the common life around him *must* be an essential source of information for him. How else can he judge the worth of the books he reads or the reports he hears?"

And if Smith does mean to say something like this, then he offers a healthy corrective to those who believed, even then, that social science ought to begin from raw sense-data open to every observer, from purely sensory facts independent of cultural ("common life") meanings, like the sensations of scarlet or orange or white marble with which Hume begins his philosophical psychology (T 5, 25). For it is indeed true that social scientists cannot afford to begin with raw, unsocialized data of this sort, that they cannot put together a picture of social practices from experience construed in such a strongly individualist way. Hume, for all his use of basic, unsocialized sensations of scarlet and white marble in the opening of the *Treatise*, is in fact the person who first put this point: "We must . . . glean up our experiments in [social] science from a cautious observation of human life, and take them as they appear in the common course of the world, by men's behaviour in company, in affairs, and in their pleasures" (T xix). And, in his essay on miracles, Hume laid out a groundwork for the kind of evidence that goes into good history and—what was at the time much the same thing—good social science. "We entertain a suspicion concerning any matter of fact," he says, "when the witnesses contradict each other; when they are but few, or of a doubtful character; when they have an interest in what they affirm; when they deliver their testimony with hesitation, or on the contrary, with too violent asseverations" (E 112–13). Hume makes clear in the next sentence that this list is not meant to be exhaustive, but even if we limit ourselves to what is on it, we get a nice set of questions to ask of any piece of historical testimony:

1. does it cohere with other reports we have?
2. are there plenty of such reports?
3. is the character of the reporters such that we ought to rely on them?
4. are the reporters disinterested, or giving evidence against their interest?
5. does the manner in which the report was delivered suggest uneasiness, possibly from an awareness that one is not telling the complete truth?[30]

Smith proves his points in WN as if he had this list in mind. He likes to pile on an abundance of evidence, all pointing in the same direction; he constantly considers the intellectual virtues of his sources, laying his opinion of their varying skills before the reader; and he worries a great deal about the interest merchants and manufacturers, especially, have in the information they provide. The only one of Hume's criteria he does not seem concerned with is the fifth one, but then it is hard to discern manner of speaking in written records, and we may presume that he made no use of oral information conveyed to him with the accent of dishonesty.

Hume's criteria for good testimony are commonsensical ones, of course, and it is not surprising that Smith would use them, or something like them. But it is worth noting that these are criteria for *historical* evidence, not for the sort of evidence one would use in astronomy or biology, nor criteria that would help one sort out good statistical studies from bad ones. These are criteria which are meant to help *interpret* data, not gather them or ready them for mathematical use, and they are criteria which, accordingly, partake to a considerable degree of the so-called "hermeneutic circle": they presume that their user already knows a great deal about human beings in general and perhaps about the society from which the testimony comes—enough to know what makes for good character among the relevant witnesses, for instance, or what would be likely to give them an interest in the facts they claim to have witnessed. A person whose main criteria for sifting evidence are Hume's is one who sees her work as a matter more of interpreting than of collecting facts.

And this brings me to the point I most want to emphasize: the degree to which all of Smith's empirical sources require substantial interpretation before they will yield evidence for anything. To arrive at his proof that money in Abraham's time was marked for fineness (WN 41), Smith must rely on a clever but hardly conclusive reading of what the phrase "current money with the merchant" means. Smith regularly engages in this kind of interpretative inference from a text or statute before him, and often draws attention to the fact that he is doing so. When he cites a Virginia merchant's testimony that he victualled his ships for 24 or 25 shillings per hundred weight of beef, he adds that only "the best beef . . . is fit to be salted for those distant voyages" (168), so the Virginia merchant must have paid something above the average price of beef. Sometimes he explicitly discusses the errors one can fall into by handling historical data carelessly. Having used a statute in support of his attempt to establish average grain prices in the fourteenth century, he remarks that this statute, since it only incidentally mentions grain prices, is "surely a better evidence of what was reckoned in those times a moderate price of grain, than the prices of some particular years which have generally been recorded by historians and other writers on account of their extraordinary dearness or cheapness" (195–6). He continues by citing a bill of fare for a feast in 1309 and noting that the prices in this bill of fare "are not recorded on account of their extraordinary dearness or cheapness, but are mentioned accidentally" (196).[31]

Nor does this concern with the proper interpretation of data end when Smith turns from texts to what he has himself observed. Smith concludes that there is a high rate of child mortality among the poor in part on the basis of the following complicated bit of evidence: (1) he has been assured by "several officers of great experience" that they cannot fill their regiments from the children of their own soldiers, yet (2) he himself has seldom seen "a greater number of fine children . . . anywhere than about a barrack of soldiers." It follows, he argues, that very few of the children about the barracks "arrive at the age of thirteen or fourteen" (97). Clearly, (2) on its own would tend to establish the *opposite* of Smith's point, especially if one assumed that child mortality mostly meant infant mortality. But Smith never takes observations like (2) on their own; he always puts them together with nonobserved facts like (1), or general principles, before drawing conclusions from them.

Smith also likes to tell us little stories to explain observed facts—a detailed account of why colliers make less than coal-heavers (121), why apothecaries charge such high prices for their products, or why grocers in small seaport towns charge so much more than retailers in other areas (128–9). He thereby suggests that the observed facts themselves do not tell their own story. One of the first things Smith tells us in TMS is that it is impossible fully to understand our fellow human beings—to "sympathize" with them—without imagining ourselves into their situations. Simply observing the external features of their actions will mislead us as to the true nature of those actions. Indeed, observation is not Smith's prime research tool, even if he engaged in far more observation, for the purposes of his work, than most other philosophers before him or since. The primary instrument for coming to grips with empirical information for Smith is interpretation or judgment,[32] not observation. This fits in perfectly with his emphasis on contextual knowledge, and is in service of what I take to be one of the central points of WN: to get the reader to notice the enormous number of fine distinctions between one economic activity and another. Once one begins to see the myriad of tiny differences between similar things that matter hugely to the way those things function economically (e.g., between the uses of gold and silver [189], the transportability of hides and wool [250], or the onerousness of taxes on hearths and taxes on windows [845–6]), one should be led to realize how very easily government attempts to control the economy will fail. And that realization naturally leads to a belief that governments should have unambitious aims, and must institute very nuanced policies to carry out even those aims—which is Smith's main point. But if it is that important to Smith to get us to focus on easily overlooked details, then it makes excellent sense for him to display throughout the need for careful interpretation of every apparent piece of empirical evidence, whether in our own experience or in written texts.

We are now in a position to see why Smith is so suspicious of a calculative approach to economic facts—of "political arithmetick." Those who want to figure out, in general, "the necessary expence of a labourer's family" are all too likely to elide the differences between one labourer's family and another (WN 95). Those who want to give a precise number to average income in a nation will need to ignore or set aside the many differences in income due to local peculiarities in geography or custom, let alone the differences due to the various "abilities of workmen" or to "the easiness or hardness of the masters" (95). Those who want to determine average profits in a nation cannot afford to get too worried about the fact that merchants often have an incentive to conceal their levels of profit (77). In each case, the attempt to come up with a body of data from which one might draw numerical conclusions requires one to regularize the facts being collected, minimizing or ignoring the differences among them, and to abstract from the difficulties of interpreting, and judging, their sources. The facts about human activities come embedded in narratives, from which they can be extracted only with great care. They do not lend themselves to regularization; they require individual attention, such that the peculiarities of each one can be appreciated. In each individual case one needs also to concern oneself with the nature of the source testifying to the fact, whether that be a writer or one's own senses, and determine whether weaknesses in the source require one to suspend conviction in the fact. Smith's work tries throughout to inculcate in his reader these habits of carefully sifting through evidence, and he is ill-served by those who use his authority to promote models of social science in which calculation, and the reduction of human events to "raw data," lie at the heart of the enterprise.

9. Providentialism

Thus far we have looked at Smith's general view of knowledge and science. I want in this section to take up a more specific aspect of his attitude toward scientific explanation: Does Smith implicitly appeal to a providential God to support his claim that markets on the whole work themselves out so as to benefit society?

Athol Fitzgibbons is but the most recent commentator to have accused Smith of relying on a Stoic faith to underwrite his "invisible hand" accounts of how free markets work. If Smith did rely on such a faith, his analyses would of course lose much of their significance for those of us who lack his faith. Fitzgibbons himself regards it as of the highest importance that any contemporary attempt to revive Smith's arguments "dispense with the mythical paraphernalia of the invisible hand."[33] But Fitzgibbons' view represents a misreading of Smith, I think, albeit one which Smith sometimes invites.

First, let's clear away some issues that cloud the main point. The issue is not whether Smith believes in a God, nor even whether he believes in a providential God—a God who runs the world for the good of human beings—but whether he *uses* the existence of a providential God as a *premise* in his social scientific arguments. More likely than not, Smith did believe in God. As we will see later (§15), the many references to God in TMS make best sense as significant parts of Smith's doctrine. By itself, that belief could be irrelevant to scientific practice. If Smith believed, say, in Spinoza's God, a rational principle behind the universe that is unconcerned with human purposes, the belief would have no tendency to lead him toward anthropocentric, and overly optimistic, accounts of social phenomena. But there is reason to believe that Smith saw God as providential, as seeking the well-being of each member of humanity. On occasion, he uses the word "Providence" as a synonym for God (e.g., TMS 185), and at one point he tells us that "the happiness of mankind, as well as of all other rational creatures, seems to have been the original purpose intended by the Author of nature, when he brought them into existence" (TMS 166). What remains is to ask whether this belief in a providential God underwrites any of Smith's claims about how social phenomena work.

And the answer to that question, I think, must be a careful "no," a no that acknowledges that at times Smith does say things that might lead one to read him otherwise. He implies, for instance, that the fact that justice helps preserve society reflects "the wisdom of God" (TMS 87), and he says that "the all-wise Author of Nature has . . . taught man to respect the sentiments and judgments of his brethren" (TMS 128).[34] In each of these passages, however, the invocation of God goes along with an entirely naturalistic, secular account of how the phenomenon in question works. Thus Smith does not *simply* say that God gave us notions of justice so that society would survive; he also shows how systems of justice arise from our natural feelings of resentment, and are enforced in part because we realize that the fabric of society would disintegrate otherwise (86). Thus, similarly, Smith gives an extended explanation of how our tendency to "respect the sentiments and judgments of others" serves our biological and social needs (13–23, 85, 104–5) before ever suggesting that an "all-wise Author" may somehow be at work behind these natural processes. Moreover, despite Smith's tendency to personify Nature, as if it had intentions and purposes, his accounts of how natural processes arise and function can always be cast in the language of evolution by natural selection—not, of course, that Smith had that language yet explicitly available to him. It is true that on a couple of occasions Smith suggests that teleology, and an appeal to God, may play a valuable role in our moral lives, approving of an attitude whereby we regard moral rules "as the commands and laws of the Deity" (TMS 165), and making respectful room for a belief that God will "complete the plan [of justice] which he himself has . . . taught us to begin" by bestowing rewards and punishments in a life to come (TMS 169). But here the beliefs in a providential God are clearly a matter of faith, not something for which empirical evidence could be given, and they serve a moral function rather than a scientific one. As far as I can see, the mention of God or Providence is not necessary to the argument of any empirical claim in TMS, much less to any claim in WN, which does not even make use of religious and teleological language. The religious language that backs up empirical explanations in TMS may be simply a rhetorical flourish, a nod to the conventions of the time, or it may be intended to allow the religiously inclined reader to see how Smith's secular, empirical explanations of human nature are compatible with the view that God establishes and rules all nature. But Smith never requires belief in God as a condition for his empirical explanations to work; he never leaves the source of any feature of human nature or human institutions mysterious, or explains them by way of miracles. I therefore agree with Knud Haakonssen when he says that "[n]othing hinges on teleological explanations" in Smith, that "wherever a piece of teleology turns up in Smith, it is fairly clear where we have to look in order to find a 'real' explanation in terms of . . . efficient causes" (SL 77). We will see the importance of this point above all when we come to consider the invisible hand (§34).

CHAPTER THREE

Moral Philosophy

10. Moral Sentimentalism

Smith's moral philosophy appears in TMS; since this is a book on WN, we need not be concerned with it in detail. But a brief sketch of what goes on in TMS will be helpful—even to the question of why so little moral philosophy appears in WN.

Smith holds, like Hutcheson and Hume before him, that what makes an act morally good or bad is the sentiment that motivates it rather than the effects it might have, and that the appropriate criterion for judging that sentiment is whether an impartial spectator would approve of it or not. He develops the notion of the impartial spectator in far more detail than either of his predecessors, showing how the feelings that ought to motivate us and the feelings by which we judge others' sentiments intimately depend upon one another, and how both arise from an imaginative projection we make into the situation of other people. We share other people's feelings when we imagine what it would be like to be in their situation, not merely when we see them laugh or cry, and it is this imaginative projection, Smith says, that is properly called "sympathy." This conception of the human capacity to share feelings as depending ineliminably on the imagination distinguishes Smith from Hume and Hutcheson, and it leads Smith to place much greater emphasis than his predecessors did on the role of imaginative literature in developing our moral capacities. He also examines, far more than his predecessors, how our moral capacities develop out of social interaction, how they express an ideal of human equality, and how, ideally, we internalize the social rewards for moral action and come to seek praiseworthiness instead of mere praise. In the most interesting and original part of TMS (Part III, which draws on insights in several of Bishop Butler's sermons), Smith shows how deeply our happiness depends on our living up to moral standards, how we aspire to and are made happy by the internalization of standards of virtue that we initially regard as imposed on us by our society. He thereby provides the century's deepest response to Mandeville. Mandeville's notion of virtue as a self-interested search for praise is undermined when we properly understand wherein our "self-interest" consists, according to Smith. No one will be truly happy who is not also truly virtuous: Happiness consists, for social beings like us, in winning the love of others by living up, internally as well as externally, to their expectations of us.

Four features of this account are particularly important for our purposes. First, Smith's definition of a morally good sentiment is just that an impartial spectator would approve of that sentiment, not that it is a variety of benevolence. For Smith's teacher Hutcheson, goodness by definition was equivalent to benevolence. For Smith it is therefore possible, as it was not possible for Hutcheson, that a sentiment directed to the care of oneself could count as morally good. An impartial spectator will not be merely neutral about but will actively approve of people taking care of their own lives and health, Smith says, and will disapprove of self-neglect and suicide (TMS 304, 287).

Second, Smith's moral theory is deeply opposed to utilitarianism, especially as that doctrine was to be developed by Bentham. Smith argues against the proto-utilitarian strains in Hume that make justice, at least, look as though it might be justified primarily for its good results rather than for the intention that goes into each just act. An action is not good if it is motivated by a vicious sentiment, for Smith, even if it should turn out to have excellent consequences for the happiness of other people. It follows that when Smith notes approvingly, in WN, that certain types of actions contribute to the public good without their agents ever intending them to have that effect, we must be careful not to confuse this endorsement with *moral* approval. If free market societies deserve moral approval—and it is not clear that Smith's moral theory really allows for moral approval or disapproval of whole societies—that will have to be for some reason other than the good effects of free market institutions. Of course, *aiming* for the happiness of others remains a morally good thing, for Smith, but it is only the aim, and not the result, that deserves moral approbation.

Third, Smith has a far more deeply social conception of the self than did his predecessors. Hutcheson and Hume both see human beings as having a natural disposition to *care* about the good of their society, but for Smith all of our feelings, self-interested and benevolent, are *constituted by* a process of socialization. Smith conceives of humanity as less capable of solipsism than Hume does, less capable of the thoroughgoing egoism that Hume, in his famous discussion of the "sensible knave," found it so difficult to refute (E 282). At the same time, Smith reconciles his social conception of the self with a respect for the absolute importance of each individual, and the capacity of each individual for independent choice. Ethical self-transformation is inspired and guided by social pressures but ultimately carried out by the individual for him- or herself; the "impartial spectator" begins as a product and expression of society, but becomes, once internalized, a source of moral evaluation by which the individual can stand apart from, and indeed criticize, his or her society. Individually free action and the social construction of the self are compatible, for Smith, even dependent on one another.

Finally, Smith envisions moral development as a task of self-transformation that is often opposed to the search for social status or material goods. Smith explains how our standards for character arise out of an attempt to balance the feelings we have as people "principally concerned" in any situation with the feelings we have as spectators to those situations. Both parties seek "sympathy," the sharing of feelings, but the person principally concerned will always have stronger feelings about the situation than will the spectator, and a balance can only be found if the former brings down the strength of his feelings while the latter brings her feelings up. From these two processes, says Smith, we get two different sets of virtues: the "awful" or "respectable" virtues by which people attempt to mitigate their natural reactions, on the one hand—the virtues of self-denial and self-command—and the "amiable" virtues of compassion and sensitivity to others, on the other. Both sets of virtue require cultivation, and the first set, which goes strongly against our natural grain, is especially hard to master. Moreover, as noted above, Smith believes that we seek ideally to live up internally to these standards, to incorporate them within ourselves: "The man of real constancy and firmness . . . does not merely affect the sentiments of the impartial spectator. He really adopts them. He almost identifies himself with, he almost becomes himself that impartial spectator, and scarce even feels but as that great arbiter of his conduct directs him to feel" (147).

"Scarce even feels" but as virtue would have us feel: Smith sees the ultimate goal in morality as a transformation such that one no longer even desires to engage in vice, cruelty, or injustice. He indeed suggests that the moral person *sees* differently than the nonmoral one, and, in particular, sees his or her happiness in a different light, as constituted in large part by virtue rather than merely being constrained by it (TMS 115–17, 146–8). We will need to bear this in mind when we consider how seriously Smith, in WN, could have regarded the mere acquisition of material goods to be sufficient for happiness. The accounts both of happiness and of virtue in TMS entail that Smith would have had to forget or change a great deal of his moral theory if he indeed came, as so many people have claimed, to believe that material self-interest was our sole motivation, and its satisfaction our sole good.

11. The *Wealth of Nations* and Moral Philosophy

This brings us to the question of whether there is a moral component to Smith's account of politics and economics in WN. For over a century, people have repeatedly asked, why would a moral philosopher write a book like WN? A commonly given answer is that WN represents Smith's abandonment of moral philosophy in favor of social science. But this cannot be right. Smith did not give up on moral philosophy after writing WN. On the contrary, he spent much of the 1780s trying to put his jurisprudential lectures into shape for publication, and his last major project, completed just before he died, was an extensive revision of TMS. A deeper claim insinuated by the question and its answer—that TMS sees people as having irreducible moral impulses while WN is governed by a view of people as exclusively self-interested (the so-called "Adam Smith Problem")—is also not right, as we will see in part II of this book. But a third claim, recently made by Vivienne Brown (ASD 43–54, 162–4), that characterizes the discourse of TMS as a moral one and the discourse of WN as an amoral one, has merit, and it is that claim I would like to examine here.

We should not accept Brown's characterization of WN as is. WN is shot through with remarks like the following:

> It is but equity . . . that they who feed, cloath, and lodge the whole body of the people, should have such a share of the produce of their own labour as to be themselves tolerably well fed, cloathed and lodged. (WN 96)

> If masters would always listen to the dictates of reason and humanity, they have frequently occasion rather to moderate, than to animate the application of many of their workmen. (100)

> All for ourselves, and none for other people, seems, in every age of the world, to have been the vile maxim of the masters of mankind. (418)

> The savage injustice of the Europeans rendered an event, which ought to have been beneficial to all, ruinous and destructive to several of [the] unfortunate countries [in America]. (448)[1]

These remarks are not morally neutral, and they presuppose that the agents they criticize are capable of living up to norms of equity, humanity, generosity, and justice. Smith's conception of social science does not preclude the introduction of a moral point of view into one's descriptions, is not at all like the positivistic social science of the mid-twentieth century, in which mixing "facts" and "norms" was looked upon as a betrayal of the scientific enterprise. Moreover, Brown reads WN as amoral in large part because she takes justice, which the book treats throughout as a constraint on economic transactions, to be a "lower-order" virtue for Smith since it is based on rules rather than on the internal dialogue of the impartial spectator (ASD 46–9). But Brown's reading of Smith on justice is tendentious. Although it is true that merely abstaining from injustice is an act that "seems scarce to deserve any reward" for Smith, he takes the *disposition to respect justice*—which amounts, as we will see later (§16), to the disposition to respect all other human beings as equals—to be a mark of high virtue. And WN often requires, of "masters," of statesmen and legislators, and of judges, that they display the disposition to respect justice and not merely abstain from acts of injustice.

In addition, we should see a certain moral impulse behind Smith's tendency, throughout WN, to project us imaginatively into the detailed circumstances of various actors in our economic environment. Recall that Smith makes imagining oneself into other people's situations crucial to sharing feelings with them—and thereby being able to feel true benevolence, justice, and so on toward them. We should therefore be alert to the possibility that passages like the following, with their sharp presentation of details in other's situations that we might otherwise have overlooked, have an implicit, if not an explicit, moral function:

> The man who works upon brass and iron, works with instruments and upon materials of which the temper is always the same, or very nearly the same. But the man who ploughs the ground with a team of horses or oxen, works with instruments of which the health, strength, and temper are very different upon different occasions. The condition of the materials which he works upon too is as variable as that of the instru-

ments which he works with, and both require to be managed with much judgment and discretion. The common ploughman, though generally regarded as the pattern of stupidity and ignorance, is seldom defective in this judgment and discretion. . . . His understanding, . . . being accustomed to consider a greater variety of objects, is generally much superior to that of [the mechanick in a town], whose whole attention from morning till night is commonly occupied in performing one or two very simple operations. (WN 143–4)

To improve land with profit, like all other commercial projects, requires an exact attention to small savings and small gains, of which a man born to a great fortune, even though naturally frugal, is very seldom capable. The situation of such a person naturally disposes him to attend rather to ornament. . . . The elegance of his dress, of his equipage, of his house, and houshold furniture, are objects which from his infancy he has been accustomed to have some anxiety about. The turn of mind which this habit naturally forms, follows him when he comes to think of the improvement of land. He embellishes perhaps four or five hundred acres in the neighbourhood of his house, at ten times the expence which the land is worth after all his improvements. . . . (385–6)

[In modern battles] the noise of fire-arms, the smoke, and the invisible death to which every man feels himself every moment exposed, as soon as he comes within cannon-shot, and frequently a long time before the battle can be well said to be engaged, must render it very difficult to maintain any considerable degree of . . . regularity, order, and prompt obedience, . . . In an antient battle there was no noise but what arose from the human voice; there was no smoke, there was no invisible cause of wounds or death. Every man, till some mortal weapon actually did approach him, saw clearly that no such weapon was near him. (699)

These are but a few of the passages in WN in which Smith gives us a brief but remarkably close phenomenology of another person's life, inviting us to imagine ourselves into that life. Given Smith's view of the importance of the imagination to moral judgment, it would be odd to suppose that these imaginative exercises serve no moral purpose. And it is indeed fairly obvious how the vignettes above help us to understand, and thereby overcome common prejudices against, seemingly stupid ploughmen, seemingly incompetent aristocrats, and seemingly cowardly soldiers. With his gift for clarifying ordinary beliefs by way of a closer than ordinary attention to detail and a greater than ordinary use of the imagination, Smith can be read as carrying out moral purposes all through WN.

But it is fair to say that moral concerns are *muted* in WN. Not only do most of the analyses in the book presume that agents will act merely to maximize material gains, but there are a number of points where one might expect moral concerns to be raised yet only pragmatic ones appear (see below, §41). It is also true that the tone of the book, as Brown says (ASD 43–6), is more "monologic," less inviting of internal debate, than that of TMS, even if the distinction between the two works is not as sharp as she supposes. WN is not shy about employing normative discourse on occasion, but it generally keeps that discourse in the background, allows it to be heard only in counterpoint to the main, purely descriptive theme. To understand better why Smith might want to subdue the moral voice in this way, it will be helpful to return to his moral philosophy a little.

Consider two additional features of Smith's moral philosophy. First, Smith puts great emphasis on the difficulty of self-judgment. The fourth edition of TMS had a subtitle: "An Essay towards an Analysis of the Principles by which Men naturally judge concerning the Conduct and Character, *first of their Neighbours, and afterwards of themselves.*"[2] According to this edition, at least, the work falls into two main parts, moving from the judgment of others to the judgment of ourselves, and in all editions, that is how Book III, the deepest section of the work, presents itself. We judge first of others, then apply those judgments to ourselves (TMS 109–13), and it is only *because* we sometimes see ourselves as if we were one of those "others" that we are moved at all to criticize ourselves and change our behavior. The self is elusive, says Smith, and does not naturally look at itself. Only after living for the approval of others for a while does it grow disgusted with groundless approval and seek "praiseworthiness" rather than praise alone (110–12). To figure out whether it is praiseworthy or not, it must however turn its tendencies to judge others in upon itself, it must develop a "conscience," and this is extremely difficult. "When we are about to act, the eagerness of passion will seldom allow us to consider what we are doing, with the candour of an indifferent person," says Smith, and when we have done acting, we all too often "endeavour to exasperate anew those unjust passions which . . . misled us" into our original action (157–8). In either case, we avoid judging our motivations honestly: "It is so disagreeable to think ill of ourselves that we often purposely turn away our view from those circumstances which might render that judgment unfavourable." Smith compares looking at oneself honestly to operating on oneself; we no more want to tear from our minds "the mysterious veil of self-delusion" than we want to open our bodies. Self-deceit is the "fatal weakness of mankind," the "source of half the disorders of human life."

Aside from a couple of powerful sermons by Bishop Butler, on which Smith is probably drawing, there is no more thorough investigation of self-delusion in all the moral philosophy of the eighteenth century. But if self-delusion is the source of half the human evils, and if it is so extremely difficult to overcome, then how should a moral philosopher—or anyone else—go about trying to *change* people morally, trying to get them to see that they are doing something wrong? Ultimately, if they are truly to change, they must see this themselves, and they will resist doing that. They will "turn away [their] view" from any circumstances the philosopher points out that present their own behavior in an unfavorable light, and they will "endeavour to exasperate anew" precisely the passions the philosopher urges them to reject. At a minimum, this suggests that a would-be moral critic needs to put his criticisms of others *indirectly*, and will perhaps do best by describing their behavior in ways they can see as wrong, without putting that moral judgment into the description. If you want to point out to me something you think I am doing wrong, but have good reason to believe that I will hear any moral criticism you express as in service of my enemies, or as a reflection of your failure to understand my feelings, then you might want to avoid any directly moral comment on my behavior and try to arouse my moral judgment, against my own actions, by way of simply describing the effects of my actions on my victims, in dry but imaginative detail. On Smith's account of self-deception, one will need all sorts of indirect discourse,[3] including apparently amoral discourse, to provoke others into seeing themselves in a moral light. This gives *moral* reason for Smith to write *amoral* political discourses. Presenting "just the facts, ma'am," without presuming to judge those facts, may often be the best way to open other people up to judging themselves. WN is in certain ways a triumph of *indirect ethics*, of an ethical teaching that may succeed in changing the reader precisely because it avoids explicitly ethical terminology.

The second feature of Smith's moral thought to which I want to draw attention is the definition Smith provides for "morality." The idea guiding Smith's entire approach to morality, I believe, is that the ordinary way we use the word "moral" is such that moral judgments are judgments of which an impartial spectator would approve. It is characteristic of Smith's method in general to try to draw philosophical definitions out of commonsensical ones, and in TMS he appeals over and over, as evidence for his points, to what "we think," "we admire," "we approve" (e.g., TMS 17, 24, 62, 178, 323); in particular, he does so to establish that "we" do not agree with Hutcheson that morality can be defined as benevolence (304). His arguments for why morality cannot be equated with prudence, or with social utility, can also be best understood as resting on the claim that we, generally and ordinarily, simply do not *mean* by "moral" what best serves either an agent's self-interest or the utility of a society; moral language is not identical with prudential or utilitarian language. Rather, when we say something is morally right we mean that it is an action of which an impartial spectator would approve. And this account of the definition of morality goes nicely along with Smith's account of the genesis of the impartial spectator. We construct the spectator within ourselves by internalizing the reactions to our own behavior by actual spectators while correcting for their misinformation (116) and their biases (129, 135). The man of true virtue seeks to act "not so much according to the light in which [other people] actually regard him, as according to that in which they would regard him if they were better informed" (TMS 116). Morality is thus not identical with the judgments of one's society, but it is identical with those judgments when corrected for partiality.

But on this account, Smith's definition of morality entails that *what our surrounding society calls "right" and "wrong" is in fact right and wrong*, subject to the proviso that the members of that society (a) have adequate information to judge properly and (b) are not being misled by passions or selfish interests. The impartial spectator is an extension or idealization of our society's mode of moral judgment. The disadvantage of this position, as many critics of Smith have pointed out, is that it veers dangerously close to relativism, dangerously close to identifying morality with what each society merely *holds* to be morality. The internal, idealized spectator avoids errors due to misinformation and passion, but otherwise it is simply an extension of external, actual spectators. In particular, it uses the same standards for evaluation as those actual ones do. If the moral standards, the basic moral sentiments, of a particular society are themselves fundamentally corrupt, say Smith's critics—if, say, a feeling of repugnance for Africans or Jews has become confused with a moral feeling, and a society's judgments of these people have been comprehensively skewed as a result—the impartial spectator within each individual will share, rather than correcting for, that corruption. It must be admitted that this difficulty of criticizing social standards represents a significant weakness in Smith's theory.[4] Yet at the same time it represents one of Smith's great strengths. For to say that our society's standards for right and wrong on the whole define what we take to be right and wrong fits the phenomenology of real moral judgment far better than the supposedly "higher" or "deeper" philosophical views by which an abstract standard—say, the principle of utility or the categorical imperative—defines what is right and wrong regardless of what our neighbors have to say. This is not the place to get into the pros and cons of moral relativism, but one reason that that view has been so widely accepted among anthropologists, even while being scorned by philosophers, is that almost everyone, in almost every society, tends in fact to share the moral attitudes of her society on an immediate, "gut" level, even if she officially proclaims a commitment to some philosophically grounded moral principle, and even if she tries, in some cases, to use philosophical argument to overcome her gut identification. Hardly anyone in America, no matter how "enlightened," *felt* that homosexuality was morally acceptable until quite recently—and hardly anyone in "enlightened" circles today can quite *feel* that homosexuality is morally wrong, even if their religion or political views might lead them to that conclusion. So Smith's yoking of moral views to social attitudes captures a deep intuition about morality, while his insistence that we correct our society's views for misinformation and bias makes some room, if perhaps not quite enough room, for people to have a critical and not merely conservative relationship to their society's attitudes. Making an internal, impartial spectator the arbiter of our moral judgments allows Smith to track the ordinary language meaning of "morality" very closely.

But the fact that Smith brings proper moral judgment so close to what, in ordinary social life, people actually judge to be right and wrong means that we should not expect him to launch external or transcendental critiques of his society's practices. Once again, we encounter his preference for immanent critique of everyday life, where critique is necessary. If everyone's society profoundly shapes everyone's moral standards, then, for one thing, who is Adam Smith to assume that the criticisms he might offer of his society could flow from a moral standard radically different from those his society taught him? And, for another, how could Smith, or any other would-be moral critic, expect his society to listen to him if he merely rejected its standards, rather than showing it how an impartial spectator, using its own standards, would condemn this or that particular action or institution?

I take Smith's conception of moral thought to give him two reasons, then, for employing a mostly amoral discourse in WN, even when he finds institutions in his society he wants to criticize. He cannot, on his own account, ever be morally persuasive unless he uses standards drawn from within his society's own moral discourse, and he cannot expect to change practices deeply rooted in people's immoral desires, and self-deceit about those desires, by way of direct assault. He therefore on the whole tries to bring out the evil in practices like slavery or the oppression of poor workers by simply laying out the relevant facts—describing the life of the working poor, for instance, so as to bring out its difficulty and dehumanization—and allowing the reader to draw his or her own moral conclusions. Alternatively, he will show what is wrong with certain institutions from a utilitarian standpoint (the inefficiency of slavery) and not stress their intrinsic evil. Once in a while, he allows himself the luxury of a direct moral exhortation, but these outbursts are relatively rare.

Of course, there are some simpler possibilities for why WN employs a generally amoral mode of discourse. One is that moral concerns are, often, irrelevant to the subject matter.[5] The components of price, and the relationship between natural and market prices, are not subjects into which moral concerns need enter—although, even here, there was once a "just price" tradition which Smith passes over in silence. Another possibility is that Smith has adjusted his rhetoric to the audience he wants to reach in WN. Since the people who can actually make the institutional changes Smith supports are politicians and the merchants who influence them, and since these people tend to be hard-boiled realists who dislike moral preaching—"practical men," as they think of themselves—Smith avoids extensive investigation of the moral aspects of economic relationships, and stresses the inefficiency of primogeniture, entail, slavery, and the like instead. As Jerry Muller has pointed out (see §2), Smith was always aware of the need to tailor the presentation of one's messages to one's audience, and the audience for WN was unlikely to be responsive to moral homilies.

Finally, as I have noted, Smith does lace the descriptive narrative of WN with a fair number of normative comments. He clearly does not believe that social science requires a strict separation between facts and values. I take that to be a mark of what I have called Smith's common-sense approach. It is part of common sense, part of our ordinary way of approaching the world, to move fluidly between factual description and moral judgment. To describe a situation that amounts to great injustice without seeming to notice that it *is* an injustice would be to describe it poorly, in most people's ordinary, unreflective view, just as to issue moral judgments without getting the facts right would ordinarily be regarded as *morally*, as well as descriptively, inadequate. What the strict positivist—influenced by Smith's friend Hume—asks us to do in the social sciences is an exercise in breaking ourselves from our ordinary view of things, in suspending that view in favor of a supposedly superior "objective detachment," and this Smith refuses to do. He is, I believe, right in this: whatever may be the case in the natural sciences, the ideal of complete "objective detachment" in the social sciences requires the scientist to react, or pretend to react, to human beings as if he or she were not one, and that is both well-nigh impossible—the values that have been suppressed sneak in anyhow—and of questionable use *even from the scientific point of view*. Do we really see other human beings more clearly if we pretend that we are not one of them? May it not instead be that the very sensory organs enabling one person to grasp what others are doing include sympathy, the ability to share feelings, interests, outlooks—what Dilthey called "Verstehen" and Gadamer a "fusion of horizons"—such that to remove our humanity, when studying other humans, is rather like removing our eyeballs so as to see better?

12. A Moral Assessment of Capitalism?

A few words, now, on the reasons for Smith's moral approval of the economic system we call "capitalism" (what he called "commercial society"). Smith seems to have four main reasons for this approval:

> (1) the broadening of free markets reduces the price of food, and of other basic goods that human beings need, thereby raising the standard of living of the worst-off. (WN 96)
>
> (2) international free trade increases peace and friendly relations among different peoples: "Commerce . . . ought naturally to be, among nations, as among individuals, a bond of union and friendship." (WN 493)
>
> (3) a commercial economy requires and is conducive to the rule of law, and to a decrease in dependency among workers: "[C]ommerce and manufactures gradually introduced order and good government, and with them, the liberty and security of individuals, among the inhabitants of the country, who had before lived almost in a continual state of war with their neighbours, and of servile dependency upon their superiors. This . . . is by far the most important of all their effects." (WN 412; see also LJ 332–3, 486–7)
>
> (4) participation in market exchanges fosters the virtues of self-reliance and self-government, virtues that are crucial to the development of good character in general. (LJ 333)

When I originally planned this book, I hoped to show that Smith's main reason for approving of free commercial economies was (4). I planned to argue that Smith saw the very impersonality of the modern socioeconomic world as capable of training us in the "awful virtues" (TMS 23, 63), the virtues by which we control our desires and emotions. I may not love my butcher and baker, I may indeed have no feelings for them at all, but to get what I want from them I must at least moderate my self-centeredness down to the point where I can present to them a plausible understanding of their needs, and a willingness to help fulfill those needs. If Smith's paradoxical way of getting at the self only through the other is at work here, it is reasonable to assume that I can achieve a more appropriate, better balanced sense of my own worth and just deserts by forcing myself to lessen my demands in the presence of others. The very fact that I need to appeal to the butcher's self-love helps me achieve self-command. And I need even more to master my own passions, of course, when I look for a job. Thus the market, by its very requirement that we appeal to other people's self-interest, can replace war as a modern training ground for self-command. This thesis is especially appealing because of the delicious irony by which what has always been considered a moral *flaw* of Smith's could be transformed into a virtue.

I still believe that something of this argument can be found throughout Smith's work. Smith explicitly says in LJ that the spread of commerce fosters virtues like probity (LJ 333, 528, 538), and he implies in WN that a certain dignity comes with our willingness not to rely primarily on the benevolence of others.[6] But in its strong version, the thesis is an exaggeration. Smith himself calls the way in which commerce helped to introduce "order and good government," and conduce, thereby, to liberty and independency, "by far the most important" of its effects. This is a political, not a moral, consequence of the free market, and WN is concerned throughout primarily with political rather than moral conditions. "Independency" does have some relationship to self-command, for Smith, but the two are not identical. The first, a political condition, helps make possible the second, moral, condition, but even *with* independency, many an individual will not develop the corresponding moral virtue. Smith is, moreover, ambivalent about the moral advantages of the commercial world, famously condemning the moral costs of the division of labor in Book V, and writing at one point in Book II that the replacement of feudalism with the commercial world has meant that a "liberal or generous spirit" has given way to a "trifling, . . . base and selfish disposition" (349). Charles Griswold characterizes Smith's attitude toward modernity as ambivalent throughout (AVE 20, 24–6), and on the value of commerce, at least, I think he is quite right.

Despite the passage describing liberty and security as the most important of commerce's effects, Smith seems elsewhere in WN to regard (1), (2), and (3) as of about equal importance, bringing out the contribution of commerce to a country's wealth, and in particular to the well-being of its poorest inhabitants, in many places, and devoting much of his criticism of the mercantilists to the way they drag their nations into wars. Montesquieu had already stressed the tie between commerce and peace, and Smith takes over the point wholeheartedly (see §60 below). And the tie between commerce and wealth could be described as the central point of the entire book, if we need to say that the book has any central point.

So I would not want to judge which of the three first reasons I have given is Smith's main one for approving of capitalism, but I think it is clear that all three are more important than the fourth, directly moral, one. The three political advantages of free commerce can *conduce* to morally good lives—it is difficult or impossible to develop a good moral character if one is starving, fighting wars, or unfree—but they do not directly make any of the individuals in a society morally good, and they do not, since nothing can, make a society *as a whole* morally good. We do not take an original interest in the well-being of society as a whole, Smith says, just in the well-being of the individuals within it: "our regard for the multitude is compounded and made up of the particular regards which we feel for the different individuals of which it is composed" (TMS 89–90). Whole societies are neither good nor evil: Moral evaluation properly fits individuals, who have sentiments and motivations, not aggregates of individuals. But societies can be more or less well suited to enable the individuals within them to live decent lives, and it is this moral function of society, rather than its ability to maximize consumer goods, that most interests Smith. By a different route, then, we see again that Smith is no utilitarian: The maximization of amoral pleasures, and their distribution to the greatest number of people, holds no interest for him. What marks a good society is that it provides its people with liberty and their basic needs. One can find practically any pleasure worth having "where there is only personal liberty" (TMS 150), and the great advantage of a well-governed over a poorly-governed state is just that in the former the subjects "are better lodged, . . . are better clothed, . . . are better fed" (TMS 186). Commerce tends to bring freedom in its train, and to improve the lodging, clothing, and sustenance of the worst off. These basic goods are all that one needs to lead a decent life—and therefore enough to make commercial society worth striving for and preserving.

PART II

Human Nature

CHAPTER FOUR

Overview

13. Philosophy and the Theory of Human Nature

Every political and moral philosopher has some theory of human nature. Often that theory gets elaborated in considerable depth—think of the discussion of the tripartite soul in Plato's *Republic*, or Kant's long discussions of our "human" versus our "rational" nature.[1] For one philosopher, human beings are essentially rational, for another they are essentially emotional; for one philosopher, they are much like, for another they are radically different from, other animals; for one philosopher, they seek union with God, for another pleasure, for a third freedom. The theory of human nature, for each philosopher, sets limits to moral expectations—one cannot expect things of people that they cannot do—and helps set moral and political goals. It is pointless to arrange one's state so as to maximize material pleasures if what people really seek is freedom or philosophical enlightenment, and it is equally silly to make freedom or enlightenment the central aim of one's politics if people are capable of taking an interest only in material pleasures.

So a theory of human nature can do a great deal of work in moral and political theory. But in the examples I have given, the theory of human nature is a theory of the human *essence*. When we ask after the "nature" of human beings we are looking for what human beings "really" want, beneath the surface trappings. We are asking, "What will fulfill our deepest yearnings?"—which may be unknown to most of us. What does our *nature*, as opposed to this or that accidental feature of our selves, lead us to desire and do? These questions are not purely empirical ones; they are also normative ones, about what human beings should be like as much as about what they are like.

We might suppose that a scientific theory of human nature will not be like this, that a social scientist like Adam Smith, in a book like WN, will employ a purely empirical account of what human beings are like, and avoid normative notions when constructing that account. Surely, to come up with a scientific account of what people are like, one needs simply to look at historical evidence, or carry out psychological and sociological studies, not bring in the morally loaded categories favored by philosophers. One might draw on statistical surveys, or run controlled experiments, or draw inferences from the work of biologists, or one might simply collect observations, from personal experience or from history, but in any case one wants the account of what people are like to reflect some empirical data set and nothing more.

But it is not that easy to distinguish the social scientist from the moral philosopher. In the first place, as we saw in Part I, to study society is to study a system in which each piece of the system has a "principle of motion" of its own—each piece is *free*. That freedom must be factored into the work of the social scientist: The possibility always exists that a human subject answering a survey, or participating in an experiment, or being observed in everyday life, is deceiving herself or deliberately misrepresenting herself to the scientist. The objects studied in social science are unlike the objects of astronomy or physics. We do not have to worry about whether a planet is misrepresenting itself, or whether its designs on the scientist might affect the scientist's designs on it. This difference leads to a difference in the way the two kinds of science handle evidence. Because social scientists need to worry about deception and self-deception, the evidence for any account they may have of human nature must be sifted in accordance with some theory about how best to *interpret* human actions and sayings. Yet any such theory of interpretation will in turn need to rely on some account of human nature, if only to determine when human beings are likely to misrepresent themselves. This is one version of the so-called "hermeneutic circle," whose importance for social science has been stressed, in recent years, by Hans-Georg Gadamer and Charles Taylor.[2]

In the second place, even for social scientific purposes, we want our account of human nature to tell us what people are *capable of* and not merely what they actually do. It is certainly possible, perhaps even likely, that only a few people ever achieve what everyone is capable of achieving. Given the right discipline or the right social conditions, perhaps everyone would be a Socrates or a Gandhi, and if so, it might be worthwhile to aim at everyone's being like that—but then we must all have been living for centuries with poor conditions for human flourishing. To be sure, one reason we have put up with these conditions is that most of us do not aspire to being like Socrates or Gandhi. But might that not be because we have been convinced, wrongly, that we cannot be like them? Even if people say, "no, even if I could be like Socrates or Gandhi, I wouldn't want to," we cannot be sure they are right. They might be deluded about themselves, about what they subconsciously want or would want if they were enlightened by better information, better self-understanding, better philosophy, and so on. We might all be badly educated, or led astray by self-destructive urges, or in some other way clouded about what we really want and can do, and if so, our self-reports will not represent what human nature is truly like. Of course our self-reports might instead be quite reliable, and we may have good reason to believe that we do not aspire to being like Socrates or Gandhi. But we do not want that good reason to fall out, tautologically, from an account of human nature that *defines* what people can and cannot do by what they in fact do or fail to do. We do not want the possibility of having strenuous aspirations for ourselves to be excluded from the picture of human nature by the mere assumption that people cannot possibly have aspirations other than the ones they explicitly avow.

It follows that accounts of human nature, while they certainly should be responsible to empirical data about human behavior, must interpret those data with some suspicion, and be open to information about what people might seek and achieve if they understood themselves differently. Smith's account of human nature, like his teacher Hutcheson's, follows this model. Hutcheson led his readers through a series of imaginative exercises to demonstrate that we are not, as Hobbes and Mandeville had claimed, purely self-interested beings. In his *Inquiry into the Original of Our Ideas of Beauty and Virtue* he asked his readers, among other things, to consider the fact that they tend to sympathize with heroic historical figures even when they themselves are heirs to the enemies of those figures, or to people who gained by those figures' deaths (OV, I.iii). By such exercises Hutcheson hoped to demonstrate, to the satisfaction of each reader, that he or she was capable of disinterested admiration for virtue: "That the perceptions of moral good and evil are . . . different from those of natural good or advantage, every one must convince himself, by reflecting upon the different manner in which he finds himself affected when these objects occur to him" (ibid., I.i). Hutcheson implied that this introspective discovery can be used to interpret the motivations of historical agents, such that we can interpret them, as well as ourselves, as acting on benevolence as well as self-interest. Smith similarly appeals to introspection to make his case that we bring our sentiments down to a level with which others can sympathize (TMS 21–2) and that we seek ultimately to be praiseworthy rather than merely praised (114). He also believes, as we have seen, that we properly share other people's feelings only by imagining how we would feel in their situations, and that that requires us to do more than just listen to what they say about themselves or observe how, externally, they behave. This use of introspection and imaginative projection to interpret human motivations provides Smith with a standard of judgment, independent of purely behavioral evidence about human nature, such that, on the one hand, he can be skeptical of some claims to disinterested motivation, and, on the other, he can suggest that some agents are more capable of disinterested action than they seem to be. Thus within the space of one famous chapter in WN we are told both that it is an "affectation" when merchants say they are trading for the public good and that the deliberations in a legislature could be more often directed by "an extensive view of the general good" than they normally are (WN 456, 472). Thus, similarly, Smith both tells us that "the greater part of men" try to better their condition by increasing their material goods, and hints—what he will say explicitly in the final version of TMS—that there is another kind of "bettering our condition," a moral kind that involves improving our character and has nothing to do with acquiring material goods (WN 341; TMS 62). Smith does not share the bias toward "expressed preferences" of his contemporary heirs in economics. Human nature always includes what people aspire to, for Smith; it is never reduced to the desires they merely happen to have.

One final point on methodology. The fact that Smith is not committed to drawing his view of human nature from empirical data alone keeps him from succumbing to historicism, as well as to the varieties of positivism, like behaviorism and rational choice theory, that came to plague social science after his day. Smith is very alert to differences in ways of human living across time, and indeed has long been regarded as a major source for the "four-stage theory of history," according to which manners, morals, laws, and all sorts of other human institutions have changed in accordance with the development of the economic base of societies from hunting to pasturage to agriculture to commerce.[3] He also has a remarkably sensitive chapter on cultural variation in morals in TMS (V.2), and he builds the importance of social and cultural influence on our expectations deeply into his jurisprudence. Nevertheless, he sees certain basic structures of human motivation as operating across all times and places. I think this is an advantage of Smith's approach, not a disadvantage, reflecting the fact that one cannot so much as discern cultural and historical variations in human beings except against the background of some basic similarities. By picking out a general structure of human motivations and aspirations, Smith can distinguish between social conditions that work against our natural impulses and social conditions that work with them. He achieves a position from which he can hold up certain social practices as, for instance, oppressing, deluding, or otherwise frustrating people. But the fact that some practices oppress or frustrate people is something we need to know even to get an "insider's" look at how a culture is experienced by its members. A transhistorical account of human nature thus gives us a more sensitive understanding of history itself than the proclamation, in the name of relativist dogma, that people always value what their societies teach them to value.

I take Smith's endorsement of general human uniformity, that is, to be a methodological device. If so, he relies on a deep but much misunderstood insight in Hume.

> Would you know the sentiments, inclinations, and course of life of the Greeks and Romans? Study well the temper and actions of the French and English: You cannot be much mistaken in transferring to the former *most* of the observations which you have made with regard to the latter. Mankind are so much the same, in all times and places, that history informs us of nothing new or strange in this particular. Its chief use is only to discover the constant and universal principles of human nature. (E VIII.i.65; 83)

This passage has been widely misinterpreted as a dismissal of cultural difference. Not only does the word "most"—emphasized in the original—tend to get overlooked, along with the many warnings Hume urges on us, in the next several pages, against carrying the expectation of human uniformity to such a length as to obscure all "diversity of characters, prejudices, and opinions" (85), but it has gone practically unremarked that what Hume declares here is more a *methodological principle* than a statement of *fact*. The chapter from which the passage comes is devoted to the argument that causal regularities are necessary to how we interpret other people's actions. We do in fact, and must, attribute general uniformity in human motivations across time because that is the only way to *interpret* the record of history—to tell which reports are likely to be accurate and which deceitful (84)—and to "collect any general observations concerning mankind" so that we can make predictions about human life in the future (85; see also 90). We all "readily and universally . . . acknowledge" a certain degree of uniformity in human actions, Hume points out, and we do so partly because the general observations generated on the basis of this acknowledgment constitute "the clue of human nature" (84–5): The uniformity principle is here clearly an assumption for gathering evidence, rather than a conclusion drawn from such evidence. It can best be compared to the contemporary philosopher Donald Davidson's principle of charity: Both are first, indispensable rules of thumb by which to gauge purported evidence about human action.[4]

Now when Smith declares that all human beings find happiness in a balance between "tranquillity and enjoyment" (TMS 149), or that people are all restless creatures, seeking to better themselves at every moment twixt womb and grave (WN 341), I believe he is similarly making an assumption of general uniformity against the background of which to interpret and explain apparent historical exceptions to that uniformity. And the proof of this particular pudding lies in the degree to which Smith does thereby explain the generosity characteristic of pastoral societies, say, or the limited appeal of Stoic principles that equated tranquility, alone, with happiness. If we think his explanations are good ones, then his methodological assumption of human uniformity is to that extent vindicated. If his explanations are poor, then we have reason to question the methodology. But this is as it should be: Empirical evidence will help vindicate or shake up the methodological principles, even as those principles are also used to interpret the evidence. There is a circle here, but not a vicious one, and Smith would not want, nor should we want, to settle the question of whether there is some basic human nature across times and places by a priori arguments alone.

We might note that Hume's main concern, in the passage I have been discussing, is to rule out *miraculous* accounts of human events. Human nature must follow the same kinds of causal regularities as other natural events if history is to be possible, and if politics is to be a science (E 90), and that means that we must be able to find some sort of uniformity in human experience. Any other assumption is as good as proclaiming each human act to be a miracle, a supernatural rather than a natural event, and leaving the interpretation of human action therefore up to faith. If human actions are as mysterious as the supposed workings of God, we will have no way of rationally judging whether reports of human actions are so much as plausible; people will believe one report of an action rather than another, or interpret a person as having one motivation rather than another, on the basis of faith alone. One specific, important consequence of this argument is that Hume refuses to credit, on scientific grounds, the claim that human beings were ever, or will ever be, much more altruistic than they are now, that under other circumstances, in a prehistoric "Golden Age" perhaps, they thrived in societies with purely communal arrangements of labor and property. Like Pufendorf before him,[5] he refuses to believe that human beings were ever so radically different than they are now that they could do without private property. The Utopians who dream up, or travelers who claim to have encountered, societies in which "men . . . [were] entirely divested of avarice, ambition, or revenge; [and] knew no pleasure but friendship, generosity, and public spirit" (84) are revealed to be liars by the principle of human uniformity. Smith will share Hume's view of utopians, of the limits of public spirit, and of the need, consequently, for private property.

14. Smith's Picture of Human Nature

Setting methodological concerns aside, now, let us sketch the main features of Smith's account of human nature.

To begin with, Smith believes that people are motivated both by self-love and by benevolence, and that they are capable of a variety of ways of controlling their own emotions, and sharing the emotions of others, via the process of imaginative projection he calls "sympathy." The virtues by which we withhold the full expression of our own emotions inspire awe or respect—they are "the awful virtues"—while the virtues by which we show compassion or friendly fellowship to others are the "amiable," the humane, virtues (TMS 23). By way of both of these kinds of virtues we become simultaneously socialized and capable of freedom: We achieve individual self-consciousness, and the consequent ability to make moral decisions, even as we find our desires and projects oriented toward the demands of our society. And guiding both kinds of virtues is the intellectual virtue by which one judges well of the appropriate means to action: prudence, which is Smith's translation of what Aristotle had called "phronesis." It is not strictly right to say that prudence is either self-interested or other-directed: In its "higher" form, it includes benevolent activity, and in itself, it is really a characteristic of the intellect rather than of any emotion.

Smith sees both self-love and benevolence as coming in various degrees. We have a moral duty to have enough self-love that we take care of our lives and health, and it is morally acceptable to have more self-love than that, but excessive self-love, the sort of self-love, in particular, that leads us to violate duties of justice or important ties of benevolence, is something that the impartial spectator would condemn and that we normally try to suppress or extirpate. Self-love can also take the form either of a concern for one's material well-being and social prestige or of a concern to develop oneself morally. It is only the first kind of self-love that can possibly conflict with virtue: Morally deserved self-approbation is "the principal object" about which everyone "ought to be anxious. The love of it, is the love of virtue" (TMS 117).[6] Self-love in this latter sense can even lead to self-sacrifice, as when a person dies trying to save someone else from a fire, so the difference between it and material self-love is immense. One might say that to apply the word "self-love" to both is to use it as a homonym, were it not that Smith has an argument by which the same structure of desires that generally leads us to material self-love can lead us to moral self-love instead (TMS 113–17).

The different degrees and forms of benevolence are equally important. Like many thinkers of his time, including his teacher Hutcheson, Smith follows the Stoics in believing that benevolence diminishes as one moves outward to the wider and wider social circles surrounding each individual. Thus we feel the strongest sentiments of love and concern for our immediate families, a somewhat weaker level of those feelings for the friends and neighbors we see on a regular basis, a considerably weaker level yet for our nation as a whole, and a very weak benevolence, but not an entirely negligible one, for "the immensity of the universe": for the happiness of "innocent and sensible being[s]" everywhere. Smith takes the progressive weakening of benevolence as we move to more and more distant sensible beings to be a natural fact that serves good purposes. Our benevolence weakens as we know less about the beings we could help—thus know less well what *would* help them—and as we have less and less power to help them. Our benevolence weakens in proportion to the "effectual good offices" we are able to perform (235). That we can feel *some* universal benevolence is important for several reasons: It plays a role in making religious experience possible, since without some concern for "the immensity of the universe" we could not worship a universal God, and it is a source on which we can draw to overcome national animosities, to reach beyond the love of country that causes war and injustice in the international arena.[7] But that we feel this universal benevolence less strongly than love of country, that love of country generally trumps love of the world, is something that politicians must reckon with if they are to persuade anyone of their policies. It is something that the author of the *Wealth of Nations*, which argues after all for free trade as something that benefits both all nations collectively and each nation individually, had to bear in mind very often. What he had to bear in mind even more often, what is indeed crucial to his argument, is that even love of country ("publick zeal" or concern for "the publick good": WN 852, 456) is much weaker than love of family and neighborhood. As we shall see in more detail later (§23), the reason Smith assumes that economic agents are mostly motivated by self-interest is not that he thinks most people are incapable of benevolence, but that he considers the *wide* benevolence by which we might care for anonymous others, throughout our nation or throughout the circles with whom we buy and sell, to be very weak, not normally strong enough to motivate economic transactions.

We will also later explore the objection that the very presentation of human motivations as running between self-interest and benevolence is simplistic and narrow, that there are many sorts of motivation left out by this scheme. We should note at the moment that the spectrum between self-interest and benevolence is not in fact Smith's only axis on which to locate human emotions. He believes that people can spontaneously feel resentment, on their own behalf or on behalf of others, and that resentment, while the basis of justice when properly channeled, can lead people to do things that are destructive both of their own and of others' interests—to die in a pointless feud, for instance. He also says that courage can motivate both noble behavior and actions that are inhumane as well as imprudent (TMS 153, 239–40, 252–3). Then, people can feel various kinds of religious awe or enthusiasm, and this too can either supplement their other moral commitments or come adrift from moral concerns and motivate the dangerous projects of fanaticism (155–6, 176–7). In TMS, Smith discusses all these different sorts of emotions in detail, while in WN, for various reasons, he plays them down, but even in WN Smith makes some reference to the self-destructive (and certainly not benevolent) "pride of man [which] makes him love to domineer" (WN 388), to the silly love of "trinkets and baubles" that can distract one from one's material and social self-interest (418–21), and to the power of religious fanaticism (795–6).

To move, now, from the sentiments that move us to the ends we seek: Happiness for Smith consists in a balance between tranquility and enjoyment, with the greater weight resting on tranquility, and with the achievement of virtue, and the recognition there is little difference between the various "permanent situations" of human life, being crucial to attaining that tranquility. Happiness depends first and foremost on our control over our own minds; external goods play a strictly secondary role in achieving it. "What can be added," Smith asks rhetorically, "to the happiness of the man who is in health, who is out of debt, and has a clear conscience?" To such a person "all accessions of fortune may properly be said to be superfluous" (TMS 45). Elsewhere he offers us a psychological theory according to which we can regain tranquility after even the greatest spasms of agony, as long as we have a chance to adjust ourselves to the source of the agony (148). In this context, he says that the Stoic view of life was "very nearly in the right" and remarks that "[t]he great source of both the misery and disorders of human life, seem to arise from over-rating the difference between one permanent situation and another" (149). Some situations do deserve to be preferred to others—it is not foolish to want to leave a state of imprisonment or great poverty—but people put far too much of their energies in trying to leave one situation for another, spend far too much passion and time on yearning for some distant improvement in their circumstances rather than recognizing "that, in all the ordinary situations of human life a well-disposed mind may be equally calm, equally cheerful, and equally contented" (149). The search for more material goods, and for a rise in social status, is almost always a distraction from true happiness rather than a contribution to it. We do need some material goods—food, clothing, and shelter, above all, and more generally, those enabling us to remain "in health, [and] out of debt"—but these are relatively easy to acquire: "The wages of the meanest labourer can supply them" (50). The most important external good to happiness is a nonmaterial one: the deserved love and admiration of friends. "[T]he chief part of human happiness arises from the consciousness of being beloved," says Smith (41); friendship is felt by everyone to be of great importance to happiness and love "sooths and composes the breast, seems to favour the vital motions, and to promote the healthful state of the human constitution" (39). Smith adds later on that "the man of true constancy and firmness" can be satisfied with his own self-regard, if he knows himself to be wrongly condemned by others, but while achieving "praise-worthiness" may thus in principle be enough for happiness, and while undeserved praise from others is certainly not deeply satisfying, most of us need the respect and friendship of others most of the time (122, 126–8). Throughout his work, and especially in passages prepared for the last edition of TMS,[8] Smith emphasized the intrinsic value of conversation to the human animal, the joy we take in simply sitting around and talking to others. Here a biographical detail about Smith may be useful: the mid-eighteenth century was a high point of club life in Scotland, and Smith belonged to a number of these clubs—political ones, intellectual ones, and purely social ones alike.[9]

This emphasis on mental and social pleasures should not lead us to think that Smith despises all material goods. He repeatedly expresses a fondness for the theater, and respect for what one can learn from it, and speaks with similar enthusiasm of fine music, good poetry, and "[t]he beauty of a plain, the greatness of a mountain, the ornaments of a building, the expression of a picture."[10] He puts, indeed, a little theory of beauty into TMS, responding to a nascent utilitarian streak in Hume that had reduced beauty to usefulness, and saying that what is beautiful is instead what *appears conducive* to usefulness, even if it is actually not useful at all.[11] Things appear conducive to usefulness when they are ordered in a certain way, and in LJ, Smith elaborates briefly what that order consists in: "A sort of uniformity mixd at the same time with a certain degree of variety gives [us] pleasure, as we see in the construction of a house or building which pleases when neither dully uniform nor its parts altogether angular" (LJ 335).[12] He draws examples of beauty from literature as well as architecture, and seems not at all inclined to doubt that artistic works, insofar as they satisfy our yearning for beauty, meet a deep human need. He also makes quite clear, in TMS and the "History of Astronomy," that philosophical and scientific achievements are intrinsically admirable, as well as satisfying to thoughtful minds (TMS 134; EPS 46). But artistic, philosophical, and scientific achievements not only directly require material goods—paper or parchment, paint and canvas, musical instruments, theatrical props, tools for experiments—but can only flourish, as Smith himself stresses, where there is an advanced economy, producing a large enough number of "necessities" that people can afford "luxuries" as well (WN II.iii; EPS 50–51). So Smith does not join Rousseau in suggesting that advancement in civilization does little or nothing to contribute to human happiness.[13] At the same time, he remains far from his contemporaries in France and Germany who saw *Bildung*—culture—as essential to human development, much less those, before and after him, who thought of art or technology as the be-all and end-all of human achievement.

Smith thus presents human happiness as primarily a social matter rather than something each person can have on his or her own; as depending more on certain moral goods than on any material goods; and at the same time as enhanced by the presence, in society if not in one's own hands, of certain material goods. We are not "utility monsters," or relentless consumers, or atomistic individuals, for Smith; we are, pretty much, the complex, primarily social, moral, and intellectual beings we always thought we were. As befits his common-sense methodology, Smith's picture of human nature coheres with our common intuitions on the subject; he does not present a counterintuitive theory of what human beings are fundamentally like. Indeed, as we shall see, Smith is more concerned to vindicate our common-sense picture of human nature against various challenges than to offer an alternative to that picture.

15. Religious Sentiments

One of those challenges was the suggestion, made by many Enlightenment thinkers including Smith's close friend Hume and hero Voltaire, that the human impulse to religious belief was entirely a product of foolish fears and a cause of bigotry and violence. Smith himself was associated by his enemies with these thoroughgoing attacks on religion, and has been read in our own day as an atheist,[14] but I think this is a mistake. He certainly criticizes religious fanaticism, and the behavior of the clergy in most churches, but at the same time he tries to redeem the basic impulse to religious belief from its Enlightenment critics. Although he does not base any of his arguments on religious premises, and makes no suggestion that religious belief is necessary for virtue,[15] he consistently gives religion an important role in morality. He calls our moral sentiments "the vice-regents of God within us" (TMS 165–6), saying that, "in this respect, as in many others," we are created after God's image (130). This is a clever variation on the way Jewish and Christian philosophers had in the past interpreted Genesis 1:27,[16] and it allows Smith to give religious resonance to his view that the search for praise signifies a deeper search for praiseworthiness: The desire for praise is the "image," in mundane social interaction, of the desire for an absolute, transmundane goodness.[17] Smith also says that it is extremely difficult to maintain universal benevolence unless one is "thoroughly convinced that all the inhabitants of the universe, the meanest as well as the greatest, are under the immediate care and protection of that great, benevolent, and all-wise Being, who directs all the movements of nature" (235). If we are convinced of this, on the other hand, we can see ourselves as "co-operat[ing] with the Deity" whenever we make other people happy (166).[18] Finally, Smith gives an extended argument for why it is morally helpful to regard religious rules as laws of the Deity, and to believe in an afterlife. Not merely our superstitious hopes and fears, but "the noblest and best principles" in our nature, says Smith, lead us to the belief "of a future state" (169). And the notion of an all-powerful and all-good Being who makes up for the injustices of this world in a life to come gives the general rules of morality "a new sacredness" (170).[19]

In this connection, we should note that Smith gives the word "sacred," which he and Hume both use to characterize the laws of justice, a much richer meaning than Hume does. For Hume, "sacred" simply means "inviolable" (E 200–201); to call a rule "sacred" is just to say that it brooks of no exceptions (T 501, 531–2). But to say that a rule should never be violated is not yet to say that it deserves awe, respect, or any of the other psychological phenomena that the word "sacred" normally calls up. The laws of nature, like Newton's law of gravity, are inviolable, but we hardly feel they are *sacred*. Hume explicitly compares the apparent superstitions that surround the claiming of property with the real superstitions that, he believes, surround religious rituals, making clear that he sees no reason why the rules of justice should be associated with awe or with any sort of taboo (T 197–200): The laws of justice are and should be, as much as possible, a rational business, not something shrouded in mysterious feelings. But one might therefore have expected him to avoid calling those laws "sacred." Smith, by contrast, has good reason to use that word. Smith says that we lay down inviolable rules, like the rules of justice, to ourselves in order to counteract the "misrepresentations . . . concerning what is fit and proper to be done" to which we may be led by "furious resentment" or passionate excesses of self-love. The rules then work precisely by way of the "awe and respect" they engender, by the fact that they mark out a region of action as if it were forbidden to us by a higher power, mark it as taboo, as something we should not even contemplate entering (160–61). Thus when Smith calls *his* rules of justice "sacred" (TMS 138, 161, 330), his usage fits in with the ordinary meaning of that word; the awe-inspiring quality of the rules, not their mere inviolability, is central to their function. Nor does the fact that we come up with the rules ourselves, that we "lay them down to ourselves," do anything to vitiate the possibility of regarding them as God's laws. If our moral sentiments are God's "viceregents within us," it is perfectly reasonable to regard the rules to which they lead as simply one way by which God's power manifests itself.

Smith's remarks on religion and use of religious language thus add up to an overall conception of religion much like the one Kant was to develop a little later on, by which belief in a providential God, and an afterlife, can help buttress and enrich morality, and is justified insofar as it does that: "religion enforces the natural sense of duty" (170). What Smith opposes, again like Kant, is the tendency of religious clergies to substitute rituals, or creedal commitments, for moral actions. He declaims with considerable asperity against those who "regard frivolous observances, as more immediate duties of religion, than acts of justice and beneficence" (170), and against those who suppose that "the futile mortifications of a monastery" could possibly be more important than the active, socially useful lives of politicians and poets and philosophers (132–4). He expresses something stronger than asperity at the way "false notions of religion" can lead people to murder those with different beliefs about the nature of the Deity (176–7; see also 155–6). It is therefore correct to see an *anticlerical* strain in Smith, and when he comes to discussing government funding for churches in WN, he recommends paying one's clergy poorly, if one must establish a religion at all, so that they can shine by way of moral qualities alone (WN 810).[20] But one can be anticlerical without being antireligious, and that, fairly clearly, is Smith's position. A well-known passage in WN talks of "that pure and rational religion, free from every mixture of absurdity, imposture, or fanaticism, such as wise men have in all ages of the world wished to see established" (WN 793). Everything Smith says about God and religion in TMS—throughout all its editions—fits in with what eighteenth-century writers considered to be "pure and rational religion." Smith is certainly no conventional *Christian*—he says nothing that would support the doctrine of a Trinity, he says in a famous letter that David Hume faced death better than "any whining Christian," and he struck the one passage indirectly referring to Christ from the last edition of TMS (92–3n)—but he belongs among the Enlightenment thinkers who looked forward to the coming of a universal moral religion, which would preserve the morally valuable parts of Judaism, Christianity, and Islam while discarding their rituals and distinctive creeds.

16. Impartiality and Equality

We spoke in §14 of sentiments that do not fit well into the spectrum that runs between self-love and benevolence. Religious sentiments and resentment both belong in that category, for Smith, and both are therefore capable of leading us to particularly selfless good behavior as well as particularly selfless evil ("fanatical") behavior. Another element of human nature that transcends both self-love and benevolence for Smith, but that motivates particularly good behavior alone, is our ability to take up the position of an "impartial spectator." Impartiality may mean that we have no feelings about what we are judging, or it may mean that we relinquish just our self-interested feelings, and enter into the feelings of each party relevant to the situation we are trying to judge. Smith at one point suggests the former, identifying the impartial spectator with "reason" and saying that its voice is "capable of astonishing the most presumptuous of our passions" (TMS 137), but on the whole he writes as if he means the latter. In any case, he believes that we can rise above our self-loving sentiments, our interest in situations we need to judge, and that doing this is essential to morality. Indeed, neither self-love nor benevolence will be truly moral attitudes, for Smith, unless they are sifted through the medium of the impartial spectator: unless we have them to the degree, and in the way, that the impartial spectator within us would approve of our having them.

Two notes on this impartial perspective. First, it is present in WN as well as TMS. Smith says at the end of WN IV.ii that the legislature would be more careful about establishing monopolies "were it possible that its deliberations would be always directed, not by the clamorous importunity of partial interests, but by an extensive view of the general good" (WN 472), and elsewhere decries "faction" and "the spirit of party."[21] He also calls throughout the book for economic transactions to be constrained by justice, which is a virtue that particularly requires impartiality, and for rulers to have "an equitable regard" for the interest of each of their subjects (471–2). The passage calling for legislators to rise above "partial interests" contains a good deal of scepticism about how often they will do this ("were it possible . . ."), but Smith seems to be hopeful that they will do so sometimes. And if they did not, if they always and unrelentingly imposed the demands of one or more partial interest on the rest of the population, then his system of natural liberty would be utterly impossible to realize politically, less even than a dream, an ideal, to strive for.[22]

Second, Smith's emphasis on impartiality brings out the centrality of human equality to his thought.[23] As he characterizes it, the position of impartiality is one from which we see other people's interests as equal in value to our own:

> [T]o the selfish and original passions of human nature, the loss or gain of a very small interest of our own, appears to be of vastly more importance . . . than the greatest concern of another with whom we have no particular connexion. His interests, as long as they are surveyed from this station, can never be put into the balance with our own. . . . Before we can make any proper comparison of those opposite interests, we must change our position. We must view them, neither from our own place nor yet from his, neither with our own eyes nor yet with his, but from the place and with the eyes of a third person, who has no particular connexion with either, and who judges with impartiality between us. (TMS 135; cf. 109–110, 228, 129)

To see others as equal with ourselves we need to take up an impartial position. In addition—what is more striking—the main *reason for* taking up the position of impartiality seems to be that we can then see others as equals. What we gain from overcoming self-love is that we can then grasp the true equality of humankind. The passage of TMS that describes the impartial "inhabitant of the breast" as "capable of astonishing the most presumptuous of our passions" goes on immediately to say that we realize, when our presumptuous passions are thus checked, "that we are but one of the multitude, in no respect better than any other in it" (137). We learn "the real littleness of ourselves," Smith says, and he uses similarly charged language over and over to assert that we make our greatest moral mistakes when we try to assert superiority over other people. In the "race for wealth," everyone is allowed to "run as hard as he can, and strain every nerve and every muscle, in order to outstrip all his competitors," but if he should "justle, or throw down any of them," the spectators will not tolerate his behavior: "This man is to them, in every respect, as good as he: they do not enter into that self-love by which he prefers himself so much to this other" (83). Again:

> What chiefly enrages us against the man who injures or insults us, is the little account which he seems to make of us, the unreasonable preference which he gives to himself above us, and that absurd self-love, by which he seems to imagine, that other people may be sacrificed at any time, to his conveniency or his humour. (96)

"Injury" and "insult" are Smith's technical terms for the harms inflicted by injustice, and here, as in the previous passage, Smith is characterizing the resentment, on our own behalf or on behalf of others, that underlies the virtue of justice. The point of the passage is to explain why even small acts of injustice seem to deserve punishment, and the argument is that even where the material harm done is slight, an act of injustice suggests that the victim is somehow less worthy than the agent, and thereby constitutes an important symbolic harm. The anger that boils out of the passage indeed captures wonderfully how we feel (and, one suspects, how Smith himself often felt) when another person seems to imagine that we "may be sacrificed at any time, to his conveniency or his humour," how bitterly we resent such a symbolic degradation below the equal worth that we think we share with all other human beings.

Now there are strands in Smith's writing that suggest quite a different picture, a sharply elitist one, in which a few people manage to be virtuous while the bulk of humanity lives out an inferior, second-rate sort of life. I will consider these passages below—most of them are, I believe, compatible with an egalitarian reading of Smith—but it is worth mentioning now that even in this strand of his thought, he is inclined to say that the most admirable people are those most inclined to see others as their equals. Describing the perfect sage, the person who most fully tries to live up to the ideal model of humanity within himself, Smith says that this person may be aware that he is superior to "the approximation to this idea which is commonly attained in the world," but

> as his principal attention is always directed towards the [ideal] standard, he is necessarily much more humbled by the one comparison, than he ever can be elevated by the other. He is never so elated as to look down with insolence even upon those who are really below him. He feels so well his own imperfection, he knows so well the difficulty with which he attained his own distant approximation to rectitude, that he cannot regard with contempt the still greater imperfection of other people. (248)

For Aristotle, the fully virtuous man (it is always a man for Aristotle) both is superior to other people and has a feeling of his own superiority; that feeling is indeed part of his virtue. For Smith, even insofar as there are "superior" and "inferior" people, one mark of the superior kind is that *they do not regard the others as inferior*; one part of their virtue is humility, which entails recognizing the insignificance of the differences among people. They are superior, in good part, because they don't consider themselves superior. Virtuous people take up the position of conscience, the stance of the impartial spectator, from which vantage point they see "the real littleness of themselves," the fact that they are but "one of the multitude, in no respect better than any other in it."

There is thus a very strong endorsement of human equality as a normative principle in Smith, of the notion that all people *ought* to be regarded as equal, and indeed a strong suggestion that the moral point of view requires us to see all human beings as equal. (Both the strong emphasis on equality, and the link between recognizing this and the moral point of view, look forward to Kant.[24]) Of course this "equality" is some sort of "equality in principle," some sort of fundamental equality in worth, and does not directly presuppose that people be equal in virtue or intelligence, or entail that they be made equal in wealth, political and social status, or happiness. Yet the normative principle does put some pressure on how we view the facts about human beings. It is difficult to believe that people really have equal worth in principle if they seem in fact to be irremediably unequal in worthy qualities, and it is difficult to see how great inequalities in goods can be justified if human equality is one's basic norm. Why should I see myself "as in no respect better than any other" human being if many others are in fact obviously less intelligent or virtuous than I am? Why should the agent of injustice see his victim as "in every respect, as good as he," if he is in fact much smarter, more creative, more beautiful, or (generally) more virtuous? If, on the other hand, we do regard people as all equally worthy, how can we tolerate great differences in the quality of life they enjoy? Normative egalitarians must grapple with two kinds of factual inequality: inequalities in human characteristics, which challenge the justification for saying that people are equal, and inequalities in human reward, which challenge one who regards people as equal to provide either an apologia or a reform program for the way goods are distributed.[25] A thinker who proclaims human equality must therefore (1) somehow explain away the facts by which people appear to be unequally worthy, and either (2) also explain away the apparent inequalities in human rewards, (3) acknowledge that there is something wrong in the inequality of human rewards but argue that the wrong is outweighed by some other moral good, or (4) support measures that might rectify the inequalities in reward. Smith, I will argue, makes moves on all of these fronts.

That people are in fact equal, in at least the capacity for virtue and intelligence, is a theme that runs through both TMS and WN. The most explicit passage in this regard is WN I.ii.4 (28–9):

> The difference of natural talents in different men is, in reality, much less than we are aware of; and the very different genius which appears to distinguish men of different professions, when grown up to maturity, is not upon many occasions so much the cause, as the effect of the division of labour. The difference between the most dissimilar characters, between a philosopher and a common street porter, for example, seems to arise not so much from nature, as from habit, custom, and education. When they came into the world, and for the first six or eight years of their existence, they were, perhaps, very much alike, and neither their parents nor play-fellows could perceive any remarkable difference. About that age, or soon after, they come to be employed in very different occupations. The difference of talents comes then to be taken notice of, and widens by degrees, till at last the vanity of the philosopher is willing to acknowledge scarce any resemblance.

I'd like to stress three features of this passage. First, Smith's use of a "philosopher" in this example is no accident. In a number of other places, he uses philosophers when he wants to show the universality of some psychological or social feature of human beings (see, e.g., TMS 34 or LJ 349). It is important to Smith to show that he himself is no exception to general humanity, and to prick his own vanity first when urging his reader to do so. Smith thus enacts his normative commitment to human equality in the very course of preaching it— and in the course of arguing for its factual correlate.

Second, the passage serves to buttress Smith's argument that the division of labor does not reflect natural divisions of talent among human beings, but is merely a way by which people can most productively use their talents for the greater good of everybody. Smith consistently plays down the importance of inborn differences in talent. In WN I.vi (65) he will tell us that "uncommon degree[s] of dexterity and ingenuity" are normally acquired "in consequence of long application," that difference in talents is a matter of difference in training, not difference in native endowment. Indeed, this line of argument really begins right at the start of the book, where the value of dividing up labor is introduced without so much as a mention of differences in talent. That differences among talents are unimportant, and that the division of labor creates such differences more than the other way around, is one of Smith's most controversial claims. Plato already maintained that a division of labor is essential to economic productivity (*Republic* 369e–370b), but he argued for a division that reflected the natural differences in human talents, and many writers, both before and after Smith, have followed Plato rather than Smith in this regard. Even the socialist Karl Polanyi agrees with Plato more than with Smith: "Division of labor . . . springs from differences inherent in the facts of sex, geography, and individual endowment."[26] Yet Smith appears to have been committed to a remarkably strong version of the claim that people are essentially equal in abilities. One of his most implausible claims—that "a great part" of the machines used in manufacturing are invented by the workmen (WN 20)[27]—reflects, in its very implausibility, his strong desire to see the humblest of people as ingenious. As we saw earlier, moreover, Smith hints strongly that he was personally "much accustomed to visit . . . manufactures" and to witness there the contribution of the workmen, and that he took a special interest in conversing with poor people (§8). In TMS there is a passage indicating that Smith took an extraordinary interest in the lives of humble people. "[W]hoever has taken the trouble to examine" the mentally retarded, he says, knows that they are far more capable than they think they are, and he then details what conversations with mentally retarded people are like (TMS 260–61). Both the content of this claim and the indication that he sought out such conversations suggest that Smith had an unusual degree of respect for a class of people who are generally overlooked even today. So the claim about the similarities between philosophers and street porters should be seen as part of a larger, energetic attempt to minimize differences in human ability.

Third, Smith often appeals to the importance of early childhood education in shaping human character, and I take this to be a mark of an attempt to show that people are much more equal, in fact, than they are generally taken to be. If fully achieving virtue is possible only via the kind of sophisticated education that Plato and Aristotle prescribe, an education that may require, as it does for Plato, mathematical and logical skills that not every human being has, and that in any case demands an investment of time that ordinary laborers cannot afford, then the virtuous will necessarily make up only a small elite in every society. For Plato and Aristotle, unabashed elitists both, this was unproblematic. Yet even modern egalitarians have often believed that some kind of extensive higher education in literature and philosophy is necessary to develop human capacities to their fullest (Kant, Schiller, and J.S. Mill are particularly good examples). These thinkers have had to struggle mightily to reconcile the egalitarianism they hold in principle with the elitism implicit in their view of education. Since he takes the education necessary for virtue to be something all human beings receive in early childhood, Smith faces no such problem. He tells us that what philosophers like Plato and Aristotle prescribed as the only route to virtue—an "artificial and refined education" in "the severest, [and] profoundest philosophy," in which one engages in "the abstruse syllogisms of a quibbling dialectic" (TMS 139, 145)—is unnecessary and in fact far inferior to "that great discipline which Nature has established for the acquisition of . . . virtue" (145). And the discipline of nature turns out to be the sort of thing that practically all children learn in their families. Smith describes how the nurse or the parents of a baby teach it some degree of "self-command" when they require it to restrain its anger, and how it learns that central virtue to an even greater degree when, as a slightly older child, it must "moderat[e], not only its anger, but all its other passions, to the degree which its play-fellows and companions are likely to be pleased with" (145; see also LJ 142–3). This playing with children outside the home is, Smith says, the beginning of "the great school of self-command" (145). The other main component of moral education is what children learn, at home, by interacting with their parents and siblings:

> Do you wish to educate your children to be dutiful to their parents, to be kind and affectionate to their brothers and sisters? put them under the necessity of being dutiful children, of being kind and affectionate brothers and sisters: educate them in your own house. From their parent's house they may, with propriety and advantage, go out every day to attend public schools: but let their dwelling be always at home. Respect for you must always impose a very useful restraint upon their conduct. (222)

Characteristically, Smith makes out moral teaching to consist most importantly of being in circumstances that train one's emotions, receiving certain kinds of emotional reactions to one's behavior, and witnessing, and trying to follow, moral examples—not of receiving any explicit instruction or grasping any philosophical principles. All the childhood teaching he endorses is inexplicit: The parents are not told to read uplifting books to their children, nor to teach them moral or spiritual truths, and the explicit learning children receive in school is played down. Similarly, in WN, Smith describes the Greek belief that an education in the arts[28] can "humanize the mind, . . . soften the temper, and . . . dispose it for performing . . . social and moral duties," notes that the Romans held no such belief, and then drily remarks that "[t]he morals of the Romans . . . seem to have been, not only equal, but upon the whole, a good deal superior to those of the Greeks" (WN 774). Smith puts the nonphilosophical "teaching" of parents and playmates ahead of what we can learn from literature and philosophical systems, in developing moral character, and thereby suggests that the achievement of virtue is open to everyone with a decent family, not something that only a formally educated elite can attain. Indeed, it is far from clear that an educated elite will be particularly good at achieving virtue. They may rather, like the Greeks who put such an emphasis on the arts, excel in certain kinds of learning while *lacking* the proper emotional structure for virtue altogether.

As against these sorts of egalitarian passages in Smith, one might mention his references to the undiscerning eyes of "the mob" (e.g., TMS 226, 253), the contrast he sometimes draws between this mob and people of wisdom and virtue, especially his remark that "They are the wise and the virtuous chiefly, a select, though, I am afraid, but a small party who are the real and steady admirers of wisdom and virtue" (62). But at least three considerations should caution us against overemphasizing this last remark. First, language deriding "the mob" is eighteenth-century boilerplate, something Smith easily may have included as part of the rhetorical conventions of his time. Second, "wise," for Smith, is almost always coupled with "virtuous," and seems to consist mostly in the recognition that one should not expect too much from life. Thus Smith's "select, . . . small party" is not a party of those with special, well-cultivated intellectual skills, just of people who attend closely enough to the beauty of virtue that they set being decent rather than being rich or famous as their goal in life. Not every human being *does* achieve this wisdom and virtue—only "a select . . . [and] small party" does—but any human being, regardless of class or formal education, *can* achieve it, and it is not impossible in principle that everyone could.[29]

It follows, third, that Smith's relegation of virtue to a select and small party is more a comment on social conditions than on human nature. That people are equally *capable* of virtue and intelligence does not mean that they will in fact develop equal virtue and intelligence. All sorts of social conditions and institutions may get in the way of their doing that. Smith believes that the advancement of the division of labor "obliterate[s] and extinguishe[s]" the nobler parts of human character in the vast bulk of the population (WN 784). He also believes that lavish churches, in which clergy live sumptuously, set up the wrong sort of role models for our emulation, and that churches like his own Scottish Presbyterian one, in which the clergy are paid poorly and therefore gain dignity only by "the most exemplary morals" (810, also 809–10, 814), can help inspire modesty and decency. Social arrangements can help or hinder people in making use of their equal capacities. If everyone begins on an equal level, but then is shaped so as to become unequal in mental or moral abilities, it will be possible to have a "mob" that gets confused, or follows blind passions, or in many other ways fails to live up to what they could be doing.

Which brings us to the other half of the problem, for a normative egalitarian, with the actual inequalities among people. We have seen how Smith tries to close the gap between the apparent inequalities of worth among people and the equality of worth he proclaims as a norm by minimizing the former; we now need to see what he has to say about how normative equality can go with actual inequality in human reward. I have said that he pursues all three of the strategies I mentioned as remedies for this problem: (1) minimizing the inequalities in reward; (2) regarding them as outweighed, even for those who get the short end of the stick, by other goods; and (3) advocating greater equality. We will look quickly at each of these strategies.

Smith's claim that people can be happy in most of the "permanent situations" of human life makes differences in material goods and social status appear relatively unimportant. If what we need for happiness is internal tranquility, above all, then the difference between one material or social situation and another will be small. There is room here to acknowledge that some situations are truly awful, and nothing Smith says here is meant to minimize the suffering of the poor and oppressed (see chapter 6). But to exaggerate the difference that more goods or a higher social status makes to one's happiness is, for him, a great moral mistake and the source of much unhappiness.

Smith also argues that inequalities in social status can be for the benefit of all, including the worst off. In the first chapter of WN, he shows how the unequal socioeconomic order of the commercial world leads to levels of productivity that enable even the worst-off person in that world to be better off than the king of a more egalitarian hunter-gatherer society. (Among hunters, he says, "[u]niversal poverty establishes . . . universal equality" [WN 712]). He also says that socioeconomic inequality helps underwrite the stability of political orders and thereby contributes to a strong and fair system of administering justice (710–15; see also TMS 226). But there is nothing more important, to the poor themselves, than a strong and fair system of justice, so social hierarchy again serves the interests of those at the bottom of the hierarchy. Moreover, by dismissing the notion, as he often does, that those at the top of such hierarchies are distinguished for wisdom and virtue (see, e.g., WN 713–14), Smith presents the division of social and material status as very much like the division of labor: a device for meeting the needs of all of us, a mechanism that equal people could therefore in principle agree to set up, not a reflection of some fundamental human inequality.

Finally, Smith urges movement toward greater equality in society, albeit to a lesser degree than other, later writers. His very emphasis on the importance of justice, throughout WN, is itself a way of urging the importance of equality: As we have seen, the rules of justice express the equality of human beings in a particularly strong way.[30] A violation of the rules of justice will irritate impartial spectators because the victim "is to them, in every respect, as good as he" who harmed her (TMS 83), and it is the "absurd self-love" by which the agent implies that he is better than we are that offends us in even small acts of injustice. So when Smith insists, as he does over and over again in WN, that the sovereign must ensure justice for all citizens, he is insisting on a legal framework that expresses the equality of all citizens. Sometimes, indeed, he couples the two terms, as when he tells us that a policy that "hurt[s] in any degree the interest of any one order of citizens, for no purpose but to promote that of some other, is evidently contrary to that *justice and equality of treatment* which the sovereign owes to all the different orders of his subjects" (WN 654, emphasis added).[31] The equality to which Smith here refers is political equality, but he also makes proposals to reduce socioeconomic inequality. He urges the abolition of primogeniture and entail, which maintained unearned gluts of wealth over centuries, and makes a number of proposals which he believes will make it easier for the poor to rise socially: the abolition of apprenticeship requirements and the laws of settlement, and the reform of a number of tax policies (135–59, 831–4, 842). He even suggests, in a couple of places, that the government arrange its taxes so that "the indolence and vanity of the rich" can contribute to the well-being of the poor (725, 842). We will return to these policies, and Smith's attitude toward what today we call "distributive justice," in part IV. For now, we need merely note that Smith's normative egalitarianism does seem to have an impact on his political proposals. The norm of human equality guides both how he interprets the facts about human nature and what he considers to be good political practice.

17. Culture and History

To return, now, to one of the methodological issues with which this chapter opened, how much is the picture of human nature we have found in Smith supposed to apply universally, to describe people in all cultures and historical periods? I have argued that Smith, following Hume, accepts a universalist rule of thumb in social science by which evidence about other cultures and historical periods must be sifted in accordance with what we know about people here and now, by which what we know about the English and the French today must be a guide to understanding the ancient Greeks and Romans. As I understand this principle, it is meant to be a defeasible one, allowing for the discovery of considerable variation among people when the evidence for that variation is sufficiently massive and reliable, but it might of course be used to ignore all human differences, to construct a picture of human nature that arrogantly reads one's local cultural characteristics into everyone who has ever lived. Does Smith's picture fall prey to this temptation? Does Smith, as Walter Bagehot once sneered, merely attempt to show "how, from being a savage, man rose to become a Scotchman"?[32]

I don't think so. First, Smith's ideal person looks more like a Roman Stoic than one of his own countrymen, both in religious conviction and in reaching for a happiness rooted in the willingness to accept one's fate rather than in commercial success or social status. Second, Smith devotes the whole of Part V of TMS to the effect of culture—what he calls "custom and fashion"—on morals and maintains there that moral standards are no less subject to cultural variation than aesthetic ones. "The different situations of different ages and countries are apt . . . to give different characters to the generality of those who live in them," he says, pointing to different standards of politeness in Russia and France, and a different balance of the gentle and the awful virtues in civilized and barbarian nations. The degree to which the noble but harsh virtues of magnanimity and self-command are developed among native Americans, he says in this context, is "almost beyond the conception of Europeans" (TMS 205). Since the notion that morality might vary in accordance with culture was by no means widely accepted in Smith's time (the very term "culture," in its modern, ethnographic sense, was not introduced until the early nineteenth century),[33] the fact that Smith devotes a major division of his book to the subject is remarkable. He does something similar, moreover, in his lectures on jurisprudence, detailing vast differences in law, political institutions, and custom among societies in different historical periods. Some of this material made its way into WN, where at least one passage suggests that moral qualities can vary with socioeconomic circumstance: that a "generous spirit" was more common in the feudal world while "a base and selfish disposition" is more common in commercial societies (WN 349). Elsewhere, Smith points out the effect of custom on fashion and on notions of respectability (113, 869–70). "[C]ustom everywhere regulates fashion," he says, noting that Dutch custom requires people to be engaged in some sort of merchant activity (113), and that English custom requires people to rent entire houses rather than just a single story of a house (134–5). The human beings in WN are by no means uniform across places and times.

Finally, it would be very odd if Smith ignored the possibility of cultural variation in human nature given the tremendous role that societal influence plays in his account both of moral development and of happiness. Society for Smith is the "mirror" through which we first see ourselves at all (TMS 110); only when we start to view our conduct "with [another person's] eyes and from his station" can we begin to judge ourselves, to set ourselves standards for how we should feel and act. (It is said to have been from Smith that Robert Burns was inspired to ask for the gift "to see oursels as others see us.")[34] But if Smith understands human nature to depend so heavily on viewing ourselves through the eyes of others, it would be extremely surprising if he overlooked the degree to which differences among different groups of those others will lead people to have different characters and aspirations. And the discussion of these kinds of differences in Book V of TMS, and here and there in WN, makes clear that he did not overlook that point.

I suggest, therefore, that we can best read the picture of human nature that emerges from TMS as a general sketch to be filled in differently in different cultures and historical circumstances. Smith gives very general names to the types of sentiment he describes, the virtues he lists, and the components he puts into happiness. It is not unreasonable to suppose that in all cultures and all historical circumstances human beings have some degree of "self-love," "benevolence" and "impartiality," of "courage" and of "awe" toward "sacred" rules, that they value gratitude and self-command, and that they find happiness in some combination of "tranquillity" and "enjoyment." These general terms leave much to be specified differently, and, especially since they constitute a picture in which opposing elements (self-love and benevolence, tranquility and enjoyment) need somehow to be balanced, they allow for quite different shadings, quite different emphases. One culture may shade virtue toward its noble but harsher elements, as Smith says native Americans do, while another valorizes compassion and puts up with a lower level of courage. One culture may shade happiness toward "enjoyment" and another toward "tranquillity"; here, too, excessive shading in one direction or another will have a price (widespread restlessness and dissatisfaction when the emphasis is too much on "enjoyment," and insufficient efforts at remedying misery when the emphasis is too much on "tranquillity").

This notion of cultural variation as a matter of shading may seem inadequate to those who think cultures have entirely different pictures of human nature, to those who want their cultural differences to be incommensurable. Smith considers such radical cultural difference to be impossible. He says that custom can lead to specific practices as shocking, to us, as infanticide—which he considers a gross perversion of morals, although an understandable one in certain conditions of society—but it can never lead to comparable moral variation in the *general* cast of a society's life: "No society could subsist a moment, in which the usual strain of men's conduct and behaviour was of a piece with the horrible practice I have just now mentioned" (TMS 211). Human nature is constrained by the general conditions necessary for any society to survive; happiness and morals can vary only within those constraints. This makes good sense: Without societies, there could *be* no socially relative variations among human beings. Smith, reasonably, presents cultural variation as possible only within a universal human nature that, in its very orientation toward society, makes such variation possible. This is a sensible compromise position on the importance of social and cultural difference, not a dogmatic insistence on thick human universality in all places and times.

18. From *Homo Moralis* to *Homo Economicus*

What is most remarkable about Smith's picture of human nature, overall, is how unremarkable it is. There is nothing counterintuitive about it, aside perhaps from the very strong claim that, I have argued, he makes for human equality. There is, in particular, nothing counterintuitive about the picture Smith gives us of our motivations. People are self-loving, but also benevolent; are benevolent to varying degrees, in accordance with how well they know the others they might care for; need self-command to use both self-love and benevolence properly; can rise above their feelings both for themselves and for others to achieve some degree of impartiality; are just insofar as they can see people in this impartial light and treat them as equals; have religious feelings, resentments, and a capacity for courage, that can serve but can also come adrift from their self-loving and benevolent feelings; and are made happiest by virtue, a lack of excessive expectations, and the high regard of others, requiring, among "external" goods, above all health, friends, opportunities for conversation, and some chance to experience natural and artistic beauty. Finally, all of these features go to compose a general picture of human beings that varies to a considerable extent with differences in culture, and with historical and economic circumstances. This may seem almost too moderate, too balanced, a view, differing only slightly from our ordinary intuitions. We might be disappointed, wanting to learn something new from our moral philosophers. But if we are disappointed in this way, then we have forgotten, or are refusing to accept, Smith's conception of the philosopher as someone who draws out what is already contained in common sense, whose virtue lies in the consistency and clarity with which he presents and organizes what we already believe. Not for Smith the counterintuitive reduction of all types of happiness to degrees and combinations of a uniform sensation of pleasure, the Benthamite project that led its author to announce proudly that there was no intrinsic difference "between pushpin and poetry."[35] Not for Smith, either, the counterintuitive reduction of all human motivations to self-love in which Mandeville had delighted.

But this view of Smith as content, nay *compelled* by his theoretical commitments, to draw an unsurprising picture of human nature, and in particular as drawing a picture in which self-love is but one of many parts of our nature, conflicts drastically with what most of us have heard about Smith, from our first introduction to him in high school or college. Did Smith not say in WN that people were purely self-interested? Is that not, indeed, one of his great contributions to economics as a science—a "great" contribution in the sense that it has helped to define the entire field, such that if one rejects the claim, one is likely to reject the field as well? If he held a different view in TMS, does that not merely show that he changed his mind between the two works, and that TMS is an intellectually less daring work, in which Smith did not yet have the courage to drop his moralism in favor of a truly scientific attitude toward the world?

It will come as no surprise that I believe the proper answer to all of these questions is "no." I do not think Smith has a different view of human nature in WN than he had in TMS, nor that he needs such a view in order to pursue economics as a science. I do not think so in part because Smith continued to work on TMS after he wrote WN, and showed no shift toward a more self-interested conception of people in those revisions, in part because, in order to uphold a purely self-interested picture of human beings, Smith would have had to abandon the commonsensical method that I take to undergird all his writing, and in part because I do not think the text of WN supports the purely self-interested picture of human nature that gets read into it. In this chapter I have discussed the historical and methodological reasons for rejecting the "purely self-interested" reading of WN; the next chapter will be devoted to the textual reasons for rejecting it. It will be followed by a chapter on the textual reasons for rejecting another, subtler reading of Smith's economics as based on a counterintuitive picture of human nature: this time one that relies primarily on TMS, and argues that Smith sees the motivations leading us to engage in economic activity as involving a "deception" or "illusion" practiced on us by nature. In both cases, the standard views of Smith understand *homo economicus* to be a radically different animal from *homo moralis.* I believe, by contrast, that the passage from *homo moralis* to *homo economicus* is and ought to be a smooth one, and that if Smith is the careful and thoughtful philosopher he seems to be, he will be concerned to have one and the same type of animal acting in both the moral and the economic realm. The remaining chapters in this section will show, I hope, why there need be no difficulty in bringing *homo moralis* and *homo economicus* together.

CHAPTER FIVE

Self-Interest

"The *Wealth of Nations* is a stupendous palace erected upon the granite of self-interest."[1] Thus George Stigler, and thus, with minor qualifications here and there, two centuries of misinterpretation of Adam Smith, especially by economists. To claim that Smith endorses the notion that self-interest governs all human relationships is severely to misread WN, especially in its relationship to other theories of human motivation at the time. The claim fits Hobbes and Mandeville, not Smith; Smith devoted considerable energy in TMS to *refuting* this aspect of Hobbes and Mandeville. Nor does anything in WN suggest that he changed his mind on this subject when he came to write about economics. We will consider in this chapter, first the context of WN, then the text, to try to get a better picture of the role Smith gives to self-interest in the economic realm.

19. WN in Context

That people are by nature "restless and selfish" was a commonplace in the eighteenth century,[2] and if we were to arrange a spectrum of early modern views on the importance of self-interest, with Hobbes and Mandeville at one end, Smith would belong well past the center toward the other end. Locke, who rejects much of Hobbes, does not disagree with him over the centrality of self-interest to human motivation. He simply thinks that our extended self-interest (incorporating, among other things, God's rewards and punishments into the calculation about whether to be good) will make clear that our bread is buttered on the side of virtue, even in the absence of a political sovereign.[3] His pupil Lord Shaftesbury certainly read him this way, and criticized him for having such a self-interested conception of human nature. Shaftesbury posited instead that we have a natural, irreducible "moral sense," by which we approve and disapprove of actions without regard to our self-interest, and argued that we act morally to achieve the *sui generis* pleasure that comes when we win the approval of this moral sense.[4] Hutcheson took up this notion, producing a series of arguments to prove that both moral approval and moral motivation are irreducible to self-interest; he felt that Shaftesbury had yielded too much to the claims of self-interest in holding that the goal of our being moral is to achieve self-approval (OV, introduction). Smith probably belongs somewhere between Shaftesbury and Hutcheson—he takes on board Hutcheson's arguments that concern for others is a basic feature of our nature, but argues against assimilating the desire for self-approval to self-interest (TMS 117, 178, 303)[5]—but even if one places him with Shaftesbury rather than Hutcheson, he would be less a promoter of self-interest than Locke, let alone Hobbes. Far from being the great spokesman for the centrality of self-interest in human life, Smith joins those who argue *against* this claim.

Now even Hutcheson, the most uncompromising promoter of benevolence in the entire eighteenth century, remarks that "general benevolence alone, is not a Motive strong enough to Industry, to bear Labour and Toil, and many other Difficultys which we are averse to from Self-love" (OV VII.viii). We are benevolent, but not benevolent *enough* to work hard: "Tho' men are naturally active, yet their activity would rather turn toward the lighter and pleasanter exercise, than the slow, constant, and intense labours requisite to procure the necessaries and conveniences of life, unless strong motives are presented to engage them to these severer labours" (SMP I: 310).

Hence, self-love is necessary in the economic sphere, and insofar as it is necessary, it is morally acceptable: "Self-Love is really as necessary to the Good of the Whole, as Benevolence; as that Attraction which causes the Cohesion of the Parts, is as necessary to the regular State of the Whole, as Gravitation." For Hutcheson, this claim is part of a theodicy. The necessity of self-love to the system of nature explains why a benevolent deity would implant such an amoral spring of action within us. Self-love is a good thing *in the universe as a whole*; it does not make the agent who acts on it laudable. Actions taken on self-love are still amoral. It is just that certain amoral actions are necessary to human functioning, and it is a good thing that God has given us a source of motivation to perform these actions.

Furthermore, for Hutcheson the feeling that is too weak to motivate industry is "general" benevolence—benevolence toward all human beings—not the more "particular" benevolence we have for friends and family. Hutcheson considers our care for friends and family to be a feeling on the same level with our self-love, but "general benevolence" to be considerably weaker:

> the depriving any Person of the Fruits of his own innocent Labour, takes away all Motives to Industry from Self-Love, *or the nearer Ties;* and leaves us no other Motive than *general Benevolence.* . . . Industry will be confin'd to our present Necessitys, and cease when they are provided for; at least it will only continue from the weak Motive of general Benevolence, if we are not allow'd to store up beyond present Necessity, and to dispose of what is above our Necessitys, either in Barter for other kinds of Necessarys, or for the Service of our Friends or Familys. (OV 182, my emphasis)

Self-love is here grouped together with "the nearer Ties," and "the Service of our Friends or Familys," and elsewhere Hutcheson talks of "the delicate ties of friendship, by which a fine spirit may be so attached to another as to bear all toils for him with joy" (SMP I: 322). The feelings we have for those we love can be as strong as self-love; we sometimes, indeed, sacrifice our interests for theirs. We simply will not normally do this for anonymous others: for the butchers and bakers we casually encounter. As we saw in the previous chapter, Smith follows

Hutcheson exactly in this distinction between general benevolence and the nearer ties, and he also follows Hutcheson in regarding self-love as essential to the economic sphere, where we primarily deal with anonymous others, while emphatically not seeing it as basic to our relationships in every realm.

Elsewhere, Hutcheson adds another concern, one that Aristotle had raised against Plato (*Politics* II.5): that even if we are to be benevolent, we want to do so of our own will, and therefore with our own goods, rather than serving as mere parts of a benevolent political system that distributes goods impersonally. What is crucial is that we each get *to decide for ourselves* whether, and how, we are going to be benevolent: "[N]o confidence of a wise distribution by magistrates can ever make any quantity of labour be endured with such pleasure and hearty good-will, as when each man is the distributer of what he has acquired among those he loves" (SMP II.6.vi, 322). Consistently with his moral sentimentalism, Hutcheson uses our feelings to bring out the value of freedom: "We all feel a sense of liberty within us, a strong desire of acting according to our own inclinations, and to gratify our own affections, whether selfish, or generous," and it is "unkind and cruel" to prevent people from acting out of this "sense of liberty" where no overriding public interest requires such intervention (SMP II.6.v, 320). Hutcheson says that "actions of kindness, humanity, gratitude . . . would cease to appear amiable," and hence to grant the legitimate pleasures of virtuous action, "when Men could be constrain'd to perform them" (OV VII.vi). It is precisely because these actions "are not matters of compulsion" that virtuous people have the "occasion of displaying their virtues, and obtaining the esteem and love of others" (SI II.iii). A distribution of goods by officials would deprive us of the opportunity to exercise and display our virtues. So we prefer a system allowing each to acquire goods for him- or herself, and then decide freely whether to be benevolent or not, over one in which "magistrates" distribute goods. A system that lets us choose whether to be benevolent will be a system that lets us act on self-love instead, of course, but a system permitting us to act on self-love will be one that allows us liberty—and Hutcheson's main concern is that we have liberty: "natural liberty," as he likes to call it (SMP II.5.2; 294).

So we have several arguments even in Hutcheson, who has never been accused of favoring self-love over benevolence, for granting self-love a central role in the economic realm. This should begin to undermine any presumption that Smith gave self-interest a new and controversial prominence in WN. That presumption should be further weakened when we note that Smith's readers did not attend to the role of self-interest in WN until long after it was published. As far as I can determine, none of WN's first readers, whether in England and Scotland or in Germany, France, or the United States, mentioned this feature of the book, either to praise it or to condemn it, nor did they see any sharp break between TMS and WN. TMS was very well-known, throughout Europe and in the United States, and it was Smith's reputation for the earlier book that garnered initial attention for WN. One would have expected a gap between the two books, if gap there is, to appear particularly sharply to Smith's readership at this point in his reception. Yet it was only much later, in the nineteenth century, when most readers knew WN well but were at best dimly aware of TMS, that people began to suggest that the two books have different pictures of human nature. This is good circumstantial reason to suspect that the supposed gap between TMS and WN lies solely in the eyes of those who misinterpret one or both of the books. Turning to the text of WN confirms that suspicion.

20. "Bettering One's Condition" in WN II.iii

Two passages are used, above all, to demonstrate WN's supposed commitment to the ubiquity of self-interest in human life. The first comes from Book I, chapter ii and can at least be plausibly construed as part of a theory of human nature that grounds the rest of the book. The fact that the second passage appears deep in Book II, and in the middle of a long argument on other matters, indicates that it is a poor source for Smith's general theory of human nature, and a close reading of the passage bears out that indication. I will therefore begin by getting the second passage out of the way, then spend more time on the first one.

Both passages get quoted shorn of their context, yet context, as usual in Smith, is crucial to understanding their import. So we should begin by noting that the second passage appears in the middle of a long discussion of the importance of saving and the dangers, real and imagined, of excessive consumption. Proponents of sumptuary laws had held that excessive luxury spending could ruin a nation. Smith grants that private "prodigality" takes away from the wealth of a nation, but argues that governments do not need to worry about this: "It can seldom happen . . . that the circumstances of a great nation can be much affected either by the prodigality or misconduct of individuals; the profusion or imprudence of some being always more than compensated by the frugality and good conduct of others" (341). Sumptuary laws are unnecessary—on 346 he will also call them "impertinent" and "presumptuous"—since most people will be frugal. But what reason do we have to believe that most people will be frugal? Smith says:

> With regard to profusion, the principle, which prompts to expence, is the passion for present enjoyment; which, though sometimes violent and very difficult to be restrained, is in general only momentary and occasional. But the principle which prompts to save, is *the desire of bettering our condition, a desire which, though generally calm and dispassionate, comes with us from the womb, and never leaves us till we go into the grave.* In the whole interval which separates those two moments, there is scarce perhaps a single instant in which any man is so perfectly and completely satisfied with his situation, as to be without any wish of alteration or improvement, of any kind. (341 ¶28, my emphasis)

Carried away, perhaps, by his own gift for rhetoric, or his Stoic delight in dishing up reminders of *vanitas*, Smith makes his case for the ubiquity of frugal dispositions in words that were to mark him as an extreme advocate of the supremacy of self-interest among human motives. Scarce a single instant of unselfishness in the whole "interval" twixt womb and grave, Mr. Smith? Surely not—perhaps only in Scotland, as some of his more malicious critics were to say. But Mr. Smith never makes any such claim, even when the italicized phrases above are torn from their context, and certainly not when they are read within it.

Even when they are torn from their context: The constancy of our desire to "better ourselves" does not preclude the presence of other desires. The passage itself makes clear that the "violent and very difficult to be restrained" passion for present enjoyment, for instance, may occur together with the desire for self-betterment, even though the two conflict. *A fortiori*, desires that do not conflict with our long-term betterment, including most of the ordinary impulses we have to help our families, neighbors, and wider society, can run alongside or even occlude the desire to better ourselves. The latter, we might say, is a long pedal note against which a variety of other interests and desires can play in counterpoint. That we may have other desires, for the good of other human beings, or for justice or fulfillment of duty or some kind of spiritual good, is not to the point, hence neither supported nor contradicted by the passage. Furthermore, far from praising or even describing the most infantile, consumerist satisfy-your-own-desires attitude, Smith here says that the ability to *defer* gratification, to postpone the immediate impulse to satisfy our desires, is normally more powerful in human beings than the "passion for present enjoyment" with which it conflicts. One could take this as praise rather than condemnation of the human motivational structure: The natural human condition here, as elsewhere in Smith, is that of the mature, socialized being rather than the unrestrained child. But in any case the passions Smith is contrasting are *both* selfish. There is nothing altruistic, just, or duty-oriented about the passion for present enjoyment, and Smith cannot possibly be construed as saying that we are governed by a desire to better our own condition *as opposed to* something more social or more virtuous.

And when they are read in context: Smith continues the passage I have quoted with the remark that an "augmentation of fortune" is merely the means "by which *the greater part of men* propose . . . to better their condition," the means "most vulgar . . . and obvious" to self-betterment. That this is but "the most vulgar" means to self-betterment suggests that there are other methods—and less "vulgar" or "obvious" ones. To anyone who has read TMS, the method that springs to mind is moral development. In TMS, Smith makes clear that virtue— the achievement of moderation and harmony in one's passions—is a deeper form of self-betterment than social status, although the intimate link between moral development and social approval often leads people to seek the latter instead of the former. Seeking fortune to improve one's social status is therefore something of an error, a confusion. Smith does not suggest that the "desire of bettering our condition" necessarily entails such a confusion. Nor does he say that savings would disappear if most people came to prefer moral to social betterment. They would then, indeed, be more likely than they are now to be frugal, and more likely to seek intelligent ways of turning their money to socially useful purposes. Later in WN, in a much less noted passage, Smith in fact describes people as saving for their children (917), a beneficent purpose. What conflicts with frugality is not intelligent beneficence but selfish prodigality, and Smith's point in WN II.iii is to show that selfish prodigality is not a matter of great public concern.

Consider, now, the italicized phrases in my long quotation from II.iii as part of this overall point. Smith is conducting a polemic against people who consider "the passion for present enjoyment" to be so dangerous, so destructive to national capital, that governments should restrict its expression by law. He urges his opponents to recognize that it is also "in general only momentary and occasional." By contrast, the desire underlying saving, "though generally calm and dispassionate," never leaves us twixt womb and grave. It is "uniform, constant, and uninterrupted," and it overcomes the worst policies, and the worst destruction of resources, carried out by governments (¶31, 36).[6] Smith hammers home the point, taking on as ugly and materialist a view of human nature as his opponents, and showing that, even on this view, the ugly, materialist desire for social status will in the end defeat the ugly, materialist passion for momentary pleasure. It is no surprise that especially cynical language appears again and again in the course of this polemic, nor that it is made vivid with bleak talk about life as an interval between birth and death. It should also be no surprise that such language does *not* appear either in the opening chapters of WN, in which Smith at least gestures toward a theory of human nature, or anywhere else in the book. We must imagine Smith, as perhaps he imagined himself, in Parliament, fighting hypocritically pious politicians who profess their great concern for the wasteful indulgences of the poor. "Foolish, violent, self-destructive passions overwhelm such weak people," they lament; "we must restrain their spending in their own long-term interest." To which Smith: "Not so, Sirs, the foolish desire to become like yourselves will restrain them without any help from us." *They* know—as perhaps you do not[7]—that any significant waste or indulgence on their part will ruin all chance they have of long-term social improvement. The threat of falling beneath the status they have achieved is constantly before their eyes; likewise, the hope that eventually they could rise, if ever so slightly. A more powerful sanction than any the government can impose will therefore keep them—mostly—saving rather than spending. The power of Smith's language, the emphatic description of the reliability of most people's desire to climb socially, can be fully explained by the polemic in which he was engaged. That ordinary people could be trusted with their own decisions about what and how much to consume was one of the least acceptable propositions of WN, to the intellectuals and politicians of its day, and at the same time one of its most important propositions, insofar as it robbed merchants of a prime argument for government control over the economy. That people always and only pursue their material self-interest may or may not be true, but from WN II.iii

Smith cannot be attached to such a view—only to the view that long-term material interests are a more reliable source of motivation than short-term material interests.

21. Self-love in WN I.ii

We come now to the most famous sentences Smith ever wrote:

> It is not from the benevolence of the butcher, the brewer, or the baker, that we expect our dinner, but from their regard to their own interest. We address ourselves, not to their humanity but to their self-love, and never talk to them of our own necessities but of their advantages. Nobody but a beggar chuses to depend chiefly upon the benevolence of his fellow-citizens. (WN 26–7)

These sentences are regularly trotted out as proof that Smith had a radically self-interested conception of human nature in WN. But is that really what they show? *Of course* we address the butcher and the baker in terms of what they can get from us! Who would ever have supposed otherwise? If Smith's point was that people are *always* motivated by self-interest he should have used a less obvious example—shown us, perhaps, like Mandeville, that charitable actions are really motivated by self-interest,[8] or, like the contemporary economist Gary Becker, that parents are so motivated in relation to their children. No self-respecting person, in ordinary circumstances, would dream of going into a butcher shop and begging for a cut of sirloin.[9] Nor does Smith deny that in extraordinary circumstances people do beg: "Nobody *but* a beggar chuses to depend chiefly upon . . . benevolence," but a beggar, of course, does so choose. Hence the passage as a whole cannot possibly make the point *that* people are motivated exclusively by self-interest. If Smith wanted to advance this Mandevillian thesis, which he is elsewhere at pains to dismiss (TMS VII.ii), he would not have appealed to the paradigm ways in which we already expect self-interest to work.

If the passage makes a poor proof for the claim *that* humans are self-interested, it offers even less to those who might hold that we *ought* to be self-interested. We come away from the passage with an appealing picture of relationships that do not require benevolence, of the reliable, independent relationship most of us have with our butchers and bakers, as opposed to the cloying, humiliating, and always uncertain life of a beggar. But it is the contrast of my life as a butcher's *customer* with the life of the beggar, and not the life or self-love of the butcher himself, that stands at center stage. The main character, the character with whom we are supposed to identify, is the one who merely *appeals* to self-love: the one who is "more likely to prevail if . . . ," who "offers . . . a bargain," who "expect[s]" his dinner, and so on. It is not at all clear that *this* character is self-interested—perhaps he is taking the meat to a charity dinner—and in any case, that is not the point: the point is to bring out his strategy, his knowledge that he can get the butcher to give him meat by offering him something in return. Unlike the beggar, or the puppy, a little earlier in the paragraph, that "fawns upon its dam," the butcher's customer can appeal to someone else's needs rather than bleating self-pityingly about his own. Thus, regardless of whether the *butcher* is self-interested, the argument of the passage depends on the butcher's *customer* being able to perceive, and address himself to, *other people's interests*. Instead of an almost Ayn Randian exaltation of self-love, we may now see these famous lines as focusing on our capacity to be *other*-directed.

Which brings us to the main point of the paragraph from which these lines come: that human beings can pursue even their individual interests *together*, that even society without benevolence need not be a hostile society, that economic exchange, even among entirely self-interested people, is not a zero-sum game. The emphasis is on the "even" in each case. No one would be surprised that people could jointly pursue activities where the tie between them was one of instinct or love. What is surprising is that joint pursuit is possible without such bonds. "A puppy fawns upon its dam," but the puppy and the dam are hard-wired, as we would say today, to work together in this way. When nonhuman animals become free of the instinctual or loving bonds that tie puppy to dam, they rarely work together: "In almost every other race of animals each individual, when it is grown to maturity, is intirely independent." At best, they may look *as though* they are working together. Two greyhounds may sometimes appear jointly to run down a hare, says Smith, but this results just from "the concurrence of their passions in the same object at that particular time." We, by contrast, intentionally cooperate in the pursuit of our interests. What differentiates us from the greyhounds is a matter of cognition: We *know* that other human beings have similar ends, and that working together can improve life for each of us rather than taking from one and giving to the other. The greyhounds and the puppy are just as self-interested as we are, but we know that self-interest allows for cooperation and they do not: *This* is the feature of human beings that "is common to men, and to be found in no other race of animals." This point serves the overall polemic of the book: to show that town and country, one nation and another, one industry and another, are not engaged in a Hobbesian struggle over wealth. They may compete on a day-to-day level, but ultimately that competition serves a joint human effort to increase the wealth of everyone.[10] *Hence* mercantilist restrictions on trade are pointless and counterproductive.

To deepen this account of the butcher-and-baker paragraph, consider its opening: "Whether this propensity [to truck, barter and exchange] be one of those principles in human nature, of which no further account can be given; or whether, as seems more probable, it be the necessary consequence of the faculties of reason and speech, it belongs not to our present subject to enquire." We are led to think that the paragraph will concern the derivation of our propensity to exchange from our propensity to speak. In earlier versions of this section, Smith had said as much. The foundation of the disposition to barter, he maintained, is "that principle to perswade which so much prevails in human nature" (LJ 493):

The offering of a shilling which to us appears to have so plain and simple a meaning, is in reality offering an argument to persuade one to do so and so as it is for his interest. Men always endeavour to persuade others to be of their opinion even when the matter is of no consequence to them. If one advances any thing concerning China or the *more distant moon* which contradicts what you imagine to be true, you immediately try to persuade him to alter his opinion. And in this manner every one is practising oratory on others thro the whole of his life. (LJ 352)

WN backs off from committing itself quite so readily to an equation between commerce and speech, leaving open the possibility that the impulse to exchange may be instead a fundamental force, like Newton's gravity, "of which no further account can be given," and remarking in any case that the issue is no part of "our present subject."[11] Nonetheless, little conversations run through the paragraph that follows, as they had in earlier versions of this material. "Nobody ever saw one animal by its gestures and natural cries signify to another, this is mine, that yours; I am willing to give this for that," says Smith. He goes on to tell us that animals fawn on one another, to get what they want, because they have "no other means of persuasion." A little later on, he tells us that "whoever offers to another a bargain of any kind" is really saying, "Give me that which I want, and you shall have this which you want." Finally, the famous lines with which we started tell us how we "*address* ourselves" to our butcher and baker, what we "*talk* to them" about. Despite the initial disclaimer about not inquiring into the relationship between commerce and speech, Smith's point in this paragraph seems to rest very much on that relationship.

Why is speech so important? In LJ, having emphasized the role of persuasion throughout human life—"every one is practising oratory on others thro the whole of his life"—and placed "barter" and "contract" within this context, Smith tells us what happens when animals join together from self-interest but lack a conversational context:

> That is bartering, by which [human beings] adress themselves to the self interest of the person and seldom fail immediately to gain their end. The brutes have no notion of this; the dogs, as I mentioned, by having the same object in their view sometimes unite their labours, but never from contract. The same is seen still more strongly in the manner in which the monkeys rob an orchard at the Cape of Good Hope.—But after they have very ingeniously conveyd away the apples, *as they have no contract they fight (even unto death) and leave after many dead upon the spot.* (LJ 352; my emphasis)

Without contracts, without discussion, self-interested animals kill each other; with discussion, they can cooperate instead. Only animals that talk can realize how exchange can be a win-win game and can construct a framework—of justice and contract—within which they can rely on each others' fair play. The greyhounds in WN may happen to pursue the same end, but they cannot do so as "the effect of any contract." They might also happen each to grab bones that the other had chewed, but they cannot have "a fair and deliberate exchange" of bones. That an exchange is "fair," we know from a later passage in WN, depends on the objects traded having a similar exchange-value. And exchange-value depends on what an object is commonly traded for. But if what it is fair to exchange for any given object depends on what is generally being exchanged for that object elsewhere in common life, then the notion of a fair exchange is essentially a linguistic one. Even if two dogs happened to exchange bones, they could not look upon their exchange as a "fair" one unless they knew what similar bones were going for among other dogs in their neighborhood. It is hard to imagine having that kind of knowledge without being able to talk.

This emphasis on speech as differentiating us from other animals recalls one of the oldest arguments in political theory. Man is a political animal, says Aristotle. He defends that point as follows:

> [T]hat man is more of a political animal than bees or any other gregarious animals is evident. Nature . . . makes nothing in vain, and man is the only animal who has the gift of speech. And whereas mere voice is but an indication of pleasure or pain, and is therefore found in other animals . . . , the power of speech is intended to set forth the expedient and inexpedient, and therefore likewise the just and the unjust. And it is a characteristic of man that he alone has any sense of good and evil, of just and unjust, and the like, and the association of living beings who have this sense makes a family and a state.[12]

With which, compare Smith:

> [The propensity to exchange] is common to all men and to be found in no other species of animal . . . [The appearance of concerted action in the greyhounds] is not the effect of any contract, but of the accidental concurrence of their passions in the same object at [a] particular time. Nobody ever saw a dog make a fair and deliberate exchange of one bone for another with another dog. Nobody ever saw one animal by its gestures and natural cries signify to another, this is mine, that yours; I am willing to give this for that. (WN 25–6)

Importantly, Smith's point is that exchange, and not political society, is natural to humans, but otherwise he follows Aristotle closely. Both make their case for the uniqueness of human social interactions by showing (a) that animal interaction is a mere response to built-in impulses ("the perception of pleasure and pain," for Aristotle; "passions," for Smith) rather than something based on speech, and (b) that what looks like speech in other animals—"mere voice" or "natural cries and gestures," respectively—is not so because it, too, is a mere expression of impulses, not a reason-guided process (Aristotle) or something that truly "signif[ies]" (Smith). Aristotle, tying speech to "reason" in his full sense of that word, moves immediately from here to the conclusion that not communication alone but communication *about* "good and evil, . . . just and unjust" is natural to man; Smith, more modestly, contents himself with a demonstration that even the most childishly self-interested of human debates is based on signification and some kind of reasoning ("This is mine, that yours; I am willing to give this for that"), and that that minimal level of intelligent communication is beyond what we can attribute to animals.

Now signification, even where it is used for no lofty reasoning, is a process by which arbitrary sounds or signs (a) get associated with objects and ideas that may not be present to the speaker at the time of utterance, and (b) get strung together in ways that make sense only if they can be evaluated in terms of truth and falsehood.[13] The ability to engage in this process accordingly requires some ability both to abstract oneself from present circumstances, and to attempt to satisfy norms for meaning and truth, rather than just to offer relief to impulses for vocal expression. To have meaning, to be signs, marks require a standard, a norm for their use, and not merely a cause. And to understand ourselves as *using* signs, as communicating, we must see ourselves as *reasonably aiming* at such standards, and succeeding or failing in our aim, rather than merely being caused to coincide or not coincide with them. Even the determinist must admit that one of the spheres of human life in which freedom most prominently *appears* to exist is our ability to speak. And this is true regardless of whether the speech in question concerns good and evil, justice and injustice, or merely our own and others' material advantages.

Thus by tying it to speech, and separating speech from mere animal cries by way of signification and persuasion, Smith connects exchange to a realm in which the possibility of human freedom is central. The connection suggests that there is something freeing about the very nature of market relationships. That impression is reinforced by the fact that the word "persuasion," on its other appearances in WN, carries favorable connotations and opposes unfavorably loaded synonyms for "power." For example:

> The pride of man makes him love to domineer and nothing mortifies him so much as to be obliged to condescend to *persuade* his inferiors. Wherever the law allows it, and the nature of the work can afford it, therefore, he will generally prefer the service of slaves to that of freemen. (388)

> [T]hough management and *persuasion* are always the easiest and the safest instruments of government, as force and violence are the worst and the most dangerous, yet such . . . is the natural insolence of man, that he almost always disdains to use the good instrument, except where he cannot or dare not use the bad one. (799, my emphasis in both cases)

We are embarrassed to persuade, yet the alternative is not only ugly but ineffective. In both cases, Smith highlights the irrationality of relying on force. And he associates persuasion with the treatment of other human beings as "free" or "independent," rather than slaves. When Smith roots market interactions in persuasion, therefore, he imports into them the freedom required for and manifest in speech. By speaking to our fellow human beings, whether in the marketplace or elsewhere, we allow them independence from us and simultaneously express our own independence from our animal impulses; we show respect to their interests and to our own; we overcome our, and forestall their, impulse to domineer; and we thereby pave the way for cooperation instead of flattery, deceit, or force. Smith thus goes Montesquieu one better: The virtues of commerce include not just peace among nations, but the moral bases of individual freedom and mutual respect.

22. Self-interest versus "General Benevolence"

Having thrust self-love out of the starring role it usually plays in accounts of WN I.ii, we must now acknowledge that it is an important supporting actor. Smith links "fair and deliberate exchanges" with the verbal argument, "this is mine, that yours; I am willing to give this for that," then contrasts such contractual/conversational relationships with a puppy fawning upon its dam and a spaniel trying to wheedle dinner out of its master. These "servile and fawning attention[s]," when successful, can arouse "good will." Human beings do not have the time to do this with every other human being whose help they need, however, so they appeal to self-love instead. By implication, the contractual/conversational relationships at the head of the paragraph are based on self-love, and they will turn out to be central to the way economies work. To repeat: The point is that human beings can pursue self-interested ends *jointly*, there is no implication that human beings are more self-interested than other animals (the puppy and the spaniel are also self-interested), plenty of room is left for "good will" in human life (the spaniel's master acts on good will), and the rhetoric of the whole piece suggests that there is something morally unappealing about relationships that depend exclusively on good will (where one party is "servile and fawning" and the other, presumably, is lordly and contemptuous), and something admirable, something "respectable" if also "awful," about the more egalitarian relationships of mutual self-interest. Still, once all this has been granted, it remains true that Smith is telling us that self-love, not benevolence, is the basis of the vast majority of economic relationships:

> In civilized society, [man] stands at all times in need of the cooperation and assistance of great multitudes, while his whole life is scarce sufficient to gain the friendship of a few persons. . . . [M]an has almost constant occasion for the help of his brethren, and it is in vain for him to expect it from their benevolence only. He will be more likely to prevail if he can interest their self-love in his favour, and shew them that it is for their own advantage to do for him what he requires of them.

The point here is certainly that benevolence plays little role in economic exchanges.[14] But *why* is benevolence economically so unimportant? Because the "co-operation" or "help" we need from others in securing our material goods, the sort of cooperation and assistance that concerns economics, is cooperation and help from "*great multitudes.*" The networks by which human beings produce and exchange their many material goods extend over large societies, sometimes over the entire human race. It is impossible, however, to know most members even of a small town well enough to expect much "particular benevolence" from them, so what we would need to rely on, if our economic exchanges were rooted in benevolence, is *general* benevolence, good will toward anonymous others, and that is a very weak sentiment. The opposition here is thus not between self-love and all kinds of benevolence, just between self-love and good will toward anonymous others. Good will toward anonymous others can take two forms. Smith calls it "love of our country" or "public spirit," when limited to people in one's own country (TMS 191, 228–32), and "universal benevolence," when extended to all people everywhere (235–7: see §14). So when Smith opts for self-love over good will as the basis of economic transactions, he is really opting for self-love over public spirit and universal benevolence. Similarly, in the invisible hand passage of IV.ii, Smith will say that the merchant has no intention to promote "the publick interest," not that he has no benevolent intentions of any kind. It is public spirit, a concern for the well-being of "great multitudes," not benevolence of all kinds, that Smith thinks we can safely ignore in economics. In this he is agreeing for once with his archrival James Steuart, who wrote that the fundamental principle of political economy is that "everyone will act, in what regards the public, from a motive of private interest, and . . . the only *public spirited* sentiment any statesman has a right to exact of his subjects, is their strict obedience to the laws."[15]

Smith is also agreeing with Hutcheson, as we have seen, and of course with Locke, Mandeville, Hume, and other writers who gave a more prominent role to self-interest in human life than he himself did. With whom might he be *disagreeing*? Well, perhaps with Rousseau and certainly with Plato, Thomas More, and the other utopians who proposed that there could be societies in which everyone worked, and exchanged goods, out of love for the common good. Hutcheson had explicitly criticized Plato and More in this regard (SMP II.6.vi, 323–4). The abbé Morelly, writing shortly before Smith, imagined a continent where everyone feels "obligated to participate in making [the land] fertile," to work joyously together and to engage only in "friendly rivalry."[16] Tomas Campanella, a century earlier, had described an imaginary "city of the sun" where the inhabitants work purely out of public spirit; the traveler who supposedly visited them reports that they "burn with so great a love for their fatherland, as I could scarcely have believed possible."[17] To this the jurist Samuel Pufendorf responded acidly, "perfect men are more easily imagined than found" (LNN IV.iv.7, p. 541). When Smith declares that general benevolence is weak in all human beings, I take it he is joining Pufendorf in dismissing the likelihood that anyone will ever find people like Campanella's supremely public-spirited citizens. The Humean rule of thumb we described in the previous chapter comes into play here: Reports presenting us with people extremely different from all those we know in daily life should be treated with extreme scepticism. Hume himself uses that rule precisely to dismiss stories of far-away lands where everyone is benevolent (E 84). And Smith, as we saw in the previous chapter, regards cultural variation in human nature as operating within a framework of general similarities, and would not expect anything as fundamental as the tendency of people to care weakly for anonymous others to vary greatly across cultures.

Smith's dismissal of concern for the public good is probably also directed against the views of those who are today called "civic republicans." Smith rejects the ideal of civic virtue, recommending private virtue in its stead. Not for Smith the notion that individuals should "belong only to the great society and be a child of the fatherland"[18] or "surrender all, even their lives, for the good of the state."[19] In WN IV.ii he writes, "I have never known much good done by those who affected to trade for the publick good." This line should be read together with a remark of Edmund Burke to Smith, in a 1775 letter, about an attempt of Josiah Wedgwood to hinder a potential competitor from entering the pottery business: "[Wedgwood] pretends . . . that he is actuated . . . by nothing but a desire of the public good. I confess a declaration of the lowest species of any honest self Interest, would have much greater weight with me, from the mouth of a Tradesman" (Corr 181). Like Burke, Smith suspects the good faith of any merchant who professes to trade for the public good, preferring them to confess honestly to self-interest. He tells us in addition that a merchant who does pursue his own interest "frequently promotes that of the society more effectually than when he really intends to promote it." Clearly the main point is, as it was for Burke, that governments should ignore the professions of public-spiritedness by which merchants ask for government protection. The lines are partly directed toward merchants specifically, since they are a class of people who often ask for undeserved and inappropriate government aid for their enterprises, but there is a more general point, rooted in Smith's particularist view of human cognition: that all people *know their own local situations* far better than they can ever know something as general as the public good. Attempts directly to promote the public good will most often, therefore, be ineffectual. Since human knowledge is highly particularist, and since sympathy, the imaginative projection by which we understand other people, is even more highly particularist, a desire to promote the public good, even when we have it, is likely to go awry. Practically all of us know far better how to help ourselves and our friends in our local situations than how to help our whole nation, or all of humankind. Smith's account of moral and political cognition is egalitarian: Experts know less than they claim to know, and ordinary people know more than they seem to know, about what will best promote the human good. It is this egalitarian view of human cognition, and not any claim about the nature of human motivation, that sets Smith most apart from his contemporaries, and that provides the essential premise for his arguments against government interference with the economy. Smith's teacher Hutcheson, his rival James Steuart, and many other political economists, did not share this confidence in ordinary people's judgment, and therefore looked to a government where the wise would guide investment, and control the labor- and consumption choices of the poor. For Smith, by contrast, the decisions made by individuals in their own local situations will almost always more effectively promote the public good than any plan aimed directly at that good.

23. Self-interest as an Assumption in WN

Commentators do not of course rely just on the two passages I have discussed when attributing a radical reduction of human motivations to self-interest to WN. Rather, they see this reduction as assumed throughout the book. In fact

WN acknowledges a number of motivations in addition to self-interest. Smith mentions "charity and friendship" as motives for lending money (113), and he remarks at one point that "publick zeal" will occasionally lead people to make great financial sacrifices in order to aid their state (852). He also presupposes, when he condemns inhumanity, miserliness, cruelty, injustice, and the like that the agents thus criticized are capable of living up to norms of justice, humanity, generosity, and kindness (see §11 above). Nevertheless, it is true that most analyses of action in WN presuppose self-interest on the part of the agents. "The consideration of his own private profit," says Smith, "is the sole motive which determines the owner of any capital to employ it either in agriculture, in manufactures, or in some particular branch of the wholesale or retail trade" (374). Earlier, he tells us that "[a] man must be perfectly crazy" who does not employ his stock "for either present enjoyment or future profit" in countries where there is tolerable security (284–5).

But our consideration of I.ii should give us a key for understanding the pervasiveness of self-interest in WN. We should bear in mind, first, that Smith's main worry in WN is about cognition rather than motivation, about how self-interest can most intelligently be employed, not about whether we act on self-interest rather than other motives. Context makes clear that the man who would employ his stock in something other than present enjoyment or future profit "must be perfectly crazy" because the alternative to doing this is letting one's money pile up uselessly, or burying it in the ground, not because rational people refuse to act on something other than selfishness. WN almost always contrasts one type of self-interested action with other types of self-interested action (selfish prodigality with selfish frugality, or investment in agriculture with investment in manufactures), not self-interested action with benevolent action.

Second, the main alternative to self-interest throughout WN is public spirit, not private benevolence, given that we are dealing with sales to and purchases from large numbers of anonymous others. When Smith says that the owner of capital is motivated solely by "the consideration of his own private profit" (374), he goes on immediately to make clear that by this he means that the capitalist never thinks about the effect of his investments on "the annual produce of the land and labour of the society." Economic agents are unlikely to care about the public as a whole, and that is just as well, since the public as a whole would not usually be well-served if they did. But motivations other than self-interest and public spirit—particular benevolence, resentment, religious feeling—are irrelevant to economic transactions. Indeed, *all* sentiments, even self-love, may be irrelevant to economics. Smith normally talks of the "interest" of an agent rather than the agent's "self-interest," let alone his "self-love." The "interest" of an agent is not really a sentiment like self-love; instead, it refers to the bundle of material goods that an agent seeks, abstracting from the purposes to which those goods may be put, the emotional yearnings they may satisfy. The interest of an agent, unlike his or her self-love, is something objective, something observable and measurable. "Interest" in this sense is shorthand for what one needs, materially, in order to pursue one's private projects, which can and normally will include caring for one's family and friends and socializing with one's neighbors. The point is that the sentiments going into these projects will not normally include any feelings for the butchers, bakers, and bankers upon whom one relies to get the material goods for the projects. From the point of view of my butcher or banker, therefore, I might as well be purely self-interested: My interests in other people do not extend to *him*. And from the point of view of the economist, we might as well view all the agents in question as if they were purely self-interested. The only other kind of motivation that might concern us would be a concern for the people with whom one trades, either individually or as a group, and that, Smith thinks, is unlikely, at least in large societies.

Third, the fact that we do not ordinarily make exchanges out of benevolence for our butcher and baker allows them, and us, an important kind of freedom. Recall Hutcheson's reasons for why we all want first to own our own goods, and then to distribute them as we see fit. We earn our bread; the baker earns his; a system of private property and mutually disinterested exchange is needed for all that; and *then*, if the baker is a friend or in some sort of need, we may act benevolently toward him. And if the baker is not a friend, and not in need, there is no reason to act benevolently toward him. He would not expect us to do so, and might well be displeased if we did: He too will feel much greater "pleasure and hearty good-will" (Hutcheson) on earning his own bread by his own labours, and then acting benevolently, if he so chooses. We all want to live in a system in which we have the liberty to be selfish or benevolent, as we choose. Smith's commitment to liberty of this kind comes out as early as the contrast between dignified conversation and "servile and fawning attention" in I.ii. He goes on to praise liberty and independence throughout WN.

Fourth, we should take the stress on private interest in WN together with Smith's suspicion of the grandiose designs of politicians. WN is addressed to lawmakers and those who influence them, who can choose to intervene in economic affairs or not. If they come to see the economic world as filled with agents who almost always act on private interests rather than public spirit, this should have the effect of disappointing any hopes they may have had of molding and directing these agents. They should become more convinced that it is hopeless to try to "superintend [. . .] the industry of private people" (WN 687), to direct the way "private people . . . employ their capitals" (456), or to launch grand "project[s] of an empire" in the name of the greater national good (947). And, as the fact that these quotations come from central passages in WN indicates, this is one of Smith's great goals. He wants to prick the hubris of statesmen filled with "the spirit of system" who think they can direct all the pieces of the human chessboard from above (TMS 234), to "awake" them from their delusions, to get them to accommodate themselves to "the real mediocrity of [their] circumstances" (WN 947). What better way to do that than to remind them, over and over again, that all these human chess pieces are motivated by their own private interests rather than by a concern for the good of their nation—that the claim that this or that grand scheme will serve the public good, therefore, is likely to fall on deaf ears? Smith is trying to get arrogant statesmen to lower the pitch of their self-love, to achieve self-command over their thirst for glory, and his theory of sympathy tells him that he can best do that by displaying to them, in detail, just how cold a reception their plans are likely to receive from the people who would be needed to fulfill them. WN not only brings out the awful virtues inculcated by the marketplace but is itself an exercise in teaching some awful virtues: the virtue of humbling one's "spirit of system," one's inclination to think one knows what will be best for all.

Finally, it is not at all clear that strong assumptions of self-interest are necessary for Smith's mode of economic analysis. What Smith clearly does and must assume is (1) that people have *rational* motivations, in their economic activity, that they are not much swayed by taboo and superstition; and (2) that, qua economic agents, they for the most part have little or no concern for other economic agents. If people produced and exchanged goods largely out of a love for their society, or a blind respect for their society's norms, or a belief that gods or spirits require them to produce certain goods, then their exchanges would fail to constitute the sophisticated signal system that Smith sees in the market. If people buy more or less corn than they need because of a love for their society, or fear of violating a traditional taboo, then, pace Smith's analysis at WN 524–34, the depth and extent of a famine will not show up properly in the prices of foodstuffs. If I buy bread from you because I care about you, or because I believe that supporting your bakery is good for our society, then the price I pay will not reflect how much I, or my family and friends, want your bread. Nor will I be led to reducing my bread purchases, and thereby conserving bread, when the price is high, or to increasing those purchases, and thereby helping to use up an abundant harvest, when the price is low. For markets to provide information and distribute goods efficiently, the agents exchanging must be rationally pursuing some interest, rather than following rules of ritual or taboo, and mutually disinterested—uninterested in the projects of the people with whom they are exchanging. But they do not need to be *self*-interested. They may care about their families and friends, their religious communities, or any of a variety of political and social projects. It is just important that these commitments not significantly affect who they buy from or sell to, or at what price they buy or sell.[20] And in a large, anonymous society, as Smith says, economic relationships will be mostly independent of these other, more personal commitments. People in such societies will not normally be making economic exchanges with family members, friends, fellow save-the-whales activists, and the like. If markets are to give information and distribute goods efficiently, it is important that the participants in the market not be interested in their trading partners; it is entirely unimportant whether or not they are interested only in themselves. And Smith makes the former but not the latter assumption.

24. Smith and Hobbes: A Response to Cropsey

Joseph Cropsey tells us that "Smith is intelligible as the disciple of Hobbes, the translator of Hobbesianism into an order of society" (PE 34). This appears to mean that for Smith self-preservation is the primary human end (3–5), and that, in particular, Smith takes self-preservation to outweigh excellence when the two conflict. "Smith elected to orient life not upon excellence but upon preservation," says Cropsey (115), noting in a footnote that one might point to the behavior of courageous soldiers in war as evidence, against Smith, that people in fact will naturally sacrifice life for excellence in certain circumstances (116n). On Cropsey's reading, then, Smith does give self-interest priority over all other concerns.

But this interpretation exactly inverts what Smith actually says. Smith is a *disciple* of Hobbes?! On the contrary: Smith devotes a chapter of TMS to a refutation of Hobbes, which concludes, "The whole account of human nature . . . which deduces all sentiments and affections from self-love, which has made so much noise in the world . . . seems to me to have arisen from some confused misapprehension of the system of sympathy."[21] In WN, Hobbes appears once, and the citation at first glance appears to be an approving one: "Wealth, as Mr. Hobbes says, is power" (WN 48). But a closer look reveals Smith to be almost reversing Hobbes's point. Hobbes had argued that wealth "joined with liberality" is power because a rich person willing to spread his wealth around can buy "friends, and servants" whose combined strength can help defend him against enemies (*Leviathan* I.x). Smith, by contrast, explicitly denies that wealth conduces to "any political power, either civil or military." Rather, he says, wealth is *purchasing* power—it gives one "a certain command over . . . all the produce of labour which is then in the market." This harmless economic point undermines, rather than buttresses, Hobbes's attempt to include wealth in the many ways people are led to carry out an endless war of all against all.

As for Smith as a promoter of self-preservation above human excellence: Smith actually says that the "wise and virtuous man" will be always willing to sacrifice his private interest to a greater public interest (TMS 235–6). He speaks repeatedly of our need, and ability, to *suppress* our desire for our own good, when that is morally necessary (e.g., TMS 25, 83, 90, 228), and describes the chief aim of human life as "to be beloved" (41), "to restrain our selfish, and to indulge our benevolent affections" (25), or "to be that thing which deserves approbation" (117)—never as, merely, to survive. He also explicitly recognizes, several times, that people both should and can live up to the ideal of the courageous soldier (90–91, 206, 236, 282). Indeed, he criticizes commercial society sharply for letting courage—"one of the most essential parts of the character of a man" (WN 787)—atrophy in the bulk of the people.

What is right in Cropsey's reading is that Smith sees the preservation of our selves, and of the human species, as the primary end that *Nature* has set for us (TMS 77), and regards self-preservation as a principle governing the motions of natural objects in general (PE 2–4). But one does not need to look to Hobbes for this doctrine—practically every philosopher from Descartes onward has shared it. Unless we want to lump all modern philosophers together in an indistinguishable mass, we need to attend to how they differ within this general framework. With regard to the question that concerns Cropsey, we might note that many philosophers, while sharing the notion that self-preservation is a basic *natural* end, have nonetheless come up with views on which self-preservation is not the primary *human* end. Kant, for instance, has no doubts at all that nature sets self-preservation as our end, but nonetheless avows that, qua rational beings rather than merely natural ones, we give freedom priority over our own survival. Smith is closer to Kant than to Hobbes on this—he allows for some tension between properly human and merely natural ends—although for Smith the properly human end is sociability rather than freedom. Cropsey in fact recognizes this feature of Smith's teaching: "[M]an is naturally disposed to reverse the natural [ranking of the virtues]. Then human nature is in some sense *sui generis*, not wholly an aspect of nature simply but partly a denial or negation of it" (PE 46). That encapsulates nicely the position, not only of Smith, but of many other modern moral philosophers, including several who greatly influenced Smith: Hutcheson, Shaftesbury, and Joseph Butler, for instance. Yet for Cropsey it is a "dubious position," which Smith occupies to try to hold on to the distinction between the noble and the ignoble "while at the same time conceding the indifference of nature to nobility" (46). The position does not seem so dubious to me, although I do not want to argue the point here. Suppose it is dubious. That still would not mean Smith failed to hold it, and it is surely a mistake to read Smith as though he were Hobbes merely because one believes that Hobbes's position, rather than Smith's, is more persuasive.

One further point: In the course of making his case that Smith is "the translator of Hobbesianism into an order of society," Cropsey identifies "society" and "polity." He says, for instance, that "Smith compares justice to the pillar, and benevolence to the ornament of political life" (PE 38). But what Smith actually says is that justice is the pillar and benevolence the ornament of "human *society*" (TMS 86). Again, on the next page Cropsey talks of Smith's "exclusion of benevolence as the principle of society," although TMS is shot through with descriptions of how central benevolence is to the workings of society. It simply shies away from making benevolence a principle of *polities* (TMS 79–81). In the same sentence, Cropsey talks of principles "of society" and principles "of political association" as if they were the same thing.[22] Now Hobbes did run society and polity together. But this is one of the main ways in which Smith *differs* from Hobbes. For Smith there is a crucial distinction between the social and the political realms. The political is the realm in which force is used to assure the maintenance of certain norms, and which therefore should and ordinarily does concern itself just with the protection of exact rights, while the social realm, which includes the political as a proper part of itself, consists also in the free-flowing sentimental relationships that allow us to become benevolent, courageous, self-commanding, and in other ways virtuous and admirable.

What is most interesting in Smith from a moral point of view is in fact that he thus separates social from political morality, restricting politics to a subset of the ways in which human beings can influence one another to uphold norms and pursue ideals. This makes Smith's liberalism distinct from, and indeed a challenge to, the liberalism of those who would maintain that human excellence is something we need to sacrifice for the sake of freedom. For Smith, the search for excellence is something to which politics is unnecessary, something we can successfully carry out by the nonpolitical, subtler and gentler forces that lead every human being to seek the praise and admiration of other human beings. It is therefore possible for a society free of "civil and ecclesiastical" domination— which Cropsey rightly identifies as Smith's main political aim (112)—to be also a society of decent, even highly admirable, human beings. It is *possible*, I stress, not inevitable or even, perhaps, likely. Smith is well aware that the free commercial society he advocates may lead people away from virtue. But he also indicates here and there that free commercial society can in some ways be helpful to the acquisition of virtue,[23] and writes most of the time as if the pursuit of excellence is at least compatible with unrestrained commerce. Today, as in Smith's time, writers on both the left and the right tend to agree that free markets are incompatible with the pursuit of virtue, and some on both sides advocate laws restricting certain kinds of market activities for that reason, while others, especially on the right, seem happy to throw the pursuit of virtue overboard. So Cropsey's assimilation of Smith to Hobbes leads him to miss one of the most interesting ways in which Smith's work serves as a standing challenge to both the critics and the defenders of capitalism who came after him. To make good the assumptions most of us have about the relationship between commerce and virtue, we need to answer Smith's presentation of a very different view of that relationship, a view by which social forces alone, without political help—"anarchic" social forces, in the literal sense of "anarchy"[24]—can lead us toward excellence.

CHAPTER SIX

Vanity

Charles Griswold maintains that the economy, for Smith, is fueled by self-deception, by "a large-scale mistake in our understanding of happiness" (AVE 224, 222). In truth, wealth is irrelevant to happiness and pursuing it requires us to plunge into "unceasing work" and constant "dissatisfaction." Nonetheless, according to Griswold, "Smith explicitly argues that the fact that most individuals are *not* perfectly happy contributes to the 'happiness of mankind, as well as of all rational beings'" (AVE 225).

Smith does not argue this, I believe, either explicitly or implicitly. In the first place, the internal quotation in the second citation from Griswold comes from a passage in which Smith says that we contribute to the happiness of human and all other rational beings when we follow "the dictates of our moral faculties," not when we pursue wealth (TMS 166). Second, far from endorsing the ironic view that the unhappiness of most individuals can contribute to the greater happiness of mankind, Smith says that "No society can be flourishing and happy, of which the far greater part of the members are poor and miserable" (WN 96). Third, Griswold's interpretation leans almost entirely on a single, albeit famous, passage in TMS (IV.i.10). He says that the *Wealth of Nations* is "painted within [the] frame" of this passage (AVE 222), and he hearkens back to it whenever he reads other Smithian writings on the relationship between happiness and "bettering our condition."[1] But TMS IV.i.10 is Smith's earliest published writing on political economy, and he later significantly altered many of the views it expresses. He did retain the passage in subsequent editions of TMS, but it makes sense to read its final meaning in the light of later texts on economic motivation rather than to read the later texts in its light.

I am devoting a whole chapter to this issue because if Griswold is right—and he represents the view held by most scholars[2]—there would remain a very serious moral gap between Smith's moral and his economic views, if not one over selfishness. If Griswold's interpretation is right, Smith urges us throughout TMS to see the pursuit of wealth as morally corrupting and conducive to unhappiness, but also applauds a social system that depends upon, and encourages, that very pursuit. This doesn't make sense. If Smith really disapproves as strongly as Griswold suggests of the pursuit of wealth, we would expect him to criticize commercial society from a moral point of view, and to recommend institutions that would correct for the delusion it fosters.[3] He does recommend such institutions to correct for the way commercial society "mutilates" the courage and intelligence of poor laborers. What accounts for the absence of any similar corrective measures against the evils of consumerism?

There is another issue at stake as well: Does Smith share the Stoic view that external goods make no difference to human happiness? In the TMS passage on which Griswold relies, Smith seems to be saying that "the beggar, who suns himself by the side of the highway" has everything one could want out of human life. From here, it would follow that material deprivation, even great material deprivation, is unimportant. Martha Nussbaum has attributed precisely this view to Smith: "Smith's account of the operations of the market, in *The Wealth of Nations*, is deeply in the grip of [the] false doctrine [that external blows do not touch what really matters]: he is prepared to let the market do its worst with little constraint, partly because he believes that the poor do not suffer at their very core, retaining a dignity that life's blows cannot remove."[4] I believe this is a misreading of WN, even if it can perhaps be imputed to parts of TMS.

Two serious moral issues, then, hang on whether Smith really believes, as TMS IV.i seems to imply, that a fully virtuous person would neither seek wealth nor be disturbed by poverty. Clarifying the implications of that passage, and its standing within Smith's work as a whole, is therefore crucial to working out Smith's views on the larger moral issues. I will begin with a close look at that text, and return later to the broader issues.

25. Vanity in TMS IV.i

It is helpful to have the offending passage immediately before us:

> The poor man's son, whom heaven in its anger has visited with ambition, when he begins to look around him, admires the condition of the rich. He finds the cottage of his father too small for his accommodation, and fancies he should be lodged more at ease in a palace. He is displeased with being obliged to walk a-foot, or to endure the fatigue of riding on horseback. He feels himself naturally indolent, and willing to serve himself with his own hands as little as possible; and judges, that a numerous retinue of servants would save him from a great deal of trouble. He thinks if he had attained all these, he would sit still contentedly, and be quiet, enjoying himself in the thought of the happiness and tranquillity of his situation. He is enchanted with the distant idea of this felicity. It appears in his fancy like the life of some superior rank of beings.

So, to begin with, the desire for wealth Smith is talking about here is not the desire that everyone has, merely to "better one's condition." It is a desire for *great* wealth, for sufficient wealth that one would no longer need to work at all, and it is a desire held by a "poor man's son" who does not really know what the life of very wealthy people is like. If he did, he would know what Smith is about to stress: that people never do "sit still contentedly" even when they have attained great wealth. All the poor man's son is likely to achieve is a life in which the "trinkets and baubles" of wealth fail to compensate for a "body wasted with toil and diseases," a "mind galled and ruffled by the memory of a thousand injuries and disappointments." So the ambitious boy in this passage aims at a fantasy; he is "enchanted"; he does not merely harbor the ordinary, realistic hope to be somewhat better off than he is now, or than his parents were. The boy wants a palace and a retinue of servants, not just the better cottage down the block that might come within the scope of reasonable expectations. His hopes do not even quite belong to the realm of the human: he wants to join "some superior rank of beings," to become super-human.

We are now told that what he needs to do, to try to realize his hopes, will go strongly against the grain of "natural indolence" he feels within himself:

> in order to arrive at [the life of this superior rank of beings], he devotes himself for ever to the pursuit of wealth and greatness. To obtain the conveniencies which these afford, he submits in the first year, nay in the first month of his application, to more fatigue of body and more uneasiness of mind than he could have suffered through the whole of his life from the want of them.

This boy who wants servants will also have to take on servile manners:

> He endeavours to bring [his] talents into public view, and with equal assiduity solicits every opportunity of employment. For this purpose he makes his court to all mankind; he serves those whom he hates, and is obsequious to those whom he despises.

The fantastically ambitious boy will, that is, "sacrifice [. . .] a real tranquillity that is at all times in his power" for an "idea of a certain artificial and elegant repose" that he will never achieve. Does this mean that, had he had more modest hopes, he could have avoided work? Of course not; he is the son of a "poor man," not of a beggar, and he, like his father, surely would have worked for a living. So the moral of this fable, thus far, is not that all attempts to secure material goods are based on vanity, not that efforts put into improving one's material condition are all pointless, just that the notion of *great* wealth as somehow raising one beyond the human lot, of a level of material possessions that enables effort and struggle to be laid aside, is a foolish illusion. The point is that power and riches are "enormous and operose machines" that produce "trifling conveniencies" at tremendous cost, and that do not solve the great problems of life:

> They are immense fabrics, which it requires the labour of a life to raise . . . and which while they stand, though they may save [the person that dwells in them] from some smaller inconveniencies, can protect him from none of the severer inclemencies of the season. They keep off the summer shower, not the winter storm, but leave him always as much, and sometimes more exposed than before, to anxiety, to fear, and to sorrow; to diseases, to danger, and to death.

Smith here expresses a traditional moralist's warnings against the temptations of excessive ambition, something that every "poor man's son" has already heard many times, and everything he says is compatible with his praise, in the final edition of TMS, of the prudent man who is "contented with his situation, which, by continual, though small accumulations, is growing better and better every day" (TMS 215). That praise is coupled with a warning against those, anxious "to change so comfortable a situation," who might go in search of dangerous "new enterprises and adventures." Throughout his work, Smith is suspicious of great risk-taking, and the parable of the poor man's son in IV.i should be taken as a part of that polemic. There is no reason to seek great wealth; one should be satisfied instead with "continual, though small" improvement in one's material situation. Nothing so far suggests that the desire for small, gradual improvement is also based on some sort of illusion.

But this is not all that IV.i contains. After the parable of the poor man's son, Smith says that most of us, most of the time, *do* desire the excessive and pointless "wealth and greatness" of the few, that we do set out to seek it. He also says that that vain desire fuels the most important developments in the history of humankind:

> And it is well that nature imposes upon us in this manner. It is this deception which rouses and keeps in continual motion the industry of mankind. It is this which first prompted them to cultivate the ground, to build houses, to found cities and commonwealths, and to invent and improve all the sciences and arts, which ennoble and embellish human life; which have entirely changed the whole face of the globe, have turned the rude forests of nature into agreeable and fertile plains. . . .

So the "deception" that leads us to desire great wealth is what inspired such major transitions in human development as the establishment of agriculture and cities. Michael Ignatieff has rightly pointed out that Smith is here rejecting the way Rousseau saw the change from "rude forests" to farms and cities.[5] For Rousseau, the coming of civilization meant also the coming of grinding poverty. For Smith, the poor are taken care of at least as well in agricultural and commercial societies as they were in hunter-gatherer tribes. The vanity of the rich, TMS tells us, turns out to give sustenance to the poor:

> The earth by these labours of mankind has been obliged to redouble her natural fertility and to maintain a greater multitude of inhabitants. It is to no purpose, that the proud and unfeeling landlord views his extensive fields, and without a thought for the wants of his brethren, in imagination consumes himself the whole harvest that grows upon them. . . . The capacity of his stomach bears no proportion to the immensity of his desires, and will receive no more than that of the meanest peasant. The rest he is obliged to distribute among those, who prepare, in the nicest manner, that little which he himself makes use of, among those who fit up the palace in which this little is to be consumed, among those who provide and keep in order all the different baubles and trinkets, which are employed in the oeconomy of greatness; all of whom thus derive from his luxury and caprice, that share of the necessaries of life, which they would in vain have expected from his humanity or his justice. . . . [T]hough the sole end which they propose from the labours of all the thousands whom they employ, be the gratification of their own vain and insatiable desires, [the rich] divide with the poor the produce of all their improvements.

And here, finally, there enters the invisible hand:

> They [the rich] are led by an invisible hand to make nearly the same distribution of the necessaries of life, which would have been made, had the earth been divided into equal portions among all its inhabitants, and thus without intending it, without knowing it, advance the interest of the society. . . . When Providence divided the earth among a few lordly masters, it neither forgot nor abandoned those who seemed to have been left out in the partition. . . . In what constitutes the real happiness of human life, they are in no respect inferior to those who would seem so much above them. In ease of body and peace of mind, all the different ranks of life are nearly upon a level, and the beggar, who suns himself by the side of the highway, possesses that security which kings are fighting for. (TMS 184–5)

The extreme stoicism of this passage is undeniable. Nature takes care of everyone, and the condition of even the poorest person is "in no respect inferior" to that of a king. If Smith had throughout his life maintained these claims, or the claim that the desire for great wealth spurs the most important of human achievements, Griswold's reading of him would be correct and Nussbaum would be right to criticize Smith for his indifference to the real harm of poverty.

But Smith did not, I believe, hold these views in his later writings. TMS IV.i was written for the first edition of TMS in 1759 and received exactly one tiny revision over the course of the thirty-one years, and five subsequent editions, in which Smith reworked his book (the word "would" was changed to "could" in ¶8). It is a beautiful piece of writing, so Smith may well have wanted to leave it undisturbed in later editions whatever he thought of some of its implications. And he did continue to endorse its main insight—that the attractions of wealth and greatness lie less in their usefulness than in their apparent suitedness to accomplish useful ends. So perhaps he did not give quite the attention to revising the passage that he might have done had he foreseen that later readers might view the entirety of WN as "painted within its frame" (AVE 222).[6] But there are ample indications, elsewhere in his writings, that the passage was a rough first stab at bringing his moral philosophy to bear on economics, not a frame for all his economic thought. To those indications we now turn.

26. TMS IV.i in the Light of WN

Perhaps the most striking clue that TMS IV.i received little later attention from Smith comes from the paragraph immediately following the one we have been quoting. Arguing that the "love of system" inspires improvements in "the public police," Smith says:

> It is not commonly from a fellow-feeling with carriers and waggoners that a public-spirited man encourages the mending of high roads. When the legislature establishes premiums and other encouragements to advance the linen or woollen manufactures, its conduct seldom proceeds from pure sympathy with the wearer of cheap or fine cloth . . . The perfection of police, the extension of trade and manufactures, are noble

and magnificent objects. . . . We take pleasure in beholding the perfection of so beautiful and grand a system, and we are uneasy till we remove any obstruction that can in the least disturb or encumber the regularity of its motions.

"Premiums and other encouragements" belong to "the perfection of police"?![7] Where in Smith's later writings would one expect to find that?[8] One can of course interpret Smith to be saying merely that the "public-spirited man" is likely to *think*—wrongly—that bounties are a contribution to the perfection of police, but that is not the most obvious reading of the passage, and it would seem at least misleading, to a reader of WN, that this mistaken object of policy should be juxtaposed with the eminently reasonable object of "mending . . . high roads." At the least, that is, we would expect a post–WN Smith, concerned to reread this chapter carefully, to have altered it so that he didn't leave the impression that he approved of bounties.

In addition, the explanation of major human improvements changes from TMS IV.i to WN. In TMS IV.i, the desire for wealth and greatness, rather than for ordinary, slow material improvement, fuels the development of agriculture and cities. Smith is probably agreeing here with Rousseau on the importance of *amour-propre*, our vain desires, to the growth of civilization. At the same time, in economic terms, he is endorsing the claim that luxury spending is crucial to growth. This is something that Hume and Mandeville had both believed.[9] But if Smith believed this when he wrote TMS, he changed his mind by the time he came to WN. In WN it is the spending of the poor, not of the rich, that makes up the overwhelming bulk of economic demand (WN 887), and in WN consumption of all sorts has become far less important to growth of the economy. Instead, we are told over and over that economic growth comes from *frugality*, that "parsimony" is even more important than "industry" (WN 337), that the great economic improvements in a nation, including those that allow for a flourishing agriculture and for the development of cities, come about through the efforts of the many ordinary individuals who accumulate capital, not the few who seek wealth and greatness.[10] The ambitious seekers after wealth and greatness, in WN, are the political leaders whose prodigality can harm the society more than that of any private individual, and who, in order to further their ambitions, lead their nations into war, which destroys national capital more than any other calamity (WN 344–6, 441–3, 661). These people *threaten* a nation's capital, and the society continues to grow only because their destructive efforts are outweighed by "the private frugality and good conduct of individuals" (345). In WN, the prudent poor man's slow accumulation of improvement, not his son's extravagant ambition, is the source of societal progress.

Finally, WN draws a distinction among the ways the rich contribute to the sustenance of the poor that is invisible in TMS, and that implies, contrary to TMS, that the ability of the poor to be happy can depend considerably upon social circumstances. TMS draws no distinction between those who "fit up the palace" and "keep in order all the different baubles and trinkets," and those who *build* the palace or *make* the baubles and trinkets. WN sees the former as unproductive, the latter as productive labor. Nor does TMS distinguish between the *food* that a landlord might directly distribute, in feasts or displays of generosity, to his servants and local peasants, and the monetary *equivalent* of food, earned by selling off his surplus, that the landlord might use to pay a construction crew or a supplier of baubles and trinkets. WN, in a passage that looks as if it were designed explicitly to revise TMS IV.i, emphatically does draw such a distinction:

> The rich man consumes no more food than his poor neighbour. In quality it may be very different, and to select and prepare it may require more labour and art; but in quantity it is very nearly the same. But compare the spacious palace and wardrobe of the one, with the hovel and few rags of the other, and you will be sensible that the difference between their cloathing, lodging and houshold furniture, is almost as great in quantity as it is in quality. The desire of food is limited in every man by the narrow capacity of the human stomach; but the desire of the conveniencies and ornaments of building, dress, equipage, and houshold furniture, seems to have no limit or certain boundary. Those, therefore, who have the command of more food than they themselves can consume, are always willing to exchange the surplus, or, what is the same thing, the price of it, for gratifications of this other kind. . . . The poor, in order to obtain food, exert themselves to gratify those fancies of the rich, and to obtain it more certainly, they vie with one another in the cheapness and perfection of their work. (WN 180–81)

Here, in the first place, the rich do not directly distribute food to the poor, and, in the second place, the poor who live off the rich's surplus wealth do so by *producing objects* to satisfy their desires—not by menial labor in rich people's homes. These subtle shifts from TMS reflect two profound refinements of Smith's thought. First, he now siphons food off much more sharply from all other goods. This fits with his concern, central to WN according to Istvan Hont and Michael Ignatieff (in NJ), that agriculture be developed to a point at which famines will permanently disappear. Second, between TMS and WN Smith devoted a lot of thought to the increased "independency" that the poorer classes gain in commercial economies, and came to recognize that menial labor, and the grand village feasts of wealthy landlords, are symptoms and causes of feudal dependency, not healthy elements of commercial independency. WN III, chapter iv above all makes this point, but it appears also in II.iii, the chapter on productive and unproductive labor: "The inhabitants of a large village, it has sometimes been observed, after having made considerable progress in manufactures, have become idle and poor, in consequence of a great lord's having taken up his residence in their neighbourhood" (336).

With these developments in doctrine comes a shift in tone. Beggars do not happily sun themselves by the side of the highway in WN, and Providence is no longer complimented for making the poor servants in the homes of the rich. Smith maintains his Stoic disregard for the "external" pleasures in which the wealthy put so much stock, but now recognizes both starvation and dependency as real hardships that do not deserve a similar Stoic dismissal as mere external pains. Economic growth alleviates real human needs insofar as it aids the poor, although it may still provide only vanities to the rich. Correspondingly, the desire crucial to economic growth is not based on illusion: Frugality replaces luxury as the most important motor of an economy, and frugality, unlike luxury, can serve realistic, and morally acceptable, desires. Unlike Hume, Mandeville, and his own earlier self in TMS, the Smith of WN does not suggest that the luxuries that please our vanity make up more than a small part of the demand providing employment to the poor. Far more important are investments that improve land, add to the housing stock, and produce everyday tools and necessities. A crucial moral implication of this move away from tracing "publick benefits," in Mandevillean vein, back to the "private vice" of vanity is that the impulse leading to wealth is no longer something rooted in fantasy, in deceit, a corruption of our true moral destiny that nature imposes on us for our material well-being. And one thing that means, for politics, is that there is no longer a tension between our recognizing and our acting on the true impulse to wealth; there is no longer a danger, as Mandeville had supposed, that economies would collapse if the masses ever properly grasped the truth about the forces leading to wealth.

Thus is the moralistic fairy tale of TMS transformed into sober economic analysis in WN. One mark of that transformation is that the invisible hand does *not* appear in the chapter on the uses of luxury, and when it does appear, in WN IV.ii, it will not be identified with "Providence." A deeper mark is Smith's small concession to the TMS story at the end of WN II.iii:

> The houses, the furniture, the cloathing of the rich, in a little time, become useful to the inferior and middling ranks of people. They are able to purchase them when their superiors grow weary of them, and the general accommodation of the whole people is thus gradually improved. . . . What was formerly a seat of the family of Seymour, is now an inn upon the Bath road. The marriage-bed of James the First of Great Britain, which his Queen brought with her from Denmark, . . . was, a few years ago, the ornament of an alehouse at Dunfermline. In some ancient cities, which either have been long stationary, or have gone somewhat to decay, you will sometimes scarce find a single house which could have been built for its present inhabitants. If you go into those houses, too, you will frequently find many excellent, though antiquated pieces of furniture, which are still very fit for use, and which could as little be made for them. (WN 347)

A restrained discussion, far from the feasts and happy servants of TMS. After two, probably legendary, examples of royal goodies falling into common hands, Smith says that the well-built housing stock that only rich people can afford to commission may spread widely across the population over ensuing generations. He will conclude with the yet more modest point that places like Versailles and Stowe do honor to their nations and offer employment opportunities to boot (347–9). He still implies that the poor cluster around the wealthy, but sometimes criticizes this "trickle down" economy rather than endorsing it (at, e.g., 336, cited above), and no longer uses it as his main argument for the "invisible hand."

27. TMS IV.I and the 1790 Edition of TMS

IV.i has a parallel chapter in the early editions of TMS—I.iii.2, in which we are told that the condition of the rich and powerful seems wonderful only when we see it "in those delusive colours in which the imagination is apt to paint it," but we are also told that nature leads us to indulge in this delusion (TMS 51–3). Even in the early editions, these are the only two places in which Smith attributes a "deception" or "delusion" to nature. Instead of praising ambition for introducing civilization, furthermore, in I.iii.2 he condemns it as a source of "rapine and injustice" (57). In the first five editions, however, the chapter did fit in with the extreme Stoic views of IV.i. For one thing, the condemnation of ambition was immediately followed by a hint that people "confirmed in wisdom and real philosophy" would despise all differences in rank. This hint closed the chapter, and there then followed a chapter on what presumably constitutes true wisdom: "the stoical philosophy." In the sixth edition, the remark about the wisdom in ignoring rank loses its rhetorically prominent placement as a conclusion, and the chapter on the stoics gets moved into the final, historical section of TMS. Not only does the latter's placement no longer suggest that Smith's own views descend from the stoics, moreover, but it loses a final paragraph that seemed to endorse stoicism and acquires instead a discussion ending in a severe criticism of stoicism.[11] Similarly, Part VI, which was entirely written for the sixth edition and which has a long chapter on the stoic virtue of "self-command," contains warnings against the dangers of a blind admiration for self-command (TMS 241–2, 250–4, 264). And chapter III.3 acquires a number of warnings against taking stoic apathy too far.[12] The final, 1790 edition of TMS thus repeatedly submerges the stoicism so prominent in earlier editions of the work.

In addition, chapter I.iii.3, on the "corruption" of our moral sentiments by our tendency to admire the rich, was added in the sixth edition, and this chapter throws deep suspicion on the notion that whatever nature implants in us is good. We have a *natural* disposition to admire, to sympathize excessively with, the rich; the structure of our moral sentiments necessitates this. But this disposition is based on a confusion and is the source of great evils: of a cruel indifference to the poor, and of a potential to seek wealth instead of virtue (62).[13] Here nature emphatically does not lead us to a good end, and one should be in serious doubt about what role a stoic god could possibly play in organizing and governing such a nature.

Finally, Smith added a series of passages to the sixth edition of TMS that importantly qualify the claim that all socioeconomic stations offer equal opportunities for happiness. The new chapter on the corruption of the sentiments argues explicitly that vanity consists in the pursuit of outstanding "wealth and greatness," not in the ordinary effort to "better one's condition" (see, especially, 64–5). The long addition to III.3 begins by expressing a very tentative agreement with the Stoics:

The never-failing certainty with which all men, sooner or later, accommodate themselves to whatever becomes their permanent situation, *may, perhaps, induce us to think
that the Stoics were, at least, thus far very nearly in the right*; that, between one permanent situation and another, there was, with regard to real happiness, no essential difference. (149, my emphasis)

Not only are we treated to a slew of weakening phrases—"may," "perhaps," "at
least," "very nearly"—but Smith goes on immediately to emphasize a qualification within the Stoics' own views on this matter: "or that, if there were any
difference, it was no more than just sufficient to render some of them the objects of simple choice or preference; but not of any earnest or anxious desire."
(Strictly speaking, Smith has already departed from the Stoics, for it was not
part of the Stoic view that external situations make any difference to happiness,
just that some of those situations are, nevertheless, proper objects of preference.)[14] Then Smith tells us that "in the most humble station, *where there is only
personal liberty*," one can find all the pleasures that the most exalted position
affords (150, my emphasis)—but there must *be* personal liberty, which makes
unacceptable the station of a slave, for instance: which the Stoic Seneca regarded as a condition just as open to the acquisition of virtue, and therefore
happiness, as any other.[15] Finally, the very passage Griswold cites to show that
the truly prudent person achieves tranquility by way of "satisfaction with one's
rank and economic circumstances" (AVE 225) in fact says that such a person
will be "contented with his situation, *which, by continual accumulations, is growing
better and better every day*" (TMS 215, my emphasis). As we have already seen in
WN, slow, gradual "bettering of one's condition" is perfectly compatible with
contentment, for the later Smith; it is only an impatient, overreaching lunge for
wealth and greatness that "might endanger, but could not well increase [one's]
. . . tranquillity" (TMS 215). Desiring gradually to better one's condition is morally harmless, and inevitable, given Smith's analysis of the workings of sympathy. Vanity is not inevitable, and is a corruption of sympathy. In Smith's later
writing, self-betterment and vanity are not the same thing.

To the textual arguments I have given for reading TMS IV.i as an early, inadequate expression of Smith's views on economic motivation, let me add a systematic concern. Smith is deeply committed to the normative equality of all human
beings (see §16). But the desire to achieve "wealth and greatness" is a desire to
stand out among one's fellow human beings, to be regarded as if one came from
a "superior rank of beings."[16] This is a desire that cannot, in principle, be satisfied for most people: its satisfaction depends on a few people achieving it while
most fail. (The end at which it aims is, in modern economists' terms, a "positional good."[17]) If this desire is basic to human nature, human reward cannot,
even in principle, be distributed equally: At best, only the wealthy and famous
will be able to satisfy the desire. Even they, according to Smith, will usually be
unhappy: "the pleasures of vanity and superiority are seldom consistent with
perfect tranquillity, the principle and foundation of all real and satisfactory enjoyment" (TMS 150). The rich, for one thing, are never rich enough; their

"superiority" needs always to be preserved against potential challengers, and even then, there are always yet greater degrees of superiority to aspire to (149–50). Only the "small party" of the wise and virtuous, who see through the frivolous glitter of social status, and aim to live up instead to an internal standard of praiseworthiness, will actually have any chance of being happy. But if both poor and rich are miserable because they are racked by an empty, insatiable desire to step above the rank of their neighbors, while a few wise philosophers can see through it and overcome it, then the lives of human beings will be thoroughly unequal. It is not as though the desire for wealth and greatness is a *trivial* corruption of our sentiments, after all. Rather, Smith believes that it destroys our tranquility, driving us instead ever onward toward illusory hopes— that it makes happiness, on Smith's definition of that term, *impossible*. So if Griswold were right, the world would consist of vast numbers of miserable people with a few smiling philosophers sprinkled among them. This picture of human life would not be one of "comic irony," as Griswold puts it (AVE 222), but something deeply tragic. One would then expect Smith, with his normative commitment to human equality, to rail against vanity, to join Rousseau in decrying the spread of *amour-propre*, and to condemn, rather than accepting with equanimity, the features of the commercial world that promote easy consumption, and the desire to rise in rank, more than any other politico-economic system has done. It would certainly be hard to understand how Smith could possibly regard commercial society as a type of society "devoted to the improvement of the human lot" (AVE 263). As Griswold admits, however, in WN "Smith does not . . . stress that [material] betterment is founded on a deception" (AVE 263), and this fits with my belief that Smith came to consider vanity, the desires provoked by the "deception" practised upon us in TMS IV.i, to be inessential to economic improvement.

It is more plausible that Smith might hold the view that Nussbaum attributes to him. As she points out, even TMS IV.i says, not that great differences in external goods are acceptable because differences in human happiness are acceptable, but that differences in external goods are acceptable because they do not fundamentally *matter* to human happiness: "In ease of body and peace of mind, all the different ranks of life are nearly upon a level." The poor, as Nussbaum puts it, "do not suffer at their very core." This view is compatible with normative egalitarianism, and as I noted in §16, it does play some role in Smith's reconciliation of his normative views with the facts about human life. But it does not constitute the whole of that reconciliation. Smith advocates greater egalitarianism for his own society, in WN, and he condemns very inegalitarian social institutions like feudalism and slavery. He also increasingly recognizes that at least some "external goods" are essential to happiness, in both WN and the final edition of TMS.[18] Hence the stress on the importance of liberty and independency, and the approval given to slow material and social improvement.

28. The Importance of Vanity

Having said all this, I do not want to deny that Smith's analysis of vanity in TMS is interesting and has valuable implications for how we understand the relationship between virtue and economic activity. My point thus far has just been to show that Smith did not consider vanity, the desire to impress others, to be the primary source of economic demand. *Pace* Mandeville, economies would not collapse if people came to their moral senses, and began to seek praiseworthiness rather than mere praise. On the contrary, by far the most important sources of demand for material goods—the sources of demand for food, clothing, and shelter—are ones of which our moral sentiments can approve. Economic growth and moral achievement are not incompatible.

Nevertheless, many of our desires for material goods *are* vain ones, and if Smith did not follow Mandeville in regarding vanity as necessary for economic growth, he did make a point of saying that the demand for vanities increases as societies get wealthier (see WN 181, 190, 193, 235, 907–8). He also provided astute explanations of why we have such a strong desire to appear superior to our neighbors, and how the acquisition of material goods helps us do that. As we have seen, for Smith the same structure of sentiments that leads us toward morality and sociability leads us also to seek just the admiration of others, and we can gain that by way of material wealth. When we have many attractive material goods, others will admire us because they will place themselves, by way of imagination, into our shoes and think they would be happy if they had our goods. Thus the mechanism of sympathy makes possible social climbing just as readily as it does the search for virtue. Since acquiring material goods seems much easier than achieving virtue, moreover, and since wealth is far more obvious, hence likely to earn sympathy, than virtue can ever be, the road to wealth generally seems more appealing than the road to virtue. So people tend to be seduced, by the very mechanism that ought to lead them to virtue, into seeking wealth instead. Even if we can overcome the temptation to seek great wealth, therefore, and even if the economic health of our nation does not require us to seek wealth, it remains true for Smith—as it remains true in fact—that many people, much of the time, are far more interested in impressing others by way of their material possessions than by way of their decency or thoughtfulness.

Smith adds to this moral criticism of humanity an intriguing analysis of the *kind* of material possessions that win admiration for their owners, of why the material possessions that especially play this role take the form of luxury goods. In the first place, he connects acquisitiveness to the desire for beauty; his explanation of what makes us desire to acquire material objects grows out of his explanation of what makes us find objects aesthetically attractive. The passages on which we have been concentrating in TMS IV.i follow an account of beauty, and Smith says explicitly that the principle he lays out for what we consider beautiful "is often the secret motive" of the economic and political projects he goes on to describe (181). As Griswold brings out wonderfully, this suggests that "the longing for beauty and harmony . . . pervades . . . human life" (AVE 358; see also 222, 330–35)—and it is an attractive, and persuasive, feature of Smith's account of beauty that he does not reduce the beautiful and harmonious to the useful. Smith anticipates Kant in finding the beauty of an object in its *suitedness to be useful* ("purposiveness," as Kant will say), as opposed to its actual usefulness. He gives the example of a man who gets annoyed by having "the chairs all standing in the middle of [his] room," and sets about re-arranging them, at the cost of "more trouble than all he could have suffered" from leaving them as they are, because he wants, "not so much the conveniency [of having his chairs readily available to him], as that arrangement of things which promotes it" (TMS 180). Kant will do a better job than Smith both of explaining why we like such purposive arrangements and of separating our liking for the beauty of the arrangements themselves from our desire to own objects manifesting such arrangements.[19] For Kant, the latter desire is vanity while the former is the love of beauty. The two are connected, but not identical. That seems right, and Smith may be faulted for not having drawn a similar distinction. But Smith's main point is unaffected by this omission. Our vanity is directed at beautiful objects, even on Kant's analysis, and our desire to own beautiful objects is vain.

And if we take the connection between vanity and the love of beauty seriously, while updating Smith's account of beauty a little, we can explain very nicely why people seem to have such an obsession with acquiring fancier and fancier luxury goods. Why do people think they "must have" the latest version of a particular kind of computer software, even if it does only a small, unimportant job better than the old one? Why will people pay enormous sums of money to get a TV screen with just a little higher resolution, or to buy a machine that makes a slightly better cup of espresso? If we take up some rich suggestions to be found in the writings of Stanley Cavell and Michael Fried, we may see our aesthetic desires as rooted in a natural human tendency to extend our capacities, to press the skills demonstrated in any given form of activity as far as they will go:

[Those who know baseball will regard it as of] "the essence of the game" . . . that it contains passages which are duels between pitcher and batter, that "getting a hit," "drawing a walk", and "striking a batter out" must have *certain* ranges of difficulty. It is such matters that the "convention" of permitting three strikes is in service of. . . . But is the *whole* game in service of anything? I think one may say: it is in service of the human capacity, or necessity, for play; [and] what *can be played* . . . is contingent upon the given capacities for human play. . . . It is perhaps not derivable from the measurements of a baseball diamond and of the average velocities of batted baseballs and of the average times human beings can run various short distances, that 90 feet is the best distance for setting up an essential recurrent crisis in the structure of a baseball game, e.g., at which the run and the throw to first take long enough to be followed lucidly, and are often completed within a familiar split second of one another . . .

There is no necessity that human capacities should train to just these proportions; but just these proportions reveal the limits of those capacities. Without those limits, we would not have known the possibilities.[20]

Cavell ties what artists do to this need for "play,"[21] this joy in stretching our capacities within a set of contingent limitations. The beauty in art is a reaching of or beyond the limits that we thought human creative capacities had, in a realm delimited by the contingencies of a medium or style. Michael Fried adds that artistic traditions result from the attempt of one artist to extend the possibilities opened up by the work of another, such that Theo van Doesburg (my example) might be seen as exploring how Mondrian's abstract studies of color can be made "purer" or projected into other geometric contexts, or Mark Rothko and Cy Twombly might be seen as trying to expand the use of abstraction to express emotions opened up by Pollock. In this way, artists create norms and paradigms for each other's work and prod each other to spin subtler and subtler variations on a particular way of seeing the world, or seeing their own medium. And it may well be that in this way, more generally, human beings are driven to seek as high a refinement as possible of each way of appreciating sensory experience: to spin as many original and subtle variations on it as possible. We may surmise that human survival has been aided, over long spans of evolutionary time, by an ability to refine our sensory apparatus further and further, so that we can, when necessary, discriminate among objects to a high degree of subtlety. The person who can tell the difference between the wine from one vineyard and the wine from the vineyard next door, or between the espresso from the $400 machine and the espresso from the $2,000 machine, is also someone who could, in other circumstances, pick up on very small changes in his or her environment that threaten danger. For this reason, or for some other, we have become creatures for whom experiencing higher and higher degrees of refinement is a basic and very important form of pleasure. Bring this together with what we learn from Smith about wanting to be admired by others for possessing beautiful objects, and we may say that we desire both to extend our capacities for appreciating experience and to be admired for having well-developed capacities in this regard. (It seems useful to our survival as a species that we would admire those among us who best develop skills of refinement, and look down on those who lack such skills.) Hence we want to own objects that display our high degree of refinement, to own the wine or espresso maker or great painting that proves to all the world that we are people "of taste."

The only problem with this desire is that we cannot reflectively endorse it.[22] It takes but a moment of reflection to realize that a great ability to distinguish among wines, no matter how well anchored in our evolutionary history, is actually of little use to human survival today, and that it represents skills that have little to do with what we deeply consider to be human excellence. It takes even less reflection to recognize that someone who merely *owns* fine wines need not be someone who actually appreciates them, and that the effort required to gain the wealth making possible such displays of "taste" could be far more sensibly directed into simply enjoying the range of tastes open to one, albeit on rarer occasions, at a lower level of material possession. When we add, as Smith certainly would, that the pursuit of great wealth—and to display more rarefied taste than most people have, one must command more resources than they do: the competition for rarefied goods, unlike ordinary economic exchanges, *is a zero-sum game*[23]—normally entails shortchanging the pursuit of virtue, and often tempts one into outright injustice, it would seem that any decent person would relinquish their desire to excel in this particular way. Smith was well aware, throughout his life, that most people either do not take the relevant moment to reflect or find themselves overpowered by the strong desire to show off nevertheless, that the vain desire to show that one has better taste than others is an extremely powerful corrupting force. But it is important to distinguish the vain from the legitimate desires for material goods in Smith's work. By the time he wrote WN, he did not believe that good people would be entirely uninterested in material objects, that material possessions were irrelevant to what Nussbaum calls the "core" of human being.

29. From *Homo Moralis* to *Homo Economicus* (Reprise)

So why do virtuous people, on Smith's account, seek material goods?

Well, first of all, they may seek food, clothing, or lodging for the sake of their health, and taking care of one's health is something Smith regards as not merely morally permissible but morally required (TMS 304). Smith talks frequently and approvingly of the desire for these three items.[24] WN opens with an account of how, first, nails, and then a day-laborer's woolen coat get produced, and later devotes enormous amounts of attention to the production of food. When Smith says that no society can be "flourishing and happy" if the greater part of its members are poor and miserable, he goes on immediately, as if this were the same thing, to say that the majority needs to be "tolerably well fed, cloathed and lodged" (WN 96). These are not trivial points. Smith diverges from a strict stoic view here, since people can survive, albeit uncomfortably, without being "tolerably . . . cloathed and lodged," and beggars in particular, like the fellow by the highway in TMS, may go for long stretches of time without any lodging. At the same time, Smith is implicitly rejecting the stress laid on luxury spending by his predecessors in political economy. In WN, the humble goods of the poor, not luxury goods, are sufficient to drive an economy. The demand for woolen coats and corn, not the frivolous fancies of the rich, is what makes the economic world go around. That means it will go around even if people were to overcome their love of vanity; a world entirely filled with decent and modest people could still have a thriving economy.[25] Smith thus distances himself from the Mandevillean economic argument that politicians need to encourage a demand for luxury goods, even as he distances himself from Mandeville's egoism and dismissal of the importance of virtue.

In addition, a virtuous person must look out for her family's needs, and since "poverty is extremely unfavourable to the rearing of children" (WN 97), the virtuous person with children will try to rise out of poverty even if she alone could manage, stoically, with a minimum of food, clothing, and lodging. This concern gives everybody a reason to "better one's condition" that is altogether independent of vanity: "those who [want to] . . . make family settlements, and . . . provide for remote futurity" must invest, and do in fact, Smith tells us, make up "a very considerable proportion" of those who buy stock (WN 917). The decent person must provide for the needs her children might have when she is gone or no longer able to work.

But a Smithian *homo moralis* can also legitimately seek material goods that have nothing to do with physical necessities. Smith's virtuous people rejoice in their friends, and sociability requires periodic shared festivities and displays of generosity. Then Smith acknowledges the pleasures, and moral education, to be found in beautiful poetry, music, theater, and the like (see especially EPS 187, 194, 204–5), suggesting that both the desire to experience art and the desire to produce it is something other than vanity. And more trivial objects of desire are unworthy of obsessive pursuit, for Smith, but need not be avoided. In his jurisprudential lectures, Smith even defends spending money on drink: "Man is an anxious animal and must have his care swept off by something that can exhilarate the spirits" (LJ 497). "Strong liquors" are therefore "allmost a necessary in every nation" (LJ 363).

Finally, Smith has a brief discussion of necessities and luxuries that sheds an intriguing light on how even a world of fully virtuous people could support economic growth. By "necessaries," he says, he means not only whatever is physically needed to survive "but whatever the custom of the country renders it indecent for creditable people, even of the lowest order, to be without" (WN 870). Linen shirts were not necessary in ancient Greece and Rome. Throughout most of Europe in Smith's day, however, "a creditable day-labourer would be ashamed to appear in publick without a linen shirt, the want of which would be presupposed to denote that degree of poverty, which, it is presumed, no body can well fall into without extreme bad conduct." Leather shoes were necessary for the same reason for both men and women in England, but in Scotland the lowest order of women might, he says, "without any discredit, walk about barefooted." Smith thus introduces a degree of cultural relativism into the necessity/ luxury distinction, while suggesting that some material goods may be necessary because *they signify moral status*. To some degree, social status will inevitably reflect moral status and a good person is rightly concerned not to be thought of as having bad morals, even if she knows that such an opinion would be unjust. Although being worthy of approbation is more important than receiving actual approbation, actual approbation can guide us in determining whether we are really morally worthy or not: the "trust and good opinion of . . . friends and neighbours, tends more than any thing to relieve [a person] from [moral] doubt; their distrust and unfavourable opinion to increase it" (TMS 122). Even the best of us have some interest in being liked and respected by others, therefore, if only to receive moral guidance and help us maintain the psychological strength to continue pursuing virtue. It follows that we have some interest in having at least that minimum of external goods that signify a respectable social status. But where a society is materially improving, whether because of technological discoveries or because of a large demand for vain luxuries, the standard of living that expresses decent moral status will steadily rise. And in such circumstances a decent person will be concerned to "keep up with the Joneses," not because he cares about social status per se, but because he cares about the customs in his society that signify moral achievement. (All this is to say nothing of the many practical ways in which changes in society may make it necessary for one generation to seek more material goods than previous generations had. In a society in which cars replace horses, it becomes necessary to own a car.) An entire society of decent people might therefore need to keep up with improvements in material goods, even though they fully recognize, as Smith says they should, that only a low level of external goods is necessary for their happiness.

I do not mean to imply that Smith ever came to reject his earlier beliefs that many people are driven by empty and insatiable desires, seek wealth instead of virtue, or imagine, wrongly, that the rich are supremely happy. The addition of I.iii.3 to the final edition of TMS suggests that he worried about these problems right up until he died. But there is plenty of room in Smith's mature thought for people to seek material improvement without suffering under any sort of delusion, or jeopardizing any sort of moral commitment. None of the desires for material things I have discussed in this section is vain. None of them leads naturally to a desire for great wealth, or suggests that great wealth is a good. But each of them makes clear that poverty can be, and often is, an evil. *Homo moralis* requires *homo economicus*; the stoic disdain for all material things is unjustified.

PART III

Foundations of Economics

CHAPTER SEVEN

Foundations of Economics

This is a philosophical companion to WN rather than an economic one. I want to stay away from the quarrels economists have over what is useful and what is wrong-headed in WN's claims about money, rent, capital, and the like.[1] But some of Smith's foundational terms and principles raise philosophical problems, and I will touch briefly on these.

30. Natural Price/Market Price

Smith sets up two dichotomies of price, in WN Book I, chapters v and vii. Both have been criticized by later economists for seeming to hold out a notion of absolute value that, it is maintained, have no place in a properly empirical theory. Medieval economic theories relied on a notion of the "just price" of commodities, the price each commodity really "should" have as opposed to the price that merchants might actually charge for it, and the great seventeenth- and eighteenth-century advance that is supposed to have made modern economics possible is the recognition that no commodity has any absolute, true price, that prices are a reflection of scarcity and need and are therefore always relative to the scarcity of and need for each good at a particular time and place. If one wants to talk in terms of justice, one might say that just prices—prices that everyone would freely agree to if they knew the consequences of the entire price structure—are in fact those prices that result from free bargaining between buyers and sellers. Or one might suspend all talk of justice and simply say that prices can never be determined by moral considerations, that they will always and only reflect the amoral contingencies that make a market in a particular good possible. Smith's talk of a "real" and a "natural" price might then seem to be a slip back toward the medieval view, especially when he says things like this: "When . . . the commodity is . . . sold for . . . its natural price [, it] is . . . sold precisely for what it is worth."[2] And it is on the basis of lines like this one that some commentators write that the phrase "natural price" is not a descriptive but a normative one, that "[t]he natural price is that price a commodity ought to be."[3]

But there is nothing particularly normative, if that means "moral," about what Smith says on either real price or natural price. To begin with the second of these dichotomies, natural price is simply the price to which a commodity will fall where a free market in that commodity operates over any considerable time.

Today we would call it "equilibrium price." Smith uses the adjective "natural" because it results where there are no "artificial" constraints—laws mandating that the object have a certain price, or legal or other forces maintaining a group of sellers in a monopoly over the product. Unlike the medieval just price, it includes the "ordinary rate of profit" that a merchant can expect to make in the particular neighborhood in which the commodity is being sold (WN 73). Smith recognizes that if the merchant cannot make this profit, he will have reason to move into some other line of work; a merchant who regularly makes less profit than his competitors do will eventually be outbid so badly in the capital and labor markets that he will have to leave the business. There is an element of thought experiment about this—conditions of sale are frequently constrained, and to come at the "natural price" of such commodities involves abstracting from such constraints in much the way that Galileo needed to abstract from friction to come at velocity—but the notion is nothing if not empirical. It provides a measure that can readily be ascertained by surveying "ordinary rates" of rent, wages, and profit, for a particular good in a particular neighborhood, and it plays an essential role in the hypothesis, introduced in the chapter in which natural price gets explained, that market prices are not arbitrary but will adjust themselves, over "any considerable time," to a level that reflects the supply and effectual demand for each commodity. The hypothesis that markets will clear when left alone depends on the possibility of a gap between actual prices and a price that reflects true supply and true demand. Natural price is Smith's way of ensuring such a gap. It is, therefore, a notion as essential to his empirical theory as the notion of motion in a vacuum is to Newtonian physics, and Smith's use of the word "gravitating," to express the relationship between market and natural prices, suggests that he had just such a comparison in mind.[4]

31. Real Price/Nominal Price; Labor Theory of Value

The empirical status of "real price" is harder to see. "The real price of everything," says Smith, "what every thing really costs to the man who wants to acquire it, is the toil and trouble of acquiring it" (WN 47). "Real price," in short, is labor price, an amount of labor that is somehow equivalent to each thing. This notion has been used by many readers to find a "labor theory of value" in WN—some of whom applaud Smith for having such a theory, while others condemn him for it—which in turn is said to have roots in a normative belief that people should work for their living, rather than in any empirical use to which the theory might be put.

Exactly why Smith argued for a labor basis of exchange value is a difficult problem, but before we come to it, let us get a more trivial objection to Smith's account quickly out of the way. Some commentators have made heavy weather over Smith's apparent wish to define the labor price of an object both in terms of the labor that goes *into* the object and in terms of the labor that the sale of that object can *command*, pointing out that these need by no means be the same.[5] But Smith was not confused on this issue: he quite clearly meant the latter, not the former. The exchange value of any commodity, he says, its value to a person who means to exchange it rather than use it, is "the quantity of labor which it enables him *to purchase or command*" (WN 47). The first line of the next paragraph may seem in tension with this definition—"[t]he real price of everything . . . is the toil and trouble of acquiring it"—but in the rest of that paragraph Smith makes clear that he is talking about the "real price" of an object we *wish to acquire*, not of an object we already own. So once again he is defining real price in terms of the labor we can command, by way of the objects we already own, not of the labor that goes into those objects. He does say that the object we offer in exchange for one we want to acquire "is supposed . . . to contain the value of an equal quantity" of labor, but the accent here is on the word "supposed," and later on in the text Smith will say explicitly that the labor going into an object will be in "proportion" to (even here: not *equal* to!) the labor that that object can command only in the earliest state of society, the state that "precedes both the accumulation of stock and the appropriation of land" (WN 65). When societies move beyond this primitive state, rent and profit, which are not reducible to labor (66–7), will make up part of the price of almost everything, so the labor an object can command need not be at all proportional to the labor required to produce it. In both this and the earlier condition, moreover, real value lies in command over labor, not in the labor "contained" in objects: "The real value of all the different component parts of price . . . is measured by the quantity of labor which they can, each of them, purchase or command. Labour measures the value not only of that part of price which resolves itself into labour, but of that which resolves itself into rent, and of that which resolves itself into profit" (67–8).

Now to the more difficult question. A labor theory of value, a theory that all value ultimately reduces to labor and that labor itself has the same value across all societies and times, appears to raise enormous difficulties, both in relation to the rest of Smith's system and in itself. In relation to the rest of Smith's system, there would seem to be great tension between his analysis of income into the three distinct categories of rent, labor, and profit and his claim that labor ultimately provides the standard by which to measure all three categories (67–8), and tension likewise between the claim that labor provides a universal, fixed standard of value (50, 54) and the recognition, in the same chapter as well as elsewhere, that the compensation of labor can vary widely (53, 116–35). In itself, the problems with the labor theory seem insurmountable. How could it be true that labor "never var[ies] in its own value" and provides the sole, "ultimate and real standard" by which to measure the value of all other commodities (51)? Will the amount of labor needed to produce a particular commodity not vary, for one thing, in accordance with the kind of technology available in each society for producing that commodity? A woolen coat may take a year or more to produce in a hunting society, but just a few weeks, or even days, in a society with sophisticated machinery. Does not the labor of different people vary in its value to others, moreover, even where equally difficult? How about the value of the same person's labor in different circumstances? It certainly seems to me that my labor has varied in its value across my lifetime. When I had no academic degree, and few marketable skills, I found it difficult to get work at more than around $4.00 an hour, and therefore considered it a bargain if I could make on my own an object that required an hour or two's labor. Today, the same object would impose an opportunity cost of many times that amount, so it certainly is not true that I would "lay down the same portion of [my] ease, [my] liberty, and [my] happiness" (50) now, as then, if I devoted an hour to making the object rather than buying it. On Smith's terms, I am to regard the good as cheaper to me now and dearer to me in the past, rather than regarding my labor as having increased in value. But that seems a strange and arbitrary inversion of the way we normally regard these things.

We also have reason to deny that labor alone sets the value of everything else. Surely both scarcity and the need for a particular commodity play independent roles in determining value. We don't value diamonds more than water just because diamonds are hard to find, and we value oil today more than we valued oil in the nineteenth century, even if it was just as hard to find then, because we have more uses for it. If I pick up a diamond in a field, or happen accidentally to come across a gold mine, I will be able to bring in great riches despite my lack of work, while if I labor long and hard to desalinate seawater, I am unlikely to get much for my efforts. One might say that locating diamonds and gold *normally* takes great labor whereas locating water normally does not, but the effort involved in locating diamond and gold mines at least underdetermines their value, and certainly underdetermines the *difference* in value between diamonds and water. For reasons like this, economists have tended to find the labor theory of value perplexing if not useless, and to suggest that Smith intended it to serve normative rather than descriptive purposes.

What Smith means is I think this:

Labor is indeed rewarded differentially in accordance with the difficulty of the task involved, as well as in accordance with "the degree of dexterity and ingenuity" it requires (65). Differences in the amount of honor or shame attached to a type of employment, the risk involved in it, the "constancy or inconstancy of employment" in it, and the degree of trust which "must be reposed in those who exercise in [it]" will also make for higher or lower wages (116–17). That said, an hour of labor in any of these different types of employment will buy very different amounts of goods in one condition of society than in another. In a society where there are plenty of goods, a street porter might give up an hour of his time for nothing less than the equivalent of a pint of beer or four loaves of bread, while a master tailor might expect the equivalent of three pints or twelve loaves, and a lawyer might refuse to take out his pen and notepad for anything less than the equivalent of fifty pints or two hundred loaves. In a society of hunter-gatherers, or one that has been hit by some natural or man-made disaster, the street porter might be happy to work for half a loaf of bread, the tailor for a loaf and a half, and there probably would be no lawyers, but if there were, they might find their services enough in demand that they could afford to ask for twenty-five loaves. Smith says, about these two conditions of society, that we have to call the goods cheap in the first one and dear in the second one, rather than calling labor dear in the first case and cheap in the second. It is in this sense that an hour's "toil and trouble" (controlling for the amount and kind of toil and trouble) is an hour's toil and trouble across centuries and vastly different conditions of society, and it can serve as an absolute measure, "never varying in its own value," against which all other values can be determined.

But why *should* it serve as such a measure? Could we not say, contrary to Smith, that labor is more expensive in the first of my two social conditions and cheaper in the second one, rather than saying that the goods are cheaper in the first case and more expensive in the second one? To some economists, it might seem that we can say this, that the price of labor is just as relative to the price of goods as the price of goods is to the price of labor, but this misses the order of explanation in any reasonable account we are likely to give of *why* the two conditions of society differ so radically. Unless we assume vast changes in human nature (which are of course possible, but for which, as regards work capacity at least, there is little evidence in the historical record), we are unlikely to suppose that the porter in the second society accepts so much less for his work because he finds carrying things easier than does the porter in the first society. Rather, the best explanation of the difference will be that goods are more *plentiful* and thus easier to come at in the first society and less plentiful, and harder to come at, in the second one. But "cheap" simply *means* "plentiful and easy to come at," while "dear" means "difficult to come at" (50–51). So it is the goods that are cheap, not the labor that is dear, in the first society, and the goods that are dear, not the labor that is cheap, in the second one.[6]

As we will see at the end of this section, measuring goods by labor rather than labor by goods has useful implications for a concrete historical task Smith wants to carry out, but it also enables him to sharpen a general question he has been implicitly raising, throughout the opening of WN, about the value of an advanced division of labor. Recall that chapter i of the book ended by comparing the standard of living of the poorest worker in an advanced economy with that of "an African king"—a king, in Smith's typology, of a hunter-gatherer society. Smith, famously, has worries about the condition of the poorest workers in advanced economies which will come to the fore in Book V, so the comparison here is not unimportant to him. And the notion of labor value as real value helps him to sharpen that comparison. Consider the fact that in chapter vi, Smith points out that "rent" and "profit," while *commanding* labor, are not themselves *based* on labor. This point will help set up Smith's sectoral analysis of the economy, and his claim that some kinds of income (rent and wages) rise with the growth of the whole economy while others (profit) do not.[7] Smith does not say, as he would if he held the normative "labor theory of value" sometimes attributed to him, that rent and profit, since they do not derive from labor, are illegitimate forms of income (although he does remark, snidely, that rent comes about because "landlords, like all other men, love to reap where they never sowed" [67]). But, by reducing all prices to command over labor, he sets things up so that we can ask the question, "is the labor price of most commodities higher or lower in an economy that allows for both rent and profit than it would be if we all labored for our goods directly?" Labor price, that is, enables us to ask the most basic question about commercial society: Do we all gain, even those of us who live by labor alone, by having a rentier and a profit-making class?

And it is largely to pose this question, I suggest, that Smith wants the notion of labor price. Chapter v opens by defining "rich or poor" in terms of one's ability to acquire commodities—"the necessaries, conveniencies, and amusements of human life." In the next sentence, it talks about the effect of the division of labor on richness and poverty, in accordance with this definition. Here we are told that after the division of labor each person can supply himself with only "a very small part" of his necessaries, conveniences, and amusements by his own labor. For the "far greater part" of those necessaries, conveniences, and amusements we must rely on the labor of other people, and we can only do that by having commodities of our own to offer in exchange. The world of exchange thus replaces what we originally accomplished by means of our own labor, and the commodities we own represent the ticket each of us has to participate in that world of exchange. It is in this context that labor is said to be "the real measure of the exchangeable value of all commodities."

Set this paragraph, now, in the context of the whole argument of Book I. The word "exchangeable" ties the opening paragraph of chapter v to the chapter that precedes it, which ended with a distinction between "value in use" and "value in exchange." Water has great use value, a diamond very little use value, but diamonds, and not water, have great value in exchange. Smith gets to this point after talking about money, which has value only in exchange, and promises at the end of chapter iv to "investigate the principles which regulate" exchangeable value, implicitly setting value in use aside as irrelevant to economics. If we back up yet farther, we find that the entire book thus far has concerned the importance of exchange. After an initial chapter telling us that the division of labor is far and away the most important factor in the expansion of production, we had a chapter explaining how the division of labor is itself made possible by the propensity of human beings to exchange with one another, followed by a third chapter maintaining that the division of labor increases in proportion to the extent of the market. Finally, chapter iv tells us how the development of money allows for an increase in the extent of markets: which, by a sequence that should now begin to be familiar, in turn encourages an increase in the division of labor, which in turn makes possible an expansion in the production of goods. So by the time we reach the opening of chapter v, we have been led through a series of greater and greater elaborations on the thought that exchange fosters an increase in the production of goods, and that exchange therefore plays a larger and larger role in human life as society progresses.

When we are told in the beginning of chapter v that labor is the real measure of exchange value, then, we are being given a measure by which to assess the *entire realm of exchange*, rather than a measure that is supposed to function *within* any particular exchange or system of exchange. We are being asked, as we have been asked since the opening of the book, to step back and survey the entire economic world in which we participate, measuring it against the world that might once have existed, and now exists only in our imaginations, in which every person makes all her "necessaries, conveniencies, and amusements" by herself. We are being asked to think of what it would take, out of our lives, to make by ourselves all the material things we use, rather than acquiring them via exchange and a division of labor. This may mean that we should imagine making our food, clothes, shelter, and toys from scratch, in a presocial world that had never seen humans other than ourselves, or it may mean that we should imagine making things in our current world, with all its machinery, but in which the other people had mysteriously disappeared. We may picture making a coat by slaughtering a goat, skinning it, cleaning and drying the skin, and so on, or by going to a warehouse, selecting some cloth, bringing it to the relevant machines, and so on. By comparing what we actually do to acquire goods with the first of these scenarios, we see quickly how much we have gained by the development of technology over the ages (itself a side effect of the division of labor, according to Smith), in which each coat can be prepared with so much less labor as to cost, in "real" terms, far less than the coat of a lone hunter. By comparing what we actually do with the second of these scenarios—and that is what yields what Smith mostly means by the "labour" or "real" price of goods— we see what we each gain, even given advances in technology, by continuing to participate in a division of labor rather than trying to produce everything we need by ourselves.

So real or labor price, in this sense, is a tool for thinking *about* economic systems rather than a measure to be used within them. Indeed, Smith sometimes presents "real" or "labor" price as something that *cannot* express the actual exchange value of any good. "[A] commodity which is itself continually varying in its own value can never be an accurate measure of the quantity of other things," he says, and labour alone gives the real price of every commodity because it "never var[ies] in its own value" (50–51). But within a network of exchange *every* commodity, necessarily, varies in its own value, depending upon the supply of and demand for the other commodities available to exchange with it; exchange value is, essentially, something relative. So labor, when Smith calls it "the ultimate and real standard" of all value, must stand beyond all exchanges. According to an argument that goes back at least to Plato, the ultimate and real standard by which to judge any set of objects that change in relation to one another must lie beyond those objects. Accordingly, labor can be "the real measure of the exchangeable value of all commodities" only if it is not itself an exchangeable value. It can measure exchangeable value only because it does not itself participate in exchange; it can help us assess the overall effect of markets only because it is itself not a market entity. It can be a measure *of* economics only because it is not an economic measure.

But that means that the labor in question cannot be the labor that people put on the market, and sell at varying prices, in societies where a division of labor and system of exchange has been established. Smith says that labor was "the first price," the "original" price of things (WN 48). His point is that labor *would be* the real price of things in a world without exchange, that it *was* the price of things before things were exchanged—when "price" was a cost to oneself, not something established by a relation with others—not that it remains such a measure in our world. And the labor that we may once have carried out before we had systems of exchange, or that we might carry out if we ceased to have such systems—if we were stranded, like Robinson Crusoe, or if all other humans died out—would indeed be a labor in which equal quantities would be "at all times and places" of equal value, in which all we would have to consider, in assessing the value of an hour's labor, would be the "portion of . . . ease, liberty, and happiness" it cost us. When we are told that labor gives the real value of commodities, we are being asked to think of labor *outside of a context of exchange*, outside of economic relationships. We are being asked to participate in a thought experiment, and a thought experiment rather more removed from ordinary empirical testing than the experiment that gives meaning, in chapter vii, to "natural prices."

A thought experiment can serve descriptive rather than normative purposes, however, and Smith's thought experiment here is meant to help make the descriptive point that the broadening of exchange relationships lowers the price of goods, not to make any normative point about the intrinsic goodness of working for a living. If we accept the notion that labor is the "real price" of goods while "money is their nominal price only," then we can see how very much cheaper goods become, regardless of their money price, where a little labor can enable us to purchase many of them. "At all times and places that is dear which it is difficult to come at, or which it costs much labour to acquire; and that cheap which is to be had easily, or with very little labour" (WN 50–51). It is not hard to imagine that in a world without a division of labor, or with a very limited one, it would take a great deal of labor to acquire even basic food, shelter, and clothing. By contrast, in the commercial world in which Smith's readers live, even a poor worker can quite easily "come at" more than adequate food, shelter, and clothing. So Smith holds at least; one might quarrel with this by contrasting life in certain miserable urban conditions with life in certain hunter-gatherer tribes. But if one quarrels, one quarrels about a fact, not a normative principle, and that is all that matters for present purposes. Smith introduces "labor value" or "real price" to help clarify a broad historical point; the notion functions as part of an historical investigation, not to express a moral sentiment.

Of course the historical investigation I have discussed so far is mostly an imaginative one. Smith's account of the genesis of exchange relationships belongs to the eighteenth-century genre that has been called "conjectural history," and that is a genre in which imaginative exercises figure prominently. In the middle of chapter v, however, Smith tries to harness his real prices to a more concrete historical project: the study of whether the value of money has gone up or down over the centuries. Smith uses corn prices as an approximation of labor prices, since corn[8] pays "the subsistence of the laborer" (53). And corn prices, "though they have in few places been regularly recorded, are in general better known" than the price of labor "at distant times and places." We may therefore "content ourselves with [corn prices], not as being always exactly in the same proportion as the current prices of labor, but as being the nearest approximation which can commonly be had to that proportion" (WN 56). So, on the assumption that labor value remains constant across centuries, and that a substance like corn, which pays the subsistence of laborers, will set the lowest price labor can bear, corn prices should enable us to measure changes in the real value of money over centuries. The theory of labor as setting real value thus gives legitimacy to Smith's later use of corn prices to trace the history of the value of gold and silver over the course of the four centuries from 1350 to his own day. And this history enables him to make one of his most important points against mercantilism: that gold and silver will not inevitably decline in value, as the mercantilists had claimed, but will on the contrary naturally "rise [. . .] with the wealth of every country" as long as the accidental discovery of new mines, like the discovery of mines in the Americas, does not keep it down (208). Again, I am less interested in the merits of this empirical claim than in the fact that it *is* an empirical claim. Labor value or real price serves Smith's empirical purposes insofar as he wants to compare economic facts across large swaths of historical time; it is not there to satisfy some metaphysical need for absolute standards that transcend market fluctuations, or to make moral points about the superiority of labor over idleness.

32. The Long Term versus the Short; Growth versus Allocation; Definition of Wealth

We can draw two further lessons out of our consideration of "natural" and "real" prices.

First, Smith's interest in making economic comparisons across centuries ties in with a theme that runs through WN: that the "wealth of nations" is something that accumulates very slowly, over long periods of historical time, not something that can be nurtured by short-term political programs. "When we compare . . . the state of a nation at two different periods," says Smith, "and find, that the annual produce of its land and labour is evidently greater at the latter than at the former, that its lands are better cultivated, its manufactures more numerous and more flourishing, and its trade more extensive, we may be assured that its capital must have increased during the interval between these two periods" (WN 343). Now comparing the "annual produce" of a country at two different periods is something one can do in the short term as well as the long term: There are fairly easy ways to come up with a means to measure that even across two consecutive years. Finding that "lands are better cultivated, manufactures more numerous and more flourishing, . . . trade more extensive" is a much more difficult business, and not one that one could easily do over a short period. Smith makes just this point: "To form a right judgment [of such changes] we must compare the state of the country at periods somewhat distant from one another. The progress is frequently so gradual, that, at near periods, the improvement is not . . . sensible" (WN 343–4). "Somewhat distant" is an understatement. Smith goes on in the next paragraph to compare the state of Britain at the restoration of Charles II in 1660 with its state in the 1770s, when WN was written. A proper grasp of the "wealth of a nation," it seems, and of whether that wealth is increasing or decreasing, requires a view that may extend over more than a century. And when we take such a view, we realize that the long-term economic health of a nation can be trusted to take care of itself.

Second, the point of the long-term comparisons is that free markets help the total stock of goods in a nation to *grow*, not that they *distribute* goods fairly, or so as to maximize people's happiness. Smith's economic theory focuses on the production of goods rather than their distribution. This point can be overlooked if one takes the account in chapter vii of how market prices "gravitate around" natural ones to demonstrate the *fairness* of market distributions. But Smith's point in chapter vii is just that free markets will allocate goods *so as to encourage efficient production*: that the natural price to which market prices gravitate gives producers the incentive to make as much of that good as they can get rid of without waste. The point is that markets allocate resources efficiently, not that they allocate resources to those who need them.

Later on, Smith provides a famous, long argument to show that free markets adequately supply the poor with basic foodstuffs (WN 524–43). But that argument turns in part on a specific feature of food (that it spoils quickly: 533) and would in any case be unnecessary if he had already shown that markets in general meet everyone's needs. What Smith has to say generally about the distribution of goods is that where there is a large supply of goods, each good will tend to be cheap and readily available (24, 50–51)—so markets, which encourage goods to multiply, will also indirectly encourage them to spread out across society. But this is hardly a solid link between free markets and optimal distribution, and Smith does not argue that markets, left alone, will always meet the needs of the poor.

Growth and distribution are linked closely enough, however, to raise a problem for Vivienne Brown's recent thesis that Smith abandons the notion that wealth consists in "low-price plenty" between LJ and WN (ASD 147–54). Opulence is defined in LJ "as a low-price, high-wage situation where the necessities of life are easily affordable by the working population," says Brown (ASD 147). In WN, by contrast, passages "linking cheapness with opulence . . . are missing" (ASD 151), and are replaced by a definition of national wealth in terms of a society's "annual revenue" or "the value of its annual produce" (ASD 179). But this attention to Smith's wording obscures the analytical connection he makes in WN between high "annual revenue" and "a low-price, high-wage situation." Furthermore, even if no explicit identification of wealth with low-price plenty appears in WN, similar language and similar ideas run through the book.

Where "the produce of the whole labour of [a] society is . . . great," Smith says, "all are often abundantly supplied, and a workman, even of the lowest and poorest order, . . . may enjoy a greater share of the necessaries and conveniencies of life than it is possible for any savage to acquire" (WN 10). Again: where a society enjoys both a lot of produce and good government, "[e]very workman . . . is enabled to exchange a great quantity of his own goods" for a great quantity of the goods of others; everyone is supplied "abundantly" and "a general plenty diffuses itself through all the different ranks of the society" (WN 22). The word "plenty" also continues to correlate with "cheapness of provisions" (WN 46, 92, 101), and high wages continue to be described as "the natural symptom of increasing national wealth" (WN 91). In WN as in LJ, opulence consists in goods being easy to "come at" —"At all times and places that is dear which it is difficult to come at, or which it costs much labour to acquire" (50–51)—and Smith shows throughout that growth in revenue and stock will correlate with high wages and a plentiful supply of goods: with, that is, the conditions that make for "low-price opulence" (ASD 147–8). What changes between LJ and WN is that *total* stock is no longer as important to Smith's analysis as *growth* in stock. In WN, Smith recognizes that a country can be "wealthy," in the sense that it has within its borders a large supply of goods, while the bulk of its people are poor: China, he says, is in this state (WN 89–90, 111–12). He now believes that a nation's revenue and stock must be continually growing for it to be "flourishing and happy" (WN 96). But this just means that growth must be added, in WN, to the conditions making possible the easy acquisition of goods for everyone. So there is no radical shift in how Smith conceives the optimum economic condition between LJ and WN, and in both there is supposed to be a link between the production of goods and their distribution throughout society. In both, also, these notions are simply linked, not brought together by an argument that free markets do as effective a job in distributing goods to those who need them, as they do in ensuring that the goods get produced. The latter is the direct effect of free markets; the former, at best, is an indirect one.

WN's focus on growth rather than distribution reflects its polemical context. The mercantilist writers Smith opposes saw a nation's wealth as a total sum that represented its glory and provided it with resources to do battle successfully with poorer nations. They argued that policies fostering manufactures and commerce increased this total sum, and were necessary in the face of the international, zero-sum competition for power. The Physiocrats, while arguing that agriculture, rather than manufacturing and commerce, were crucial to wealth, shared the mercantilists' "sum total" view of what wealth was. We have some reason to believe that Smith did not see national wealth this way, that he had a distributive rather than an aggregative conception of wealth—at the end of the first chapter of WN, for instance, he appeals to the condition of a European peasant as a mark of Europe's wealth—but he could not have made political headway against his opponents had he framed his economic views in such completely different terms. For polemical purposes, he needed to take on an aggregative view of national wealth, even if his own primary interest in a country's total amount of goods lay in the effects of that totality on distribution. Where there is a "great multiplication of the productions of all the different arts" and a healthy network whereby those goods can be exchanged, he says, "a general plenty diffuses itself through all the different ranks of society" (22). But he talks for most of the book about what allows the general plenty to arise rather than about how it diffuses itself. This makes it hard to know where he would stand in the very different polemical context we inhabit today, where distribution rather than production dominates debates over political economy. We will return to this theme in part IV, when we take up distributive justice.

33. Productive and Unproductive Labor

Imagine that, for a year, politicians, servants, everyone in the entertainment industry, and "churchmen, lawyers, physicians, [and] men of letters of all kinds" (331) continued to work on their regular schedule, while all farms, manufacturers, freight transport, and sales outlets shut down. What would happen? Well, the scenario is only barely imaginable, because short of some miraculous profusion of fruit on trees in public parks, or other equivalent of manna, the politicians, churchmen, lawyers, etc., could not continue to work. Within a very short time, everyone would run out of their provisions at home and begin to starve, freeze, and have no means of getting around except their feet.

By contrast, if all the politicians, entertainers, churchmen, and the like went on strike for a year, while the farms and manufacturers and transporters and retailers kept to their regular schedule, perhaps the quality of life would be diminished but life itself could certainly go on. There are indeed whole societies without entertainers or men of letters, but none without some way to produce and distribute food, clothing, and shelter.

This is all that Smith means by distinguishing between productive and unproductive laborers and saying that the productive ones maintain both themselves and the unproductive ones (332). Unproductive laborers are a luxury, productive ones a necessity. Smith says that unproductive laborers include "some . . . of the gravest and most important" professions as well as some of the "most frivolous" ones, and we know from elsewhere that he certainly does not have contempt for poets and philosophers (e.g., TMS 134). So he does not mean to equate "unproductive" with "lazy" or "wasteful." His point is just that a country can afford to enlarge its unproductive sphere, however worthwhile it may be, only in proportion to the extent of its productive sphere.

Smith also wants to make two other points, one of which should be welcome to modern economists while the other is troublesome. The welcome point is directed against the Physiocrats, who had originally introduced the distinction between productive and unproductive labor. For the Physiocrats, only agriculture could be productive. All production must be rooted in "nature" (*physis*), they felt—in the end, all other production depends on those who draw out the resources of nature. Smith responds by recognizing not only that manufacturing can give farmers an incentive to produce more than they would otherwise do, and that the manufacturing goods of a country can be exchanged for agricultural produce from elsewhere, but that the work of merchants, by transporting goods from one market where they are in abundance to another where they are scarce, also enhances the produce of a nation: "Unless a capital was employed in transporting, either the rude or manufactured produce, from the places where it abounds to those where it is wanted, no more of either could be produced than was necessary for the neighborhood" (361). So the merchant, too, is a productive laborer. To return to the imaginary scenario with which this section opened, suppose that all retail stores (to take just one branch of the commercial sector) were to close for a year, while everything else remained as it is. Only those who lived on or near a farm could survive for long in such a situation, and very soon all commercial transport and all manufacturing would close along with the stores. So commercial activity is very much a part of productive labor in any economy with an advanced division of labor. It is indeed very much a part of what nature produces, as long as we are willing to extend the word "nature" to include the proclivity, in *human* nature, to increase production by dividing up labor, and then to exchange the results. Smith is to be commended for deepening what should count as "nature" for economic purposes, for allowing the work of merchants to be included in the *physis* that determines the degree to which nations can allow for "unproductive" activity.

What is more troublesome, and what has inspired many of the objections against Smith's distinction between the productive and the unproductive, is his attempt to link "productive" labor to something that "lasts for some time at least after that labour is past" (WN 330). Using menial service as a model, Smith says that unproductive labor does not "fix or realize itself" in a vendible commodity. Your valet lays out the perfect suit for you. You enjoy the convenience, as well as the respect you get later in the day because you are so well turned out. But what the valet did cannot be resold, or "stocked and stored up" to add value to something that will later be resold. It "adds to the value of nothing."[9] The acts for which menial servants get paid "generally perish in the very instant of their performance, and seldom leave any trace or value behind them, for which an equal quantity of service could afterwards be procured." The service can be sold just once, to the person who first enjoys it. After he or she enjoys it, it disappears. So it cannot be resold, cannot be exchanged for anything else. For the same reason, it cannot be added to the general produce of a nation. It cannot contribute to the plenty of the nation and the consequent cheapness of its goods.

There are two problems with this analysis. First, unproductive labor is not generally as ephemeral as menial service. Second, ephemeral goods are not necessarily immune to resale. The first problem may strike us immediately in a way that it did not strike Smith because we now have ways of preserving what were in Smith's day necessarily ephemeral events. Smith could compare the performance of a play to the work of a menial servant because the play, like the valet's laying out of a suit, gave satisfaction only to those who actually attended it. By way of film and sound recordings, practically all art and entertainment can be turned into a "vendible commodity" today, and sold and resold many times in return for other goods. The work of an actor very much "fixes and realizes itself in some particular subject" when that work is captured on film. That was not so in Smith's time, which helps explain why he saw artists and entertainers as not producing anything that could, for instance, be sold to other countries in return for food. Yet even in his own day, the work of "men of letters" was not ephemeral, nor was the work of a lawyer or physician, which could permanently change a person's legal condition or state of health. An enhanced state of health might help a person work better, moreover, and an enhanced legal condition might enable a person to attract loans for investment more easily. So it is not at all clear why work that leads to these results should count as "unproductive."

In addition, ephemeral goods can, in a sense, be sold again under some conditions. Smith seems to believe that there can never be a regular market for something ephemeral. But this is not true. Consider a nation that has a highly developed tourist industry. Here the attractions of flashy theater, or of hotels with wonderful service, can draw in consumers on a regular basis, offering their goods in return for the *repetition* of an event that, in itself, is ephemeral. The theatrical event or hotel service does "leave a trace or value behind it," for which an equal quantity of another good can be procured: in the reputation of the event or hotel, which can draw in ever new customers. We might say that a proper understanding of the good produced is that it consists in a repetition of certain events across time, that the actor and the chef sell, not *this* particular performance or fine meal, but a series of performances or meals. In this way, services can be sold in a regular market just like any palpable good, and can form a part of a nation's stock. There are nations today that draw most of their goods from other countries in return for tourist services.

Of course that was not true in Smith's day. But it is unclear that he should be excused on this count. One would expect that his sound inclusion of commercial activity within the class of productive labor, his recognition, central to the whole argument of WN, that exchange makes production possible, would have prevented him from assuming that the ephemeral cannot make a regular contribution to market value. For the merchant, too, does not "leave a trace" on the goods he moves and sells. The merchant buys corn wholesale from the farmer and then sells it to a retailer, at a considerable markup. Nothing changes in the *corn* as a result of this; the corn does not get any "value added." Or rather: The corn gets no value added unless we count the very movement from one locale where it commands a lower value to another where it commands a higher one as itself a way that a good can increase in value. Smith clearly does seem to do that, else he would not include merchants among productive laborers. But the same logic entails that the actor "adds value" to his theater, the good waiter "adds value" to his hotel, and so forth. If "value added" can consist in anything that enhances the demand for a good, then unproductive as well as productive laborers should be able to add value to a nation's goods.

The connection Smith draws between unproductive labor and the ephemeral

ties in, however, with another, very intriguing theme. Smith maintains that unproductive labor conduces to dependency and idleness while productive laborers tend to be independent and industrious (332–3, 335–6). The argument
for this connection seems to be as follows: Because the unproductive laborer
does something that entertains or instructs one particular person, or group of
people, at a particular time, he or she is dependent on the favor of that person
or group for further employment. The productive laborer has an item to sell
that he can take around to any one of a number of people. If he is insulted or
abused by a particular customer, or if he simply dislikes that customer, he can
"stock and store" his product until he finds other people to whom to sell it. The
productive laborer has many customers, and rests his reputation primarily on
his work, so as long as he is honest and good at what he does, he cannot easily
be ruined by any single nasty or unhappy customer. As Smith says in a later
chapter, a tradesman or artificer "derives his subsistence from the employment,
not of one, but of a hundred or a thousand different customers," and although
he is "in some measure obliged to them all," he is not "absolutely dependent on
any one of them" (419–20). The unproductive laborer, by contrast—the menial
servant, especially—has nothing to store if his master rejects his work, and
cannot simply shop his work around to other "customers." He will indeed find
it very difficult to work for anyone else unless his master gives him a good
reference. Hence he often has to put up with insult and abuse, or at least
subdue his independence and do his master's will rather than his own. He is
clearly dependent, and his dependency is one reason he is likely to be idle: He
loses his independent will, his autonomy, his internal motivation to work.

There is also another reason. Unproductive laborers are paid out of revenue
rather than capital, Smith says (333, 336), which means that whether they are
employed or not depends on how much discretionary income people happen to
have at any particular time. They will therefore be employed quite haphazardly,
and the irregularity of their work can breed in them habits of idleness. "Our
ancestors were idle," says Smith, "for want of a sufficient encouragement to
industry" (335).

The ancestors of which Smith speaks are the common people of feudal times,
most of whom lived in relationships of dependency to a lord and many of
whom were menial servants. This is one of the places in which Smith takes to
task his own earlier stoic embrace of menial servitude, in TMS IV.i, as a way by
which Providence distributes the bounty of the rich to the poor (see §26
above). Both here and in WN III.iv, Smith draws a sharp distinction between
the kind of labor characteristic of feudal society and the kind of labor characteristic of a commercial society, portraying the former as conducing to idleness,
dependency, and poverty while the latter encourages industry, independence,
and a comfortable standard of living. The point of II.iii is that rich countries
have a great many productive laborers while poor countries are filled with unproductive ones (334–5)—the wealth of a nation correlates strongly, here, with
the dignity and high wages of its common workers.

Does this admirable normative conclusion require the distinction between productive and unproductive labor, or the intricate links Smith draws between that distinction and industry/idleness and independency/dependency? It is true that some unproductive workers are employed irregularly, and may therefore incline toward habits of idleness, but not all are: Smith again thinks too much of actors and servants, and not enough of physicians and lawyers. It is also true that many unproductive laborers depend heavily on their employer's good will for continued employment, or for a chance of working elsewhere, but that also does not hold for all types of unproductive labor—whereas it does hold for productive laborers in a factory setting. (Smith seems to have in mind mostly small *independent* craftspeople and farmers, not factory workers, when he talks of "productive laborers.") Where a large market develops for service or entertainment, moreover, actors, waiters, and the like may be able to carry their credentials more easily with them from one employer to another, if only because many potential new employers are likely to see them in action and not have to rely on a reference. Of course even today references can be extremely important, and workers in all sorts of settings are heavily dependent on their employers' opinions of them. Workers also tend, today, to have a labor-schedule set for them, and then get monitored by their employers, rather than to produce things independently: and this imposed discipline often does conduce to habits of idleness, of disinclination to work whenever one is not being supervised. The habits of idleness and dependency do not, however, necessarily lead to poverty; they are just morally corrupting. So Smith's analysis of how the relationship between employer and employee can encourage or discourage certain character traits is a morally illuminating one, which brings out problems in the modern, corporate workplace as accurately as it does in the feudal, servile one. But it is not clear that that analysis is any longer of economic use, if indeed it ever was.[10]

34. The Invisible Hand[11]

WN is filled with explanations of social institutions in which a result beneficial to society is reached without any agent directly intending that result. In the second chapter of Book IV, this mode of explanation is used to argue that merchants will naturally tend to direct their investments toward domestic industry, even without any government regulations to that effect, and even though they are interested in their own gain rather than the good of their societies. In this context, Smith says that each merchant is "in this, as in many other cases, led by an invisible hand to promote an end which was no part of his intention" (WN 456). The vivid phrase he uses has been lifted from the passage to characterize Smith's view of economic activity in general.[12] Whenever people are left alone to pursue their own interests, Smith is said to believe, an invisible hand ensures that they will benefit society as a whole. The question then arises, does Smith have some sort of empirical or mathematical proof to show that this must be the case, or is he tacitly relying, as the metaphor of an "invisible hand" might suggest, on a Stoic or Christian notion of Providence, beneficently guiding all human activity behind the scenes?[13]

The first thing to say about this question, and the interpretation of Smith that prompts it, is that it draws far too much out of the famous sentence in WN IV.ii. The phrase "in this, *as in many other* cases" has been overlooked, for one thing. Smith provides us with a number of cases in which an individual's unconstrained pursuit of his or her interest will not benefit the society. In WN II.ii he talks of "projectors" who developed irresponsible ways of raising money that brought on a crisis in British and Scottish banking. In V.i.g, he says that only when a church offers modest pay to its clergy, and pays them equally so as to *remove* any inclination they may otherwise have to "better their condition" materially, will the clergy be appropriately learned, decent, and independent.[14] Here individual self-interest and the well-being of society are in potential conflict, and the self-interest must be guided in a certain way if it is to serve society. More generally, as Anthony Waterman puts it, Smith does not see actions on private interest as benefiting society where they are taken "within the wrong sort of institutional framework."[15] This means, above all, that societies must provide a framework for action that includes proper rules of justice, but the church discussion indicates that Smith allows for institutional design, even beyond the establishment of justice, to direct private interest in better and worse ways.

So Smith is by no means pronouncing a universal rule in WN IV.ii. It would be odd, moreover, if such a rule appeared in this context. Smith is in the midst of making a relatively small point (that merchants will tend to base even their "carrying trade" in their home ports), and has adduced a few plausible but weak generalizations about merchant behavior in support of that point. If he wanted to proclaim that an invisible hand *always* guides individual economic decisions toward the good of society, we would expect that proclamation at the opening of the book, as part of his grounding theory of economic activity. The theory Smith gives us there does support the claim that individuals generally promote the social good in their economic behavior without intending to do so, but there is no hint that this holds in all cases, much less that it is guaranteed to hold by either empirical or metaphysical laws.

Nevertheless, one recent scholar suggests that Stoic optimism ultimately provides the warrant for Smith's invisible hand claims, that those claims rest on a belief in a benevolent deity who governs nature for our benefit.[16] If so, Smith's views on economic policy would be far less interesting than they have seemed to his many non-Stoic readers. Fortunately, the Stoic reading of WN's invisible hand is demonstrably wrong. It is true that the two other occurrences of the phrase "invisible hand" in Smith's work have providential overtones. In the early "History of Astronomy," Smith says that ancient religions attributed certain sorts of events, but not all events, to "the invisible hand of Jupiter" (EPS 49). In TMS, Smith maintains that the rich are "led by an invisible hand" to share most of their wealth with the poor, and follows up this claim by saying that "[w]hen Providence divided the earth among a few lordly masters," it did not forget the poor (TMS 184–5). But in WN the mention of an invisible hand is not conjoined with any reference to Providence, and there is no invocation of either that term or any related notion in the entire book. Indeed, as we have seen

(§26), WN does not share the optimism Smith expresses in TMS's "invisible hand" passage about economic relationships always benefiting the poor as well as the rich. The blanket optimism of TMS would in any case render pointless Smith's efforts to demonstrate that free commercial economies promote a great expansion of material wealth. If people are happy regardless of their economic condition, then whether their society has a greater or smaller stock of material goods, and whether they themselves are employed or not, should be irrelevant to them. Smith's views on economic policy should then be that a mercantilist or Physiocratic or indeed a feudal economy is just as good as a free trading economy, since Providence will take care of everyone under any sort of economy. He does not say that, of course. So the central "invisible hand" argument of WN, the argument for the greater beneficent tendencies of unguided than mercantilist or Physiocratic economies, cannot by any stretch of the imagination be construed to depend on a general, metaphysical optimism according to which Providence will make sure that everything turns out for the best in all economies.

What does the argument depend on? Simply, I think, on the empirical premise that, normally, *society makes possible the opportunities for any individual to gain.* More precisely, if inelegantly:

> (IH:) Where people act freely rather than under threats of violence, long-term opportunities for any one individual to better herself are made possible by the needs and wants of her society.

Like ants or bees and unlike bears or tigers, human beings acquire material goods only in society, which means that an opportunity for one person to gain will normally so much as *exist* only if the needs or desires of other people make it possible. In general, people will pay you for something only if they need or want that something. The "invisible hand" thus represents social forces, not Providential ones. An individual may think he is pursuing only his own interest by making or selling a certain good, but it is the needs of society that create the niche within which he can gain by making or selling that good, and his gains, therefore, will serve the good of society whether he intends to do so or not.

If this seems disappointingly obvious, that is partly because we expect too much of the invisible hand passage. Smith himself does not write the passage as if it offered particularly striking news. Rather, here and throughout WN, he treats the fact that society shapes the opportunities for each of us to gain as something that ought to be uncontroversial, once one reflects on how the division of labor comes about. That the role to which self-interest draws the merchant is normally one that maximizes the economic gain he can provide for the whole society follows trivially from the account Smith has been giving of economic roles since the beginning of the book. It is no wonder that, two paragraphs after invoking the "invisible hand," Smith recalls the description of the division of labor he gave in Book I, chapter ii:

> The taylor does not attempt to make his own shoes, but buys them of the shoemaker. The shoemaker does not attempt to make his own cloaths, but employs a taylor. The

farmer attempts to make neither the one or the other, but employs those different artificers. All of them find it for their interest to employ their whole industry in a way in which they have some advantage over their neighbors. (WN 456–7)

The invisible hand sentence depends on the fundamental economic principle of WN: that human beings, alone among animals, have the understanding to realize they can get more for themselves by participating in a system in which each one labors to produce goods for all.[17]

Neither the invisible hand sentence nor its underlying principle is really trivial, moreover. In the first place, as the principle (IH) we have drawn out of the sentence makes clear, it is true only on the condition that people are not threatened by violence. That is where the advantage of commercial economies over feudal economies, and free commercial economies over mercantilist or Physiocratic ones, comes in. In a feudal economy, the lords hold threats of violence over their serfs, and in protectionist commercial economies, governments use their threat of violence to prevent some kinds of trades from taking place. It is crucial, for Smith, that mutually beneficial trade can take place only where governments protect individuals against all threats of force by other individuals, and refrain from using their own force to interfere with exchanges unless absolutely necessary.

In the second place, there are a number of empirical, eminently defeasible assumptions built into the claim that people unconstrained by violence will trade for mutual benefit. One might deny that claim by saying that people don't generally know what they need or want, and can therefore be fooled by clever merchants—and there is a long-standing tradition that criticizes free market economies in just this way. Or one might consider differentials in wealth to constitute something like a threat of violence, such that wealthy merchants can force poorer people to buy things at prices much higher than they want to buy—and this too is a claim put forward by a long line of critics of the free market. Smith rejects the first of these claims, insisting repeatedly that ordinary people know very well what they need to know to make their economic choices (138, 346, 456, 531). To the second, he says that any sort of force a particular merchant might have over a particular market at a particular time will normally be dissipated by competition from other merchants who hope to gain by undercutting the first one (77, 329, 361–2). Here competition thrives on the needs of the people oppressed by the would-be monopolist. Once again, social needs structure the opportunities for gain, and gain entails the satisfaction of otherwise unmet needs.

On the deepest level, the point of Smith's invisible hand accounts of social phenomena is that society structures both the means available for any individual to attain his ends and his very conception of those ends. The opening chapters of WN show that opportunities for an individual to "better" himself are normally made possible by the needs of his society, and chapters I.iii and III.1–3 of TMS make clear that what he will *count* as bettering himself normally arises out of the influences upon him, via sympathy, of his friends and neighbors. In

WN, the stress is on the fact that we are animals who need the assistance of others like ourselves, a point made as early as the second chapter: "In almost every other race of animals each individual, when it is grown up to maturity, is intirely independent, and in its natural state has occasion for the assistance of no other living creature. But man has almost constant occasion for the help of his brethren" (26). We are structured to help each other, regardless of our intentions; we would not survive otherwise. The would-be arrow-maker in WN I.ii finds that he can make a living off of arrows only because significant numbers of his fellow tribespeople want arrows, and this example is supposed to encapsule the way that the needs of other people, and the trade motivated by those needs, determine the range of things each of us can do to increase our possessions. In WN IV.ii we learn in addition that the way trust and mutual understanding work, among human beings, leads us to favor our own society over its rivals. The merchant naturally knows and trusts his fellow citizens better than foreigners, and therefore favors trade at home over trade abroad (454).[18] And in TMS, we learn that our desires *themselves*, not just the means to satisfy them, are shaped by our attempt to have just those feelings that our friends and neighbors can sympathize with.[19] Consequently, as Smith stresses in TMS IV.i, even when social forces lead us into a false conception of our ends, what we do to pursue these illusory goods will benefit the society that has misled us.

It follows from this highly socialized conception of the self that individuals will generally promote the public good regardless of whether their own interest is furthered, harmed, or left alone by their actions. In TMS IV.i, the agents led by the "invisible hand" contribute to the public good without particularly advancing their own good, and in Book III of WN, feudal lords promote the good of society even as they *destroy* their own favorite good (power over their vassals). What powers Smith's invisible hand are the forces by which societies shape individuals, and lead them generally to serve each other's ends. If societies did not do this, they would not survive; Darwinian evolution is an excellent tool for explaining the processes Smith describes. There is nothing mysterious about them, nothing unnatural, nor need they be rooted in any divine "Author" of nature.

Of course, Smith's general view of the power society has over individuals, no less than any of his specific claims about how this power works toward societal benefit, is open to controversy. What matters for our purposes is not the truth of these claims but their empirical status, and their defeasibility testifies to that empirical status. Smith uses plausible but defeasible empirical claims to underwrite his invisible hand explanations, and his invisible hand itself consists in a set of social forces, not metaphysical ones. The beneficent tendencies nudging individual economic decisions in the direction of a society's good arise from general facts about human nature. None of these facts are underwritten by metaphysical guarantees. None of them are even universally true: for which reason the invisible hand works, as Smith says, only "in many cases," not in all.

PART IV

Justice

CHAPTER EIGHT

A Theory of Justice?

Smith's theory of justice has been identified by many recent commentators as both his most important contribution to political thought and the central link between his moral philosophy and his political economy.[1] I think it is neither as central nor as successful as that. Nevertheless, the emphasis given to justice in recent interpretations has been a helpful corrective to earlier tendencies to view Smith as a utilitarian.[2] He certainly was not a utilitarian, saying in the *Wealth of Nations* that one should never sacrifice justice to utility except in cases of the "most urgent necessity" (WN 539; cf. also 188), and criticizing the proto-utilitarian strands in Hutcheson and Hume throughout his moral philosophy. Laws of justice, and the rights they protect, are of the utmost importance to him, not something to be passed over in the name of the greatest happiness for the greatest number. Yet in WN Smith plays down his own theory of justice, and it is important to try to assess, as has not been done in recent commentary, what the significance of this fact might be. Moreover, the commentators who emphasize Smith's views on justice tend to see him as laying the groundwork for the modern libertarian critique of the welfare state, and this, I believe, is a mistake. Smith does not have the absolute, presocial conception of property rights that would make it unjust to use redistributive taxation to help the poor. He would almost certainly oppose state socialism, and he might well be suspicious of welfare programs administered by large bureaucracies, but even here, his reasons for suspicion would come from sources other than his views on justice. His general approach to the functions of the state may well be closer, in fact, to welfare state liberalism than to libertarianism. Since the difference between these two is so central to modern political debate, the details of interpretation that lead one to see him as an ancestor of one camp rather than the other are worth spelling out. I shall, accordingly, devote three full chapters to the subject: one to Smith's views on what he calls "justice in its proper sense"—the protection of individuals against harm to their life, body, reputation, or property— another to property rights, and the third to Smith's place in the history of what today we call "social" or "distributive" justice.

35. Some Puzzles about Smith's Treatment of Justice

i. At the end of TMS, Smith identifies justice as the one virtue that can and should be delineated precisely, and "natural jurisprudence" as a subject that deserves much more attention than it has received. He promises "another discourse" that will lay out "the general principles of law and government" that ought to hold in all nations, and we know that he carried out a discourse that more or less meets this description in his lectures at Glasgow. Yet he published, as the *Wealth of Nations,* a version of only the last part of those lectures, the part concerning "police, revenue, and arms," and while he worked on a manuscript on natural jurisprudence up until his last years, he ordered the manuscript to be burned at his death (the lecture notes survive by accident). Why did he publish the end of his jurisprudential lectures before their beginning and middle? WN seems to have been originally intended as the last section of a tripartite project: a book on morality (TMS), a second book on jurisprudence, and a third book, or perhaps a concluding section of the second book, on economics and other policy matters (WN). In this project, the whole would be structured to move from general moral concerns, through their (partial) incarnation in law, to their (yet more partial) realization in policy. There would also be a deeper connection between the second and third parts of the project. Smith says throughout both LJ and WN that a fair and effective system of justice is an essential condition for economic growth, and he also says in LJ (333, 486–7) that a commercial economy, by raising the standard of living of the poor and offering them "independency," helps prevent crime and encourage virtues of probity and self-respect. A somewhat truncated version of this point appears also in WN (412), where it gets called "by far the most important" of commerce's effects.

In this tripartite form, Smith therefore had a project with a clear central thread, a project that develops political concerns out of moral philosophy much as Aristotle did in moving from his *Nicomachean Ethics* to his *Politics.* But without its middle unit, the project falls apart. So Smith's decision to publish WN before working out a publishable version of LJ, and then to take a job as Commissioner of Customs and work only sporadically on LJ for the rest of his life, looks like a change of mind about the way moral philosophy and politics ought to be linked, a decision that reflections on politics and economics can stand alone, and need not be rooted in moral theories, even about justice.

ii. This structural point about the place of WN in Smith's overall project fits well with the content of WN. There is barely any discussion of what constitutes justice in WN, and no explicit reference to TMS, on the subject of justice or on anything else.[3] Smith appeals to justice in the course of many arguments, but he never explains what it is. He had said in TMS that explaining the general principles of "natural" justice was a central task for political philosophers, but he does nothing toward that end in WN. He had also developed an account of rights in LJ, and of justice as the protection of rights, but again, this does not show up in WN. The words "right" and "rights" are not used often, and do not appear in Smith's index to the book.[4] So the impression many of Smith's nonphilosophical readers have long had of WN, that it is a work in which moral issues, even about justice, are downplayed or ignored, is not a foolish one.

iii. That there are some general rules of justice according to which the positive laws of every society can be judged is very important to Smith. It is important partly because he believes, as many in his time and since have done, that moral principles ought to govern relations *between* societies, that laws of war and peace ought to hold internationally (LJ 545–54, WN 626–7). It is also important because he wants to criticize certain laws and institutions in his own society, and he needs a standard of judgment independent of those laws and institutions to do so. In WN, he criticizes primogeniture, entail, slavery, the British laws of settlement, and a host of restrictions on free trade. It would help him a great deal in doing this if he could point to some standard of "natural justice" showing that these laws and institutions are unjust.

But the nature of his moral views makes it difficult for him to do so. TMS links the function of morality so closely to the maintenance of society, and makes so much room, accordingly, for the legitimacy of social and historical variation in the way the moral sentiments play themselves out, that it is odd to see Smith writing at all of "general principles which ought to run through and be the foundation of the laws of all nations" (TMS 341). The whole notion of "natural jurisprudence" is an anomalous one in the context of a moral philosophy like Smith's, and it is not surprising that there are tensions, throughout his lectures on jurisprudence, between the attempt to bring out universal principles behind all law and a fascination with, and sympathetic explanation of, the historical forces that have led to massive variations in law across cultures. Knud Haakonssen sees a deep and subtle reconciliation, in Smith's writings, between the natural basis of justice and its historical incarnations; Charles Griswold suggests that Smith's entire project of natural jurisprudence conflicted so deeply with other elements of his thought that it could not be completed. I agree with Griswold rather than Haakonssen.[5] As Griswold says, Smith nowhere shows us in TMS how his general, unchanging principles of justice might be derived from moral notions. And if they are, instead, to be drawn out of history,

> the problem is obvious: How can history yield general normative principles that are always the same? Is not the process [of deriving such principles from history] either circular or inherently impossible? *Qua* system, the principles of natural jurisprudence would have to be complete. But as dependent on the experiential or historical, the system would have to be open-ended. (AVE 257)

Smith's projected natural jurisprudence was never published, Griswold suggests, "because it could not be written" (37 n61).

iv. Sometimes justice in TMS seems to be a merely negative virtue, such that an individual may "fulfil all the rules of justice by sitting still and doing nothing" (TMS 82). Elsewhere, Smith suggests that we need to build within ourselves a disposition to respect the laws of justice (TMS 158–61, 174–5), and that developing such an internal discipline requires a great deal more than "sitting still and doing nothing." Griswold elaborates this point beautifully:

[T]he just person is not *simply* someone who consistently follows rules that prohibit doing harm to others. Rather, the just person is governed by a reverence for rules of justice and a determined resolve never to be guilty of hurting others without just cause. Smith's language in this regard is striking. He speaks over and over again of the just person's "conscientious," sacred," and "religious" respect for the . . . rules of justice. Even when sitting still and causing no harm throughout his life, the just person demonstrates a "habitual reverence" for the principles of justice. . . . [S]ociety "cannot subsist among those who are at all times ready to hurt and injure one another" [TMS 86]. The just person not only abstains from hurting others; he is not ever *ready* to hurt others without warrant, and this is a fixed disposition of character. (AVE 237)

But this cannot be the same justice that, according to Smith, needs to enforced. It is crucial to Smith's case for the enforcement of justice that *only overt acts* of injustice need to be punished. Only overt acts of injustice inflict "real and positive harms" on individuals, and threaten the continued existence of society. Nothing need be or should be done to enforce the *disposition of character* to respect justice; attempting to enforce that would interfere with the very liberties of conscience that justice is designed to protect. Yet if justice consists in both an enforceable disposition to refrain from certain acts and an unenforceable disposition to respect the laws prohibiting those acts, it would seem really to be *two* virtues. I shall call these two kinds of justice "political justice" and "moral justice," respectively, and suggest that Smith carves the former out of the latter.

36. Smith's Different Accounts of Justice

The tension between "moral" and "political" justice is but one instance of the way in which Smith seems to have several different accounts of justice. The views of justice in (i) Smith's pre-TMS lectures on morality, (ii) various sections of TMS, and (iii) Smith's lectures on jurisprudence differ subtly but significantly from one another, so that it is hard to attribute to Smith any consistent thesis about what justice consists in. Smith scatters at least four separate discussions of justice around TMS alone (78–91, 154–63, 269–70, 329–42), and it is not at all clear that even these accounts are compatible with one another.

   i. *In the pre-TMS lectures*: Smith states the "libertarian" view of justice that is commonly attributed to him in a fragment of his early lecture notes, probably written shortly before the first edition of TMS:

That civil Society may not be a Scene of Bloodshed and disorder every man revenging himself at his own hand whenever he fancies himself injured, the Magistrates in all Governments that have acquired considerable Authority employs the power of the commonwealth to enforce the practice of Justice, and to give Satisfaction to the injured . . . When our benevolence to each particular person is exactly proportioned to the importance of those circumstances which point them out to our favourable regard, we are, by a metaphor, said to do them Justice, and we are said to do them injustice when it is otherwise. When we chuse rather, for example, to do a good Office to a new acquaintance than to an Old friend we are said to do Injustice to the latter. This, however, is a different Species of Injustice from that which we have been treating of above. It does not consist in doing hurt, but in not doing good according to the most perfect propriety. In the Schools it has been distinguished by the name of distributive justice, as the former, which can alone properly be called Justice, has been denominated commutative Justice. In the observation of distributive Justice consists the proper exercise of all the social and beneficent Virtues. It cannot be extorted by force. The violation of it does no positive harm, and therefor, exposes to no punishment. The Rules which determine the external actions which it prescribes, are loose and unaccurate and fall short of that exact precision, which . . . is peculiar to the Rules of what is properly called Justice.[6]

Justice alone may be enforced by governments, and justice must be enforced. Justice properly consists simply in the abstention from "doing hurt" to our neighbors; it is but metaphorical to call benevolence "distributive justice." And one important reason why "justice" must be limited to its "commutative" sense is that the rules for not doing hurt to our neighbors can be made precise, while the rules for doing good to them are always "loose and unaccurate."

iia. *In TMS 78–81*: It looks as if Smith began his discussion of justice in TMS by simply transcribing what he had written for his lectures, but then stuck complicating phrases and sentences throughout the passage, and never quite reconciled the original account with its later qualifications. At first the discussion in TMS seems exactly like the one in the lecture notes:

> Beneficence is always free, it cannot be extorted by force, the mere want of it exposes to no punishment; because the mere want of beneficence tends to do no positive evil. . . . There is, however, another virtue, of which the observance is not left to the freedom of our wills, which may be extorted by force, and of which the violation exposes to resentment, and consequently to punishment. This virtue is justice: the violation of justice is injury: it does real and positive hurt to some particular persons. (TMS 78–9)

But then, barely a page later, it becomes less clear that only justice may be enforced:

> Even the most ordinary degree of kindness or beneficence . . . cannot, *among equals*, be extorted by force. . . . A superior may, indeed, sometimes, with universal approbation, oblige those under his jurisdiction to behave . . . with a certain degree of propriety to one another. The laws of all civilized nations oblige parents to maintain their children, and children to maintain their parents, and impose upon men many other duties of beneficence. The civil magistrate . . . may prescribe rules . . . which not only prohibit mutual injuries among fellow-citizens, but command mutual good offices to a certain degree. (80–81, my emphasis)

On one page Smith says that beneficence is "always free," that it "cannot" be extorted by force; on the next, he says that beneficence is only free "among equals," that established governments, which introduce "superiors" among once equal human beings, rightly enforce "many . . . duties of beneficence."[7] Which is it? Can beneficence never be enforced, or is that the case only before governments are instituted? I think we must simply recognize a contradiction here, between a relatively straightforward view that Smith initially held, and a more complicated view that he later tried to insert in the middle of the straightforward one, without appropriately weakening how he had formulated the latter. No talk of "superiors," much less any suggestion that "civilized nations" may enforce virtues other than justice, appears in the fragment from Smith's lectures. Indeed, if we compare what Smith says about the job of the "magistrate" in the two places, it looks as if he is trying specifically in TMS to revise his earlier views: "The civil magistrate is entrusted with the power *not only of preserving the public peace by restraining injustice*, but of promoting the prosperity of the commonwealth, etc." The "not only" (repeated a few sentences down) seems directed, as much as anything, at the restricted notion of the magistrate Smith himself had earlier held.

I believe the tension here is rooted in a deep problem that I will develop later in this chapter: Are there any sharp criteria by which to distinguish "real and positive hurt," against which justice is supposed to protect us, from the mere absence of good? Unless we can find such criteria, we will be unable to set justice off sharply from other virtues, to formulate it in precise rules, and to use it as a constraint on otherwise beneficial government action.

iib. *In TMS 82–91*: Shortly after the passage I have just considered, Smith tells us that justice rules out acts that would destroy society. Justice is "the main pillar" upholding the "edifice" of society; it "raise[s] and support[s]" the whole "immense fabric of human society" (TMS 86). Both the idea and a closely related image can be found in Hume (E 305), and Pufendorf and Hutcheson also argued that justice must be enforced because without this use of force, society would disintegrate. Pufendorf, Hutcheson, Hume, and Smith are probably all in part nodding to Hobbes here, but they are also registering a significant disagreement with Hobbes. For Hobbes, *all* morality was necessary to society, and all virtues therefore could be enforced. People will kill each other "for trifles, as a word, a smile, a different opinion" (*Leviathan* I.xiii.49), so in the name of peace, governments can try to extract even such virtues as gratitude and "complaisance" from the population (ibid., I.xv), and can regulate such things as the expression of "words" and "opinions." There is no morality without government, for Hobbes, and all morality serves to prevent society from disintegrating into civil war; all moral principles can, therefore, be enforced. For Pufendorf, Hutcheson, Hume, and Smith, this is true only of a limited subset of moral principles. Acts that violate "perfect rights," to use Pufendorf's and Hutcheson's terminology, must be prohibited, else there will be constant violence, but people are motivated to other virtues and moral principles by an innate sociability or benevolence, and are led to live up to those other virtues and principles, where their benevolence might fail, by the gentle sanction of other people's approval and disapproval. So once society is in place, and the linked forces of sociability and approval/disapproval have a realm in which to operate, governments need not, and should not, use their powers for most moral ends. They need only to prevent acts of injustice—acts that would threaten the very existence of society.

Hume contributed a curious twist to this tradition. Unlike other virtues, justice was not really a natural moral trait at all, he believed—not a trait of which we have a natural disposition to approve. He pointed out that the rules of justice often mandate actions which in themselves offend our moral sense. We punish poor thieves trying to feed their families in order to protect the property of misers and debauchees (T 482). We guard the right to inherit of those who don't need inheritances. In these cases our immediate—"natural"—moral sympathies, which account fully for our approval of kindness, gratitude, courage, and other virtues, do not explain why we approve of justice. Justice, says Hume, consists in a scheme of laws by which disputes can be settled. Since the relative absence of violence that comes of observing the scheme is, in the long run, in everyone's interest, over time people come to approve of justice. But this sense of approval is a new, "artificial" feeling, grafted on to our natural ones.

The central concern of Smith's discussion of justice in TMS is to fend off this suggestion of Hume, to argue that the rules of justice do indeed have a natural basis in our moral sentiments, and are justified by something they do for individuals, not just for society as a whole. Smith argues that, while the scheme of justice does serve the interests of society, it more immediately protects each individual, and our approval of it in particular cases can be explained, like the approval of other virtues, by way of an immediate, natural feeling. That feeling is resentment, which has been implanted in us to insure that we protect both ourselves and our fellow human beings against grave harm:

> Resentment seems to have been given us by nature for defence . . . It is the safeguard of justice and the security of innocence. It prompts us to beat off the mischief which is attempted to be done to us, and to retaliate that which is already done; that the offender may be made to repent of his injustice, and that others, through fear of the like punishment, may be terrified from being guilty of the like offence. (TMS 79)

This means both that a victim of harm will tend to resent and retaliate against harm to himself, and that "every generous spectator" will not only approve of such conduct but will "enter so far into his sentiments as often to be willing to assist him." Even in a condition without civil government, says Smith, when "one man attacks, or robs, or attempts to murder another, all the neighbours take the alarm, and think that they do right when they run, either to revenge the person who has been injured, or to defend him who is in danger of being so" (TMS 81).[8] Smith denies that justice is an artificial virtue. "[R]etaliation seems to be the great law which is dictated to us by Nature," he says (TMS 82), and it is nature which implants in us the impulse to resent injury, and to sympathize with the justified resentment of others. Legal systems merely formalize—and, importantly, moderate—this natural impulse.[9] But that is to say that the impulse leading to the creation of legal systems is an impulse by which we resent harm to *individual* people—to ourselves, or to individual others—not just to that artificial entity, "society as a whole."

At the same time, Smith does believe that justice serves the interests of society. "Society . . . cannot subsist among those who are at all times ready to hurt and injure one another" he says. It can subsist, "though not in the most comfortable state, without beneficence; but the prevalence of injustice must utterly destroy it" (TMS 86). So Hume is right that the scheme of justice protects societies against crippling violence, and thereby makes them possible. But this is a sort of side effect of justice, not its primary function nor the main reason we approve of it. Rather, our respect for justice rests in our concern for each of the individuals in a society; it is an indirect, and unintended, effect of this protective concern for other individuals that society is thereby made possible. (We see here an example of how Smith uses an incipient version of an evolutionary argument: a principle implanted in us by nature has one effect that we directly intend, and another, quite different effect by which it promotes the survival of our species.) We are explicitly conscious of the large-scale social benefits of justice only when we need to persuade the "young and licentious" who ridicule, and thereby display a lack of understanding of, the sacredness of rules of justice, or when, in exceptional cases, the laws of justice require something against which all our natural moral sentiments rebel (TMS 87–91).

So Smith's version of the thesis that justice is the "main pillar" holding up the edifice of society rests on the claim that the acts making society impossible are just those inflicting "real and positive harm" on individuals. Such acts arouse a desire for revenge in the victim and all who witness the infliction of harm, which without a system of justice would lead to an endless series of feuds, a Hobbesian war of all against all. The rules undergirding society and the rules prohibiting gratuitous harm against individuals will therefore be one and the same.

If this equation holds, it should be very helpful: We should be able to discover the natural rules of justice, and the corresponding harms they prohibit, from two directions instead of just one. We could either develop a clear and precise list of acts that inflict "real and positive harm" on people or a clear and precise list of acts whose commission threatens the existence of society. But I am not convinced that the equation does hold. Would society really be impossible if people's reputations were poorly protected against slander, if governments deprived people of most property rights, if chastity was widely violated? The actual existence of societies, now and in the past, in which false rumors abound, in which property is regularly confiscated by army and government officials, or in which the very notion of chastity has practically disappeared, makes this an implausible claim. That widespread killing and physical brutality can destroy a society is clear—Idi Amin's Uganda demonstrated that vividly—but people seem to be willing to put up with a great deal of "real and positive harm" short of this extreme. Justice cannot be limited to the prohibition of killing and physical brutality, however, and Smith certainly does not so limit it.

iii. *In LJ*: The notes we have on Smith's lectures on jurisprudence raise a new problem. As Knud Haakonssen has emphasized, Smith's jurisprudential lectures make heavy use of the notion of rights; the entire course is structured around kinds of rights and their violations (NL 132–48). Both TMS and WN, by contrast, seem to go out of their way to *avoid* the language of rights, even where it was used by Smith's contemporaries. Thus Hutcheson talks of the "imperfect rights" by which relatives, friends, benefactors, and the miserable may claim our good offices, asserting that some of these relationships give rise to imperfect rights that "ascend" almost to the level of perfect ones (SI II.ii.iii). Smith makes the same point by saying: "But of all the duties of beneficence, those which gratitude recommends to us approach nearest to what is called a perfect and complete obligation" (TMS 79). Here "duties" and "obligation" do the work that "rights" did for Hutcheson. Hutcheson lists our perfect rights—including rights to life, bodily integrity, and independent judgment—defining "natural liberty" by their means and "justice" as the protection of liberty. Smith does no such thing in TMS. Instead of defining justice in terms of rights, he speaks of the "rules" or "laws" of justice. Where Hutcheson has a "sacred right to property," Smith has "sacred laws of justice" guarding property (SI II.vi.ii; TMS 84). In WN, there is one reference to "the sacred rights of property" (WN 188); elsewhere in the book, Smith describes property as "sacred and inviolable" without using the word "right."[10]

Whether Smith is properly a friend or a foe of rights-talk is thus unclear. LJ goes in one direction; TMS and WN, his published works, in another. Smith's work as a whole displays at best an ambivalence about rights-talk. That ambivalence is again, I think, a symptom of Smith's uneasiness about whether the hurts that justice protects us against could be formulated as clearly and precisely as he had originally hoped. For a "right" is supposed to be a clearly delineable feature of ourselves, or our relationships to others, whose infringement can be discerned with equal clarity. The infringement of a right is always a real and positive hurt, and real and positive hurts are always supposed to be formulable as the infringement of rights. That is at least the connotation of "right" as it had been used in strictly legal contexts: They were created either by positive laws or by explicit contracts, and were thereby given precise delineation, and a promise of enforcement, by the sovereign who proclaimed the law or in whose domain the contract was sealed. We can see why Smith might have been drawn to such a notion as a way of capturing the clear, precisely formulable harms that justice was supposed to guard against. We can also see why he might have been uncomfortable with that notion, if he increasingly saw deep problems with the notion of precisely definable "real and positive hurts."

37. A First Argument for the Precision of Rules of Justice

That justice can be formulated in precise laws is an essential premise of Smith's attempt to define a universal or "natural" justice. If justice were like other virtues, in which what is called for by the virtue can only be determined within each social context by the impartial spectator, we could not expect to find a theory of it that could determine "the foundation of the laws of all nations" (TMS 341). That justice must be formulated in precise laws is also essential to the use of it to bar the state from engaging in activities that require many ad hoc, potentially arbitrary, decisions—like the micromanagement of an economy. So determining where the precision of the laws of justice comes from in Smith is crucial to finding the core of his various accounts of justice.

We have seen above that Smith rejects Hume's thesis that justice is artificial. Yet he agrees with Hume that justice is sharply different from the other virtues, and begins his own account of justice by acknowledging "that remarkable distinction between justice and all the other social virtues, which has of late been particularly insisted upon by an author of very great and original genius" (TMS 80).[11] But if the remarkable distinction does not rest on the fact that justice is artificial, what does it rest on? In the passage from which this quotation comes, it seems to rest on the fact that justice is enforceable. As we have seen, however, Smith immediately throws into doubt whether justice really is unique in lending itself to enforcement. And elsewhere in TMS he cites *precision*, not enforceability, as the feature of justice that makes it unique:

> The general rules of almost all the virtues, the general rules which determine what are the offices of prudence, of charity, of generosity, of gratitude, of friendship, are in many respects loose and inaccurate, admit of many exceptions, and require so many modifications, that it is scarce possible to regulate our conduct entirely by a regard to them. . . . There is, however, one virtue of which the general rules determine with the greatest exactness every external action which it requires. This virtue is justice. The rules of justice are accurate in the highest degree, and admit of no exceptions or modifications, but such as may be ascertained as accurately as the rules themselves, and which . . . flow from the very same principles with them. (TMS 174–5)

Smith elaborates this point at some length both here and at the end of TMS (327–30, 340–42), and refers throughout WN to the importance of an "exact" administration of justice. The important point at the moment is that precision and enforceability are two different qualities, and it is not clear in which of them Smith wants to locate justice's uniqueness. Of course, justice could happen to be *both* uniquely precise *and* uniquely enforceable, but this would be an odd coincidence. Surely either one of the two is the true reason for justice's uniqueness or they are intimately related.

As it happens, the two are supposed to be intimately related, although Smith never spells out that relationship. The fact that he fails to do that is unfortunate, because a great deal turns on how we construe the relationship. The basic idea is that enforceable laws must be precise because if people are liable to punishment for doing something, they need to know in advance what that something is. This is a very ancient principle of justice, to be found, for instance, in Aquinas's requirement that laws be "promulgated" to those to whom they apply.[12] It is unfair to punish people unless they know in advance that what they are doing is wrong. Practically no legal system has been oblivious to this principle. It follows that laws should state precisely what is permitted and what is forbidden, and that any virtue that doesn't lend itself to being defined in such precise terms should not be enforced. The question that remains is this: Is justice a "naturally" precise virtue, which therefore lends itself to enforcement? Or do we need to *impose* a precision upon justice *because* it must be enforced? It is unclear, that is, in which direction the inference between precision and enforceability is supposed to go. Is there some realm of just acts which, unlike the realm of beneficent or grateful or courageous acts, can be precisely defined and therefore enforced, or is it necessary to *carve out* some precise realm of just acts, and unnecessary to carve out similarly precise realms of beneficent or grateful or courageous acts, because justice, but not those other virtues, must be enforced? Haakonssen, the most thoughtful and comprehensive commentator on Smith's jurisprudence, takes it as clear that Smith endorses the first of these possibilities; I think Smith wavers between the two and ultimately plumps for the second. This difference, as we shall see, has extremely important implications.

Haakonssen takes the core intuition in Smith's account of justice to be the recognition of a certain asymmetry between pain and pleasure. Pain, both when we suffer it and when we observe it, makes a greater impression on us than pleasure. Therefore (so the argument goes) we are clearer and more certain about the presence of pain, and its beginnings and endings, than about the presence or absence of pleasure. Avoiding pain is also more important to us than achieving pleasure. It follows that laws to ban "real and positive hurt" are both more necessary to us and can be more precisely formulated than laws to promote positive goods:

> The rules of justice are precise because they are derived from spectator reactions which are unusually 'universal' and 'distinct', namely the 'pungent' feeling of sympathetic resentment occasioned by 'real and positive hurt.' Smith's idea seems to be that clarity and accuracy are transferred in the following chain; the action (negative: hurting), the reaction (resentment and punishment), the spectator-reaction through sympathetic resentment (sympathetic resentment and assistance in punishing), and the general rule arising from spectator reactions. (SL 86; see also 83–7)

This seems a clear enough string of associations, moving from the universal sharp impression of harm, through the related universal ability we have to recognize when other people are harmed, to the possibility of formulating and enforcing laws harming those who cause harm to others. There is a view of justice captured in the slogan, "Your right to swing your arm ends at the point of my chin." The slogan suggests that human beings can all literally *see* the point at which harm begins. If Haakonssen is right, every sort of harm is as readily obvious as the blow to the chin in this slogan, and Smith developed an entire conception of natural jurisprudence from the insight, brilliant in its simplicity, that these harms can be easily and precisely recognized by all human beings in all cultures. For excellent biological reasons, we can, and must, pick

out harm far more readily than either good or the absence of good; it is therefore both more possible and more necessary to enforce the virtue preventing
harm than any virtue promoting good. A whole theory of justice, we might
think, can rest on this insight into the asymmetry between harm and good.

The only problem is that the insight is false. Harm is an essentially *social*
category, not a physical one, even in the case of harm to one's body. Even
invasion of the body is not necessarily a harm, else surgery and sexual intercourse, to name just two of many activities, would be unjust. Neither invasion
of one's body, nor physical pain, nor any other presocial, purely biological fact
will define harm in its juridical sense; both invasion of the body and pain can
be desired, accepted, or merited, such that they are permitted or even required
by justice, and figuring out exactly what does and should count as the relevant
kinds of desiring, accepting, and meriting depends irremediably on social
norms and practices. It is therefore not true that we can find in raw human
biology a clear, precisely delineable type of "real and positive hurt" to serve as a
basis for a clear and precise notion of justice across all societies. In particular,
contra Haakonssen, the pungency of a harm does not entail its precision. We
may feel a pain very strongly, yet not be sure exactly wherein the wrong done to
us lies, or exactly who should be blamed for it. If I lose my job after having
been slandered, I may be unsure whether the depression and anger I feel is
caused by the slander or the fact of unemployment, and I may be unsure
whether the agent of my misfortune, and object of my anger, is most appropriately the people who spread the slander, my boss who believed them, or
myself, if, say, I did not defend myself well, or did something that made the
slander plausible.

We may also feel both a pleasure and the deprivation of an expected pleasure
quite precisely. You give me an uncalled-for gift, or disappoint an expectation of
mine by being too ill to perform your new Schumann piece for me, and I know
exactly why I am pleased or mildly upset. I am a recipient of beneficence in the
first case, and a victim of bad luck in the second; in neither case am I likely to
have a very pungent feeling; yet I can identify both my feelings and their causes
more precisely than in the instance of slander described above.

Furthermore, harms need not be more pungent than the deprivation of
goods. Compare mild injustices with gross failures of beneficence. Suppose I
jostle you, or take a nickel from your desk, or walk off with your pen. Do you
really, in ordinary cases, suffer a great and pungent pain from this loss? And if
you do, will an impartial spectator feel a pungent resentment on your behalf?
Smith says that the truly infuriating pain that arises in us on any occasion of
injustice, no matter how small, comes not from the loss itself but from the
implied attitude of the agent that he or she is superior to you, that he and you
are not equals: "What chiefly enrages us against the man who injures or insults
us, is the little account which he seems to make of us, the unreasonable preference which he gives to himself above us, and that absurd self-love, by which he
seems to imagine, that other people may be sacrificed at any time, to his conveniency or his humour" (TMS 96). I think this is right, and it explains well

why we sometimes prosecute even small thefts, and can be enraged by even minor assaults or slanders. Still, we normally do not prosecute when the infringement is *very* small, and if someone gets furious about the loss of a nickel or a pen, or about being lightly jostled, our sympathies as spectators are unlikely to go out to him or her. Indeed, if the victim persists in seeking redress for such an act, we may well sympathize with the agent instead, and tell the victim not to be such a fusspot, not to insist so arrogantly on her rights.

By contrast, suppose I bear children and then entirely neglect them, letting them suffer or even die on their own. Or suppose I walk by an elderly person who has slipped and fallen on the sidewalk, late on a bitterly cold night, and do nothing in response to her calls for help. Not supporting one's children is a failure of beneficence rather than an injustice for Smith (TMS 81),[13] and as long as I am not, say, a doctor or police officer, my blithely passing by the fallen elderly person, even if she then dies, is also but a failure of beneficence. Yet I surely do "real and positive hurt" in both cases, much more so than when I take your pen or jostle you, and impartial spectators are likely to feel a furious resentment against me. In a wonderful and terrible scene, a wife in Lillian Hellman's *The Little Foxes* deliberately sits still while her husband, calling out for help she could easily render, dies in front of her. Most people who see the play will probably consider the wife a murderess, but she might well not be convicted of murder in any court, and she certainly does not violate commutative justice as Smith, and the jurisprudential tradition before him, defined it.

Now we can of course simply *stipulate* that some kinds of beneficent action count as duties of justice—we can pass Good Samaritan laws, and claim that they enforce duties that properly belong to justice—and we can also set the bar for what counts as theft or battery high enough that taking nickels and pens, and jostling people, won't count as violations of justice. But to make these moves is simply to concede the point I have been arguing: that the "natural" borders of justice are blurry, not sharp, and that they cannot be clarified by way of a prelegal, presocial notion of harm. Moreover, this is not really a problem just about the borders of the concept. Taking a pen or a nickel may be a huge deprivation in some impoverished societies, and jostling may in some cultures, or some circumstances, be a grave insult. Failing to raise a child, by contrast, might be acceptable where the society as a whole has institutions to take care of all its children, and it might be at least understandable in a desperately poor society. Failing to help the fallen elderly person might similarly be excusable where great dangers face anyone out late at night—during a civil war, say—or where there is a regular emergency service patrolling the streets. So what should count as the boundary between justice and beneficence will vary enormously according to cultural, political, and historical circumstance. It can move inward, to put in doubt what may seem to us core cases of justice, or outward, to embrace within the fold of justice acts that seem to us, here and now, clearly in the province of beneficence. And it can shift around, so that what is barely a hurt at all in one culture will be a real and positive hurt, even a terrible one, in another.

Smith recognizes most of this. In TMS, he wanders off from his own proclamation of the exactitude and precision of the laws of justice to acknowledge
that, when we consider justice as a moral rather than strictly legal virtue, many
of its aspects are "impossible to determine . . . by any general rules that will
apply to all cases without exception."[14] In LJ, he says that injuries to reputation
vary in accordance with the attitudes of different nations toward honor (LJ 123–
4), and describes in detail the history by which what counts as property has
been gradually extended over time. He also recognizes that the kind of pain or
hurt relevant to the justice of contract law depends crucially on the "reasonable
expectations" we have of acquiring a piece of property (87–93). Expectations
are indeed central to the kind of pain justice is concerned with in general. It is
not pain as a purely biological phenomenon, the pain that can be defined by
reference merely to nerve endings or wounds to the body, that constitutes "injury" in the justiciable sense. If you hit me, even very hard, in the course of a
boxing match, that it is not justiciable injury, nor is it injury if I am cut with a
knife in the course of a religious or social ritual I have freely undergone. I am
injured, as opposed to simply *hurt*, where I had a reasonable expectation that I
would be protected from hurt. But expectations, let alone reasonable expectations, are strongly dependent on the social practices and norms in the context
of which they get formed. I will probably not have an expectation of escaping
hurt if I agree to participate in boxing matches, and I cannot have a reasonable
such expectation. Indeed, the positive laws of our society play a significant part
in determining what we reasonably expect. So if the injury punishable by justice
depends on what I expect or reasonably expect, it must be something relative to
social practices, including positive laws, not something that can be picked out
by natural and universal sympathies, and upon which all societies' laws might
therefore be based. No appeal to the natural pungency of pain, or of sympathy
with pain, can enable Smith to develop "the general principles which ought to
run through and be the foundation of the laws of all nations."

Smith himself provides yet deeper resources for this point about the socially
relative structure of injury. A running theme of TMS is the way that our pleasures and pains, especially the ones that we care most about, are structured by
our desire to receive approval from others in our society. We want to have the
kinds of pleasures that others can enter into sympathetically, and we want to
avoid especially the kinds of pains that will bring on contempt from others. The
kind of disappointment of reasonable expectations that constitutes "injury," in
the sense relevant to justice, is thus very likely to be something that no impartial spectator could understand without first knowing the pleasures and pains
typically approved or disapproved of in each society.

38. Critical Jurisprudence and the Problems in Defining "Harm"

If justiciable harm is a socially relative category, it will be difficult to find any
laws of justice that must be realized by every society. It will therefore be very

hard for Smith's account of natural justice to get any critical bite on each society's norms and practices, as he wants it to do. If we swallow the fact that "harms" and "reasonable expectations" are socially structured, what can we say, in the name of natural and universal justice, about the following cases?

a. X is a wealthy man in a society where concubinage is widely accepted. Partly for this reason, he has been willing to enter into a loveless marriage; like many other men he knows, he seeks his sexual pleasure, and has always expected to seek his sexual pleasure, outside of marriage. His concubines have likewise planned their lives around the understanding that concubinage is acceptable: They would not want to be regarded as prostitutes, and if that was the standard attitude toward concubinage, they would have settled for a lower standard of living along with a respectable marriage. X's wife may suffer under the system, or perhaps she too was willing to settle for his lovelessness, along with his wealth, because she knew that they would not have to be very intimate.

Abolition of concubinage would violate reasonable expectations central to the lives of X and his family, and therefore be unjust to them. Yet concubinage may well itself perpetuate harms that justice should rule out; it may well be that no one *should* expect to live under such a system.

Suppose now that a reformer arises in this society. She will, first, find it not all that easy to convince others in the society that concubinage really is an injustice—given that the wives and concubines themselves do not necessarily regard themselves as "harmed." Second, she will face a difficult practical dilemma: How can the systematic injustices of concubinage be ended without perpetrating individual injustices against the people whose lives are based on that system?[15] Given Smith's strong commitment to the notion of harm as the violation of reasonable expectations, and of injustice as primarily a matter of harm to individuals, he has little help to offer the reformer as regards either of these difficulties.

And that is a serious problem for him. Not only does he himself have to avoid calling concubinage "unjust" when he criticizes it (LJ 151–3), but very similar difficulties arise for other systematic ills that he does regard as unjust, like primogeniture and slavery.

b. Society X castrates some of its young boys, so that they will be fine singers. Society Y expects its young girls to undergo clitoridectomy, so that they will direct their energies away from sexuality. Society Z expects its young children to participate in violent and risky sports, like boxing or rugby. All of these societies systematically urge their members, at an age when consent can at best be partial, to inflict serious damage on their bodies. Are they all unjust? If some are and some are not, what differentiates them?

One thing that seems to matter is the way in which the people suffering regard the pain imposed on them. If the boys in society X *welcome* castration, and see it as an expansion of their ability to sing rather than a destruction of their ability to procreate, that might make us feel it is not unjust, and we are similarly less likely to feel the sympathetic resentment that picks out injustice where the boxers are enthusiastic about their sport. Still, we may suppose that many of these people have been deluded by superstition, ignorance, social pressure, and the like. People *ought* to resent clitoridectomy, we may say, and they *would* do so if they fully understood what was happening to them. But now perceiving the harm in injustice, far from being the straightforward exercise that Smith suggests all human beings can do, would seem to require first clearing away a lot of cultural debris. Clearing away such debris might well be an important and admirable job, but it is not supposed to be necessary in order to grasp what counts as "real and positive harm." Nor will it be easy to be sure that such debris is not getting in our own way, when we look at possible injustices in our own society. (I suspect that the vast majority of my readers feel quite sure that Z does not belong in the same class with X and Y. But how sure can any of us be that this feeling reflects more than a cultural bias?) Nor, finally, will it be easy to know just when our clearing has been adequately done: the cultural debris in question forms an indeterminately large obstacle to the perception of injustice.

c. Society X exposes its infants. (Smith calls this "murder," at TMS 210, although he also attempts to explain it sympathetically.) In society Y, parents stop supporting their children at six years old, and do not provide them with any education. In society Z, rich people refuse to give up enough money to ensure that poor children have adequate housing, health care, or nutrition.

When I attempt to take up the position of the impartial spectator, I see little difference among these societies, and my resentment goes out more or less equally to each of them. Others would vehemently disagree, at least as far as Z is concerned. One thing I and these others might agree on, however, is that there is no sharp line, no precise line, between the degrees of "harm done" in the three cases. But that suggests that there is no natural law of justice that everyone, by taking up the position of the impartial spectator, will find to cover these cases. One who condemns X as unjust can plausibly say the same about both Y and Z, while one who finds Z just can make a plausible case for the justice of X and Y as well.

On Smith's own account, it is hard to say that what is wrong with all three societies is just a lack of "beneficence." Smith himself says that the exposure of infants counts as murder, and in any case his account of justice turns on what kinds of acts move the impartial spectator to sympathetic resentment on the victim's behalf, to the feeling that someone ought to be punished for what the victim has suffered. I feel great resentment on behalf of both the abandoned and the desperately poor child, and can sympathize readily with a call to punish those who have let them suffer. Hence I think these are cases of justice. That others are likely to disagree simply demonstrates the variability of our capacity for resentment, of our vicarious sympathies with "harm."

What all these examples bring out is the elusiveness of "natural rules of justice independent of all positive institution" (TMS 341), so long as the harm that justice is meant to rule out gets defined in accordance with people's reasonable expectations. The point of the project to which Smith gestures at the end of TMS is to provide a critical standard by which one might determine when a society systematically perpetuates injustice in its laws or policies. Natural justice is unnecessary for determining whether a society violates its own rules; the point is to try to figure out when the rules themselves are unjust. But identifying systematic injustice is precisely what Smith's notion of pain, and spectator-resentment, cannot do. What people reasonably expect under the laws and norms of one society will not be what people expect under the laws and norms of another society; so what is harmful in one society will not be what is harmful in another society; so what is just in one society will not be what is just in another. How then to find a level of justice independent of all positive institution, independent of all law?

39. A Second Argument for the Precision of Rules of Justice

Setting aside, now, the question of what content one might give to the principles of "natural jurisprudence," let us return to the formal question of why the laws of justice must be precise:

i. One reason to reject Haakonssen's account of Smith's argument for the precision of rules of justice, in addition to the philosophical concerns I have raised about it, is that Smith himself does not draw an inference from the pungency of pain to the precision of laws against inflicting pain (as Haakonssen admits on SL 86). Instead he gives different, conflicting reasons for that precision. The differences and conflicts suggest that Smith himself was unsure how the argument was supposed to go, which makes it attractive to seek a good reconstruction of his view, out of the various arguments he has given us.

And the best hope for such a reconstruction lies in an argument Smith makes that certain formal features of rules express and enhance human liberty and equality. The rules of a game or a club establish a certain equality among people, in their capacity as players or members. Smith draws on this fact, to make a point about justice, on several occasions:

> In the race for wealth, and honours, and preferments, [every one] may run as hard as he can, and strain every nerve and every muscle, in order to outstrip all his competitors. But if he should justle, or throw down any of them, the indulgence of the spectators is entirely at an end. It is a violation of fair play, which they cannot admit of. (TMS 83)

> The government and laws hinder the poor from ever acquiring the wealth by violence which they would otherwise exert on the rich; they tell them they must either continue poor or acquire wealth in the same manner as they have done. . . . [A]s every club or society has a title to say to the severall members of it, Either submit to the regulations we make or get you about your business, so the community may say to the

individualls who are members of it, Either make your behaviour agreable to our laws and rules or depart from amongst us. (LJ 208–9; see also 204, 313)

Games are constituted by rules. You will not *be* playing soccer if you insist on picking up the ball with your hands. Clubs require rules of this sort in order to pursue joint activities, and rules of selection if they want to provide a safe and intimate space for association. Rules of a game or club are "practice rules"; they help to constitute a practice, to orient it toward a goal and to enable the participants in it to co-ordinate their activities, and to plan them in advance.[16] No social practice is possible at all without this kind of rule. The rules thus bring people together, but at the same time they help each person plan his or her individual activities. If I know that my club expects me to do something, I can arrange my club activities in accordance with that expectation, and my non–club activities so that they do not conflict with my duties to the club. The fact that the club has rules *both* coordinates my activities with those of my fellow club members *and* gives me room to act on my own. By making social expectations predictable, rules thus expand the degree of individual liberty within society. This conception of law is one of Smith's main themes in both LJ and WN:

> The courts of justice when established appear to a rude people to have an authority altogether insufferable; and at the same time when property is considerably advanced judges can not be wanted. The judge is necessary and yet is of all things the most terrible. What shall be done in this case? The only way is to establish laws and rules which may ascertain his conduct; . . . for when it is known in what manner he is to proceed the terror will be in great measure removed. (LJ 314; see also 287)

And it is this aspect of rules, their ability to guard our liberty against arbitrary interventions with our liberty, that requires them to be precise:

> [A]n other thing which greatly confirms the liberty of the subjects in England . . . [is] the little power of the judges in explaining, altering, or extending or correcting the meaning of the laws, and the great exactness with which they must be observed according to the literall meaning of the words . . . [T]he liberty of the subjects was secured in England by the great accuracy and precision of the law and decisions given upon it. (LJ 275, 282; see also 280)

Practice rules need precision. To fulfill their function of coordinating activity, and of enabling individuals to plan their participation in such activities in advance, they need to let us know, clearly and exactly, what others are likely to do, and what we may and may not do. Such precision gives us a sphere within which we can act freely. To a degree, it doesn't even matter what the rules *are*, as long as they are precise. They can be absurd, requiring anyone in the public square on Tuesdays, say, to jump up and down. Even requirements like this one preserve a sphere of liberty as long as they are precise. If this were the only rule in my society, I would be completely free every day except Tuesday, and could even do what I liked on Tuesday as long as I avoided the public square.

What we have said so far, that is, allows for the possibility that systems of justice could vary greatly in content while sharing the same form. Neither games nor clubs require any *particular* set of rules, and insofar as Smith compares the rules of justice to these sorts of rules, he implies that the rules of justice could likewise vary from one society to another.[17] To look forward to an example that will be important to us later on, this "game" conception of justice allows for the possibility that one nation might prohibit private property in capital goods, another permit private property in capital goods but outlaw inheritance, while a third granted the whole gamut of property rights demanded by radical libertarians, and, as long as all three made their rules clear and precise, all three would be equally just. Of course, one of these systems might be more efficient than another, one might make most of its people happier than another, or one might be better suited to a particular culture or historical period than another, but none of these would be reasons *of justice* for distinguishing among the three. Justice would be neutral among them. Alternatively, it might turn out, as a matter of empirical fact, that enforcing the rules under one of these systems was more prone to corruption and arbitrariness than enforcing the rules of the others. Then justice would give us a reason to oppose this system, but even then the strength of the reason would depend on the nature of the fact making the system prone to bad administration. If it were possible to overcome that fact—by finding a more precise formulation for the rules, say, or by providing better education or different incentives to the administrators—then justice would return to its posture of neutrality, vis-à-vis the three arrangements.

Differences among property arrangements along the lines I have described are, however, precisely what modern debates about justice tend to take as their subject. So if Smith does not have more to say about justice than we have seen so far, he will contribute little to our debates.

ii. Clear and predictable rules can include rules that distinguish arbitrarily among people. A rule restricting the use of a club dining room by the race, religion, or sex of some members of the club might be perfectly clear and predictable, as might a rule arbitrarily favoring a similar subclass of players of a game. On most conceptions of justice, and certainly on Smith's, the rules of justice cannot be like these club or game rules. Rules of justice do not only have to be clear and precise; they need to be general, in two senses of that term. First, to continue with the game or club comparison, they must be general across the players of the game or members of the club. One of the things that game and club rules accomplish is a sense, among the participants, that they willingly belong to the same group. Of course, a club can discriminate against some of its members, but then those members are likely to leave, or belong only resentfully. Such a club will not enable all its members to experience the pleasure, intimacy, and mutual moral support that comes of association with others, and we know that Smith sees these ends as the most important function of society. If these ends are to be accomplished, each individual who joins a group must be able to see the rules defining the group or group activity as respecting him or her as much as they respect every other participant. The spectators to the race for wealth and honors will not allow one competitor to "justle" another,

Smith says, because "[t]his man is to them, in every respect, as good as he" (TMS 83). Rules of justice need to express the fact that fundamentally everyone is as important as everyone else. They need to establish a basic equality in the social context within which we live, even though, given that basic equality, we may hold "races" creating some inequalities. So rules of justice that favor one group in society over another, or one individual over others, will defeat one of the central purposes for which they are formed.

What I have said so far allows, however, for rules that favor *members of the entire society* to which they apply over people outside that society. For Smith, as again for most theorists of justice before and after him, these would not be rules of justice. This brings us to the second sense in which rules of justice must be general. A feature of justice of great importance to Smith is that it expresses a fundamental equality among all human beings (cf. §16). Rules of justice arise from "the general fellow-feeling which we have with every man merely because he is our fellow-creature"; they express a feeling we can and ought to have even toward "an odious person" (TMS 90); they express the one moral feeling that must not be limited to members of a particular society but go out instead to everyone.[18] Smith discusses, and partly endorses, our natural preference for our own society over other societies, but at the same time condemns the injustices inflicted by one nation on others (WN 448, 588–9, 626–7). We do not normally need to be benevolent across national borders—"our effectual good offices can very seldom be extended to any wider society than that of our own country" (TMS 235)—but we do need to be just. Not inflicting gratuitous harm is a universal duty, transcending borders.

The rules of justice are thus supposed to provide ground rules, not merely for *each* society, but for the society of *all* human beings. They are supposed to represent rules that every human being can accept, and that protect a crucial aspect of every human being. Hence Smith wants to find "natural rules of justice" that precede, and properly constrain, the positive laws and institutions of every nation. He cannot allow that rules of justice will vary completely from one place to another as game and club rules do—he needs to find some content that all such rules ought to share.

iii. Can we perhaps derive the content of these natural rules of justice from the liberty promised by their form? We have seen the difficulties involved in delineating a universal notion of harm, but perhaps we can do better by way of a universal notion of liberty. We would then have a picture in which the content of natural jurisprudence neatly matched its form.

Drawing on Locke and Hutcheson, and looking forward to Kant, Smith in fact often links injustice to the violation of liberty. (e.g, WN 138, 405, 530). For Hutcheson, justice protects our "natural liberty," which includes our rightful powers over our lives, bodies, possessions, and consciences. Without these rightful powers, we could not act on our own, which means we would be unable to develop any virtues and we could not be held responsible for any actions. If we have duties to God, for instance, we could not fulfill them, since God requires "the service of the heart"—an intentional, deliberate turning toward Him. In the name of religion, then, there must be religious freedom: Christianity, properly construed, requires the freedom of religion, for Hutcheson. Smith may have given religion a lesser place in the moral life, but he fully shared the notion that moral achievements are worthless unless they are reached freely. Freedom, for Smith, is a condition for the development of the moral excellences that he considers so crucial to our happiness. Smith sees social forces as essential to moral development, but the ultimate moral achievement as a free incorporation of one's society's moral norms into one's conscience (TMS Book III). So one way of cashing out what it means to say that society cannot "survive" without justice is to say that it cannot survive *as a morally valuable entity* if it does not preserve the liberty of its members. A society cannot *simply* say to its members, if they don't like its rules, "get you about your business"; its rules must be rules that protect all its members' liberty. The principles of natural justice will then be those principles that best enable societies to protect liberty.

But this does not solve the content problem. Saying that justice protects against violations of "liberty" rather than against "positive harm" will not give us precise and universal rules about when and how liberty is infringed. Exactly what counts as "liberty" still needs to be defined, and that can be as difficult as defining "harm." Many different cultural practices that involve apparent acts of force against the body, and many different political arrangements regarding property, are regarded by those who live under them as fully compatible with liberty. Many cultures will also insist that certain kinds of moral and/or theological knowledge are necessary for liberty: only a well-educated person or only a believer in the true God, they will say, has the knowledge by which he or she can exercise truly free choice. Perhaps the individuals living in some of these cultures have been socialized or politically manipulated to believe in a *false* notion of liberty, but to make that point we need a universally acceptable account of what liberty is, and Smith has no such account. Kant, of course, later attempted to develop one, but the fact that both socialists and radical libertarians have plausibly considered themselves to be following Kant should give us pause if we think that precise rules about property can be derived from his account. I don't mean by this offhand remark to trivialize the Kantian tradition. But it seems fair to say that the history of that tradition does not offer much hope that a solution to Smith's difficulties in developing natural jurisprudence will be found by substituting the protection of "liberty" for the protection against "real and positive harm."

iv. Smith's conception of justice gives us reason to add one more formal constraint on laws, in addition to clarity and precision: that there be few of them, that societies try not to use law to do much more than protect liberty. Smith warns us explicitly that the attempt to enforce every sort of virtue "is destructive of all liberty, security, and justice" (TMS 81). He also describes both people who wantonly inflict injuries on others and people who have "too violent a propensity" to resentment—the passion upon which justice is based—as "wild beasts" that threaten the very existence of society (TMS 40, 86). This suggests that excessive law enforcement is as dangerous to society as lawlessness. The sovereign, after all, needs to use violence in the attempt to minimize violence. Those who punish crimes need to do something unnervingly similar to the very activities they are punishing, and in his early fragment on justice, Smith noted that "Improper punishment, punishment which is either not due at all or which exceeds the demerit of the Crime, is an injury to the Criminal, . . . and if inflicted, exposes the person who inflicts it to punishment in his turn" (see TMS 390). Systems of justice are engaged in a delicate business, having to prevent harm without themselves inflicting excessive harm. So one constraint on those systems is that they not try to do too much, that they consist not only of clear and precise laws but also of *few* laws, no more than necessary.

But how many are necessary? Smith himself sees the legislator as having some tasks in addition to the protection of liberty: all "civilized nations," he says, "impose upon men many . . . duties of beneficence" (TMS 81). Even if we stick to the protection of liberty, moreover, it is hard to know what exactly is necessary for that task. As we shall see later on (§56), Smith implies that adequate education may be a condition for having liberty, that liberty may require certain mental and material conditions, and not just the absence of violence. Smith also describes many types of burdens as "oppressive" (e.g., WN 393–4, 401–2, 853, 862) whether or not they involve directly preventing people from what they want to do. His use of the word "liberty" thus seems to be broad and vague, as is the ordinary use of that word. To determine what laws represent the proper minimum for a nation to enact, however, we would need a precise definition of liberty. Without that, the formal constraint calling for law not to do too much can tell us little about the content that legal systems ought to have. Perhaps because Smith was aware of this, his warning against enforcing every sort of virtue is embedded in two sentences that call, with remarkable vagueness, for the lawgiver to steer judiciously between a Scylla of too few laws and a Charybdis of too many:

> Of all the duties of a law-giver, . . . this, perhaps, is that which it requires the greatest delicacy and reserve to execute with propriety and judgment. To neglect it altogether exposes the commonwealth to many gross disorders and shocking enormities, and to push it too far is destructive of all liberty, security, and justice.

40. Reconstructing Smith's Theory of Natural Justice

We have drawn reasons from Smith for justice to be expressed in clear, precise and general rules, but not much of an account of what the content of these rules should be. The reasons we have drawn from Smith for the rules of justice to be precise have nothing to do with there being a precise content out there for those rules to map. The harms that human beings undergo are no more precisely delineable than the goods they seek; no original insight Smith may have had into the asymmetry between pain and pleasure enabled him to formulate precise rules of natural justice. Rather, he drew on arguments to be found as far back as Aristotle and Aquinas according to which the rule of law is more conducive to liberty, and expressive of equality, than the rule of magistrates. Justice must operate according to rules, and those rules must be clear, precise, and general, because grounding society in clear, precise, and general rules protects the basic liberty and equality of each human being. Such rules enable people to coordinate their activities so that each can predict the behavior of the others, and each can, therefore, plan his or her individual actions. General rules in addition give people the sense that they are part of a group that respects each of them, and thereby make possible the many ways in which society can provide us with pleasure and moral education. But none of this implies that there is a type of human experience that naturally lends itself to being promoted or prohibited by way of clear, precise, and general rules. Nothing about the form that justice must take, or the reasons we have for insisting on that form, guarantees that there is a content out there fitted to that form. Instead of drawing the precision of justice from the precision of human harms, we now face the possibility that we might need to come to the realm of harm with a demand for precise rules already in hand: that we might need to *carve out* some precise set of harms to protect people against, out of all the possible harms they might undergo.

I don't think Smith would have welcomed this conclusion. A good deal of his language does imply, as Haakonssen suggests, that he thought there was some natural realm of harms that the laws of all societies ought to prevent. Not just any clear, precise, and general rules will accomplish what Smith regarded as the proper ends of justice. Rules mandating that everyone jump up and down on Tuesdays would be silly interferences with what each of us wants to do, and rules mandating that everyone profess faith in Christ or Mohammed or Moses, no matter how well intended, would be grave violations of freedom.

But it is very unclear how Smith could possibly bring the formal features of justice together with any particular content. We might say that silly and oppressive rules have been eliminated, as candidates for rules of justice, by the requirement that we seek the minimum number of rules necessary for freedom, but we can't really know which these are unless we can say what freedom is. Can we perhaps rely on a common-sense understanding of freedom? Smith has no philosophical account of freedom, but if he is a common-sense philosopher, as I have suggested (§4), perhaps he doesn't need one. Perhaps we should understand him as relying on our common-sense intuitions that we can be free while lacking many positive goods—free beings presumably need to determine, each for him- or herself, what will *count* as a "positive good"—but that our freedom will be limited or destroyed when others hurt our bodies or goods or prevent us from moving. So the rules of justice, the rules that protect our liberty, ought just to prevent us from what we regard, in common sense, as "real and positive harm."

Even within common sense, however, "real and positive harm" is a vague and contentious phrase. Nor is it likely that Smith could find any implicit principle in common sense that would determine a more precise definition for it, especially if that definition needs to hold across all cultures and historical periods. Unlike Kant or Bentham, Smith does not base ethics on a fundamental principle, from which notions like "harm" might be derived. He uses instead, for justice as for every other virtue, an appeal to the sentiments of the impartial spectator. But sentiments vary widely according to context, as he himself stresses, and it is not usually possible to formulate precisely what the deliverances of the impartial spectator will be in every context. This is, in general, an advantage of Smith's theory. The impartial spectator issues in psychologically astute moral judgments *because* it reflects the nuances of social contexts. But such sensitivity to context makes it hard to see how the impartial spectator could ever provide us with a set of precise laws that hold across all societies.

So we face a dilemma: either leave the attempt to give content to the rules of justice with the vague, but perhaps universally acceptable, gesture that such content should protect the innocent from harm, or try to make that gesture precise at the cost of losing the universal acceptability of the rules we propose. Our notion of justice can either be universally acceptable but imprecise, or precise but not universally acceptable. Or we can let justice prescribe formal conditions on the enforced rules of every society, and give up the hope of finding similar conditions for the content of those rules.

None of these are attractive options, and I don't think Smith clearly endorsed any of them. But if we put together the various things he says on this issue, we might reconstruct his considered position as follows.

1. Justice requires certain formal conditions of the positive laws in all societies: that they be clear, precise, and apply equally to everyone.
2. Justice also ought to have a certain content, corresponding to its form, by which states should enforce only those laws that protect individuals against harm and maximize their liberty. This condition, however, cannot be spelled out in a clear and universally acceptable way.
3. One can therefore demand that every society meet the first condition, but only gesture toward the second one, hoping that over time, and under favorable historical circumstances, the laws of every society will evolve in content toward a minimal set protecting liberty. Exactly which set this is, or whether there is even only one, cannot be determined.
4. Putting (1) together with (2) and (3), we can say that every society ought to carve out for itself a segment of the vague arena of "protecting individuals from harm," or "protecting every individual's liberty," that it can enforce with precise and general rules. (1) is essential if the laws themselves are not to oppress the individuals who live under them, so it takes priority over (2) and (3). It is therefore better for every society to acknowledge that its laws do not perfectly express the content of justice than to try to realize that content more fully at the cost of the form of law.
5. It follows that we can straightforwardly accuse a society of injustice that employs imprecision or lack of generality in its legal system so as to favor

some individuals and harass others (LJ 423, 426), or that harms individuals who, by its own standards, are not deserving of harm, but that it is more appropriate to try to unveil pervasive cultural superstitions, or point out the advantages of a different conception of "harm," when we think the content of a society's legal system is misguided. We might say: When a society's legal system lacks the proper form of justice, or upholds that form in theory but violates it in practice, then the society should itself be able to see the system as unjust. When its system seems to lack the proper content of justice, on the other hand, the society may need to alter other moral concepts before it can see its laws as unjust.

If Smith holds a view along these lines, that would explain why he so often suggests an evolutionary account of how laws come to be invested with a properly just content. Punishments "are gradually mitigated to the proper pitch in the advances of society," he says, which means they sometimes become milder and sometimes more severe (LJ 114, 121, 131, 132); contracts are enforced, as they always by natural right should be, only quite late in the history of every society (98, 472); and it takes a very sophisticated society to begin to give proper protection to people wrongly accused of a crime (119, 121–2). To be sure, Smith sees the evolutionary process here as working its way toward the *right* content for justice—he is not a relativist—but he has no resource for distinguishing between the "right" and the merely "historically conditioned" responses of an impartial spectator, and he shies away from ever laying out principles for determining this right content. In any case, his method allows convention and history a more essential role in even the basic principles of jurisprudence than he seemed to want, when he described his ambitions at the end of TMS.

41. Smith's Critical Jurisprudence in LJ and WN

We said at the beginning of this chapter that Smith seems to have wanted a doctrine of natural jurisprudence in good part because he wanted to criticize some of his own society's laws and institutions as unjust. Natural jurisprudence would provide a clear moral basis for political economy: good political economies would rest on and promote just laws and institutions.

But the project of developing a detailed natural jurisprudence failed, I have argued, leaving Smith with some universal formal conditions on any system of justice, and not much more than vague gestures in the direction of "protecting liberty" and "avoiding harm" as guidelines to the universal content of justice. To what extent, then, could he still use natural jurisprudence when he wanted to criticize his nation's political economy? To what extent was a critical jurisprudence still available to him, as a tool for critical, and not just descriptive, political economy?

Well, according to principle (5) in my reconstruction above, Smith had tools for directly criticizing the form of a society's legal system and for indirectly criticizing the content of its laws, by way of moral values that the society itself already holds. This seems to be exactly what he does when criticizing policies and institutions in LJ and WN. When he criticizes legal systems in LJ, whether in his own nation or elsewhere, he rarely makes direct use of the feelings of the impartial spectator that are supposed to provide the basis for natural jurisprudence. Rather, he acknowledges that systems allowing for polygamy and unrestricted divorce, for example, are not really unjust since all the participants in the systems know what they are getting into when they marry; their reasonable expectations are not violated. As a whole, however, the systems make both the women and the men involved in them miserable and are therefore "very inconsistent with a well-regulated police" (LJ 150). Similarly, he accuses the custom of entails of being "absurd in the highest degree," argues that it does not follow from a proper respect for the dead, and shows how it conflicts with the economic interests of society—but he does not call it unjust (LJ 70–71). He does introduce his attack on primogeniture by calling it "contrary to nature, to reason, and to justice" (LJ 49), but in the course of carrying out the attack he is content to point out the hardships imposed by that institution, rather than describing those hardships as justiciable injury. Even as regards slavery, which clearly inflicts unmerited pain and obstruction of liberty on individuals, he prefers to bring out the inconveniences of the system than to stress its injustice. Smith's jurisprudence is thus critical and not merely descriptive, as Haakonssen has argued (SL chapter 6), but the criticism, especially when directed to the content rather than the form of a legal system, tends to be immanent, showing how institutions or laws conflict with purposes already held by the society in which they exist, rather than transcendent, appealing to a natural standard of justice beyond that society's values.[19]

This reluctance to characterize the content of laws and institutions as unjust continues into WN. Smith again brings out the foolishness of primogeniture and entail (WN 383–4, 423), this time without once using the word "unjust," and condemns slavery, in the harshest language, as an expensive way of catering to "the pride of man" (386–90, 586–7), but never quite calls it "unjust." (He does say that it rests on "violence" (387), however, and that is a term he usually associates with injustice.[20]) Monopolies, he says, artificially raise the price of goods and labor (78–9), are "a great enemy to good management" (163), and lead to an inefficient investment of a nation's resources (608, 628–34); he does not say they are unjust.[21]

He does, however, describe monopolies that serve as rulers over distant countries as almost always exercising power "unjustly, . . . capriciously, [and] cruelly" (WN 754; see also 635–8). "Folly and injustice seem to have been the principles which presided over" the entire European enterprise of establishing colonies in Asia and the Americas: "the folly of hunting after gold and silver mines, and the injustice of coveting the possession of a country whose harmless natives, far from having ever injured the people of Europe, had received the first adventurers with every mark of kindness and hospitality" (588). Smith freely hurls the words "injustice" or "oppression" at the behavior of European colonists toward the native inhabitants of the countries in which they settled (589, 626, 636, 754). Why is he comfortable using the term here, while avoiding it in the condemnation of primogeniture, entail, monopoly privileges, and slavery? Well, in the first place, here the harm done by the acts he has in mind—acts of outright theft and murder, along with the use of law to benefit a ruling population at the expense of their subjects—is much more severe and obvious than the harm done by primogeniture, entails, and monopoly privileges. But the harm done by slavery is equally severe and obvious, so that cannot be the whole reason for the difference in language. I think the rest of that difference is accounted for by the fact that, to condemn the evils of European colonists toward natives, Smith need not make any controversial remarks about the content of justice. What was wrong with such behavior was unjust according to every conception of justice his readers may have held.[22] Calling slavery unjust was another matter. He needed a detailed theory of justice to persuade his readers of that, and he had no such theory.

Smith is also generous with the label "unjust" for various sorts of restrictions on the poor. Apprenticeship laws, which restrict entry into many professions, are "a manifest encroachment upon the just liberty both of the workman, and of those who might be disposed to employ him" (WN 138). The 1662 law of settlement enabled parishes to expel laborers who might become a charge upon them, but this is "[t]o remove a man who has committed no misdemeanour from the parish where he chuses to reside," which is "an evident violation of natural liberty and justice" (157). When Smith decries violations of natural liberty and justice in WN, he likes those violations to be "evident" ones. Or at least he likes to *make them out as* evident. As it happens, it was far from evident to everyone that the Statute of Apprenticeship and laws of settlement were unjust, but it was part of the most widely shared conceptions of justice in England (a) that property in material things was founded upon labor, and (b) that expulsion from one's home was a form of criminal punishment. From (a), Smith extrapolates the claim that property in labor itself must be yet more deeply rooted than property in material things: "The property which every man has in his own labour, as it is the original foundation of all other property, so it is the most sacred and inviolable" (138). He then uses this fundamental property in one's labor to oppose the Statute of Apprenticeship, and to oppose other laws restricting people's "natural liberty to exercise what species of industry they please" (470, 529–30, 539, 582). Similarly, from (b) Smith infers that the law of settlement was a form of unjust punishment. In both cases, his strategy is to suggest that a particular application of the concept of injustice follows directly from the understanding of that concept his readers already share. What Smith does *not* do is challenge that shared understanding, or try to ground it in more fundamental moral principles.

I think that Smith, realizing that his project of developing a full-scale natural jurisprudence was internally flawed, decided in WN to finesse the issue and write the book with a conception of justice that his contemporaries would take as uncontroversial. Principles of justice certainly play a major role in WN. But the fact that Smith includes in WN no discussion of what justice, liberty, or even property consists in, and that his appeals to justice, and to property rights, always rely on a conventional notion of justice, should give pause to those who have tried to claim originality for Smith's account of justice, or to claim that WN should be read with the distinctive features of that account in mind. There are many new and controversial notions in WN, but the claims he makes about justice are not among them.

This point is reinforced by the fact that Smith often couples "justice" and "utility" when he defends a point, and especially when he suggests that justice demands of us an act that may look contrary to society's utilitarian interests. In one passage, Smith first justifies a high standard of living for "servants, labourers, and workmen" as something that increases the "conveniency" of society, and then adds, "It is but equity . . . that they who feed, cloath and lodge the whole body of the people, should have such a share of the produce of their own labour as to be themselves tolerably well fed, cloathed and lodged" (WN 96). A similar coupling occurs when he criticizes laws restricting the exportation of corn. A free trade in corn, he argues first, will help palliate dearths and prevent famines. Then he adds: "To hinder, besides, the farmer from sending his goods at all times to the best market is evidently to sacrifice the ordinary laws of justice to an idea of publick utility, . . . an act . . . which can be pardoned only in cases of the most urgent necessity" (539). Earlier in the same section, he says that laws attempting to regulate the activities of wholesalers are "evident violations of natural liberty, and therefore unjust"—but in the same sentence he calls them "as impolitick as they [are] unjust" (530). That justice, and the liberty it protects, greatly encourages economic production, is of course a central theme of Smith's (see, *inter alia*, 284–5, 345, 393, 405, 470–71, 540, 910). What is unjust is impolitick and contrary to conveniency; and what is contrary to conveniency is, often, unjust. Most of the time, utility and justice do not come apart enough in WN for us to know which Smith would choose if they conflicted. On the one occasion in which he does pose a conflict between the two, he plumps for utility over justice. Calling for a restriction of bank notes to sums of five pounds and up, Smith concedes that such a law would be "a manifest violation of . . . natural liberty," yet says that it would nonetheless be justified:

> [T]hose exertions of the natural liberty of a few individuals, which might endanger the security of the whole society, are, and ought to be, restrained by the laws of all governments; of the most free, as well as of the most despotical. The obligation of building party walls, in order to prevent the communication of fire, is a violation of natural liberty, exactly of the same kind with the regulations of the banking trade which are here proposed. (WN 324)

To be sure, the exception Smith here proposes is pressed upon the law, in his opinion, by necessity, and Smith follows a long tradition of jurisprudence in holding that justice itself allows necessity to rewrite the ordinary laws of justice (see §53 below). But the fact that in this one case in which there is even a prima facie conflict between justice and utility Smith opts, prima facie, for utility over justice, should give us pause if we want to argue that he brings justice in as a *constraint* on the pursuit of utility, that he rules out policies, on grounds of justice, that he might otherwise have welcomed. No such position is clearly stated in WN, only the much less informative view that the long-term pursuit of utility almost always requires acting in accordance with laws of justice, that the two concerns rarely diverge.[23]

So Smith's views on justice do play a role in WN, but it is a background role, not the foundational one that he may originally have wanted them to play. They help underwrite his argument that governments should proceed by way of a minimal number of clear, precise, general laws, rather than by giving ad hoc powers to local administrators. They also help bring out the importance of human liberty, and the great wrong done to slaves, to native peoples in distant countries, and to the poor, by policies violating their liberty. But the dependence on convention that Smith was unable to eliminate from justice led him to avoid appealing to "natural jurisprudence." Instead of invoking general principles of justice that should hold in all times and nations, he argued against policies and institutions primarily by showing their "inconvenience" or by invoking moral notions that he knew to be already widely accepted among his readers.

CHAPTER NINE

Property Rights

42. Property as Central to Justice

We have seen that Smith succeeds in justifying absolute principles about the *form* of any legal system, and in gesturing toward a vaguely defined realm of liberty and security from harm that every legal system ought to protect, but that this is compatible with systems of justice that have very different content, systems that protect different sorts of marital, contractual, and property arrangements. It is the last of these issues that I want to stress now. Even someone unpersuaded that justice in general has an ineliminably conventional component for Smith will have to grant that Smith allows systems of property to vary enormously in accordance with the historical circumstances of each society.[1] But property rights are the central concern of justice, for Smith as for the jurisprudential tradition before him, and raise the most difficult questions about the relationship between justice and political economy. So even if it were possible to find a purely natural basis for some principles of justice, allowing convention to gnaw at the roots of property will leave us with little guidance, from natural jurisprudence, on how to settle the fundamental controversies of political economy.

Property is "the grand fund of all dispute," says Smith (LJ 208), and it is one overarching purpose of justice to settle disputes. Hume had argued that establishing rules for property was practically the *sole* purpose of justice, since violent disputes arise primarily when people attempt to take material possessions from one another. Our self-love, and love for our near and dear, could rarely lead us into conflict with other people were it not for competition over material goods:

> There are three different species of goods, which we are possess'd of; the internal satisfaction of our mind, the external advantages of our body, and the enjoyment of such possessions as we have acquir'd by our industry and good fortune. We are perfectly secure in the enjoyment of the first. The second may be ravish'd from us, but can be of no advantage to him who deprives us of them. The last only are both expos'd to the violence of others, and may be transferr'd without suffering any loss or alteration; while at the same time, there is not a sufficient quantity of them to supply every one's desires and necessities. . . . *[E]nvy* and *revenge*, tho' pernicious, . . . operate only by intervals, and are directed against particular persons, whom we consider as our superiours or enemies. Th[e] avidity alone, of acquiring goods and possessions for

ourselves and our nearest friends, is insatiable, perpetual, universal, and directly destructive of society. (T 488, 491–2)

Hence property and justice co-arise, for Hume: "The same artifice gives rise to both" (T 491). Without a system of justice, there will be no property. Without property, there will be no need for justice:

> No one can doubt, that the convention for the distinction of property, and for the stability of possession, is of all circumstances the most necessary to the establishment of human society, and that after the agreement for the fixing and observing of this rule, there remains little or nothing to be done towards settling a perfect harmony and concord. (T 491)

Smith does not go as far as this—he regards injury to life, body, and reputation as subjects for justice quite independent of injury to property, and he allows, more than Hume does, for dark, nonrational passions to motivate such injuries even where no property is at stake—but he does grant that conflicts over property will be by far the main concern of any system of justice. In a passage that seems designed to echo, and mildly revise, the ones from Hume's *Treatise* cited above, Smith writes:

> Men who have no property can injure one another only in their persons or reputations. But when one man kills, wounds, beats, or defames another, though he to whom the injury is done suffers, he who does it receives no benefit. It is otherwise with the injuries to property. The benefit of the person who does the injury is often equal to the loss of him who suffers it. Envy, malice, or resentment, are the only passions which can prompt one man to injure another in his person or reputation. But the greater part of men are not very frequently under the influence of these passions; and the very worst men are so only occasionally. As their gratification too, how agreeable soever it may be to certain characters, is not attended with any real or permanent advantage, it is in the greater part of men commonly restrained by prudential considerations. Men may live together in society with some tolerable degree of security, though there is no civil magistrate to protect them from the injustice of those passions. (WN 709)

It is not true, as Hume had said, that the absence or settlement of disputes over property would allow for "perfect harmony and concord" in society, but people would at least live together "with some tolerable degree of security." So justice is concerned centrally, if not solely, with providing rules to minimize or eliminate struggles over property.

Now one reason rules for property raise so much greater difficulty than rules defining and prohibiting murder or bodily injury is that "property" can mean many different things. The paradigm case of possession, and the one from which all Anglophone accounts of property after Locke tend to begin, is the scenario in which a lone individual enters a hitherto unowned forest and plucks an apple from the trees growing wildly there. Practically no one, not even a die-hard Marxist, will deny the right to possession in this case. But suppose now that the lone individual returns to society and gives his apple to someone he loves. Does she have the right to pass it on to someone she loves better than him, or does the act of gift constrain her ownership of what she has received? Or suppose our apple-picker, on return to society, exchanges his apple for a small tool—while hiding the fact that the apple has a worm in it, or while manipulating or misleading his partner in the exchange into undervaluing the tool. Does he now properly "own" the tool, or does the tool-maker really still own it and have a right to take it back and throw away the apple? Suppose we say he does not properly own the tool, but the person with the rotten apple never complains, and our apple-picker holds on to his embezzled tool for many years. Does he then acquire a right to it, by virtue of long possession, or does the person cheated out of the tool have a right to reclaim it at any time, no matter how long he put up, uncomplainingly, with the original injustice?

These are but some of the issues that make it difficult to determine what "property" means. Possession by one's own efforts is one thing; possession by way of gift is another; possession by way of exchange is still another; and possession by long occupation or use (what the natural law tradition called "prescription") belongs to yet a fourth category. And we have not yet even mentioned possession by way of contract, "accession" (close connection with the things we already own), or "succession" (inheritance), let alone the problems, still debated today, of what exactly people can be said to own when they buy stock in a company, invent a machine, or create a work of art. If our apple-picker exchanges his apple for a *promise* of a tool, to be delivered within three weeks, what rights does he have over the tool-maker should the latter fall sick and be unable to complete the work? If he throws the apple casually aside, does he have a right to the apple tree that might happen, through no further effort of his own, to spring up from the seeds? And if he dies, does his mere request, at the moment of death, that Joe Schmoe acquire ownership over all his apples rightly transfer possession of those apples to Joe Schmoe? If he says nothing at the point of death, do his next of kin automatically have more right to his apples than anybody else? (And if so, *which* next of kin: his wife, his children, his brothers and sisters, . . . ?) Finally, apples are at least concrete items with a ready use, so we can determine in fairly uncontroversial ways what they are, when someone has picked them, and what counts as "making use" of them. It is far less easy to say what counts as the relevant new idea in an invention or work of art, when someone has created it, and what sorts of production or performance properly count as "making use" of that idea.

Smith is not only aware of all these complexities in the notion of property: he stresses, throughout his jurisprudence, that notions like prescription, inheritance, and copyright laws have become part of what is considered "property" by way of complicated historical processes. "All laws which extend property beyond the person of the possessor," says Smith, "are of later introduction than those which constitute property, and are not at all necessary to its existence" (LJ 309). In hunter-gatherer societies, "property begins and ends with possession, and they seem scarce to have any idea of any thing as their own which is not about their own bodies" (LJ 460). The "idea of property . . . is further extended" among shepherds, and "receives its greatest extension" when societies turn to agriculture (loc. cit.). Property in land is an idea that shepherds and hunters never have: "An Arab or a Tartar will drive his flocks over an immense country without supposing a single grain of sand in it his own" (loc. cit.). And accession, prescription, and succession are extensions of property that would not occur to the members of a pre-agrarian society. Moreover, the rules for establishing these extensions are fairly arbitrary: "Nature has fixed no period for prescription, and accordingly it varies according to the stability of property in a country" (LJ 462). Many of the rules of inheritance are "very whimsicall" (LJ 62). Indeed, succession by way of testaments is in general "one of the greatest extentions of property we can conceive" (LJ 38), and tends to wring tortuous justifications out of philosophers of law (LJ 63). In many respects, then, Smith not only admits but emphasizes the conventionality of laws of property, the fact that they come about in response to the circumstances, needs, and traditions of each society, rather than following from some basic law of nature.

But this is not to say that Smith considers systems of property to be *entirely* conventional and historical, to have *no* basis in nature. Hume comes close to such a position. Justice demands "*that possession be stable*" (T 502, emphasis in original; see also 497), but it does not demand any specific regime of stable possession. Possession can be stable under very different systems of property: under both capitalist and socialist ones, for example. As long as we all know, for certain and in advance, that no one can own capital goods or inherit property, we will not even attempt to challenge the state's right to these goods, and a fully socialist state can thereby have as stable a regime of property as a fully capitalist one. On Hume's account, justice gives us no intrinsic reason to prefer either of these regimes to the other,[2] or indeed to prefer any rule governing possession, no matter how silly, over any other—as long as that rule settles disputes over property and thereby enables possession to be stable. Hume gently mocks, as we shall see, the standard rules that jurists have given for just possession, finding in them mostly the work of fancy or imagination rather than reason. Smith does not follow him this far along the road of equating property with artifice. He acknowledges, at the beginning of his lectures on jurisprudence, that there is no clear derivation of our right to property from self-evident principles. The "original of the greatest part of . . . natural rights . . . need not be explained," he says—it is "evident to reason" that wounds, restraints on liberty, and defamation of character are wrong. "The only case where the origin of naturall rights is not altogether plain, is in that of property"; only the basic principles of property do not "at first appear evident" (LJ 13). But the point here is that the derivation of the "original" of property is not immediately *evident*, not that there is no such derivation, and Smith proceeds to give us an account of how the "original" of property, its basic or core notion, is in fact a natural right. This basic or core notion will not go beyond present possession, but it will establish that some sort of ownership is part of the natural liberty all of us want from our societies, that to have at least certain of the objects we call "ours" taken away from us constitutes an injury analogous to bodily wounds, physical restraint, or slander. I shall argue that Smith's justification for a natural right to present possession displays the conventionalism that I have attributed to his entire theory of justice, and in any case present possession does not, even in Smith's eyes, justify the vast array of rights and claims that make up a sophisticated system of ownership, but it would be unfair to suggest that Smith himself considered the "original," the basic or core notion, of property to be purely a matter of convention.

43. Utilitarian Accounts of Property

One more preliminary, before we turn to Smith's account of property's "original." It is crucial to bear in mind that to call protecting property a part of justice means for Smith that property is an essential part of an *individual's liberty*, not that it contributes to a *society's utility*. Justice in general for Smith is something that may not be sacrificed "to an idea of public utility, to a sort of reasons of state" except where there is "the most urgent necessity" (WN 539). Smith argued in WN, as we have seen, that following the rules of justice would generally promote social utility as well, but he never believed that the main *purpose* of laws of justice was to contribute to social utility; their direct and primary purpose is instead always to protect individuals. This is indeed a point of great importance to Smith, for which he argued against the nascent utilitarianism of Hutcheson and Hume. Thus when Smith himself gives utilitarian arguments for certain rules of property, he is not, on his own terms, showing how they are called for by justice.

This needs to be said because Smith does in fact give utilitarian justifications for some rules of property. Short-term copyright protection for authors he calls "an encouragement to the labours of learned men" (LJ 83; cf. WN 754), and he says it may on occasion be reasonable to grant a joint stock company temporary monopoly privileges over some branch of dangerous trade so as to recompense the merchants involved for taking risks from which "the publick is afterwards to reap the benefit" (WN 754). He also says repeatedly that the protection of individual property rights in general is a spur to industriousness and essential to long-term growth. When people "are secure of enjoying the fruits of their industry, they naturally exert it to better their condition" (WN 405). We may presume then that Smith would agree with the utilitarian arguments of his teacher Hutcheson, and friend Hume, for private property:

> Whatever method . . . is necessary to encourage a general industry must also be necessary for the support of mankind; now without a property ensuing upon labour employed in occupying and cultivating things fitted for the support of life, neither our self-love, nor any of the tender affections, would excite men to industry. . . . [N]o man would employ his labours unless he were assured of the fruits of them at his own disposal; other ways, all the most active and diligent would be a perpetual prey, and a set of slaves, to the slothful and worthless. (Hutcheson, SI II.v, p. 150)

Render possessions ever so equal, men's different degrees of art, care, and industry will immediately break that equality. Or if you check these virtues, you reduce society to the most extreme indigence; and instead of preventing want and beggary in a few, render it unavoidable to the whole community. . . . Who sees not . . . that whatever is produced or improved by a man's art or industry ought, for ever, to be secured to him, in order to give encouragement to such *useful* habits and accomplishments? That the property ought also to descend to children and relations, for the same *useful* purpose? (Hume, E 194–5)

These are very old arguments for individual property, to be found in Aristotle and Aquinas,[3] as well as in practically every thinker in the natural-law tradition after Aquinas. Smith agrees that people will not be motivated to work unless their property is protected: "When people find themselves every moment in danger of being robbed of all they possess, they have no motive to be industrious" (LJ 522).[4] He does not, however, offer this as a *justification* for property rights: The motivational function of private property is for him a secondary effect of property, not its ground. The justification of a right, for Smith, must lie in the just claims of the individual whose right it is, not in any good that the guarantee of such rights does for society as a whole. The boilerplate natural-law arguments for the utility of individual property rights are thus something Smith offers independently of the arguments he gives for why such property rights are, in themselves, justifiable. Far from emphasizing them, as he is commonly thought to have done, Smith distances himself from utilitarian arguments for property rights.

And he is smart to do so. For utilitarian justifications of laws of property, or of any other laws of justice, are slippery, and need not support the absolute protection of individual liberty that Smith wants from such laws. If, contrary to the empirical claims of Hume and Hutcheson, the system of private property, despite its incentives to industry, on the whole makes people more miserable than some communal arrangement would do, then the justification for that system falls away. It likewise falls away if clever political scientists and psychologists are someday able to dream up a way of motivating people under systems of communal ownership, or if technology someday allows us to produce most of what we want with little or no effort on the part of live human beings. Hutcheson himself acknowledges that utilitarian considerations alone might lead one to favor a centrally controlled system of distributing goods, rather than the system of private property, if only "a wise political constitution could compel all men to bear their part in labour, and then make a wisely proportioned distribution of all that was acquired, according to the indigence, or merit of the citizens" (*System* II.vi.6, 322). He considers it very unlikely that such a constitution could actually come about, but leaves this, as he should, an empirical matter, not a matter of principle. What might rule out such a constitution even if it were possible are arguments from "natural liberty," not utility. It is these arguments that Smith wants to emphasize; only these reasons, not utilitarian ones, could underwrite an absolute and universal justification of a right to property. Smith, like Hutcheson, attempts to draw them out of a famous passage in Locke.

44. Locke, Hutcheson, and Hume on "Original" Ownership

Locke's justification of property is complex, and it has utilitarian elements.[5] But it was of the utmost importance to Locke to argue, contra Hobbes and others, that at their root property rights are not dependent on the institution of political society, that the practice of claiming goods as one's own rests on pre-political principles. The demonstration of this included a passage that became one of Locke's best-known contributions to moral and political philosophy:

> Though the earth and all inferior creatures be common to all men, yet every man has a property in his own person; this nobody has any right to but himself. The labour of his body and the work of his hands, we may say, are properly his. Whatsoever then he removes out of the state that nature hath provided and left it in, he hath mixed his labour with, and joined to it something that is his own, and thereby makes it his property. . . . He that is nourished by the acorns he picked up under an oak, or the apples he gathered from the trees in the wood, has certainly appropriated them to himself. Nobody can deny but the nourishment is his. I ask, then, when did they begin to be his? when he digested? or when he ate? or when he boiled? or when he brought them home? or when he picked them up? And it is plain, if the first gathering made them not his, nothing else could. That labour put a distinction between them and common; that added something to them more than nature, the common mother of all, had done; and so they become his private right. (ST V.27–8)

No one needs to consent to this original act of acquisition, Locke adds: "If such a consent . . . was necessary, man had starved, notwithstanding the plenty God had given him." So the original act of claiming property precedes all social intercourse; property precedes society, and the political and legal institutions protecting property merely ratify the presocial activity of acquisition that we need to engage in to make use of God's plenty. This activity of acquisition is presocial in another sense as well: social norms are unnecessary to determine when it has taken place. In each of Locke's examples, here and in the following few paragraphs, property is claimed by means of a mechanical interaction between people or animals (already owned by people) and other matter, not by means of such intrinsically social acts as the statement, "This is mine." Locke speaks of apples and acorns being gathered and eaten, of "the grass my horse has bit, the turfs my servant has cut, and the ore I have digged," of water drawn into a pitcher, of a deer being killed. In each of these cases, a human being or animal changes the physical state of a piece of matter. Social actions may of course *recognize* these physical changes, but that recognition does not in any way *constitute* the change. The words, or other social acts, by which we recognize them are not essential to the change actually taking place. The act that establishes property is a transaction between two types of physical matter, between two bodies, a literal "mixing" of the exertions of human bodies with other material objects. In one example, Locke notes that a hunter is thought to have property in a hare even when he is just pursuing her and has not yet caught her, but he explains this by way of the fact that the hunter "has employed so much labour . . . to find and pursue her": his labor "mixes" with her running away and thereby "remove[s] her from the state of nature wherein she was common" (ST V.30).

We can see the importance of this point by contrasting Locke with the version of Locke that appears in Hutcheson. In his *Short Introduction to Moral Philosophy*, Hutcheson begins by saying that it is "trifling to imagine that property is any physical quality or bond between a man and certain goods" (SI vi, 152); in his *System of Moral Philosophy*, he says that difficulties about the nature of property arise from the "confused imagination" that property is a "physical quality or relation" (SMP II.v, 318). Nevertheless, he grants that first occupation gives a right to property. One who "first occupies any of the spontaneous fruits of the earth," like acorns or apples, or who "by any act of labour" makes things hitherto unused more available for human use, is "deemed justly the proprietor for these reasons" (SI 152). Labor sinks to but one mode of "occupation" here. That is not Hutcheson's main point, however. More important is the justification he gives for his Lockean conclusion: that the desires that go into first occupation in these cases are "innocent" ones and that it is morally evil, a sign of malevolence, arbitrarily to block other people's innocent desires:

> [T]he first impulses of nature toward supporting ourselves, or those who are dear to us, point out the right of the first occupant to such things as are fit for present use. The obstructing this innocent design must appear morally evil, as it is ill-natured to hinder any man to take his natural support from the things granted for this purpose by God and nature.

> We all feel a sense of liberty within us, a strong desire of acting according to our own inclinations, and to gratify our own affections, whether selfish, or generous: we have a deep resentment of any obstruction given to these natural desires and endeavours; . . . and we must disapprove it as unkind and cruel, where no important publick interest requires it, whether we meet with it ourselves or see others thus opposed in their innocent designs. From these strong feelings in our hearts we discover the right of property that each one has in the fruits of his own labour. (SI II.vi.v, 317–18, 320)

Moral goodness is in all cases the expression of benevolence, for Hutcheson, and moral evil of malevolence. Accordingly, he justifies the "original" of individual property by saying that the initial claim of an individual to a hitherto unclaimed bit of matter is good because a benevolent spectator will approve of it.[6] And the spectator will approve because the *motivation* for the claim is at worst innocent and at best (when designed for the support of "those who are dear to us") morally good. So what makes good an individual claim to property is an intention, not a physical transaction, and its goodness is determined by the bestowal of approval by other, well-meaning human beings. The claim has no moral worth outside of society; it makes no sense where isolated individuals move among apples and turf and deer. It remains true that we have a right to the "fruits of our labor," but the emphasis has now been shifted from the physical act of labor to the intentions motivating that labour, and the feelings that those intentions will inspire in a benevolent observer. Indeed, Hutcheson gives examples of first claims to property in which *only* an intention, not a body, "acts on" a chunk of matter: "One who has fitted out ships for a descent upon unoccupied lands, towards the occupation of which no previous labour has been employed by others, would be wronged if another hearing of the design made greater dispatch and prevented him, and afterwards refused to make a division" (SMP II.7.ii). Where "the design" of someone else is previously known, "'tis immoral and unjust for another, without necessity, to prevent or intercept his advantage" (SMP II.6.v, p. 318n; see also SI vi, p. 153).

But designs or intentions, unlike physical acts, cannot be known by an unsocialized, purely "natural" human being. I signal that I am fitting out ships for an expedition to unoccupied lands by way of a series of conventional gestures—announcements, contracts, forms—and by acts, like buying provisions at merchant-marine stores, that can only be understood by someone who understands the language and practices of the society from which I am leaving. Many philosophers today would argue, more generally, that intentions cannot so much as exist without being couched in language, or some similar symbolic system. Intentions just *are* potential gestures to other intentional beings, potential moves in a communicative game. Unlike animal passions or dreams or mere mental driftings and musings, intentions come into existence only when they are capable of being signaled to some other intentional being. We say that a person has not yet *formed* an intention when he or she is incapable of communicating any intention to us. We will not even say of ourselves that we have formed an intention unless we can put into words what that intention is. It follows that the central act in the acquisition of property, on Hutcheson's account, *is already a social one*, not a purely physical transaction that requires only protection by society. At least implicitly, property for Hutcheson can be acquired only within a social group, a group of interacting language-users who can recognize and approve of one another's intentions; it is not a presocial feature of human life.

What is implicit in Hutcheson will be explicit in Smith. But before Smith came Hume, who did not accept even the tempered naturalistic account of property to be found in Hutcheson. Not only is it "trifling to imagine that property is any physical quality or bond between a man and certain goods," for Hume; it is trifling to imagine that any configuration of our natural moral sentiments gives rise to rights of property. The motivations to perform acts of justice, and to approve of such acts, are "artificial," for Hume, not natural, and the motives that lead us to claim and respect property co-arise, as we have already seen, with the artifice of justice (T 491). Accordingly, the relationship of property comes about "from human conventions" (489–91). Moreover, unlike both Locke and Hutcheson, Hume famously calls the state of nature "a mere fiction"

(493).[7] Since the whole purpose of setting up the state of nature, in Locke and Hutcheson, is to determine the natural rights that people have before entering society, and since property is a prominent such right for Hutcheson and practically the sole one of interest to Locke, this dismissal of the state of nature also serves to point up the artificiality of property.

And when Hume comes to the rules that determine who properly owns which goods, he utterly rejects Locke's notion that one can "mix" one's labor with any material things (T 505n). Occupation or first possession, he says, is a good rule for determining the ownership of certain things only because property must be made stable somehow and "first possession always engages the attention most" (505).[8] It is an arbitrary feature of our imagination that leads us to associate ownership with first possession, and the other rules that determine property are also "principally fix'd by the imagination, or the more frivolous properties of our thought and conception" (504n). Hume says that "we never shall find satisfaction" if we look to reason or the "public interest" to settle questions about what rules should establish property (506n). The whole subject seems indeed so philosophically embarrassing to him that he relegates most of his discussion of it to a series of footnotes. Locke's plucked apple and Hutcheson's unoccupied lands both appear in these notes; Hume endorses neither the principle that labor establishes possession nor the principle that intention establishes possession, but sees both as connections in the imagination or "fancy" that people rely on because they need *some* relationship on which to base possession. Sometimes he seems to be mocking all philosophical debates over where possession begins or ends:

> A wild boar, that falls into our snares, is deem'd to be in our possession, if it be impossible for him to escape. But what do we mean by impossible? How do we separate this impossibility from an improbability? And how distinguish that exactly from a probability? (T 506, in the main text)

> Suppose a *German*, a *Frenchman*, and a *Spaniard* to come into a room, where there are plac'd upon the table three bottles of wine, *Rhenish*, *Burgundy*, and *Port*; and suppose they shou'd fall a quarrelling about the division of them; a person, who was chosen for umpire, wou'd naturally, to shew his impartiality, give every one the product of his own country: And this from a principle, which, in some measure, is the source of those laws of nature, that ascribe property to occupation, prescription, and accession (T 509–10, in the footnotes)

Behind the flippancy is a serious point. Hume insists that the relationships we are inclined to regard as determining possession depend on the imagination, and that the factors working on the imagination "run so insensibly and gradually into each other, that 'tis impossible to give them any precise bounds or termination" (T 506n). We can *draw* sharp lines distinguishing these cases, if we like, if sharp distinctions help us settle disputes and keep the peace, but there are no sharp lines defining possession to be found "out there," in nature or reason. This is very similar, and I think not accidentally so, to what he had said, much earlier in the *Treatise*, about personal identity. In his account of the identity we ascribe to our minds or selves, he had similarly found a notion brought forth by the imagination, with blurred borders, which is a source of confusion and error, and where we try vainly to cut through the confusion and error by imposing on it some principle of reason. There, too, he saw different principles working on the imagination, sometimes at cross-purposes (see especially T 257–8), and there too he described us as cutting through the dilemmas that arise from these different principles by way of convenient fictions. The identity we attribute to objects in general, and especially to our minds, is "only a fictitious one," and it is founded, like all fictions, in the workings of the imagination rather than in any principle of reason (T 259). Some of these workings are exactly the same ones that produce notions of property. We allow identity to a changing object in accordance with the proportion between the size of the change and the size of the object changed (so we think of an object as "the same" if it undergoes a relatively small change, but not if it undergoes a relatively large one), and we allow a small object to come with the ownership of a large one by way of "accession," but not a large one to come with the ownership of a small one (T 255–6, 510–11n). We attribute identity to objects where we see but gradual and insensible change, and we attribute property where lands bordering upon rivers "insensibly and imperceptibly" change by way of "alluvion" (T 256, 511n). The fact that our thoughts cause one another—"one thought chaces another, and draws after it a third" (T 261)—helps us attribute identity to the self; the fact that parents cause their children to exist helps explain the transmission of property via "succession" (T 511–13 and 513n1). And when Hume discusses both the notion of identity and the notion of property, the dependence he finds on principles of imagination rather than principles of reason leads him to dismiss the standard philosophical debates over that notion. "[T]he nice and subtile questions concerning personal identity can never possibly be decided" (T 262), he says; in very similar language, he declares that disputes among philosophers about property are "impossible to be decided" (T 507–8n; see also 504n, 506).

The parallel between personal identity and property is no coincidence. "Property" is a term we use for things owned by a self; it consists in the things that are "proper to" a self. If there is no self, there can be no property, and if the self is socially constructed, so, *a fortiori*, is property. Hume rejects views of Locke in both sections of the *Treatise* we have been considering, denying in Part I that there is a substantial self to be found by way of the reflexive acts of consciousness (vs. Locke's account of the self in the *Essay Concerning Human Understanding*) and in Part III that there is a substantial notion of ownership to be found by way of the "mixing" of consciously driven activity with material stuff in the world (vs. Locke's account of property in the *Second Treatise*). He does not quite say that the identity of human minds is a consequence of social conventions, but the notion of selfhood as something the imagination creates to serve various purposes at least opens the way to seeing ascriptions of selfhood as arising from social interests. Then the self would be as conventional as property. Even if we don't go this far, taking away the notion of a substantial self makes it impossible for property to *attach* to anyone, for there to be any essential relationship between things and persons. Without a substantial self, there is nothing for property to be but a set of conventions, justifiable, if at all, in terms of the interests or convenience of society.

45. Smith on "Original" Ownership

Thus we have a Lockean basis for property slowly getting transformed, at the hands of the Scots, from a "natural" relationship between an individual and the material world into a relationship that gets *constructed* between individuals and the material world by the society in which those individuals live. When we turn to Smith, I believe we can best understand him as retreating from the radical conventionalism of Hume without quite returning to the naturalism of Hutcheson, let alone of Locke. Smith tries to see property as socially structured but not fully invented by societies. Like both Hutcheson and Hume, he abjures talk of "mixing" one's labor with material objects, and like Hume, he allows that our perception of our selves comes always via society (TMS 110–13). But he does not endorse Hume's full deconstruction of the self, and seems throughout his moral writings to take for granted a substantial notion of personal identity, albeit one mediated by social interactions.[9] Correspondingly, he tries to develop an account of property by which a reasonable basis can be found for some kinds of possession within the social nature of the human being.

To get at this, let us begin with Smith's treatment of the hunting example Hume discussed at T 506, quoted above. Locke, Hutcheson, Hume, and Smith all discuss the question of whether a hunter has property in his prey before he actually catches it. Locke, recognizing that the hunter's labor has not yet made any mark on the hare he is hunting, nevertheless says that the hare "is thought to be his . . . during the chase," because the labor employed by the hunter "to find and pursue" the hare marks her out for himself, out of "the state of nature wherein she was [hitherto] common" (ST V.30). He could have strengthened the case for a mixing of labor with the object here by noting that the hunter's labor *has* physically affected the hare, insofar as she is tired out. Hutcheson adds this point for him—"He who *wounded or tired out* any wild creature in the chace, so that it becomes an easy prey, . . . has a property begun, and is wronged by any who intercept his prey, or frustrate his labours" (SI II.7.ii, 325–6, my emphasis)—but the example appears in the middle of one of Hutcheson's paragraphs on the innocence of our designs to acquire goods for ourselves, and on the whole Hutcheson downplays the importance of actual labor in this example. His reason for offering the example is indeed to bring out the fact that property is claimed by one's intentions more than by what one actually does. The hunter is wronged when his innocent intentions to catch the hare are frustrated, regardless of whether he was the first actually to hold the hare in his hands.

Hume contrasts the hunting case with a version of Locke's apple-picker:

> A person, who has hunted a hare to the last degree of weariness, wou'd look upon it as an injustice for another to rush in before him, and seize his prey. But the same person, advancing to pluck an apple, that hangs within his reach, has not reason to complain, if another, more alert, passes him, and takes possession. What is the reason of this difference, but that immobility, not being natural to the hare, but the effect of industry, forms in that case a strong relation with the hunter, which is wanting in the other? (T 506–7n)

Of course, for Hume the "strong relation" in the last sentence is but a relation *in our imaginations*, not in reality, and his point is not to buttress the labor theory of property, but to show how much the principles of property depend on quirks and whims of our fancy. The whim here is an understandable one—immobility is indeed natural to apples and unnatural to hares—but Hume has deliberately constructed the two cases so that the difference between them looks trivial. The cases come in a footnote to the passage about the "wild boar that falls into our snares," where Hume expressly denied that one could use anything other than convention to "mark the precise limits" between the circumstances in which the boar would and would not properly be "deem'd to be in our possession."

Smith, in LJ, denies that either the hare or the boar is properly "mine." He justifies this by assimilating Hume's hare case to Hume's apple case:

> If I was desirous of pulling an apple and had stretched out my hand towards it, but an other who was more nimble comes and pulls it before me, an impartial spectator would conceive this was a very great breach of good manners and civility but would not suppose it an incroachment on property.— . . . But if one should attempt to snatch it out of my hand when I had the actual possession of it, the bystander would immediately agree that my property was incroached on . . . Let us now apply this to the case of the hunters. When I start a hare, I have only a probability of catching it on my side. . . . If one in this case should come and take the game I had started and was in pursuit of, this would appear a great tresspass on the laws of fair hunting; I can not however justly take satisfaction of the transgressor. . . . But if he had violently or theftuously taken from me what I had actually in my possession, this would evidently be an atrocious transgression of the right of property. (LJ 19)

It is interesting that Smith denies a type of property claim that Locke, Hutcheson, and Hume had all accepted, but what is most remarkable about this passage is that Smith bothers to try to find a philosophical settlement for this issue at all. Using Hume's own juxtaposition of examples and thus surely aware of Hume's claim that these cases do not lend themselves to principled settlement, Smith nonetheless goes to great lengths to try to provide an entire schema of reasonable distinctions between breaches of "manners and civility" and breaches of property in both the apple and the hunting cases. Indeed, in shortening the passage for easier reading, I left out yet another variation on both the apple and the hare cases, in which we physically hold the apple or hare for some time, then drop it and someone else grabs it. Smith calls this sort of grabbing "a very heinous affront," "very near to an infringement of property," but, like the first case, not actually a violation of that right. That Smith was willing to enter into the minutiae of these cases, confidently distinguishing what is "very near" to a violation of property rights from what actually crosses that sacred boundary, shows that he did not share Hume's attitude that the entire terrain was beyond or beneath a philosopher's regard. Rather, at least in LJ, he seems to have thought that he had a philosophical principle by which to define the fundamental rules of property.

That principle is the judgment of the impartial spectator, which Smith introduces into Locke's primordial apple-picking scene:

> How [is it] that a man by pulling an apple should be imagined to have a right to that apple and a power of excluding all others from it. . . . From the system [of TMS], you will remember that I told you we may conceive an injury was done one when an impartial spectator would be of opinion he was injured, would join with him in his concern and go along with him when he defended the subject in his possession against any violent attack, or used force to recover what had been thus wrongfully wrested out of his hands. This would be the case in the abovementioned circumstances. The spectator would justify the first possessor in defending and even in avenging himself when injured . . . The cause of this sympathy or concurrence betwixt the spectator and the possessor is, that he enters into his thoughts and concurrs in his opinion that he may form a reasonable expectation of using the fruit . . . The reasonable expectation therefore which the first possessor furnishes is the ground on which the right of property is acquired by occupation. (LJ 17)

As I said earlier, what was implicit in Hutcheson becomes explicit in Smith. Hutcheson rooted property in the innocent or well-meaning "designs" people have when they exercise labor to gain goods for themselves or their loved ones, implicitly appealing to the approval we, as benevolent beings, will have of such intentions. Smith explicitly places an impartial spectator on the scene with the apple-picker and the would-be apple thief. Locke's silent forest, devoid of all human beings but one lone apple-seeker, whose act of gathering fruit will be ratified as "property" only once he returns with his apple to society, becomes in Smith's hands a place where there are already at least three notional people: the apple-picker, one who would do injury to the apple-picker, and an impartial spectator to decide between the two.[10] The virgin forest has become a little social scene, and the possibility of property arises only where there is a possibility of conflicts between people, and of the settlement of such conflicts by impartial spectators—who stand in, as we have seen (§11), for society as a whole. So Smith's primal scene of ownership is not a presocial one. But unlike Hume, he *has* such a primal scene, at least in LJ, which bespeaks a belief that ownership is not a mere creature of the "fancy," that it has roots in emotions to which we are naturally prone, and which we can feel impartially—morally— not just on our own behalf.

Two notes on this difference between Hume and Smith. First, Smith does not accept the sharp distinction between nature and convention or "artifice" that Hume relies on in his account of justice. It is natural to humans to come up with conventions and artifices, certainly natural for us to live in societies, so the fact that property begins to make sense only where there is the language, and shared sentiments, to settle quarrels over apples does not mean that either property, or the language and sharing of sentiments on which it depends, is unnatural. We may recognize someone's claim to an apple as justified only where our imaginations converge in approving of that claim, but *that is natural*—that is the natural way for human beings to come to moral agreement.

Second, and relatedly, Smith does not share Hume's attitude toward the imagination. The imagination is a source of "fictions" and mistakes for Hume, which we may have to accept as constituting much of our daily, common-sense way of thinking, but which, as philosophers, we can accept only reluctantly, trying "incessantly [to] correct ourselves by reflexion, and [to] return to a more accurate method of thinking" (T 254). If rules of property arise from the whims and errors of the imagination, therefore, the philosopher must treat them with amused disdain, recognizing that their true justification lies in their usefulness, not in the supposed natural relationships they claim to reflect. For Smith, by contrast, much of human life and thought is *legitimately* carried out in the medium of imagination. We construct our scientific theories and our social worlds by way of our imaginations, and the philosopher can no more "get beyond" the imagination to look down on its products with amused disdain than can any other human being. Smith is reconciled to the imagination, we may say, in a way that Hume is not. If we want to stay away from these sweeping characterizations of their methodologies, we can note alternatively just that Smith, much more than Hume, understands our emotions and desires as so shaped by our imaginations that we are always living for "goods" or "ends" that we have first, quite literally, imagined. I may want a particular kind of house, while my counterpart in a nomadic tribe may want a particular kind of tent, but we both come to our goals by way of what, in interaction with our friends and neighbors, we have come to imagine as "a good home." In this context, it makes perfect sense that what will count as my "owning" my house, or my counterpart's "owning" his tent, depends inextricably on the quirks of the typical imagination in our respective societies. If "owning" around here includes a right to exclude annoying relatives from my home, but does not include any such right for my nomadic counterpart, that is no odder, no more unreasonable, than the fact that I desire a house while he desires a tent. The dependence of property rules on the imagination does nothing to make them arbitrary, for Smith.

Neither of these points gives Smith any sharp rebuttal to Hume's charge that property is *conventional*. They suggest rather that property is in fact conventional, but that being conventional is compatible with being both natural and reasonable. Perhaps that is Smith's main point. Nevertheless, a natural jurisprudence is supposed to give us grounds for criticizing positive laws and institutions in some nations and times, and it is unclear whether Smith's version of the apple-picking scenario provides a basis for ruling out any set of property arrangements at all. Smith himself says that the scenario shows how property in its "originall" was limited to "actual possession" of a thing, how it "was conceived to end as well as to begin with possession," and was "confined to what was about ones person, his cloaths and any instruments he might have occasion for" (LJ 17, 18–19, 20). But this much possession is compatible with the most extreme communist experiments. Even in Mao's China, in Pol Pot's Cambodia, and in the most radical cultic communes of the 1970s, people did not ordinarily get their clothes ripped off their back or have instruments torn out of their hands. So if all property beyond actual, immediate possession counts as an "extention" of the original concept, as Smith says in these pages, then it seems that the original concept does no interesting jurisprudential work. Of course, the impartial spectator is supposed to come back, on Smith's account, to help draw limits to property in some of its extended senses as well as its original one. But when Smith brings the impartial spectator back to help justify the moves from present possession to more sophisticated types of property, he does a less persuasive job than he did in the initial case, if only because he tends to give only very cursory remarks to justify what he claims the impartial spectator would say. Thus he says, for instance, that "accession" (property in the natural products of something one already owns, as when a shepherd claims ownership of the milk of his sheep) is a natural and "originall" mode of acquiring property, like occupation, because "there would seem an impropriety" in allowing the milk of a sheep to anyone other than the person who tamed the sheep. He does not say *why* "there would seem" an impropriety in this.[11] His appeals to the spectator, for this and for all the other extensions of property, are peremptory, and presumably supposed to be immediately evident. But it is very hard to know how the spectator would actually judge in these cases. For, on Smith's own account, these extensions come about historically, and the impartial spectator who comes in to adjudicate matters of, for instance, inheritance is therefore a product of history, not a representative of universal humanity. How then can we derive from *this* spectator standards for judging whether a particular stage of human history has come to a legitimate extension of property or not? If a society at some stage of its history were to extend property in an unjust way (measured by ahistorical, universal standards of justice), how would an impartial spectator *shaped by that society* know it had made such a mistake? Would not that impartial spectator be socialized so as, incorrectly, to acquit its own society from the charge of injustice? Here convention and nature conflict, and the conventionality of property, in its extended forms, may make it impossible to find a point outside the system of conventions from which that system might reasonably be judged.

In fact that problem may infect Smith's version of the primal scene as well. Smith suggests that in the absence of rules about property, any impartial spectator would look on the one who actually picks the apple as owning it, while regarding the one who merely reaches toward it but gets intercepted by "an other who was more nimble" as having no strict right to ownership. But is it really true that *any* impartial spectator, in any society and state of society, will react this way, or is Smith perhaps reading certain conventions, about property or apple-picking, from his own society into what he attributes to the impartial spectator? And how is he, or are we, supposed to *tell* what is natural and what merely a projection of customs, in a situation like this? Smith presents these reactions of the impartial spectator as if they were self-evident. But they are not. What if the slow reacher is a child, or very old, or lame, and the nimble one is a track star?[12] What if the reacher is starving, and the nimble one well fed? Perhaps you will say that these are just *different* cases from the ones Smith describes, that in Smith's account it is clear we are dealing with competitors for an apple tree of fairly equal strength and needs. But even if that is so—and Smith does not say that it is—how would the impartial spectator draw a sharp line between Smith's case and the ones I am proposing? How old, how lame, or how hungry would the apple-reacher have to be to trigger a different reaction in the spectator from the one Smith describes? Suppose, also, that in some society very young or old, very hungry, or somewhat injured people made up the bulk of the population, so that the cases I describe were the *usual*, the most common ones. Is it not reasonable to expect that the *general disposition* of the spectator would then be to favor apple-reachers over nimble interlopers, to reverse the judgment Smith gives about the priority of physical possession over activity directed at possession?[13] How is Smith so sure that the "natural" human tendency, before conventions and rules, will give physical possession priority over actions directed toward possession?

The point of all these questions is not that Smith is *wrong* to identify physical possession as the first, "natural" mark of property. The point is just that Smith cannot prove he is right. Smith cannot say, for instance, that the impartial spectator gives property to the possessor because the possessor's body is physically "mixed" with the apple, as Locke would have said. His whole approach to the issue sets aside the troubled move from physical relationships to moral claims in Locke, and rests property instead, like other moral claims, on the way human sentiments respond to events in the physical world. More generally, Smith does not have a grounding moral rule, like Bentham's utilitarian standard or Kant's categorical imperative, from which to derive the "correct" response to the apple case. Instead, here as elsewhere, the deliverances of the impartial spectator are supposed to *precede* all moral rules (TMS 159–60), are supposed to be themselves the grounding intuitions from which morality is developed. What the impartial spectator would say is supposed to be the court of final appeal, settling the question of what originally counts as property. Sometimes, in TMS, Smith will give an argument for what the impartial spectator is likely to say based on the psychological forces that construct the spectator. He hypothesizes, for instance, that admiration is a response to unexpectedness, and accounts for the admiration we give to virtues that require great effort, like self-command in the face of "dreadful calamities," by the unexpectedness of such behavior (TMS 48). He does not offer any such argument to derive the judgment he attributes to the spectator in his property cases, however, relying instead on the hope that his intuition about that judgment is self-evident. But we have a number of competing intuitions about these cases, no one of which is self-evident or has a clearly stronger grounding in the nature of the impartial spectator than the others. It is just one intuition against another, when we ask whether the impartial spectator, in the absence of convention, would favor the physical possessor over the aged or starving apple-reacher, and it is very hard to see how Smith can give us any criteria for determining which intuition is correct.

I will suggest below that it was the difficulty of settling disputes like this that led Smith to leave the whole discussion of the original of property, with its apple-pickers and hare-hunters, out of WN. Smith over-reached, I think, when he attempted to derive a founding moment of property, a first sharp line to demarcate possession, from the impartial spectator, and he seems to have recognized that. In TMS, Smith is most convincing when he uses the impartial spectator to account for very general moral insights: that hatred and anger, because they are the emotions most likely to be experienced differently by agent and spectator, are the emotions of which "we ought to be [most] doubtful"; that easy-to-come-by virtues are merely "approved" while difficult ones are admired; that performing the ordinary offices of love out of duty is rather contemptible, while performing some offices of honesty out of duty, because difficult, is admirable (TMS 34–8, 25, 172–3). *General* features of justice, like the fact that it expresses a filtered version of resentment, can also come out in this way, but it is unlikely that the feelings of the impartial spectator will guide us to any specific rules. When Smith gives us his apple-picking and hare-hunting scenarios in LJ, he is himself primarily interested in drawing out the general result that property is rooted in our sympathy with other people's reasonable expectations rather than in either Locke's mixture of labor with matter or Hutcheson's sympathy with the innocent exercise of liberty: "[t]he reasonable expectation therefore which the first possessor furnishes is the ground on which the right of property is acquired by occupation."[14] And this we may want to grant Smith. But his further claim, that actual physical possession will clearly trump intention to possess in the first, "natural" rule of property, I think we can treat only as conjecture. The variety of circumstances surrounding claims to possession, even in a stripped-down primal setting, make it very difficult to be confident that every impartial spectator would accept any given rule of ownership.

Still, I do not want to insist too much on this doubt about Smith's defense of present possession. It is not implausible that an impartial spectator, in any state of society or stage of history, will regard ripping objects from a person who presently possesses them as an injury of much the same type and gravity as battery. To say that, however, does not require Smith's detour via the reasonable expectations of the apple-picker. It cannot be because the nimble interloper who winds up with the apple in his hands has a reasonable expectation of eating it, after all, that he takes priority over the person who was reaching for it: *both* of them had reasonable expectations of eating the apple. If the interloper nevertheless has a better claim to the apple, that can only be because the apple now forms a continuum with the exterior of his body, and ripping it out of his hands is indistinguishable from inflicting physical injury on his hands. But this means that Smith has accomplished much less than he may have hoped by placing his impartial spectator at the primal scene of property: He has merely assimilated a minimal paradigm of ownership to the natural injury of bodily harm.

Smith's initial scenario therefore does not get us far. It certainly does not offer anything like an account of initial ownership that might be used to justify complex systems of property. In most cases, it may be true that ripping food out of someone's hand, or clothes off someone's back, will be as obvious, as "natural," an injury as murder and battery. But if so, we will have a natural right just to what we immediately, physically possess, and that will not be enough to establish anything like the systems of property on which most societies, and especially societies with an advanced economy, must rely. These systems require, as Smith himself says, vast *extensions* of the right to what one presently possesses, extensions which cannot be derived from present possession itself, and which Smith can justify with his impartial spectator only by relying on peremptory declarations of what that spectator might say. And Smith himself acknowledges that many of the extensions have no basis at all in "nature," in the deliverances of the spectator (LJ 82–3, 400). They are justified purely by their utility. Sometimes they are useful—like limited copyright and patent laws—and sometimes they are not (like most other monopoly privileges), but in all cases the rights in question are invented, not natural ones, and are not necessary for individuals to have liberty.

46. Property in WN

It is the absence of any attempt to justify property that is most striking in WN. Smith brings many ideas and passages from his jurisprudential lectures into WN, but he never mentions his primal scene of ownership, nor so much as alludes to the fact that he had once attempted to offer a philosophical foundation for property rights. Instead, he talks mostly of the *utility* of protecting property, which, as we have seen, does not for him count as a direct moral defense of any right. In addition, he hardly ever uses the phrase "property rights." On one occasion, he condemns a law for sacrificing "the sacred rights of private property . . . to the supposed interests of publick revenue" (WN 188), but his argument here turns on the word "supposed" rather than the words "sacred" and "rights," since the law in question overrode property rights for the mercantilist purpose of encouraging the discovery of hard metals, and Smith thinks this is not a genuine "interest of publick revenue" at all.

Elsewhere, Smith several times refers to the justice of securing "to every man . . . the fruits of his own labour" (WN 540; see also 405, 610). "It is but equity," he says, that the poor workers who create food, clothing, and lodging for everyone "should have such a share of the produce of their own labour as to be themselves tolerably well fed, cloathed and lodged" (WN 96). He also, famously, declares: "The property which every man has in his own labour, as it is the original foundation of all other property, so it is the most sacred and inviolable" (WN 138).[15] On all these occasions, he writes as though he endorsed the Lockean theory grounding rights to property in the mixing of labor with material things. The passage on 138 uses the Lockean account of the foundation of property to defend a yet more fundamental freedom of activity,[16] which is an interesting way of deriving worker's rights from rights to property, but it is essential to this interesting move that Smith write as if he agreed with the Lockean account. In LJ, as we have seen, the whole tendency of his argument is to *reject* this view, following out the criticisms of Locke to be found in Hutcheson and Hume. Smith does have his apple-picker say, in response to one who would take the apple away, "I have gone [to the forest] already and bestowed my time and pains in procuring the fruit" (LJ 17), but this, as Knud Haakonssen has pointed out, at most makes the bestowal of labour "*one* of the circumstances which would . . . tend to induce a spectator to sympathize with one's expectations of the use of the thing as reasonable."[17] Property, in LJ, gets claimed on the basis of "reasonable expectations," not because of any direct link between labor and the fruits of labor.

Why, then, does Smith write in WN as if he shared Locke's views on property? It is implausible to suppose that he came to embrace an uncritical Lockeanism, given the devastating critique of Locke's "mixing" metaphor that he knew from Hutcheson and Hume, and given his general philosophical antipathy toward the sort of scientific reductionism implicit in this "mixing" metaphor, toward an approach to moral questions that tries to reduce them to mechanical ones. But the absence of LJ's account of property from WN certainly suggests that Smith was uncomfortable with his own arguments for property, and it may be that Smith decided to use Lockean language precisely because he did not want to enter into controversy over the justification of property. This would then be the best example of the general strategy that, I have argued, Smith employs in WN regarding matters of justice: he tries to finesse them, putting his case for his policy recommendations in widely accepted, noncontroversial terms so as to persuade people who might not share his philosophical views. Locke's approach to property was the standard one in Smith's day, pleasing both to businesspeople who wanted the state to leave them alone and to radicals like Thomas Spence who believed in everyone's right to the fruits of the land. Moreover, on the whole it suited Smith's rhetorical purposes very well. He was able to use it both to bolster his case against government management of the economy and to defend the right of workers against apprenticeship laws and wage caps. Locke's language was thus convenient to him. But there is no reason to think he had any deeper commitment to it than that. And when the strength, and presocial status, of Locke's property rights might have raised a problem for the recommendations he wanted to make, he simply avoided the phrases that he otherwise found so useful. As we shall see in the next section, he ignored Locke's views on taxation, for example, entirely.

47. Taxation and Property Rights

There is a view abroad today, especially in certain sectors of the American electorate, that a presumption of injustice hangs over all taxation, which can only be rebutted if the government uses the money it collects for purposes that every taxpayer can agree to. "It's *your* money," has been a rallying cry of many political leaders, including George W. Bush in his 2000 presidential campaign, to justify large tax cuts. It goes with this view that governments should carry out only minimal tasks: protecting citizens against crime and military attack, primarily, and perhaps responding to other large-scale dangers that private institutions cannot handle. Fostering virtues or controversial moral views will be clearly illegitimate, underwriting the arts and sciences only slightly less obviously so, and running welfare programs, or other systems to help the poor, will at best be very dubiously justifiable. If there is any disagreement in the society over whether government should carry out a task, the libertarians I am describing tend to say, then it is wrong for the government to force individuals, by way of taxation, to give up their property for that task.

This view is not nearly as obvious as its proponents seem to think. When I earn money, by way of investment or salaried work, the conditions making it possible for my efforts to bear fruit are due in no small part to the efforts of my society and my government. My efforts will fail if I am not protected against theft and attack, if there are no decent roads in my area, if environmental blight or urban drabness keeps people away from my storefront, or if the general population is so poorly educated, ill, or despairing that I can find no customers or good workers. It is therefore quite reasonable to look on my earnings as *not* purely "my" money, as the product, rather, of a *collaborative effort* between me and my neighbors and political officials, and to suppose that I owe some of those earnings back to the society, and government agencies, that have helped me. It is this view, not the libertarian one, that Smith endorses:

> The subjects of every state ought to contribute towards the support of the government . . . in proportion to their respective abilities; that is, in proportion to the revenue which they respectively *enjoy under the protection of the state*. The expence of government to the individuals of a great nation, is like the expence of management to the *joint tenants of a great estate*, who are all obliged to contribute in proportion to their respective interests in the state. (WN 825, my emphases; see also 844)

Society creates the conditions under which financial success is possible, and has therefore a rightful claim to share in that success.

If one wants to find a seventeenth- or eighteenth-century intellectual ancestor for the alternative, libertarian view, one should look to Locke. Locke makes property a presocial right, regards the protection of property rights as the central task for which governments are established, and declares that it is a condition of legitimate government that the "supreme power [not] take from any man any part of his property without his own consent" (ST §138). It turns out, a bare page or so later, that what "his own consent" means, in this passage, is "the consent of the majority" of the people, and that that can be expressed by way of the people's representatives in the legislature. So even Locke, far from proclaiming an *individual* right to consent to or dissent from any proposed taxation, as at first he seems to do, allows a majority vote of the legislature to override any such individual right. Still, it is fair to say that Locke sees in taxation a threat to justice, sees tax monies as presumptively the property of the taxpayers, and declares that a government that ignored this presumptive right would be illegitimate.

Smith declares these views of Locke to be of a piece with the fallacy in the latter's contractual theory of government:

> It is a rule laid down by Mr. Locke . . . that the people have a right to resist whenever the sovereign takes their money from them without their consent by levying taxes to which they have not agreed. Now we see that in France, Spain, etc. the consent of the people is not in the least thought of; the king imposes what taxes he pleases. It is in Britain alone that any consent of the people is required, and God knows it is but a very figurative metaphoricall consent which is given here. . . . No doubt the raising a very exorbitant tax . . . would, as well as any other gross abuse of power, justify resistance in the people. But where this power is exerted with moderation, tho perhaps it is not done with the greatest propriety . . . and tho not even a figurative consent is requir'd, yet they never think that they ought to resist tho they may claim the liberty of remonstrating against it.—Government was established to defend the property of the subjects, but if it come to be of a conterary tendency, yet they must agree to give up a little of their right. (LJ 324; see also 435)

People in fact go along with taxation, Smith says, whether their consent has been explicitly solicited or not. They have, we might say, a reasonable expectation that they will be taxed, which is enough to bestow considerable legitimacy on taxation. Smith is inclined to dismiss Locke's worries on this subject. Taxation comes with government. People "must agree" to give up a little of their property in order to maintain governments. What governments do, even aside from protecting property, is important enough to justify taxation, and one ought generally to trust that the taxes get raised for these important purposes. One who objects to taxation really objects to government itself. All governments must and do impose taxes on their subjects, and subjects are and should be willing to go along with such taxes in much the same way, and to much the same degree, that they are willing to go along with the existence of government. Indeed, Smith believes that people are generally proud to pay taxes. The fact that the government taxes them is a mark of their citizenship, a sign that they are free: "Every tax . . . is to the person who pays it a badge, not of slavery, but of liberty. It denotes that he is subject to government, indeed, but that, as he has some property, he cannot himself be the property of a master" (WN 857).[18] Governments expand everyone's liberty, protecting each of us against other people's love of domination, and the fact that we pay taxes to support the government is but a sign and a consequence of the freedom we thereby receive. As we saw above, Smith proclaims that people have a duty to pay for government, and that the more revenue they "enjoy under the protection of the state," the more they ought to contribute to the state's upkeep.

So Smith does not see in taxation any presumptive challenge to our rights of property. He does worry about injustice in the *way* taxes are imposed. Haakonssen says that Smith regards the revenue system as "rais[ing] very serious problems of justice because it involve[s] forcible infringement of liberty, privacy, and property of individuals" (SL 96). As far as "property" goes, this is incorrect, and none of Haakonssen's citations support such a claim.[19] But it is true that Smith worried about the invasions of liberty and privacy involved in certain modes of tax collection. Taxes that are "arbitrary" or "uncertain," that are not made "clear and plain" by law, will help tax-gatherers line their own pockets, which is a great and ever-present danger in every system of revenue collection (WN 825–6, 867). Taxes are also oppressive if gathering them requires too great an interference with people's private lives. Taxes that require a businessperson to "shew his books" to the authorities impose a hardship that amounts to a serious "breach of liberty" (LJ 531, WN 848). A tax on home-brewed liquors will require the irksome intrusion of tax collectors into the privacy of people's homes, and should therefore be imposed on the materials for the liquor rather than on the final product (WN 936). A real estate tax on the windows of a house is preferable to one on the hearths of a house, because to count hearths the tax-gatherer must enter every room of a house, while he can count windows from outside (845–6). (This last detail is an occasion on which Smith's stress on imagining the situation of others does moral work for him: only by actually visualizing a tax collector going through someone's house does one recognize the advantages of the window over the hearth tax. A focus, like that encouraged by abstract moral rules, on the financial burden of the tax would miss this point entirely.) In general, any tax that subjects people to "the frequent visits and odious examination of the tax-gatherers" is unnecessarily painful and oppressive, and thereby inflicts injustice (827; see also 848–50, 853, 867, 888, 898–9, 927).

Taxes can also be unjust if they are unequal (WN 825–6). The first of Smith's four maxims for taxation requires that tax burdens be distributed across all types of revenue, and that they be levied in accordance with people's ability to pay them (825). Equality in taxation can be hard to determine, however (828–9, 836, 837, 867), and the maxim calling for it may conflict with other requirements of justice (826, 868). The maxim that taxes should impose an equal burden on every citizen's ability to pay can therefore at most be a good rule of thumb and Smith says, about a tax that falls heaviest on the rich, that "in this sort of inequality there would not, perhaps, be any thing very unreasonable" (WN 842).[20] Inequality "of the worst kind" is the kind in which a tax falls more heavily on the poor than on the rich (WN 846; see also 893). Smith here invokes a kind of justice that Haakonssen does not mention, something much like what today we call "distributive justice," a notion he is often thought to dismiss. We shall have more to say about this in the next chapter.

Finally, Smith objects to many taxes because they are inefficient: either they cost too much to raise, or they "obstruct the industry of the people" (WN 826). In this context, it is correct to associate Smith with a dislike of high taxes. High taxes can burden the economy, diminishing people's ability to invest in promising branches of business. When Smith called for "easy taxes," in his early 1755 paper on political economy,[21] he was surely looking for taxes to be as low as they can be while still meeting the public needs. (I deliberately leave open here what should count as "public needs."[22]) But this concern comes under the heading of *utility*, not of justice. There is nothing *unjust* about even a very poorly conceived tax, which requires a ridiculous amount of expense to raise or which blocks the development of a richly promising economic channel.

It is therefore right to say that Smith sees a number of possible injustices in the way taxes are imposed on people, but wrong to suppose that he regards taxation, in itself, as even a prima facie threat to property. That makes sense, given the conventionalism of his view of property. Most claims to property are a far extension from the small core of possession protected by natural right, for Smith, and it is perfectly reasonable for the laws that make possible this extension to constrain the rights they create with a duty to pay taxes. Indeed, I take Smith's lack of anxiety about taxation, his dismissal of the notion that taxes can only be legitimate if they have the explicit consent of the taxpayers, to be a confirmation of the conventionalist reading I have given of his general attitude toward property. Were he convinced that property is a natural, presocial right, he would be more worried about the potential of taxation to take away that right. His claim that taxation is a duty we owe society, in return for the many ways in which it enables us to acquire wealth, presents property as a *creation* of society, something that develops out of our relationships with others, not something that comes into existence in a transaction between each of us and nature, and that, in the transition from nature to social contract, we need to guard jealously.

48. Inheritance and Property Rights

Having described one respect in which Smith himself dismissed a possible tension between rights in property and governmental action, let me conclude this chapter by mentioning two, linked, respects in which, although Smith himself did not draw antilibertarian conclusions from his own views on property, he inspired some of his followers to do so. The first is the possibility that government might abolish or heavily tax inheritances, and the second is the possibility, which many hoped would take place in part by way of abolishing inheritance, that governments might take it on themselves to redistribute wealth to the poor.

The abolition of inheritance is a prominent plank in socialist programs from Babeuf in the 1790s to Marx and Engels' *Communist Manifesto* in 1848. Nevertheless, it is not intrinsically a socialist idea; it can easily be argued that the "work ethic" on which American *capitalism* is based—according to which financial rewards should be earned by one's own efforts—militates against people gaining wealth merely by receiving it from their parents.[23] The "bourgeois radicalism" that fueled the American Revolution and the early French one, with its attack on established, hereditary privileges, is very much the sort of movement one would expect to criticize inheritance while remaining attached to the notion of private property.[24] Tradespeople want to run their economic affairs by them-selves, and to own and manage whatever they acquire by their efforts, but they do not tend to be overly fond of inheritance practices, which primarily serve to keep large estates intact over many generations, as indolent father hands his wealth down to indolent son. The attack Smith launches on primogeniture and entail is directed at this infringement of the "work for your living" principle, and it is but a small step away from an attack on inheritance itself.

So it is not surprising that students and admirers of Smith were prominent among those who, in the wake of the French Revolution, called for a drastic diminution of the right to inherit property. Thomas Jefferson, who called WN "the best book extant" on political economy,[25] at about the same time famously wondered whether all hereditary privileges should be abolished since "the earth belongs in usufruct to the living" (he did not specifically mention inheritance, however).[26] Tom Paine, who considered himself a disciple of Smith's on political economy, recommended a steeply progressive estate tax in his *Rights of Man*.[27] Most importantly, Smith's student John Millar espoused "a change in the inheri-tance laws such that only testaments for a limited part of a man's property [would be] enforced."[28] Millar was a firm believer in private property and in the Smithian notion that social change should come via reform of standing law, rather than via revolution, and he saw the reform of inheritance as entirely compatible with this respect for property and for law. Haakonssen corrects those who see Millar as calling for Parliament to distribute property: "He only wants Parliament to abolish the old inheritance laws and then let the distribu-tion of property run its own course" (NL 177). The form of Millar's proposal is thus fully in line with Smith's emphasis on the need for governments always to act by way of clear, precise, and certain laws.

How about the content of the proposal? Are there sources in Smith's own writings to support limitations on the principle of inheritance? Well, in his lectures on jurisprudence, which Millar attended, Smith conjectures that intes-tate succession to family members was originally based on the fact that families in primitive societies produced most of their goods together, so that each per-son's goods were already legitimately claimed by the rest of the family before he or she died (LJ 39); by implication, there was no right to inheritance indepen-dently of a right to the fruit of one's own labor.[29] About testamentary succession, he says that it is "one of the greatest extentions of property," and that "there is no point more difficult to account for than the right we conceive men to have to dispose of their goods after death." If the dying person has not already trans-ferred her property *before* her death, how can she possibly transfer it afterwards? After she dies, she no longer has property rights—how then can she transfer such rights to someone else? Smith says this is a puzzle that led philosophers, absurdly, to bring in the immortality of the soul (LJ 63), as if in this one area the dead remained party to civil disputes among the living. He goes on to propose his own solution to the puzzle, but the questions he had raised would surely have already sown grave doubts, in his students' minds, about the legit-imacy of inheritance.

His solution, moreover, is more than a bit halfhearted. The point of death, he says, is "so momentous . . . that every thing that is connected with it seems to be so also. The advices, the commands, and even the very fooleries of the dying person have more effect on us than things of the same nature would have had at any other period" (LJ 64). In the mood of reverence for our friend or relative that we have at this moment, everything we say takes on the aura of a solemn promise, and that solemnity holds us in its grip for a good while afterward. So if we promise to disperse the person's property in a certain way, we keep to that promise after his or her death, regardless of whether we can reasonably justify the promise any longer in terms either of utility or of justice. We are "forced by [our] piety" to go beyond what reason and nature might demand (LJ 64). The suggestion that piety to the dead is an irrational principle hangs heavy over Smith's account of inheritance. He is, moreover, unwilling to allow this piety to dictate too much: "we do not naturally imagine that this regard [for the will of the dying] is to last for ever" (LJ 65). The regard wears off after a while—hence entails are unjustifiable. We don't, and shouldn't, have regard for the wishes of a man who died 100 years ago or more (LJ 65).

But this is a tricky move. If we are so overwhelmed by reverence at the moment of death that we want to respect every wish of the dying person, then why *shouldn't* we take seriously, and try to fulfill, his wish that "this house stay in my family forever"? Surely people do greet these wishes too with tearful solemnity, and respond to them by resolving to do whatever they can to fulfill them after the person dies. And in fact many people, even if not Smith himself, have a certain piety toward very ancient commitments of this kind. Think of the loving care many religious people devote to the graves of long-dead saints, or the indignation aroused even in secular people by proposals to overturn the terms of a bequest that founded a local museum. So if testamentary succession rests on the feelings we *actually* have about the dying and the dead, it would seem to justify entail as well as inheritance—a result Smith very much does not want. Smith himself more or less admits this equivalence, although in a back-handed way: "The making of entails came in . . . soon after the introduction of testaments. When once the notion of the will of the deceased directing his succession for one step [came in,] it was no difficult matter to suppose that it should extend farther" (LJ 69). But we can just as well say: When once the notion of the deceased directing succession for many steps comes into question, it is no difficult matter to question whether it may be so directed even for one step. Doubts about entail naturally bring in their train doubts about inheritance itself.

As we might expect by now, the entire discussion of how inheritance can be justified in jurisprudential terms is omitted from WN. Smith calls it "cruel and oppressive" to deprive children of any part of their inheritance if they were living with the parent who died, but he says it "may . . . be otherwise with those children who . . . are said, in the language of Roman law, to be emancipated" (WN 859). He countenances an estate tax on children who have homes of their own as quite in accordance with justice and no more "inconvenient" than any other tax or duty. He does worry about "taxes on the transference of property from the dead to the living" when they make life more difficult for a financially straitened seller who must get rid of what he or she has inherited (WN 862). But his concerns about inheritance taxes focus throughout on questions of utility, on whether, in a world in which inheritance is sometimes the only means of succoring young children, and is at other times a burden on already needy people, taxes on inheritance will add an unnecessary source of suffering. He does not suggest that estate taxes are inherently unjust, that people have any natural right to pass their goods down to their children, or that children have any such right to acquire what belonged to their parents. Knud Haakonssen has written that the reasons Thomas Reid gave for the legitimacy of private property "are such that it is not a long step to arguing for the abolition of private property" (NL 207). Exactly that can be said about the reasons Smith gave for the legitimacy of inheritance. With friends like Smith, the principle of inheritance hardly needed enemies. Smith did not quite dismiss the basis in natural jurisprudence for inheritance, but he weakened that basis, and paved the way for the more radical suggestions of his students and admirers.

49. Redistribution and Property Rights

Practically all commentators say that Smith rejects the notion that the state should pursue distributive justice. Istvan Hont and Michael Ignatieff write that Smith's views "effectively excluded 'distributive justice' from the appropriate functions of government in a market society," that he "insisted" that only commutative justice could be enforced (NJ 24). Donald Winch speaks of "the restriction of the application [of the notion of justice] in the *Theory of Moral Sentiments* to commutative as opposed to distributive justice" (RP 100). Charles Griswold describes Smith as having made a "decision to focus on commutative justice and for the most part to assimilate distributive justice to [the private virtue of] beneficence" (AVE 250).

All of these commentators are glossing Smith's remark, in the course of a history of moral philosophy at the end of TMS (269), that the kind of justice that "may be extorted by force" is the kind that bars injury to our neighbors, while the phrase "distributive justice" uses the word "justice" in a different sense. Similarly, in a brief explanation of natural law terminology at the beginning of LJ (9), Smith remarks that distributive justice concerns imperfect rights, like the right to praise of "a man of bright parts or remarkable learning" or the right of a beggar to charity, and that this is not the kind of justice that can be enforced, or with which jurisprudence is concerned. Each of the commentators above writes as though Smith is doing something new or controversial in these remarks—"exclud[ing]" something from the notion of justice (Hont and Ignatieff), "restrict[ing]" the concept in some way (Winch), or making a "decision" to define the concept in a certain way (Griswold)—which in turn gives the impression that, before Smith, there was a tradition that did include distributive justice among "the appropriate functions of government," that Smith is abandoning to private beneficence a function that the jurisprudential tradition before him had given to the state.

This impression is quite wrong. Distributive justice was already a private virtue, not a job for the state, in the natural law tradition that Smith inherited, and had little or nothing to do with the distribution of property.[30] Far from rejecting anything in this area, Smith simply ratified what the tradition said on the subject. If anything, as we shall see, he contributed to the changes in moral outlook that made possible the modern notion of distributive justice, the notion used to justify socialism and welfare state liberalism. We will elaborate these claims in the next chapter, but I want to mention here that it was, again, Smith's students and admirers who proposed some of the most important programs for using government funds to help the poor in the 1790s. We have seen that John Millar was regarded as a believer in redistribution, and it is certainly true that his object in proposing limitations on inheritance was to diminish social and economic inequality (NL 177). Tom Paine included his steep estate tax in a bundle of policy proposals that amount to one of the first comprehensive plans for educating poor children, supporting the elderly, and providing work and basic needs to the unemployed. He shared his admiration for Smith with Condorcet, who promoted WN avidly in France during the revolution; both men were, as Donald Winch writes, "egalitarians of the social insurance variety."[31] Such radicals as William Godwin and Richard Price also expressed admiration for Smith, as did Jeremy Bentham.

There is something right about the instinct of all of these figures to find in Smith a passion for the rights of the poor akin to their own, even if he would probably have rejected some of their proposals. Smith is known to have disliked Price, and one cannot imagine him going along with Godwin's rejection of private property. Similarly, Bentham's program in aid of the poor involved such extreme control over poor people's lives that Gertrude Himmelfarb rightly sees his claim to Smith's mantle as misguided.[32] Himmelfarb tends to look on all Smith's "left-leaning" admirers as misunderstanding him, however, while playing down the distance between Smith and such "right-leaning" admirers as Frederick Eden and Edmund Burke (although she does not overlook the problems in assimilating the later, conservative Burke to Smith).[33] But in this Himmelfarb reads Smith too much through the lens of his modern-day reception. Donald Winch, navigating carefully through the same charged waters, finds Paine much closer to Smith, on economic matters, than Burke, and acknowledges Condorcet's abiding interest in Smith and adherence to "the main lines of Smith's teachings" (RP 168, 228). Neither he nor anyone else, moreover, doubts Millar's deep roots in Smith's thought. I think the "left-leaning" followers of Smith have at least as good a claim to his legacy as the "right-leaning" ones do. Smith's concern for the poor pervades all his work, as Himmelfarb herself stresses, and he never shows himself averse to the government's raising funds from the wealthy in order to help the poor. He proposes several state policies for helping the poor in WN, including a couple of redistributive measures. The belief that he would oppose all state redistribution of property is based on a misunderstanding of one or two texts and the entire context of his work. In particular, it arises from a confusion between the Aristotelian and the modern notions of distributive justice. The next chapter will be devoted to disentangling the two notions, and restoring Smith's proper place in the history by which one gave way to the other. We will then be able to see that Smith's popularity among radical advocates of the poor, in the decade after he died, was no foolish error: He inspired their proposals, and took some steps in their direction himself.

CHAPTER TEN

Distributive Justice

*Man is by Nature directed to correct, in some measure,
that distribution of things which [Nature] herself would
otherwise have made.*

(TMS 168)

50. Two Meanings for "Distributive Justice"[1]

"Distributive justice" in its modern sense calls on the state to guarantee that property is distributed throughout society so that everyone is supplied with a certain level of material means. In its Aristotelian sense, "distributive justice" referred to the principles ensuring that deserving people are rewarded in accordance with their merits. So the ancient principle had to do with distribution according to merits, while the modern principle demands a distribution independent of merit. *Everyone* is supposed to deserve certain goods regardless of merit, on the modern view; merit-making is not supposed to begin until everyone has such goods as housing, health care, and a decent education. We can be quite sure that this is not what Aristotle had in mind, when he wrote about people being rewarded in accordance with their virtues, or participating in political life in accordance with their social status.[2]

How can we get from the Aristotelian to the modern meaning of the phrase? "Justice," unlike "wisdom" and "charity," historically has been understood as a secular and a rational virtue, whose demands can be explained and justified without appeal to any religious faith; to be a virtue that governments can and should enforce, and that indeed ought to be the prime norm guiding political activity; and to be a virtue that, if only because politicians need to organize their plans around it, ought to take as its object practicable, readily achievable goals. Thus ensuring belief in Christ has never been held to be a project for *justice* since the goodness of this project, if it is good, cannot be explained in purely secular and rational terms. Thus securing warmth in friendship is not considered an object of justice since it depends on the uncoerced feelings of individuals. And thus guaranteeing to everyone freedom from illness has never been included among the objects of justice because, so far at least, it is impossible. Finally, justice, in general, has long been seen as a matter of "giving to everyone their due," and distributive justice in particular was originally defined by Aristotle as a matter of dividing up rights, offices, and goods in accordance with people's merits. So to arrive at the modern notion of distributive justice, from what "justice" generally means, one needs to hold:

1. that a certain number of material goods, is everyone's "due," that everyone *deserves* such a thing,
2. that the fact that they deserve it can be justified rationally, in purely secular terms,
3. that this distribution of goods is practicable: that attempting consciously to achieve it is neither a fool's project nor, like the attempt to enforce friendship, something that would undermine the very goal one seeks to achieve, and
4. that the state, and not merely private individuals or organizations, ought to be guaranteeing the distribution.

These four premises are closely linked, but it is particularly important, and particularly difficult, to get from Aristotle's distributive justice to our premise (1). To look to people's "merits" ordinarily means looking to their distinctive qualities or to what they have done, while to say that *everyone* deserves something implies that they deserve it independently of what is distinctive about them or what they have done. From the point of view of the Aristotelian tradition, this makes no sense. Moreover, for most moral and political thinkers in the premodern world, the poor appeared to be a particularly vicious class of people, a class of people who *lacked* merits. Even those who believed strongly in helping the poor regarded such help as undeserved: It was to be bestowed as a matter of grace, an expression of the benevolence of the giver.

I use the word "grace" advisedly. Most premodern proponents of charity, or of the communal sharing of wealth, did so on religious grounds that violate premise (2). Nor were our other premises widely held. Premise (3) is still much debated, and its contradictory was taken for granted in almost every society until the late eighteenth century. And premise (4) is something one really does not hear at all until "Gracchus" Babeuf's conspiracy at the end of the French Revolution. Premise (4) really depends on all the others: only if people deserve some set of material goods, if they do so for reasons that can be explained without appeal to religion, and if it is a practical and not a far-fetched goal to give them what they deserve in this respect, can it be reasonable to expect the state—an entity that dispenses what is owed to people and not what it would merely be nice for them to have, that, at least in the modern world, is supposed to abjure religious justifications for its actions, and that aims at feasible goals— to take upon itself the distribution of these goods.

Smith's optimism about the productive possibilities of a free market helped to make (3) begin to look plausible. Despite his posthumous reputation for "laissez-faire" absolutism, he also made some recommendations that implied an acceptance of (4).[3] But his most important contribution to the modern notion of distributive justice was to provide grounds for (1) and (2), clearing away a lot of superstition and prejudice according to which the poor, far from having a right to increased material means and social opportunities, deserve precisely the socioeconomic station they already occupy. More than anyone else before him, Smith urged an attitude of respect for the poor, a view of them as having equal dignity with every other human being, and without this view, the notion that they deserve not to be poor could not have gotten off the ground.

51. Smith's Contribution to the Politics of Poverty

That Smith does not have any principled opposition to using the state to redistribute wealth should be clear from the fact that he makes recommendations to do just that. Wealth can be redistributed either by a direct transfer of property from the rich to the poor, or by taxing the rich at a higher rate than the poor, or by using tax revenues, gathered from rich and poor equally, to provide public resources that will mostly benefit the poor. Smith makes proposals that fall under both the second and the third heading.

The most important of these is the advocacy of public schooling. In both LJ and WN, Smith cites the mind-numbing nature of certain kinds of labor as one of the greatest dangers of an advanced economy, and says that the state should take steps to ensure that the laboring poor have an education fostering in them the capacity for moral and political judgment (WN 782–9), and giving them "ideas with which [they] can amuse [themselves]" (LJ 540). Building on institutions that already existed in Scotland, he recommends that all states underwrite local schools that teach reading, writing, and "the elementary parts of geometry and mechanicks" (WN 785).

In addition to this proposal, Smith suggests that luxury vehicles pay a higher road toll than freight vehicles, so that "the indolence and vanity of the rich [can be] made to contribute in a very easy manner to the relief of the poor" (WN 725). He also advocates a tax on house-rents, in part because it will fall heaviest on the rich: "It is not very unreasonable that the rich should contribute to the publick expence, not only in proportion to their revenue, but something more than in that proportion" (WN 842). And, as Gertrude Himmelfarb has pointed out, although Smith harshly criticizes the laws of settlement, he "conspicuously did not . . . challenge" the English Poor Law[4]—the most significant government program to help the poor in his day, and one that came under criticism, then and later, as too expensive and as sapping the incentives of the poor to labor.[5]

This is about all one can find in Smith in the way of *positive* programs to help the poor. He advocates the lifting of apprenticeship statutes, residence requirements for poor laborers, and sumptuary laws, but these are all *negative* proposals, aimed just to remove obstacles to people's freedom. If his positive programs seem a bit meager to us, we should remember, first, that Smith seems to have believed that an unrestricted economy could achieve a 100 percent employment rate (WN 470–71), and second, that he was writing at a time when common wisdom held that the poor needed to be *kept poor*, else they would not work, that only necessity prevented the poor from wasting their time in drink and debauchery. Most writers also held that poor people needed to be restrained from luxury spending, and taught habits of deference so that they remained in their proper social place and did not ape their superiors. In this context, to propose *any* government programs that would allow wages to rise, and poor people to aspire to the goods and learning of the middle and upper classes, was to swim mightily upstream.

But by far the most important contribution Smith made to the history of state welfare programs was to *change the attitudes toward the poor* that underwrote the restrictive, disdainful policies by which the poor were kept poor. "More important than this or that policy [in Smith]," Himmelfarb rightly says, "was the image of the poor implicit in those policies." And she sums up a consensus among scholars when she writes, "if the *Wealth of Nations* was less than novel in its theories of money, trade, or value, it was genuinely revolutionary in its view of poverty and its attitude towards the poor."[6]

Smith's picture of the poor may be one we take for granted now, but that is in good part the effect of his work. Smith has indeed changed our notion of what "the poverty problem" *is*; his predecessors regarded it as the problem, primarily, of how to cope with the vice and criminality of the lower classes. On the whole, they did not think the world should, much less could, do without a class of poor people. Until the late eighteenth century, most people in Christian countries believed that God had ordained a hierarchical organization for society, with the truly virtuous people occupying positions of wealth, or power, at the top, and "the poor and inferior sort" at the bottom.[7] Of course, the people at the top were supposed to help those at the bottom—but not enough to raise them above their proper place. Alms-giving was understood as a means to redemption, in Christianity as in many other religions, and the existence of the poor was seen as an integral part of God's plan for human life: "God could have made all men rich, but He wanted there to be poor people in this world, that the rich might be able to redeem their sins."[8] This teaching was virtually unquestioned in medieval times, but even in 1728 the common wisdom about the social order was expressed in these words of Isaac Watts, a renowned advocate for the poor: "Great God has widely ordained . . . that among Mankind there should be some Rich, and some Poor: and the same Providence hath alloted to the Poor the meaner Services."[9] As Daniel Baugh sums up the situation:

> In . . . 1750, . . . there were two widely held attitudes toward the poor existing side by side. . . . The dominant one supposed that the poor should never have misery lifted from them, nor their children be encouraged to look beyond the plough or loom. It reflected traditional notions of social hierarchy and was reinforced by economic theories about labor and motivation. The other attitude was derived chiefly from Christian ethics. It held that the duty of the rich was to treat the poor with kindness and compassion, and to aid them in times of distress. This benevolent attitude did not provide a suitable basis for policy-making; rather it was a reminder of conscience, of the fact that the ill-clad, filthy laboring masses habitually viewed with contempt by their betters, were equally God's creatures, whom a Christian community could neither exclude nor ignore.[10]

And the major breakthrough in getting beyond both of these attitudes, says Baugh, "came in 1776, when a philosopher of great learning, penetration, and literary persuasiveness published his *Inquiry into the Nature and Causes of the Wealth of Nations.*[11] Smith combated both the explicit condescension of the first view and the implicit condescension of the second one. He was a virulent opponent of the notion that the poor are inferior in any way to the well-off. Over and over again, Smith pricks the balloon of vanity upholding a contemptuous picture of the virtues and skills of the poor. He presents the poor as people with the same native abilities as everyone else: "The difference in natural talents in different men is, in reality, much less than we are aware of." Habit and education make for most of the supposedly great gap between the philosopher and the common street porter, even though "the vanity of the philosopher is willing to acknowledge scarce any resemblance" between the two (WN 29).[12] To those who complain that the poor are naturally indolent,[13] Smith declares that, on the contrary, they are "very apt to over-work themselves" (WN 100). To those—and these were legion, even among advocates of the poor—who saw indulgence in drink as a vice characteristic of poor people, Smith replied that "Man is an anxious animal and must have his care swept off by something that can exhilarate the spirits" (LJ 497).[14] To those who complained that the poor were affecting the manners of their "betters," and should be prevented from buying luxury goods both in the name of natural social hierarchy and in the name of their own financial health,[15] Smith says that it is "but equity" for the lower ranks of society to have a good share in the food, clothes, and housing they themselves produce (WN 96), and that it is "the highest impertinence and presumption, . . . in kings and ministers, to pretend to watch over the economy of private people." He adds, about these kings and ministers: "They are themselves, always, and without any exception, the greatest spendthrifts in the society" (WN 346). The poor, he believes, tend to be frugal rather than prodigal: practically everyone, including practically every poor person, saves in order to rise in social standing (WN 341–2; see §20 above).

This is not the end of the list. Smith defends the religious choices of poor people against the contempt and fear of his Enlightenment colleagues, pointing out that the religious sects that poor people tend to join, while sometimes "disagreeably rigorous and unsocial," provide laborers in a vast and anonymous urban setting with community and moral guidance (WN 794–6). He repeatedly demonstrates that it is better for poor workers to be independent rather than dependent on their "superiors" (139, 335–6, 378–9, 412–20). He even tries to excuse, if not quite to justify, the mob violence characteristic of struggles between workers and their masters (84).

In the context of the eighteenth century, then, Smith presents a remarkably dignified picture of the poor, a picture in which they make choices every bit as respectable as those of their social superiors—a picture, therefore, in which there really are no "inferiors" and "superiors" at all. Individual people may be good or bad, of course, but Smith urges his readers to see the average poor person as much like themselves: equal in intelligence, virtue, ambition, and interests with every other human being, hence equal in rights and desert, in dignity. It is this picture of the poor as equal in dignity to everyone else, and as deserving, therefore, of whatever we would give to our friends or expect for ourselves, that sets up the possibility of seeing poverty as a harm, as something that, since we would not have it inflicted on anyone we loved or respected, we should not be willing to have inflicted on anyone. Seeing the poor as like one's friends and oneself invites the question, "don't they deserve not to *be* poor?" One would rather one's friends and acquaintances work from choice rather than need, that they have a buffer against hunger or homelessness should they lose their jobs, and that they have enough education, health, and financial resources to lift themselves out of a miserable social condition if they try. So once we come to respect the poor as equals, it is but a small step to ask, "should there not be education, health care, unemployment protection, etc. for *everyone*?" But first we need to see the poor as equals. It is essential to the modern notion of distributive justice that one believe the poor *deserve* certain kinds of aid, but one is unlikely to believe that if one takes the poor to be naturally or divinely appointed to the bottom of a social hierarchy, or to be inherently vicious and indolent. The possibility that people might have a right not to be poor, that the state, in the course of enforcing human rights, should attempt to abolish poverty, is one that could open up only once Smith's dignified portrayal of the poor replaced the views, which had reigned unquestioned for centuries, by which poverty went with a difference in kinds of people, not merely a difference in luck.

Two final notes on Smith's picture of the poor. First, it fits in with the strong moral egalitarianism I attributed to Smith in §16. Smith is reluctant to acknowledge that the division of labor is based to any significant degree on differences in talents. He would rather see even the philosopher and the street porter as equal in natural endowments. I don't think we need to accept quite this view—although it is not entirely implausible, if we take into account the great influence of early childhood care on the development of talents—but its very extremity helps us appreciate how strong a version of the doctrine of equality Smith held.

Second, it is deeply appropriate if the dignified picture of the poor is, as I believe it is, Smith's most novel contribution in WN. For then WN's greatest triumph is a shift in our moral imaginations—it leads its readers to *imagine* the poor person differently—and it was the central teaching of TMS that how we imagine others is what most profoundly shapes our characters and moral attitudes. By putting us, vividly and in detail, into the situation of the poor, Smith overturns ancient stereotypes against them. That WN pulls off this dramatic shift in the human imagination suggests a much stronger, if implicit, tie between TMS and WN than has heretofore been recognized. It is a wonderful illustration of the "indirect ethics" I have attributed to Smith (§11): of the way Smith accomplishes ethical ends without actually mentioning ethical terms, writes so that ethical concerns come, as if naturally, to the surface without having to be dragged there by preachy pronouncements.

52. A Brief History of Distributive Justice

What is supposed to block any argument from Smith for distributive justice is the view that the tasks of that virtue belong to individuals, not to the state. Smith does identify the phrase "distributive justice" with beneficence (TMS 269–70),[16] and he issues a warning that enforcing beneficent offices is a delicate task—pursuing it too far will destroy "liberty, security and justice," while neglecting it altogether "exposes the commonwealth to many gross disorders and shocking enormities" (81; see above, §36). But, in the first place, the fact that a task is a delicate one does not mean it should not be pursued. Many commentators emphasize just the first horn of the dilemma that makes the task delicate, and so impute to Smith the view that beneficence and other virtues should be enforced only very rarely and reluctantly. But there are *two* horns to Smith's dilemma, and he no more considers it permissible for a government to stand idly by "gross disorders and shocking enormities" than for it to violate liberty, security, and justice.

In the second place, Smith is not talking about what today we call "distributive justice." The confusion that arises from the two different meanings of this phrase can be cleared up by a bit of history. I would like to get at that history by way of a response to Istvan Hont's and Michael Ignatieff's deep and influential article, "Needs and Justice in the *Wealth of Nations.*" Hont and Ignatieff say that Smith's conception of distributive justice represents a sharp break with the jurisprudential tradition he inherited, that he conceived of property rights in a much more absolutist way than his predecessors had, and that he therefore did not allow for aid to the poor to be conceived of as a state duty, a matter of justice. The natural-law tradition coming out of Aquinas, they maintain, had regarded aid to the poor as a matter of justice, requiring it both under the heading of a "right of necessity" and as a condition on property rights. This interpretation of intellectual history is, I think, exactly inverted. In the remainder of this chapter I will try to show, first, that Smith does not break with the earlier jurisprudential tradition on distributive justice, except in small ways that bring it closer to its modern meaning; that the right of necessity that Aquinas had established for the poor does not amount to anything like modern distributive justice, and that in any case Smith accepted that right; and finally, that Smith also follows Aquinas and his followers on the relationship between property rights and distributive justice—once again breaking from them, if at all, only in ways that helped to ground, not to undermine, modern redistributivism.

Aristotle draws a twofold distinction in the notion of justice, first between a sense, later called "universal justice," in which the word can include all the virtues—the sense in which Plato had used the word in the *Republic*—and a more "particular justice" that pertains only to legal and political actions, and second, within the latter, between "distributive justice" and "corrective justice." The former calls for honor or political office or money to be apportioned in accordance with merit—"all men agree that what is just in distribution must be according to merit" (NE 1131a25)—while the latter calls for wrongdoers to pay damages to their victims in accordance with the extent of the injury they have caused. Aristotle's discussion of this distinction is devoted to the different ways in which "distributive" and "corrective" justice represent a norm of equality. In the former case, the equality consists in the fact that everyone is rewarded in proportion to his or her merits, such that it is unjust for unequals in merit to be treated equally or equals in merit to be treated unequally (1131a23), whereas in the latter case, equality requires every victim of wrongdoing to be compensated equally, regardless of merit: "it makes no difference whether a good man has defrauded a bad man or a bad man a good one . . . ; the law looks only to the distinctive character of the injury" (1132a4–5).

So it is essential to Aristotle's distributive justice that it involves a notion of merit: the whole contrast between it and corrective justice turns on the relevance of merit. We compensate even bad people who have been injured, paying attention just to the degree of harm done, but we distribute goods to people only insofar as they deserve them. And the case of distributive justice that most concerns Aristotle is the case of how political participation (the ability to vote or hold office) should be distributed, to which he returns, later on, in the *Politics*.[17] He does mention once casually that distributive justice can arise in connection with the distribution of material goods as well: when partners in a business venture need to disburse common funds in proportion to each person's contribution to the venture (NE 1131b29–30). What he does not raise even as a possibility is that the state might be required by justice to organize the distribution of material possessions among its citizens. Even when he takes up Plato's proposals for communal ownership of material goods, in *Politics* II.5, he never so much as mentions the possibility that *justice* might require—or forbid—a redistribution of goods by the state. Nor had Plato defended his proposals that way. What Plato had suggested, and what Aristotle denies, was that the communal ownership of goods would help temper the material desires of a state's rulers, prevent corruption among them, and create bonds of friendship between the citizens and their rulers. He did not suggest, and it did not occur to Aristotle to deny, that all citizens, much less all human beings, *deserve* an equal share of material goods—deserve, indeed, any share of material goods at all.

The debate between Aristotle and Plato set the stage for what "distributive justice" would mean until the end of the eighteenth century. A series of writers, like Thomas More and Tomas Campanella, would follow Plato in arguing that the communal ownership of material goods could bring friendship to the community's citizens and help prevent political corruption, while other writers, notably James Harrington and Jean-Jacques Rousseau, argued that political corruption could be mitigated by more modest redistributions of goods. (Occasionally, in the Christian world, religious arguments would be added to these political ones, to the effect that a community that truly wants to express the spirit of Christ in its midst needs to abjure private property. One can find this line of thought running from the community of apostles mentioned in Acts 4:35

through the founding principles of many monastic orders to the language and practices of the Anabaptists in Münster, in 1535, and the British Diggers in 1649.) Other writers, including Aquinas, Pufendorf, and Hutcheson, attacked these schemes, and defended private property on much the same grounds that Aristotle had used against Plato. What no one said was that distributive justice requires the state to override or abolish private property rights, that the poor deserve any particular share of the society's material goods. And since no one said this, no one bothered to deny it either.

Given the strong link Aristotle had made between distributive justice and merit, moreover, it is hard to imagine how any premodern figure *could* have argued that justice requires a redistribution of material goods to the poor. The poor were regarded in the Christian West as, at best, people of inferior virtue who gain by having better people placed above them—they then learn proper respect and have role models to guide their behavior—and at worst as people so vicious that they deserve, even need, for their own moral well-being, to remain poor.[18] Even John Bellers, a Quaker who proposed the most thoroughgoing program to eliminate poverty before the late eighteenth century, hoped that his proposals might remove "the Profaneness of Swearing, Drunkenness, etc." among the poor, noting that these "evil Qualities" should be taken as a reason for his proposals, not against them: "For the worse [the poor] are, the more need of endeavouring to mend them."[19] Bellers thus follows in a long tradition by which aid to the poor can be justified only by charity, not by justice. The poor, wretches that they are, deserve nothing; but the well-off Christian, who is himself unworthy of Christ's redemption, has a bond with these undeserving people and should help them despite their lack of merit. But they certainly do lack merit. To suppose that the poor *deserve* help, that they *merit* even minimal charitable aid, let alone a permanent, substantial share of material goods, would have seemed preposterous.

Now after the time of Hugo Grotius talk did begin to be heard of duties of "distributive justice" toward the poor. It is crucial to this talk, however, that the phrase "distributive justice" began to be used as a synonym for charity. Grotius himself distinguished between "expletive" and "attributive" justice, the former of which corresponded to Aristotle's "corrective" justice while the latter was closer to Aristotle's "universal" justice: it embraced all "those virtues which have as their purpose to do good to others, as generosity, compassion, and foresight in matters of government" (LWP I.viii.1; 37). The main distinction between the two, for Grotius, was that the former but not the latter can be enforced. Grotius's "attributive justice" seems indeed connected to what he calls "the law of love": it mandates acts that reflect our willingness to go beyond the letter of any law.[20] As such, generosity to the poor is a prime example of attributive justice, although it is not the only one.[21]

Grotius's followers include Samuel Pufendorf, an important influence on Hutcheson and Smith, who formulated clearly an important distinction between "imperfect" and "perfect" rights to which Grotius had pointed.[22] Attributive justice responds to imperfect rights, rights that cannot be enforced. Expletive justice enforces perfect rights. It now becomes possible to say that a poor person has some sort of right—an "imperfect" one—to material aid, but it is of the nature of this kind of right that it should not be enforced.

Thus when Smith remarks that distributive justice cannot be enforced, he is merely reporting the traditional view he had inherited. Indeed, he and his teacher Hutcheson help to push that tradition in the direction by which the modern notion of distributive justice could come to birth. Following Pufendorf, Hutcheson characterizes "imperfect" rights as the claims we make on "the charitable aids of others" (SI II.iv.v). Perfect rights include our right to life, bodily integrity, chastity, liberty, property, and reputation; imperfect rights consist in the claims we make to positions and honors we have earned by our merits, and to the help of our friends, neighbors, and relatives (SI II.iv.iii–vi). Hutcheson says that the obligations corresponding to imperfect rights "are of such a nature that greater evils would ensue in society from making them matters of compulsion, than from leaving them free to each one's honour and conscience to comply with them or not" (SI II.ii.iii). Imperfect rights come in "a sort of scale or gradual ascent through . . . insensible steps," however, gaining in strength in accordance with the merits and needs of the person claiming help, and the closeness of the bond between that person and the one from whom she asks for help, until at last we reach some imperfect rights "so strong that they can scarce be distinguished from the perfect" (loc.cit.). The notion of imperfect rights rising, at some point, to the level of perfect ones seems to be new with Hutcheson, a suggestion that distributive or attributive justice may not be purely a matter of "love" in some cases.

On each of these points, including the last one, Smith is Hutcheson's faithful student. Quoting Hutcheson and Pufendorf, Smith distinguishes between perfect and imperfect rights, connecting the first to commutative justice and the second to distributive justice (LJ 9), and including in the first rights to life, bodily integrity, chastity, liberty, property, and reputation. Distributive justice comprises not just duties to the poor but duties of parents to children, of beneficiaries to benefactors, of friends and neighbors to one another, and of everyone to people "of merit"; all these kinds of relationships therefore also give rise to imperfect rights. Perfect rights may be enforced; imperfect ones generally should not be, and to try to do so can be "destructive of liberty, security, and justice" (TMS 81). But duties of beneficence vary in their strength in accordance with the claimant's "character, . . . situation, and . . . connexion with ourselves" (TMS 269), and at their strongest, some of them "approach . . . what is called a perfect and complete obligation" (TMS 79). Once civil government has been established, the strongest of these may be underwritten with force; "all civilized nations" rightly enforce the obligations on parents and children to take care of each other and "many other duties of beneficence" (TMS 80–81). More explicitly than Hutcheson, Smith avows the legitimacy of using state power to "impose upon men . . . duties of beneficence." So Smith moves the jurisprudential tradition *closer to*, not farther away from, a recognition that people in certain circumstances may have a strict, properly enforceable right to beneficence.

When he associates "distributive justice" with beneficence, or says that the "right" of a beggar to our charity is so-called "not in a proper but in a metaphoricall sense" (LJ 9), he is merely reporting the common sense of his moral and legal tradition. When he says that governments do and should enforce certain duties of beneficence, he steps a little beyond that tradition—if only a little, and with warnings that to enforce such duties can endanger government's proper task.

It is therefore entirely untrue to say, as Hont and Ignatieff and many others do, that Smith rejected a conception of distributive justice held by his forebears, by which the state had a duty to direct or supervise the distribution of property. Rather, he accepts, as a matter of terminology, a historical distinction by which "commutative justice" means protection from injury and "distributive justice" is a catch-all term for all the virtues by which an individual does good to his or her fellow human beings. Distributive justice in this sense therefore has little or nothing to do with the distribution of property. The distribution of *political office* was a matter for distributive justice, according to Aristotle. Later, defenders of universal suffrage, like the Levellers, often framed their arguments in terms of justice. But basic patterns of property ownership in a society were not generally considered a matter for state constitutions to determine—and where they were, as in the writings of Plato, More, Campanella, or Rousseau, the argument for re-organizing property was not put in terms of justice. Not a single jurisprudential thinker before Smith—not Aristotle, not Aquinas, not Grotius, not Pufendorf, not Hutcheson, not Blackstone or Hume—put the justification of property rights under the heading of distributive justice. Claims to property, like violations of property, were matters for *commutative* justice; no one was given a right to property by distributive justice. As we shall see below, even the famous "right of necessity," by which those in extreme need may make use of the goods of others without permission, falls under the heading of commutative justice, for Aquinas and his followers.

In addition, in its post-Grotian sense distributive justice was by definition a virtue of individuals rather than states. I display my civic pride, or generosity, or great honesty, when I act on distributive justice; the state has no such personal virtues to display. It makes no sense to accuse the state of violating distributive justice, in this context, and to have the state forcing individuals to comply with distributive justice would lead people to display the outward signs of a virtue whose essence is an unforced, inner feeling of goodwill. The state would succeed simply in making us hypocrites, not in instilling the virtue at which it aimed.

It was shortly after Smith's death that the idea that states had a duty of justice to support the poor appeared on the scene. Smith died in 1790, shortly after the French Revolution began, and we have no explicit record of any comment by him about that revolution.[23] This is unfortunate because it was among the French Revolution's supporters that the modern notion of distributive justice seems to have first come into its own. Tom Paine introduced a ground-breaking poverty program for the state to undertake in his 1792 *Rights of Man*; a right to socioeconomic equality was discerned by many in the French Constitution of 1793; and "Gracchus" Babeuf and his friends made such a right explicit in their 1796 conspiracy. Babeuf declared that nature had given everyone "an equal right to the enjoyment of all wealth"; the right to equal wealth here is clearly meant to stand next to the other natural "rights of man" that had been declared at the outset of the Revolution, is clearly meant to be what Pufendorf would have called a "perfect" right. Indeed, for Babeuf this right to material equality was the most important of all perfect rights. The right to equality in wealth is the first principle in the twelve-point summary that was published of Babeuf's views, and the second is that "The *aim of society* is to defend this equality, often attacked by the strong and the wicked in the state of nature, and to increase, by the co-operation of all, this enjoyment."[24] Thus Locke's argument for the purpose, and source of legitimacy, of all states—that the state can enhance and better preserve the rights we have in the state of nature—is here applied to one right that Locke never considered such: the right to equal economic status. Given the Lockean view of legitimate government, it would follow that only communist states can be legitimate. One cannot find an argument like this anywhere in the earlier writings of the Western political tradition.[25]

Of course later believers in distributive justice did not necessarily support quite such a strong notion of its importance, nor did they, generally, insist on strict equality. But Babeuf is not just the first major figure to promote communism as a practicable and secular goal; he is also the first to propose that justice requires any sort of material redistribution at all. There were many preachers of human equality before Babeuf, but there was hardly anyone who felt that that equality translated into a perfect, enforceable right to some number of material goods. Only from Babeuf's time onward does this translation of human equality into economic rights begin to seem, to some, a practicable goal, and one that follows from what people "deserve." After Babeuf, but not before, it makes sense to speak of a position about the nature of justice, well-known enough that political writers had to come to grips with it even if they rejected it, according to which justice, and not merely beneficence, guarantees to the poor a share in all wealth.

It follows that it is absurd either to condemn or to praise Smith because he did not insist that justice requires a redistribution of goods. Smith was never called upon to comment on the idea of helping the poor by a redistribution of property, much less a notion that justice demands such a redistribution. The many views, and proposals, of this kind with which we are acquainted arose after he died. We can extrapolate what he might have said about them, but we must recognize that what we are doing in that case *is* extrapolation, not a straight reading of history. Moreover, although there are grounds on which to say that Smith would have objected to the speed of change, the contempt for law, and the enthusiasm for centralized government of radicals like Babeuf, there are no grounds for saying that he would have dissented from the moral spirit, of sympathy for the poor and anger at oppression, that animated their proposals. Indeed, he is better seen as someone who shared that spirit, whose writings helped encourage the attitudes out of which modern distributive justice was born.

53. The Right of Necessity

What, now, of Hont and Ignatieff's claim that modern distributive justice is entailed by the long-standing "right of necessity," made famous by Aquinas?

In the question of the *Summa* concerned with property ownership and theft (II-II, Q 66), Aquinas devotes one article (A7) to the claim that people may claim *as their property* anything they need if they are in imminent danger of dying without that thing. When an individual is in danger of starvation, she may pull fruit off a tree or drink from a well, regardless of who owns the tree or well, and the food and drink she needs *belong* to her, as long as she needs it, not to the person who ordinarily has title to it. Similarly, one may make use of medicine if one is about to die without it, or shelter, if one is caught in a terrible storm, or anything else one needs for immediate survival. Private property, says Aquinas, is permitted to human beings because it is ordinarily a good way by which everyone can both satisfy her own needs and help to succor the poor. But there are cases that fall outside this ordinary pattern, and when a need is "so manifest and urgent, that it is evident that [it] must be remedied by whatever means be at hand," then the fundamental purpose of property takes precedence over the ordinary rules of property, and it becomes "lawful for a man to succour his own need by means of another's property, by taking it either openly or secretly: nor is this properly speaking theft or robbery." It is worth noting that by giving people a property right in what they need to survive an emergency, Aquinas brings the right of necessity under the rubric of *commutative* justice, not distributive justice, and there it would remain, in its subsequent treatments by other natural law thinkers.[26]

It is also worth noting how very limited this "right of distress" is, for Aquinas and for all who followed him on this. Aquinas places the seventh article of Q 66, which justifies taking property in need, right after two articles making clear that theft is always a mortal sin, even when one merely keeps a lost item one happens to find. Having now affirmed a strong view of the centrality of property rights to the general "order of justice" (A5, R3), article 7 enables him to make legal space for the desperately needy in cases that *by definition* lie far outside the way the normal order of social life proceeds: that by definition are "abnormal." And that space is circumscribed very tightly, as the first objection and its reply make clear. The first objection quotes the *Decretals* of Gregory IX: "If anyone, through stress of hunger or nakedness, steal food, clothing or beast, he shall do penance for three weeks." The reply declares that this line applies to "cases where there is no urgent need." So the "stress of hunger or nakedness" does not constitute "urgent need"! Only where a need is "so manifest and urgent" that there is *no* other way of satisfying it—only where "a person is in some imminent danger, and there is no other possible remedy"—does the right of distress come into play. As Aquinas has conceived it, this right can hardly be enforced, much less institutionalized: in most cases, it will be very difficult to determine whether a person who takes food, say, was truly starving or merely "hungry" at the point when he took the food, and although a judge might commendably believe the poor person in all cases, it would also be understandable, and excusable, if the judge regularly took the prosecution's side. Aquinas provides no guidance for how a human court should distinguish between "urgent need" and mere "hunger or nakedness," and his placement of this article right after an article on the mortal sin of theft, and right before two articles on the degrees of sinfulness in different types of theft, suggests strongly that he is primarily concerned with the judgments of the heavenly court, not the earthly one. God knows when needs are urgent, and the person who takes property presumably knows whether her need was urgent. That person can be assured that if she really was in need, she has not committed a sin and does not owe a penance. What human law, and human courts, are to do about these cases doesn't seem to concern Aquinas much, and he certainly does not translate this marginal kind of case into a general call for human law to redistribute property.

Grotius, who was a jurist rather than a theologian, discusses the right of necessity with more of an eye toward its application in human legal systems, but otherwise he follows Aquinas closely. The right to use someone else's property in times of dire need is not a mere extension of the law of love, he says, but a true right, originating in the fundamental principles that ground the order of property itself (LWP II.vi.1–4, 193). Once again, however, this right is severely constrained. "Every effort should be made to see whether the necessity can be avoided in any other way, as for example, by appealing to a magistrate, or even by trying through entreaties to obtain the use of the thing from the owner" (194). One is not allowed to make use of the right "if the owner himself is under an equal necessity," and one should, if possible, make restitution of whatever one uses after the necessity is over (194–5). The right of necessity "may not be carried beyond its proper limits" (194), and Grotius makes clear that these limits are narrow ones: "He who is rich will be guilty of heartlessness if, in order that he himself may exact the last penny, he deprives a needy debtor of all his small possessions; . . . Nevertheless so hard a creditor does nothing contrary to his right according to a strict interpretation" (759). The law of love asks that the rich not impoverish poor debtors, but the strict law, the law that enforces rights, does not. So the poor have no right not to be poor, no right even against rich people who would claim "all [their] small possessions"; they just have a right, in the direst of cases and when all other means of survival are closed off to them, to use what they need to stay alive.

Once we keep in mind that, for both Aquinas and Grotius, the right of necessity is distinct from the demands of benevolence, and that it is the unenforceable latter and not the enforceable former to which the poor normally appeal when they need help, it becomes clear that Hume merely maintains the natural law tradition intact on these matters, and does not alter it in favor of a more absolutist view of property rights. Alasdair MacIntyre has suggested otherwise:

[W]hat the rules of justice are taken to enforce [,according to Hume,] is a right to property unmodified by the necessities of human need. The rules of justice are to be enforced in every particular instance . . . , [even] in the face of that traditional figure, the person who can only succor his family . . . by doing what would otherwise be an act of theft. The tradition of moral thinking . . . shared . . . by Aquinas . . . saw in such an act no violation of justice, but Hume, asking the rhetorical question "What if I be in necessity, and have urgent motives to acquire something to my family?" sees such a person as one who may look [only] to the generosity of "a rich man."[27]

But MacIntyre misrepresents Hume. For, despite the presence in it of the word "necessity," the passage he cites (from T 482) is not Hume's response to the possibility of a right of necessity. That comes in the second *Enquiry*, where what he says could easily have been said by Grotius:

Where the society is ready to perish from extreme necessity, no greater evil can be dreaded from violence and injustice; and every man may provide for himself by all the means which prudence can dictate, or humanity permit. The public, even in less urgent necessities, opens granaries, without the consent of the proprietors; as justly supposing, that the authority of magistracy may, consistent with equity, extend so far. (E 186)

It is important to note that for Hume the point is more that justice falls away altogether in the face of necessity, such that opening granaries is, strictly speaking, neither wrong nor right, than that a special *kind* of justice applies to cases of necessity, but he is clearly trying to accommodate what the earlier jurisprudential tradition had called "the right of necessity" within his own theory. Before and after this passage, he gives examples of other cases where necessity overrules the usual laws of justice—after a shipwreck, in a siege, in a famine—all of which closely resemble the examples that Grotius gave of the right of necessity (cf. LWP 193).

Like Aquinas and Grotius, moreover, Hume distinguishes the right of necessity from the normal course of justice, in which the poor may appeal only to the beneficence of the rich. The passage MacIntyre quotes comes from Hume's characterization of that normal course of justice. And what Hume says there fits in perfectly with the earlier natural law tradition. For Aquinas, poor people ordinarily need to appeal to the obligation upon rich people to "communicate [their external goods] to others in their need,"[28] and for Grotius, as we have seen, the law of love, but not law in the strict sense, imposes on the rich an obligation to refrain from taking all of a poor debtor's "small possessions." Hume is no less insistent than Aquinas and Grotius that morality demands that we help the needy: "A rich man lies under a moral obligation to communicate to those in necessity a share of his superfluities." But the rich man does not violate *justice* if he fails to live up to this obligation. Thus Hume, despite his famously original defense for justice and property rights, does not introduce any new notion of how strictly, vis-à-vis human needs, they are to be enforced. Rather, he holds the same two-sided view that we have seen in his predecessors. In ordinary cases, the poor must rely on beneficence for their claims on the property of the rich, but they may justly take property without permission in cases of extraordinarily urgent need.

Where does Smith fit into this tradition? Hont and Ignatieff, who rightly place Hume within the tradition, wrongly imply that Smith gave more limited scope to the right of necessity. Smith invokes the right of necessity three times in his *Lectures on Jurisprudence* (LJ 115, 197, 547), endorsing it as properly a part of justice implicitly in the first two cases and explicitly in the third: "necessity . . . indeed in this case is part of justice."[29] About the opening of granaries, he writes:

> It is a rule generally observed that no one can be obliged to sell his goods when he is not willing. Bu[t] in time of necessity the people will break thro all laws. In a famine it often happens that they will break open granaries and force the owners to sell at what they think a reasonable price. (LJ 197)

Smith may be quoting Hume in this passage, as the editors of LJ suggest; at any rate, he seems to find the opening of granaries just as acceptable as Hume does. Hont and Ignatieff overlook the passage entirely, and its resemblance to Hume, which leads them wrongly to contrast Hume and Smith on this matter (NJ 20–21). Stressing the words "most urgent," in Smith's remark that "the ordinary laws of justice" may be sacrificed to public utility "only in cases of the most urgent necessity" (WN 539), and the words "less urgent" in the passage from Hume quoted above, they maintain that Smith has a stricter notion of when human survival might trump laws of justice. But the remark of Smith's on WN 539 occurs in a discussion that has nothing to do with opening granaries, and in any case it declares just what the tradition defining the right of necessity had always held. Everyone who upheld a right of necessity believed that it obtained only in urgent and extreme cases.

Hont and Ignatieff make a similar error when, quoting LJ to the effect that beggars have a "right" to our charity "not in a proper but in a metaphoricall sense," they see this as implying that Smith (here together with Hume) wants to replace the ancient right of necessity with an unenforceable duty of benevolence: "It was to this discretionary sentiment that [Hume and Smith] looked to the relief of the necessities of the poor in any emergency" (NJ 24). But Smith is once again simply *following* the traditional jurisprudential view. Every thinker who recognized a right of necessity before Smith and Hume, including Aquinas, took the "discretionary sentiment" of benevolence to be the proper source of aid to the poor in all but life-threatening cases. Smith would differ from the tradition he inherited only if he held, as he does not, that the poor must rely on the benevolence of the rich *even* in life-threatening cases.

What leads Hont and Ignatieff astray is that they assimilate certain positions in the eighteenth-century debate over famine policy to the right of necessity. Not only the opening of granaries, but laws imposing a maximum price on grain, or against exporting or "engrossing" it (buying it up early in the season, so as to sell it at a higher price when supplies grow short), all derive, they suggest, from the logic behind the ancient right of necessity (NJ 18–20). This is something of a confusion. Even the opening of granaries, as Hume points out, is only dubiously justified by the right of necessity, and any set of *laws* cannot possibly fit under the *exception* to all law that Aquinas and Grotius carved out for cases of extreme and urgent need.[30] The right of necessity is, by definition, an exception to the ordinary course of justice and not a part of that course. It is designed precisely for emergencies, for cases where one cannot "appeal to a magistrate" (LWP II.II.vii; 194), for circumstances where the ordinary legal and political framework fail. Law and policy are general tools, meant to cover the usual, more or less predictable run of affairs. To the extent that certain disastrous circumstances fall outside of that usual run of affairs, a right of necessity is proclaimed as a stopgap measure, preserving human life until the normal framework can take over again. It follows that no law or general policy could possibly be an extension of the right of necessity. If law and policy can handle a set of circumstances, that set of circumstances cannot be the sort of exception to which "necessity," in this sense, applies. Thus the opening of granaries is quite far from the sort of situation that Aquinas and Grotius had in mind (a mob opening a granary has time to bake bread, and therefore time to appeal to a magistrate), and all laws, including those policing the grain market, are by definition not an exercise of the right of necessity. If a famine or dearth is predictable enough that laws can prevent or limit it, then it is something that can be dealt with by the ordinary course of justice, and not by an extralegal device.

And if we turn, now, to the course of ordinary law and policy that Smith recommended for the prevention of famine, we find that Hont and Ignatieff make his views appear more counterintuitive than they were. Like his Physiocratic predecessors, Smith proposed that law and policy deal with famine by lifting all restrictions on the grain trade rather than by capping prices or preventing the exportation of corn. Hont and Ignatieff are right that Smith thought such a policy would end the threat of famine forever, and they draw out the moral consequence of this view beautifully when they say that he thereby hoped to "explode the whole antinomy between needs and rights" that underlay the concept of a right of necessity, that he hoped the subsistence of the poor would thereby become "a matter [n]either of benevolence [n]or of the drastic justice of grave necessity" (NJ 24; see also 22, 25). They are also, of course, right that in proposing a fully free market in corn, Smith disagreed radically with the economic common sense of his time. He had a sophisticated argument to show that the common sense of his time was wrong on this, that it failed to understand the way markets in foodstuffs worked, and that it therefore maintained measures preventing the investment in agriculture that would end famines in the long run. Allowing the free export of corn, and allowing corn merchants to make a handsome profit by engrossing corn, would encourage investment in agriculture, which in turn would eventually make for good harvests every year; allowing the free importation of corn would alleviate dearths in the meantime; and removing price caps on corn would make people "feel the inconveniencies of a dearth somewhat earlier than they otherwise might do" and therefore prevent the dearth from turning into a famine (WN 533).

These proposals do include the notion that people can put up with a "dearth," and that in many circumstances in which food is scarce governments should maintain free market policies anyway. What Smith never said was that these policies should be pursued in the face of *starvation*. Hont and Ignatieff distort Smith's views at this point, making it look as if Smith was blinded to immediate human suffering by the beauty of his long-term vision. Smith's views on the corn trade, they say, earned him "the reputation, even in his own day, of being a dogmatic 'projector' for the application of long-term models of natural market processes" to issues of short-term policy.[31] They rightly attribute to Smith the belief that "if . . . the market in food were freed of meddling interventions, in the long run . . . the labouring poor would never go hungry," but then they wrongly imply that he somehow overlooked the fact that "human beings starve in the short term rather than in the long" (NJ 14), and insisted that governments may not meddle in food markets even where such meddling is necessary to prevent famine (18). They suggest that Smith differed with James Steuart and the Abbé Galiani over whether the price of food "should be regulated, in times of grave necessity . . . , by the government" (14; see also 15–18).

But Smith did not oppose the regulation of grain prices, or grain exports, "in times of grave necessity." He explicitly allowed for regulating the price of bread in some cases: "[w]here there is an exclusive corporation [of bakers], it may perhaps be proper to regulate the price of this first necessary of life" (WN 158). And he declared that a small country in conditions of dearth may legitimately forbid the exportation of corn:

> The demand of [some] countries for corn may frequently become so great and so urgent, that a small state in their neighbourhood, which happened at the same time to be labouring under some degree of dearth, could not venture to supply them without exposing itself to the like dreadful calamity. The very bad policy of one country may thus render it in some measure dangerous and imprudent to establish what would otherwise be the best policy in another. . . . In a Swiss canton, in some of the little states of Italy, it may, perhaps, sometimes be necessary to restrain the exportation of corn. (WN 539)

Both of these passages contain the word "perhaps," and both allow measures, in the face of bad policy, that Smith disapproves of in general. Nevertheless, they make clear that preventing immediate starvation was of paramount importance to Smith, just as it was for Galiani, that he was neither an absolutist about the property rights of farmers and corn merchants nor a theorist with so fixed a gaze on the long term that he could not recognize the need, in some cases, for short-term solutions that ran counter to his long-term goals. Smith's endorsement of the right of necessity was as full as that of all his predecessors—and for him, as for them, it made very little difference to long-term law and policy.

54. Smith and Natural Law Views of Property

Finally, now, to Hont and Ignatieff's claim that the natural law tradition had always understood property rights as a response to the demands of distributive justice. When we see what is wrong with this claim, we can bring the issues about distributive justice we have discussed in this chapter together with the discussion of property rights in the previous chapter. We will also see how much Smith is a *source* for the notion that property rights ought to be justified in a context of distributive justice, rather than someone who tried to undo an earlier coupling of the two. Hont and Ignatieff were among the first to show how much can be learned by placing Smith within the natural law tradition, and they thereby bring out a question of central importance to WN. But they read the natural law tradition in exactly the wrong direction, and this blinds them to the true significance of their own point about Smith. For in fact concern for those excluded from a system of private property becomes more, not less, prominent as the tradition proceeds, and none of the earlier thinkers they cite is nearly as concerned as Smith is with the question of how to reconcile property rights with the needs of the poor.

Hont and Ignatieff see the problem of securing "justice as between haves and have-nots" as haunting the natural law tradition's approach to the justification of property rights. They argue that Aquinas begins from the assumption that the world belongs properly to all human beings in common—that God originally gave the world "to the collective stewardship of the human species as a community of goods" (NJ 27)—and then allows for individual property rights under the strict condition that such rights be used to meet the needs of the poor. But this badly distorts Aquinas's view. Aquinas does not suppose an original "collective stewardship of the human species" over material goods; he explicitly *denies* that natural law recommends collective ownership (II-II Q 66, A2, R1). Rather, he believes that before private property was instituted people participated in what is generally called a "negative common," in which it is legitimate for anyone to use any good. This is a far cry from "collective stewardship," which implies a communal organization of production and distribution like that of the apostolic community in the book of *Acts*, and which Aquinas actually considers to be a *violation* of the natural order: He says that individual ownership of goods, as opposed to common ownership, is not merely legitimate but "necessary for human life."

Nor is the main problem about property rights, for Aquinas, the possibility that the poor might thereby be kept from the means for their subsistence. He does mention that possibility, but only in a digression from his main theme. His overarching concern is to refute a type of extreme religious asceticism, according to which individual ownership of material goods gets in the way of true communion with Christ. In particular, he wants to refute a pair of linked theological propositions: (1) that all material things belong to God alone, and (2) that God licenses the use of His things, at most, to the species of human beings as a corporate body, not to individual people. Property rights get justified in articles one and two of *Summa* II-II, Question 66. The first of these argues, against a claim that people do not naturally own things since they cannot change anything's nature, that God allows us a power to use things, if not to change their nature, and that that power is indeed a proper expression of the image of God residing in man. Drawing on both Biblical texts and arguments from Aristotle, Aquinas concludes that God grants us a "natural dominion over external things." The second article condemns as heretics those in the early church who regarded individual ownership of things (along with marriage) as blocking salvation, and argues that people best express their "natural dominion over external things" by way of individual property rights. The early heretics who get thus condemned may well be standing in for more contemporary theological opponents. As Richard Tuck has pointed out, one of Aquinas's purposes here is to challenge "the life of apostolic poverty as practised . . . by the great rivals of his Dominican order, the Franciscans."[32] But that is to say that the opponents with whom Aquinas is wrestling are people who feel that property rights constitute a religiously impermissible attachment to material things, not people concerned with the injustice of a distinction between rich and poor. That communal ownership of goods also maintained the poor was incidental to this religious vision. It was not uncommon, after all, for an entire community, constituted in this way, to be poor, and such poverty was a badge of honor, not something to regret or resolve. Aquinas rejects the radical other-worldliness of these communities. As he does throughout his theology, Aquinas integrates God more fully with His creation, and the worship of God more fully with a delight in that creation, than do his more mystical predecessors and peers. In any case, Aquinas is worried first and foremost about a theological question concerning the place of material goods in a Christian life, not, except incidentally, about the relationship between property ownership and the poor.

Grotius does not share these theological concerns, but his defense of property rights is similarly unprovoked by a worry about "justice as between haves and have-nots." Instead, he takes up property rights as a part of his investigation into the law of war and peace. He is concerned about such issues as how property rights can give rise to a just cause of war, and what kinds of property can legitimately be claimed, in the course of war, to secure provisions for an invading army. The origin of property rights comes up largely as a basis for considering the extent to which the sea, and other large waterways, properly belong in common to all human beings, and should not be controlled by one country to the prejudice of others. And the justification Grotius gives for property rights turns essentially on the fact that without such rights, people get into constant conflicts. So, again, the question of how the poor may get their needs met is very much an incidental one, yielding a side-constraint on a system of property rather than a structuring feature of that system.[33]

When Locke, now (ST V.34), offers his famous justification of property rights as a way of increasing the "benefit and . . . conveniences of life" available to all human beings, as dependent, ultimately, on labor, and as resulting, when carried out most fully, in a world in which "a day-labourer in England" can live better than an Amerindian king, he may be denying any claim of the needs of the poor as against property rights, but he at least makes the effectiveness of property rights in helping the poor more important to their function than do Aquinas and Grotius. But the issue still lurks a little behind his main concerns. The claim that property depends on labor served Locke's political purposes as part of an argument that taxation requires the consent of the people. Kings had no right to collect taxes without the consent of Parliament, since taxes come out of people's property, and property, however much it might be shifted around by systems of positive law, is rooted in a prepolitical right to own the fruits of one's labor. In the course of defending this claim, Locke wants to show how very useful labor is for the multiplication of goods, and part of his demonstration of *that* point involves the remark, picked up by Smith, that an Amerindian king, ruling over people who fail to improve their land by labor, "feeds, lodges, and is clad worse than a day-labourer in England" (ST V.41). So Locke makes this point to bring out the tremendous productive power of labor, not to show that property rights deal justice to the poor.

It is Hume who first does the latter, and Smith develops the argument more fully. Hume begins his discussions of justice and property, in both the *Treatise* and the second *Enquiry*, by stressing the way in which particular acts of justice may seem silly or cruel taken on their own. In the *Treatise*, this is what leads him to ask why I have no right to take a rich man's property even "if I be in necessity, and have urgent motives to acquire something to my family?" In the *Enquiry*, he defends the inequalities of property after first conceding

> that nature is so liberal to mankind, that, were all her presents equally divided among the species, and improved by art and industry, every individual would enjoy all the necessaries, and even most of the comforts of life; nor would ever be liable to any ills, but such as might accidentally arise from the sickly frame and constitution of the body. It must also be confessed, that, wherever we depart from this equality, we rob the poor of more satisfaction than we add to the rich, and that the slight gratification of a frivolous vanity, in one individual, frequently costs more than bread to many families. (E 193–4)

Having said this, Hume goes on to argue that any attempt to establish complete equality will (a) reduce the entire society to poverty, (b) require extreme restrictions on liberty, and (c) undermine the political structure that is supposed to ensure the equality itself. It follows that it is better for everyone, including the poor who suffer from inequality, to live under a system of private property than to try to replace it with an equal distribution of goods. Property, like the virtue of justice that protects it, has clearly *bad* effects in particular cases but provides, as an entire scheme, far more good than harm to everyone.

Smith sets up a view of the same general kind with an even greater emphasis on the ways in which systems of private property burden the poor. In both sets of lecture notes published in LJ, as Hont and Ignatieff rightly emphasize, Smith begins his discussion of political economy with a vivid dramatization of the injustice that seems to be involved in the division between rich and poor:

> Of 10,000 families which are supported by each other, 100 perhaps labour not at all and do nothing to the common support. The others have them to maintain beside themselves, and . . . have a far less share of ease, convenience, and abundance than those who work not at all. The rich and opulent merchant who does nothing but give a few directions, lives in far greater state and luxury and ease . . . than his clerks, who do all the business. They, too, excepting their confinement, are in a state of ease and plenty far superior to that of the artizan by whose labour these commodities were furnished. The labour of this man too is pretty tollerable; he works under cover protected from the inclemency in the weather, and has his livelihood in no uncomfortable way if we compare him with the poor labourer. He has all the inconveniencies of the soil and the season to struggle with, is continually exposed to the inclemency of the weather and the most severe labour at the same time. Thus he who as it were supports the whole frame of society and furnishes the means of the convenience and ease of all the rest is himself possessed of a very small share and is buried in obscurity. He bears on his shoulders the whole of mankind, and unable to sustain the load is buried by the weight of it and thrust down into the lowest parts of the earth. (LJ 341)

The poor worker is Atlas, holding up the human universe: Smith calls up here a picture that might have served as a program for the heroic monuments to the worker that were put up under socialist regimes in the 1930s and 1940s. The passage is very Rousseauvian—except that there is no passage in Rousseau himself that brings out the unfairness of the division between rich and poor quite so clearly.

And the parallel passage in the early draft of WN tells us explicitly that that division is unfair. It begins:

> Supposing . . . that the produce of the labour of the multitude was to be equally and fairly divided, each individual, we should expect, could be little better provided for than the single person who laboured alone. But with regard to the produce of the labour of a great society *there is never any such thing as a fair and equal division*. In a society of an hundred thousand families, there will perhaps be one hundred who don't labour at all, and who yet, either by violence or by the more orderly oppression of law, employ a greater part of the labour of the society than any other ten thousand in it. (ED 4, my emphasis)

That the most wealthy gain their wealth "by violence or by the more orderly oppression of law" is a yet more stunningly Rousseauvian suggestion than anything in the LJ passage. Smith also tells us outright that it is an *unfair* division of goods that leads to what he is about to characterize, as in LJ, as the "burial" of the poor beneath the weight, which they uphold, of the rest of society. What he will go on to say, also as in LJ, is that this "unfair and unequal" division of goods still leaves the poorest workers much better off than even the richest people in more egalitarian societies. Here we get Locke's Amerindian king (LJ 339, 489, 563), who is materially worse off than the poorest day-laborer in

England. Smith thus gives us essentially the same justification for inequalities that John Rawls would propose two centuries later: they are acceptable if and only if the worst off people are better off than they would be under a more equal distribution of goods.

Now in its published form, WN does not include the detailed breakdown of employments in society, rubbing our noses in the inverse relationship between hard work and comfort, that appears in LJ and ED. Nonetheless, the point about the poorest people in commercial societies being better off than the king of a more egalitarian tribe provides the famous, dramatic ending of the opening chapter—and the dramatic placement of the point here makes it more effective, rhetorically, than it was either in Locke or in LJ and ED—and Smith continues to note that systems of private property primarily protect the rich against the poor, and only indirectly benefit the poor themselves (WN 710, 715). Finally, the bitter irony about the place of the poor that so marks the passages in LJ and ED shows up in many of Smith's comments in WN on the way masters try to keep their workers poor.

It is worth noting the difference in tone between Hume and Smith on this issue. Smith takes over both the question Hume had raised about the justification for protecting property rights against the needs of the poor and the answer Hume had given to that question, but the issue has a great deal more prominence, and a very different emotional coloring, in Smith's thought than in Hume's. Hume sets up what we might call "the paradox of justice" (compare NJ 42)—the paradox that the very system that claims, by way of protecting everyone's rights, to respect all human beings equally in fact serves to sanctify *un*equal distributions of property—but that paradox is for him but one illustration of a philosophical point: that justice is an artificial virtue, whose foundation rests on utility rather than immediate approval. For Smith, the paradox is a matter of concrete moral and political import. The detail he lavishes on the disproportionate effort, and meager reward, of poor workers in commercial societies is astonishing, such that, even if in the end he praises commercial society for making those workers better off than people were in earlier stages of civilization, he seems not to want our endorsement of our own stage of society to be wholehearted.

So it is Hume and especially Smith who first present the system of private property as standing under a presumption of unfairness because of the way the poor suffer to provide luxury for the rich. Both Hume and Smith have an answer to that presumption, but they contribute something new to the discourse on property simply by making this presumption central to their accounts. It seems absurd, even immoral, to Smith and Hume, that misers and scoundrels should be able to claim large amounts of property while hard-working people make do with virtually nothing. Only once we understand that a system of strict property rights on the whole protects the liberty of everyone, and in the long run leads everyone to be better off than they would be under an egalitarian system, should we accept such rights as justified. Far from hiding or ignoring the paradox of justice, Hume and Smith frame their defense of property rights by posing it as starkly as possible. In this mode of presentation, they differ from Aquinas and Grotius, for whom the tension between property rights and the needs of the poor at most lurks dimly behind concerns about God or war. Hume and Smith are the first to make the suffering of the poor *the* problem for the justification of property rights. What Hont and Ignatieff call the "antinomy" between needs and rights, between "need claims" and "property claims" (NJ 2, 42) thus only comes to the fore when the natural law tradition enters the modern world. After Hume and Smith, some radicals came to deny that property rights are justified at all, to maintain that justice requires the abolition of private property. But the radicals who made these moves were piggy-backing on Hume's and Smith's question: "how can property rights be justified if they protect the rich while making the poor miserable?" They *answer* that question differently, rejecting the story by which property rights, in the long run, actually help the poor. But it is Hume and Smith, more than anyone earlier in the natural law tradition, who taught them to ask this question in the first place.

I do not mean to imply that Smith would necessarily have defended the modern welfare state, let alone modern socialism, or that his latter-day followers are wrong to invoke him when they complain about welfare programs administered by large bureaucracies. Smith does prefer government to work through a small number of clear, general laws than through officials making ad hoc decisions; he worries about both the inefficiency and the danger to liberty of anything that involves interference in people's lives on a daily basis. But he does not say, nor would it be true, that all attempts to redistribute resources need involve bureaucratic power in this way, and he did not think that redirecting resources to help the poor was in principle beyond either the capability or the rightful province of the state. On the contrary, in his conception of the poor and of what the poor deserve, Smith helped bring about the peculiarly modern view of distributive justice: the view according to which it is a duty, and not an act of grace, for the state to alleviate or abolish poverty.

PART V

Politics

CHAPTER ELEVEN

Politics

The truth in the libertarian reading of Smith comes from his cynical, dismissive view of politics. Many libertarians justify their opposition to government inter-vention in individual affairs by the belief that it is unjust to tell people how to act, except in those cases where their actions would inflict violence or fraud on others. We saw in part IV of this book that Smith does not believe it is always wrong to interfere with what individuals do, even aside from cases in which they engage in violence or fraud. He does not admire self-interest, like Ayn Rand, nor think that interference with it is unjust, like Robert Nozick. But he does believe that government officials tend to be ineffective, corrupt, and vainglorious, and that government action is therefore a poor solution to most social ills. Smith's hostility to politics has philosophical roots, and it distinguishes him from both a long tradition, later identified with the left, that values political action as intrin-sically worthwhile, and a variety of religious and nationalist traditions that either look to government as a source of moral teaching or glorify the state, and see the extension of their nation's power as intrinsically worthwhile. In this chapter we will examine what Smith has to say about politicians and how this view affects his attitude toward democracy, citizenship, and war.

55. Moral Vices of Politicians

Smith takes a dim view of the virtue of politicians, and hence of their ability to guide others toward virtue. His description of the statesman as "that insidious and crafty animal" (WN 468) is perhaps his most famous swipe at politicians, but there are many other passages, both in WN and in TMS, where he indicates that political office tends to attract, and produce, particularly vain, arrogant, and otherwise unadmirable people. He grants that "a wise man" can occa-sionally play a valuable role in shaping or reforming his nation's political consti-tution (TMS 231–2), but he abjures the notion, held by many of his contem-poraries, that political leaders are in a good position to shape the moral opinions, or regulate the moral practice, of their fellow citizens. Hutcheson had said that sovereigns should take care to instruct their citizens in principles of virtue, which for him included natural religion.[1] Smith says that "a temporal sovereign, though he may be very well qualified for protecting, is seldom sup-posed to be so for instructing the people" (WN 798). He also tells us that kings and ministers are "always, and without any exception, the greatest spendthrifts in the society" (WN 346), that successful warriors, statesmen, legislators, and founders of political parties tend to be filled with "excessive self-estimation and presumption," and that when they are successful, we enter into their self-admiration by sympathy and therefore overlook the imprudence and injustice with which their enterprises are beset (TMS 250–52). He grants that successful political leaders are often courageous, but warns that their courage tends to go together with cruelty and violence (TMS 55, 64–5, 152–3). Even where it is not accompanied by violence, moreover, the vanity of politicians is likely to lead them to arrogant attempts at imposing their will on the populace. Politicians are apt to be "wise in [their] own conceit" and therefore to be drawn to a "system" that fails to respect the independent projects of the people it is supposed to serve (TMS 185, 233–4). This arrogance is enough to mark political leaders, on Smith's terms, as less than virtuous: humility is essential to truly good people. We considered this point in an earlier section (§16), where I argued against a view of Smith as an elitist, but even if he is an elitist, it is clear that most politicians will not belong to his elite.[2] (This, in sharp contrast with Aristotle, for whom Pericles was an ethical paradigm.) It is not clear whether politicians will even normally be ethical enough to carry out their own proper tasks. Smith tells us that an impartial concern for the public good is supremely important in politics (WN 471–2, TMS 231–3), but he also makes clear that that concern tends to be in lamentably short supply among those who occupy government positions, and that it tends to be most lacking where, as during war or civil strife, it is most needed (TMS 154–5). Recall that Smith believes we are most capable of benevolence with regard to individuals we see and know well, that our moral sentiments fade as the group of people we affect grows larger and more anonymous. True devotion to the good of a large public will therefore be rare, and it will be relatively easy, for one whose decisions affect many people he will never see, to behave callously and unfairly. Add in the tendency to "excessive self-admiration" that drives people toward success in politics, and it is small wonder that political leaders will rarely be models of ethical achievement.

One of Smith's sharpest differences with his teacher Hutcheson shows up in this view of the character and skill of politicians. Hutcheson says that it is "natural to men to esteem and admire any singular abilities discerned in others; such as courage, wisdom, humanity, justice, publick spirit," and that people therefore "commit their important interests" to people of such dispositions, and "have a zeal to promote them to honourable offices and powers of managing the common concerns of society" (SMP III.iv.i; 213). Smith says that virtuous qualities are "invisible" and "always disputable," that societies therefore have never "found it convenient" to bestow rank and power on the basis of those qualities, and that political office instead drifts to the less admirable but more "palpable" qualities of age, fortune, and aristocratic birth (WN 711, 711–13). He adds an analysis of what attracts people to positions of power that makes the prospect of finding a virtuous class of politicians look very dim:

If to each [of the American] colon[ies], . . . Great Britain should allow . . . a number of representatives . . . ; a new method of acquiring importance, a new and more dazzling object of ambition would be presented to the leading men of each colony. Instead of piddling for the little prizes which are to be found in what may be called the paltry raffle of colony faction; they might then hope . . . to draw some of the great prizes which sometimes come from the wheel of the great state lottery of British politicks. Unless this or some other method is fallen upon . . . of preserving the importance and of gratifying the ambition of the leading men of America, it is not very probable that they will ever voluntarily submit to us. (WN 622–3)

With what impatience does the man of spirit and ambition . . . look around for some great opportunity to distinguish himself? No circumstances, which can afford this, appear to him undesirable. He even looks forward with satisfaction to the prospect of foreign war, or civil dissension; and, with secret transport and delight, sees through all the confusion and bloodshed which attend them, the probability of those wished-for occasions presenting themselves, in which he may draw upon himself the attention and admiration of mankind. The man [born to] rank and distinction, on the contrary, . . . shudders with horror at the thought of any situation which demands the continual and long exertion of patience, industry, fortitude, and application of thought. Those virtues are hardly ever to be met with in men who are born to . . . high stations. (TMS 55–6)

The latter passage gives us a choice between two kinds of unadmirable people as natural candidates for government work, and goes on to tell us that "all governments, . . . even . . . monarchies" tend to prefer the ambitious types who delight in war and civil dissension over their lazier but more pacific aristocratic counterparts. In any case, the glittering prizes of politics are attractive incentives precisely for those people who most hunger for attention—which is the very opposite of the character type, inwardly directed and concerned with praise-worthiness rather than praise, who is likely to develop into a paragon of virtue. There is thus a competition, for Smith, between the incentives that lead us toward fame and the incentives that lead us to moral development, and those who act on the first type of incentive are drawn away from, not toward, the second. Excessive attention to "the clamour of the man without" distracts us from proper attention to the quiet voice within. The noise of public admiration is something that the sage avoids, while those who seek it in place of the more honest judgment of "the man within" are people who have lost a crucial part of their ability to direct themselves by conscience (TMS 130–31; see also 247–8).[3]

In the passage from WN above there is also considerable scorn for the supposed value to society of what politicians do. Political office appears as a mere prize in a lottery, to be "raffled" off to American leaders as a way of buying compliance from them. Smith seems unconcerned about whether the lucky winners would do a good job in their offices, for the people they represent or for Britain as a whole; he is concerned just about "preserving [their] importance and gratifying [their] ambition," so that they will desist from the war in which they are engaged. Allowance must be made for the rhetorical context of the passage—in 1776, British readers might be more likely to heed a proposal for American representation in Parliament if it was couched in terms contemptuous of the American leaders—but it is hard, here or elsewhere, to find Smith ever taking the content of what political leaders do very seriously. Political office is a job like any other, for him; it arises as a special occupation, like other jobs, with the advancement of the division of labor; it reflects, therefore, a real human need but it does not deserve the veneration, as the highest of human callings, that the populace, and classical philosophers, have bestowed on it. What "dazzles" about political office is in reality worth no more than what dazzles in lottery prizes.

There are occasions on which Smith thinks a political leader can perform a very important function in society, and on these occasions he believes it to be of great importance that decent, thoughtful people step into the breach. He condemns those who would value the life of monks and friars above the "statesmen and legislators" who have been the "protectors . . . of mankind,"[4] and he tells us that a person of "real political wisdom" and deep patriotism is needed to help bridge divisions in society, and carefully alter a constitution, in times of civil faction (TMS 231–2). A person who accomplishes this, Smith says, "may assume the greatest and noblest of all characters, that of the reformer and legislator of a great state" (TMS 232). On the basis of these passages, Donald Winch has tried to recover a civic republican strain in Smith, to argue that he did indeed think politics could be among the highest of human achievements (ASP 159–60). But that times of crisis require people of virtue to hold political power does nothing to suggest that political power is generally a good arena for the display of virtue, and Smith clearly takes the achievements of great reformers and legislators to be *exceptional to,* not paradigmatic of, the behavior of most politicians. It is because virtue is in general so difficult to combine with politics that any politician who does display virtue must be unusually admirable. When faction or other deep political disturbances arise in a state, one who overcomes the moral pitfalls of politics to help forge a well-reformed constitution can rightly be counted "the greatest and noblest of all characters." But it is precisely because people are normally drawn into politics by their vices, and are led moreover into greater partiality by their participation in it, that the legislative reformer is so admirable. What Smith has to say positively about the virtues of the great legislator in times of unrest is parasitic on his view of the normal course of politics as vicious.

I therefore agree with Vivienne Brown rather than Winch on this subject. Brown has shown brilliantly how the distinctive feature of WN, in relation to similar literature of its time, is "the elimination of the legislator/statesman . . . as a guiding force in setting up the constitution, establishing an ongoing programme of legislation, managing the economy, or promoting public virtue" (ASD 210–11; see also 120–40, 209–12). Smith does not see virtuous politicians as having any regular role in promoting the good of society, although he does think they are necessary on occasion. But it is the notion that the ordinary, normal flow of social life needs guidance by wise leaders that is behind most of the paeans in classical literature to politics as a realm where virtue can shine. It is that notion, too, among modern admirers of the classical view from James Harrington to Hannah Arendt, that has inspired the belief that participatory citizenship is an essential component of the human good. Smith, by contrast, developed a conception of morality which "excluded the development of a political personality" (ASD 211). The moral and the political personality conflict, for him; the one does not grow naturally out of, let alone complete, the other.

56. Cognitive Vices of Politicians

It is, however, not so much a view about morality as a view about cognition that provides the deepest reason for Smith's distrust of politicians. This comes out in some of the best-known passages of WN. Two closely related ones are the following:

> What is the species of domestick industry which his capital can employ, . . . every individual, it is evident, can, in his local situation, judge much better than any statesman or lawgiver can do for him. The statesman, who should attempt to direct private people in what manner they ought to employ their capitals, would not only load himself with a most unnecessary attention, but assume an authority which could be trusted, not only to no single person, but to no council or senate whatever, and which would nowhere be so dangerous as in the hands of a man who had folly and presumption enough to fancy himself fit to exercise it. (WN 456)

> [Under the system of natural liberty, e]very man, as long as he does not violate the laws of justice, is left perfectly free to pursue his own interest his own way, and to bring both his industry and capital into competition with those of any other man, or order of men. The sovereign is completely discharged from a duty, in the attempting to perform which he must always be exposed to innumerable delusions, and for the proper performance of which no human wisdom or knowledge could ever be sufficient: the duty of superintending the industry of private people, and of directing it towards the employments most suitable to the interest of society. (WN 687)

Both passages tell us that it is "folly" or a "delusion" for any single person, or even any group of people, to think he or they could ever know enough to guide the many economic decisions of the individuals in a great society better than those individuals can do themselves. As discussed earlier (§§5, 7, 22), Smith sees human knowledge as highly particularist, as far better at grasping the details of particular events than at generalizing from those events. Indeed, he trusts self-interest to govern economic decisions in large part because he believes it leads us to attend appropriately to details. Like other animals, we perceive details better when they matter to what we care about. Hence people should always be left alone to secure what is necessary for their own self-interest; they will care more about it than a lawgiver or statesman would, and they will therefore know it better. Self-interest gives the individual *cognitive* advantages, vis-à-vis whatever is in his or her interest, over the statesman. Smith does not say that people should always be allowed to act on self-interest, or that they should be immune to state oversight in matters where something more than their self-interest is at stake. "The law ought always to trust people *with* the care of their own interest," he says (WN 531), not that the law should always trust people *to* care about their own interest. Here, as in the lines from 456 quoted above, Smith decries *paternalistic* legislation—legislation designed to help people better than they can help themselves—not legislation designed to protect one group of people from others.

And he has a similarly narrow target in the lines from 687, which form part of the famous conclusion to Book IV. Smith does not tell sovereigns that the system of natural liberty discharges them from *all* duties that might involve interfering with private actions, merely that it discharges them from "a" duty of this kind. What duty is that? The duty to *direct capital and labor toward an increased production of goods*. It is this duty that requires knowledge that no human being could possibly have. It is this duty, moreover, against which the whole long polemic of Book IV has been directed. What Smith has been showing throughout Book IV, and to some degree throughout the whole of WN, is that "systems of preference and restraint"—mercantilist and Physiocratic systems—invariably misdirect the investments of a society, draw too much stock toward one species of industry, or force too much away from another species of industry.[5] They are therefore inferior, for the purpose of increasing a nation's total stock, to simply letting industry find its own course without government direction. Economic growth is not a task for governments to undertake, and the sovereign is therefore relieved of the duty of guiding "the industry of private people . . . towards the employments most suitable to the interest of society."

Nothing follows from this about government duties other than those supposed to promote economic growth. Nothing Smith says in the conclusion to Book IV suggests that the distribution of goods, let alone the control of externalities like pollution, or the development of institutions, like educational institutions, that foster freedom, should be left in private hands alone. Smith does not say, nor could he plausibly argue, that his economic arguments show anything about *all* government duties. When he tells us that every man should be left free to "pursue his own interest" (within the limits of justice), context makes clear that he means only that such freedom is the best way to pursue economic growth. He is not proclaiming a libertarian principle of government in general. Indeed, the third category of duties he proceeds to give the sovereign—the duty of creating or preserving those public works and institutions "which it can never be the interest of any individual, or small number of individuals" to create or preserve but which will "frequently do much more than repay [their cost] to a great society"—is broad enough to include practically all the tasks that modern welfare liberals, as opposed to libertarians, would put under government purview. Smith's third category describes institutions that help society without turning a profit. Institutions to help the poor, but which the poor cannot themselves afford, are prime examples of that sort of institution. Smith himself puts his public school proposal under this heading, and the terms of the third duty would in principle allow for public housing, health care, unemployment insurance, and much else. Institutions that provide education or foster virtues that people do not think they need would also fall under this category. For modern libertarians, this latter type of institution, especially, is morally offensive. They believe government should not do things to try to change the individuals they represent. Smith, by contrast, shows no unease about including institutions to foster courage and intelligence, and to dampen religious enthusiasm, within the sovereign's third duty. So it is a grave mistake to read Smith's objections to mercantilist and Physiocratic policies as similar in principle to the modern libertarian claim that governments should do no more than protect us all against physical harm.

One person who makes this mistake is Gertrude Himmelfarb, when she writes that Smith's proposal for widespread public schooling runs "against the grain of his own doctrine." "Having spent the better part of two volumes arguing against government regulation," she says, "he now advanced a scheme requiring a greater measure of government involvement than anything that had ever existed before."[6] But Smith had *not* spent the better part of WN arguing against "government regulation" per se; he had spent the better part of WN arguing against government regulation *in the name of increasing national wealth*. Wealth is maximized by private efforts undirected by the government, he showed in Books I to IV, rather than by government attempts to steer resources into any particular economic channel. From the fact that governments should leave wealth-production alone, however, it does not follow that governments should leave every social process alone. Smith's general view of politics, as Himmelfarb recognizes,[7] is that governments should foster their subjects' freedom as much as possible. Yet the fostering of freedom may require that governments provide certain institutions as well as that they refrain from imposing certain laws. People are deprived of some part of their freedom if they are led into "gross ignorance and stupidity" (WN 788), if they become incapable of "bearing a part in any rational conversation" and of "forming any just judgment concerning many even of the ordinary duties of private life" (WN 782). People who lose their rationality, lose their ability to "form just judgments," also lose their ability to make informed— free—choices. Fostering rationality and the capacity for judgment is therefore a way of *restoring* liberty to them. In this light, Smith's proposal for governments to help underwrite schooling, and even to require some level of education of all children, is needed to *protect* the people's liberty.[8] His argument for government provision of schooling to all thus follows directly from his doctrines, rather than running against their grain. And if there are other institutions that similarly foster freedom, Smith's doctrines would require governments to make sure they too exist.[9]

But the limitations Smith describes on what anyone can know about their society should give pause to those who are confident that governments can carry out even the task of protecting freedom successfully. Taken together with his scepticism about the judiciousness, decency, and impartiality of those who go into politics, this is what gives punch to the libertarian reading of Smith.

Anyone convinced by the arguments that culminate in WN 687–8 can impute a task to government only with great reluctance. As Charles Griswold says: "A burden-of-proof argument suffuses Smith's writing in political economy; the state may intervene in all sorts of ways, but those who would have it do so are required to show why it should in [each] particular instance" (AVE 295).

For Smith himself, the burden of proof is met in a number of cases. Smith proposed a government limitation on the private notes of credit that circulated in his day (WN 323–4), and endorsed a series of interventions that his government had already made in the way such notes were drawn up (WN 325–7). He also proposed small public schools, militia training for everyone, and a requirement that anyone entering the professions be trained in "science and philosophy" (WN 796). These are fairly small-scale proposals, as befits one who distrusts the competence and virtue of government officials, but they are not the proposals of a person with principled objections to governmental shaping of society. Whether Smith would have countenanced the more thoroughgoing projects of the modern welfare state is not easy to say. He probably would not have objected to any of them in principle, but they would each have had to meet his "burden-of-proof argument" against the ability of governments to handle any task, and many of them would fail that test.

57. Problems with the "Private Sector"

Emma Rothschild has recently made a point of great importance, correcting some common myths about Smith:

> The objects of Smith's obloquy are not only the institutions of national government; they are also, and even especially, the oppressive government of parishes, guilds and corporations, religious institutions, incorporated towns, privileged companies. One of the most insidious roles of national government is indeed to enact, or confirm, the oppressive powers of these intermediate institutions. The criticism of local institutions, with their hidden, not quite public, not quite private powers, is at the heart of Smith's politics. (ES 108)

Modern libertarians often respond to the problems inherent in government agency by suggesting that social issues be turned over to the private sector. By the "private sector" they mean corporations, churches, and other voluntary organizations, as well as individual citizens, families, and neighborhoods. They do not just mean, that is, that individuals can solve their problems of poverty or environmental degradation all by themselves (although they usually think this is more possible than the advocates of big government assume). Rather, they believe that the interest of many large businesses, and the beneficence of churches and other voluntary organizations, will direct them toward helping to solve these problems, and that these "private" groups are more likely to act effectively and efficiently than the government will. There is good reason to think Smith would have rejected all of this. It is not clear that large, organized bodies like

General Motors or the Catholic Church should count as "private" entities at all,[10] and Smith's analysis of what is wrong with politicians in any case applies to the leaders of these entities as well.

Smith makes clear that large churches and corporations are much like government, wielding power that interferes with the way individuals would otherwise act in their local situations, and that where they compete with government for control over the society, it is better to put that control in the hands of government. Government is after all a body specifically entrusted to use power for secular, civic ends, and a body that in most nations, certainly in republics, is to some degree restrained by the citizenry. Neither churches nor corporations need be restrained in this way, and they are certainly not bodies entrusted by the citizenry with secular, civic purposes. Smith stresses, moreover, that the interest both of churches and of merchants can be, and often is, opposed to the public interest (WN 266–7, 797), and that when these groups achieve secular power, they tend to use it to promote, respectively, absurd, factious doctrines or private, material gain. The rule of merchants, he says, "is, perhaps, the worst of all governments for any country whatever" (570; see also 637–8, 752). And he describes the medieval Catholic Church as "the most formidable combination that ever was formed against the authority and security of civil government" (802).

The extreme incompatibility between business habits and concern for the public good is a major point of WN; Smith is very worried about the great influence merchants had over political decisions in Britain and intends his separation of economy and state at least as much to protect the state from the corruption of economic interests as to protect the economy from the ineptitude of political forces. He regards the political influence of churches as just as baleful as that of merchants, however, and for similar reasons supports a separation of church and state (792–6). Indeed, he compares churches to corporations: "The clergy of every established church constitute a great incorporation" (797). He then devotes much of his chapter on religious institutions to the politics by which church leaders get selected, and to the various ways in which large churches have tried either to subdue or to ally themselves with temporal sovereigns. He describes churches as rivals to political sovereigns, pointing out that the Catholic Church's medieval role in supporting the poor gave it "the command of a great temporal force" (802). From the point of view of the public good, it was a great victory when governments finally wrested control back from the church: "the liberty, reason, and happiness of mankind . . . can flourish only where civil government [, as opposed to the church,] is able to protect them" (802). Smith recommends that governments in future take care not to delegate any part of their power to business and religious interests, that they keep those interests from "the performance of [any] part of the duty of the sovereign" (733). Without government support, Smith believes, without any sort of alliance with government, both business and church groups will naturally split themselves up into smaller and smaller entities over time, and he considers it far better for societies to be filled with many small, competing economic interests and religious institutions than with large gluts of economic or religious power. So the last thing Smith would ever propose is a delegation of state tasks like welfare or education to for-profit or religious enterprises. Rothschild rightly says that Smith would oppose anything tending "to enact, or confirm, the oppressive powers of . . . intermediate institutions," like churches and privileged companies.

To say that governments should not "enact or confirm" the power of religious and business organizations is not, however, to say that those organizations are themselves political entities. But large organizations of any kind need a structure of governance much like that of a political unit, and Smith discusses business governance in explicitly political terms throughout WN V.i.e and church governance in those terms in V.i.g. More deeply, Smith's analysis of the problems with politics applies without alteration to large religious, business, and other "private" institutions.

In the first place, the leaders of a large church or business tend to be socially prominent in the same way that political leaders are, and rank in these organizations therefore offers incentives that are just as corrupting of morals as political rank does. People like Bill Gates or Pope John Paul II are very much in the public eye, and the yearning to be thus acclaimed by "the man without" makes up a great part of the motivation leading people to try to achieve positions like Gates's or the Pope's. In the case of church leaders, the incentive to preen oneself publicly rather than to develop oneself internally is in fact more dangerous than the comparable incentive in politics, since church leaders are normally taken to be moral exemplars while political leaders are not. This means moral corruption in the church will damage the moral fiber of the population in a way that moral corruption among politicians will not. It also means that leadership positions in the church will tend to draw in people willing to lead a life that often adds hypocrisy to moral shallowness, thus people whose characters are even worse than the sort of people who find politics appealing.

Smith makes all these points about churches and their leaders at WN 803–8. He offers moral criticisms of business leaders at WN 267: they are "an order of men, . . . who have generally an interest to deceive and even to oppress the publick, and who accordingly have, upon many occasions, both deceived and oppressed it." Their line of work inclines them to an extremely narrow focus on their own and their friends' interests, to the exclusion of the interest of their competitors let alone of the public as a whole (144–5, 266–7, 456, 461–2, 734). People who achieve prominence in the business world are not prone to hypocrisy, and to leading people astray, as church leaders are, but their situation does habituate them into pursuing their own interests without even the pretense of looking to the wider, moral concerns that politicians and church leaders are supposed to take up. This narrow, very selfish, uncitizenly attitude, what Smith calls their "mean rapacity, the[ir] monopolizing spirit," means that merchants are particularly unsuited "to be the rulers of mankind" (493).

In the second place, the cognitive problems in judging what will be best for every individual in all the many local situations in a great society are just as great when the people who try to direct those situations from afar are merchants or church leaders as when they are politicians. Smith draws our attention to parallels between problems in running a large corporation and problems in running a state. A "spirit of faction" can run through the stockholders of a joint stock company (WN 741), just as it may run through the citizens of a state. The stockholders always employ others to direct the day-to-day affairs of the company, moreover, and these directors, "being the managers rather of other people's money than of their own," cannot be expected to "watch over it with the same anxious vigilance" that a person would show if he were taking care of his own interest (WN 741; see also 737, 739–5). Again, Smith believes that self-interest normally motivates due attention to detail, that cognitive skill and emotional energy are linked (see §5). Since corporate leaders will often lack the proper motivation for their job, their capacity for good judgment will not be properly engaged. "[E]very individual . . . can, in his local situation, judge much better than any statesman or lawgiver can do for him" (WN 456), but this crucial premise for the invisible hand holds only where the individual regards a local situation as "his," not where he is carrying out the orders or looking after the interests of someone else. Consequently, "[n]egligence and profusion . . . must always prevail, more or less, in the management of the affairs of [a joint stock] company" (WN 741). Smith claims that this is the reason why joint stock companies are so very anxious to secure a monopoly over the trade in which they engage: They are run so poorly that they can succeed only with such a monopoly (WN 741, 755).

Note that it is inessential to this argument that a corporation be chartered by the government. People who combine an admiration for Smith's critique of government activism with a fondness for large corporations tend to play down the critique of corporations in the chapter I have been quoting by saying that that critique applies only to concerns, like the East India Company, *established by the government*, and that Smith had nothing to say, because he did not foresee, the large private firms made possible by the coming of general limited liability, about a century later. As K. N. Chaudhuri points out, however, the British East India Company was in many ways "the direct ancestor of the modern giant business firm."[11] And although Smith is particularly incensed by the quasi-governmental role given to the East India Company—"No other sovereigns ever were, or from the nature of things, ever could be, so perfectly indifferent about the happiness or misery of their subjects" (WN 752; see also 637–8, 754)—a good deal of the problem he sees in corporations has to do simply with size. "[A] joint stock company, consisting of a small number of proprietors, with a moderate capital, approaches very nearly to the nature of a private co-partnery," he says, "and may be capable of the same [high] degree of vigilance and attention" (WN 744). By contrast, the South Sea Company, because it had "an immense capital divided among an immense number of proprietors," was bound to be rife with "folly, negligence, and profusion" (WN 744–5; see also 755).

There are deep connections among Smith's view of moral community, trust in the invisible hand, and distrust of politics. Because human beings are built to attend to one another as individuals, and as individuals whose emotions and needs vary greatly in accordance with minute differences in their circumstances, they can best care for one another, monitor and scrutinize one another's behavior, and lead each other to aspire to standards of propriety and virtue, in small, close-knit communities.[12] Within these communities, each of us surveys the others, subtly checks and guides each other's behavior, and cares to some extent about all of the others, so the monitoring and socialization in which we engage is egalitarian and, therefore, allows for a considerable amount of individual freedom. I try not to stifle you, since you and I have equal power and I don't want to be stifled myself. So in small communities we can keep each other acting for the benefit of all without using force or even much explicit rebuke. We can, peacefully and spontaneously, achieve a balance between socialization and individual freedom.

In a similar way, small economic units in a large society can allow each other freedom of action and satisfy their own interests while simultaneously meeting the needs of the society. Those who own small economic units will find it in their interest to run them directly, and the units will normally have to both satisfy an independently existing source of demand and live up to social standards for good business behavior. Since the interests driving the action of each unit will be directly engaged with the social needs that the unit serves, each unit is likely to promote the public good, as if by an "invisible hand." Each unit is also likely to operate without trampling on either its workers' or its competitors' or anyone else's freedom. Human beings "love to domineer," and our pride is indeed so great that we will sacrifice our material self-interest in order to lord it over others (WN 388; see also LJ 186, 192). Where economic units are small, however, the number of such units prevents any one of them from being able to stifle the others, from taking its laborers for granted, or from attempting to control what other elements of the society might be doing.

As a community expands, each member of that community becomes more anonymous, and more likely, therefore, to drop into "obscurity and darkness" (WN 795). The degree to which each individual cares about the others, knows how to help them, needs to worry about his or her own conduct, or even knows how to promote his or her own interests, drops off markedly. One consequence of this is that people's moral traits will atrophy, and Smith has a moving, very astute discussion of the way working-class people can lose their virtues when they move from a country village to a large city (WN 795–6). Another consequence is that in order to keep their members from harming one another, such large communities need to create a caste of people charged explicitly with monitoring behavior, and dispensing rewards and punishments. Governance replaces the natural, egalitarian processes of mutual monitoring and mild social pressure. Hierarchical relations replace egalitarian ones, fear replaces persuasion, and obedience to authority replaces independence. Herein lies the fundamental reason why government force is so inferior to social forces in guiding human behavior, but what is troubling about government power here is just as troubling in the power structures that large corporations and churches must set up to accomplish their ends. When a firm is large enough that its owners and workers do not know one another on a face-to-face basis, when it is large enough to need a level of "middle managers" between its owners and its every-day policies, then one can no longer trust it either to treat its workers decently or to serve its own needs, let alone the public's needs, very well. And when a church is large enough that its clergy can jockey for power over one another, directing their energies into love of domination rather than into setting a moral example, and when it is large enough that face-to-face contact between clergy and parishioners no longer keeps the clergy in moral check, then it comes to be just another temporal source of power, hypocritically hiding its oppressive work behind the pretension that it offers higher, moral teachings. When either a firm or a church gets this large, moreover, the number of resources it controls tends to be large enough for it to seek the aid of government, with which it becomes yet more able to interfere with the actions of individuals across society, and to pursue its own, partial interests against the interests of the society as a whole. The natural human ability, by way of sympathy and approval and disapproval, to tame the natural human yearning for domination decreases the more individuals join forces in large, organized groups, and works best when people are dispersed into very small units, interacting constantly with one another without preventing each other from doing what each judges it best to do.

When Smith maintains that this or that social problem can best be handled by "private people" (WN 687), therefore, he means to leave the problem strictly up to the interaction of *individuals*, perhaps in families or other small units, not to turn it over to large organizations. Indeed, where small-scale individual inter-actions will not solve a problem, he prefers to put that problem into the hands of government than to turn to large organizations outside government. Govern-ments, after all, have at least an official commitment to the public weal, and the political sovereign has an interest in maintaining this commitment. In elected governments, officials may lose their job if they abandon the public good in obvious ways, and even in unelected governments, the safety of the ruler de-pends crucially on whether he or she is perceived by the populace to be con-cerned for the public good.[13] The sovereign is therefore more likely than any other element of the society to look out impartially for the interests of everyone, how imperfectly soever he or she may carry out this task, and Smith turns to the sovereign when he thinks such impartial concern is needed. Thus it is "the wisdom of the state only" which can render soldiering into a special occupation (697), and it is the interest of the state that Smith considers to be most closely linked to the educational needs of the poor (788). The state is also the agent most likely to counter oppression by powerful individuals and groups within society. Smith praises states for breaking the power of feudal landowners (401–5), and looks to the state to end slavery, lamenting that a democracy, because it will be run by slaveowners, is less likely to end slavery than a monarchy (LJ 182, 187). Similarly, he says that regulations in favor of workers are "always just and equitable" (WN 157–8). The fact that the state has a structural stake in being perceived as impartial enables it to look out for the weaker elements in society, those who might otherwise be squelched in the struggle among partial interests.

Finally, Smith sees the state as the only power able to mediate impartially between warring factions within the society, and to transcend partial interests enough to provide trustworthy information on certain subjects. Even if its deliberations are directed all too often "by the clamourous importunity of partial interests" rather than "by an extensive view of the general good," it is still the legislature that is in the best position to look out for the needs of all the various sectors of a great society (WN 471–2). When sections of a country are divided by "rancorous and virulent factions," it is also only "the coercive power" of a strong central government that has any chance of restoring peace (WN 945). Similarly, that governments are more likely to be impartial than other agents in society leads Smith to see them as the proper agents for issuing public information. On several occasions, he accepts the need for government to put its mark on certain products so as to secure consumers against abuse (WN 40, 138). When he recommends that the state require "the study of science and philosophy" of anyone who wants to enter the professions (WN 796), he implies that the state will determine what *counts* as "science and philosophy." In all these ways, the state can achieve goods that no other agent can, because it alone is designed to stand above partial interests. As much as Smith decries the failings of government, he regards it as playing a number of irreplaceable roles in society.

58. Law over Policy; Well-designed Institutions[14]

There is thus a profound tension, even a paradox, in Smith's attitude toward government. Smith believed government was in principle the appropriate agent to handle many social problems, yet he distrusted the people who work in governments so much that he thought they often should not attempt such solutions. His reasons for preferring government solutions to social problems are deep ones: Only governments so much as purport to take up the impartial perspective, vis-à-vis an entire society, from which conflicts among partial interests should be solved. And his reasons for distrusting government officials are also deep ones: those who hold government office tend to be amoral or corrupted by their office, and the knowledge government officials can have of local situations is almost always poorer than the knowledge people in the middle of those situations have. So the tension here is not an easy one to resolve. One can neither simply abandon the government's role to the private sector nor expect that better education, say, would produce adequately decent and wise candidates for political office. To some extent, Smith does lean toward the first of these options, suggesting that society can run better on its own than one might imagine. He also has some other ways of navigating between the Scylla and Charybdis he has set up. Above all, he recommends that government actions be enshrined as much as possible in general laws, rather than in bureaucracies making ad hoc decisions, and that new laws and institutions be designed with an eye toward how they will most easily fit in with existing practice and custom. Both of these strategies reflect an interest in making government as little dependent as possible on either the knowledge or the moral character of individual officials.

To begin with the first: Smith evinces a strong preference, throughout both LJ and WN, for the rule of law over the rule of persons. Brown says that LJ fits in well with the legal writing of its time, "which accepted the superiority of judicial practice over the work of the legislator" (ASD 120), and this captures nicely Smith's belief that fair administration of established law is far more important to freedom and security than new laws aimed directly at freedom and security. It is also true that Smith sees the independence of the judiciary from the other branches of government as essential to freedom: "One security for liberty is that all judges hold their office[r]s for life and are intirely independent of the king" (LJ 271; cf. WN 722–3). At the same time, Brown's formulation is not quite right, for Smith argues that the work of the legislature is essential to restraining the judiciary from becoming itself a means of arbitrary rule:

> The judge is necessary and yet is of all things the most terrible. What shall be done in this case? The only way is to establish laws and rules which may ascertain his conduct; . . . for when it is known in what manner he is to proceed the terror will be removed. . . . The growth of the judicial power was what gave occasion to the institution of a legislative power, as that first made them think of restraining the power of judicial officers. Laws instituted at the beginning of a society . . . would appear to be the greatest restraint imaginable on the liberty and security of the subjects; but afterwards they evidently appear to tend to the security of the people by restraining the arbitrary power of the judges, who are then become absolute or nearly so. (LJ 314–15)

Again, as regards the specific tradition of law in Britain, Smith says: "[a] thing which greatly confirms the liberty of the subjects in England . . . [is] the little power of the judges in explaining, altering, or extending or correcting the meaning of the laws, and the great exactness with which they must be observed according to the literall meaning of the words" (LJ 275; see also 282–5). So Smith does not particularly venerate the English *common law* tradition, with its reliance on precedent rather than written law and room for judges to interpret those precedents, and it is not quite true to say that he gives "judicial practice" priority over "the work of legislators." Rather, he both wants the legislative to put a strict check on the power of judges and sees an independent and strong judiciary, bound by the letter of the law, as essential to liberty. Both the legislative and the judicial branches of government are preferable for Smith to the work of "that insidious and crafty animal, vulgarly called the statesman or politician, whose councils are directed by the momentary fluctuations of affairs" (WN 468). Both the legislature and the judiciary, oriented as they are toward "general principles which are always the same," are more likely to be impartial, and to place clear and predictable limits on individual action, than the executive branch of government. As Smith says in the passage from LJ quoted above, "when it is known in what manner [government officials are] to proceed, the terror [of them] will be removed." Individuals have freedom in proportion to the degree to which they can predict how the government will treat them; arbitrariness is the greatest threat to liberty.

Smith therefore dislikes laws (like the settlement laws or certain kinds of taxation—see WN 153 and 825–6) that put too much power in the hands of individual government officials, and laws (like most trade restrictions) that change too much in the short term. Laws that fluctuate often are unpredictable and make room for partial interests, like the merchant interests that shaped bounties and import restrictions, to have too great a say in government. Smith prefers governments to employ (1) long-term strategies, (2) enacted in simple and clear laws, (3) that reflect the interests of all the different sectors of society (WN 654), and particularly of the weaker sectors (WN 157–8), and (4) that fit in as much as possible with a country's history and current practice. (Laws that institute sharp changes from past custom will interfere with individual action much as arbitrary or quickly fluctuating laws do.)

These four features mark all of Smith's own proposals for political change. With them in hand we can see that Smith was in his own way a reformer, not the political quietist he is sometimes taken to be. In the beginning of WN, Smith says that "philosophers" are people who, by "observ[ing] every thing" and thereby "combining together the powers of the most distant and dissimilar objects," come up with "inventions" (WN 21). In parallel drafts of this passage (LJ 492, 570), he lists "political" and "commercial" philosophers among the subdivisions of philosophy, suggesting that he is thinking of himself, among other people, as one of those who observe widely and thereby bring together things normally held apart. But if the passage is self-referential, Smith must have thought of himself as an inventor! I suggest that his policy proposals are meant to be his "inventions." Thus his proposal for altering the coinage, so that people would no longer have incentive to melt down silver coin (WN 61–2), his elaborate scheme for resolving the dispute with the American colonies (622–3, 944–5),[15] his proposal to prohibit the circulation of bank notes smaller than 5 pounds (WN 323–4), his recommendation for taxes that would encourage agriculture (831–4), for publicly funded schools (785), and for a union with Ireland (944–5) can all be seen as his inventions, the products and useful consequences of his philosophical work.

Placing these inventions in the context of WN I.i, where the mechanical inventions described are all improvements on existing machines, gives us a nice idea of the *scale* of policy proposals Smith favored. The philosopher, like the boy who improved "the first fire-engines," comes up with a small shift in method, designed to fit one cog better into an already ongoing complex process, to hook a small piece of a machine here with another piece there. A thorough understanding of the process being altered, and a deep sensitivity to how it might be improved with as little disturbance as possible to its general workings, are required for such innovation. In the philosopher's case this means: A vast and deep knowledge of the natural environment, human psychology, economic processes and history may allow one to envisage a small shift in current policy, a regulation that can easily be integrated into ongoing practices, or a new institution that is not too expensive and is likely to have few wildly unforeseeable consequences. A philosopher's policy proposals must operate the way a good mechanical invention does: must fit in with its surroundings and thereby gently enhance an existing system, so as to bring about a new equilibrium rather than simply destroying the old one. In a work published five years before WN, Smith's student John Millar characterized these sorts of proposals, and the type of politician who promotes such proposals, in terms of which Smith would surely have approved:

> It is . . . extremely probable, that those patriotic statesmen . . . whose laws have been justly celebrated, were at great pains to accommodate their regulations to the situation of the people for whom they were intended; and that, instead of being actuated by a projecting spirit, or attempting from visionary speculations of remote utility, to produce any violent reformation, they confined themselves to such moderate improvements as, by deviating little from the former usage, were in some measure supported by experience, and coincided with the prevailing opinions of the country.[16]

Political inventions that "deviate little" from current usage, and fit in with the way ordinary people already see the world, may well turn out not only to be less dangerous but to have greater impact than the sweeping changes proposed by utopian revolutionaries. A Rube Goldberg machine produces nothing, and is too complicated to build even if it did produce something; James Watt's improvements to the steam engine revolutionized an industry. Similarly, the French Revolution mostly brought on new repression while the American First Amendment had a vast transformative effect on society, both in America and across the world.[17] One reason for the plausibility of Smith's proposals is that his new laws, small schools, and so on are all designed so that people will have strong incentives to make them work. Smith is careful to mesh his proposals with people's self-interest, which means he does not need to make unrealistic expectations of people. The utopian expects vast changes in human nature; the Smithian tinkerer works with human nature as it is. Ironically, this means that small Smithian changes are more likely to improve human beings than grand utopian plans. Institutional changes that do not entirely shake up a society are ones its members can integrate into both the ethical and the procedural norms they already have. They can therefore figure out fairly easily how to adapt themselves to the changes. Such changes can therefore work vast social transformation over time. Revolutions, by contrast, rarely so much as get a grip on the societies they are supposed to transform. After the initial flush of enthusiasm, people fail to understand, or know how to live with, the new changes, which means that the revolution must either disappear or be taken over by an elite willing to rule by force. Smith's striking philosophical idea is to see that *radical political change works through conservativism*, through gradual changes that conserve even as they transform. This is neither a Burkean presumption in favor of tradition over conscious planning, although it may often look like it, nor, of course, either a Benthamite or a Rousseauvian fondness for the wholesale re-structuring of society.[18] The uniqueness of the position has, I believe, not yet been properly appreciated.

59. Republics versus Monarchies; Civic Republicanism

What worries Smith about politics applies to all forms of government, whether they are responsible to voters or not. Bad character and inadequate knowledge will plague politicians in monarchies and republics alike, and the inferiority of political force to social forces will hold regardless of governmental form. Smith is therefore more concerned to urge that governments act in limited ways, and use general laws and simple institutions when they do act, than to defend any particular form of government. Nor does he concern himself much, as Rousseau did, with the type of citizen a system of politics produces. Nevertheless, he does engage a little with these issues, making characteristically nuanced contributions to both.

Smith endorses republics over monarchies, but with enough qualifications that one may be tempted to take what he says as no endorsement at all.[19] He is recorded, in LJ, as holding the following view:

> In a republican government, particularly in a democraticall one, <?utility> is that which chiefly, nay almost entirely, occasions the obedience of the subject. He feels and is taught from his childhood to feel the excellen<c>y of the government he lives under; how much more desirable it is to have the affairs of the state under the direction of the whole than that it should be confined to one person; that in the one case it can hardly ever be abused and in the other it can hardly miss of being so. (LJ 318–19)

Note that the main advantage of republics, here, is that they guard against the abuse of power, not that they express the general will of their citizens, or enable citizens to develop their political personality. There is moreover a suggestion that the claim that republics are superior to monarchies is something of a party line ("He . . . is taught from his childhood to feel . . ."). Nevertheless, Smith says nothing to contradict the party line, if that is what it is, and he goes on shortly afterward to praise the Whigs, the British party that preached utility and the utilitarian advantages of republics, over the monarchical Tories:

> The bustling, spirited, active folks who can't brook oppression and are constantly endeavouring to advance themselves, naturally join in with the democraticall part of the [British] constitution and favour the principle of utility only, that is, the Whig interest. The calm, contented folks of no great spirit and abundant fortunes which they want to enjoy at their own ease, and dont want to be disturbd nor to disturb others, as naturally join with the Tories and found their obedience on the less generous principle of [authority]. (LJ 320)

Republicanism is similarly contrasted with "oppression" in WN (584–5). There Smith also describes the liberty of the American colonists as due to their republican form of government, and seems to approve particularly of the fact that the king does not "corrupt" the American legislatures, that they are "more influenced by the inclinations of their constituents." In addition, he praises the colonies for having no hereditary nobility, no one with "privileges by which he can be troublesome to his neighbors" and reports, with apparent approval, that the colonists have more republican manners than their counterparts in the mother country (WN 584–5). It is not unreasonable to suppose, indeed, that Smith's suggestion that the British constitution "would be completed" by American representation in Parliament, his endorsement of a full union between the two with the British capital perhaps moving, in the course of time, over to the American shore (WN 624–6), is intended to help lead Britain itself, gradually, toward greater republicanism.[20]

At the same time, Smith has serious reservations about republics. The greatest of these we have already touched upon: He believes republics are less likely than monarchies to abolish slavery. In a republic that has slaves, slaveowners will inevitably constitute a powerful segment of the electorate and the government will find it very difficult to overcome their interest in preserving slavery (LJ 181, 187). In a monarchy, "there is some greater probability of [the] hardships [of slavery] being taken off. The king cannot be injured by this; the subjects are his slaves whatever happen; on the contrary it may tend to strengthen his authority by weakening that of his nobles" (LJ 182). The king is therefore more able to act as "an impartiall judge"—a central role for all government, as we have seen above—and to override the partial interests that deprive a class of human beings of their freedom. For this reason alone, Smith is not sure anyone of decent moral sentiments should welcome the spread of republicanism:

> The greater <the> freedom of the free, the more intollerable is the slavery of the slaves. Opulence and freedom, the two greatest blessings men can possess, tend greatly to the misery of this body of men, which in most countries where slavery is allowed makes by far the greatest part. A humane man would wish therefore if slavery has to be generally established that these greatest blessing<s>, being incompatible with the happiness of the greater part of mankind, were never to take place. (LJ 185)

It is unsurprising in this light that Smith was unsympathetic to the American revolutionaries, and would have preferred a union under the British crown to American independence; he presumably saw a purely republican government as likely to maintain slavery indefinitely. Needless to say, his misgivings in this respect were entirely justified.

But how about if slavery does *not* "have to be generally established"? Is there anything wrong with republicanism *aside* from its tendency to maintain slavery? Well, in the first place, Smith's argument that it is difficult for republics to override the partial interests of their most powerful citizens transfers readily from the case of slavery to ways in which the rich may trample on the rights of the poor even when the poor are not slaves. In the second place, Smith dismissed the notion that even a fully democratic republic would really reflect the will of all its citizens, as Rousseau may have thought it could. In the modern age, most people, and especially most poor people, will not have the time to participate adequately in their nation's governance:

> In the modern republicks every person is free, and the poorer sort are all employed in some necessary occupation. They would therefore find it a very great inconvenience to be obliged to assemble together and debate concerning publick affairs or the tryalls of causes. Their loss would be much greater than could possibly be made up to them by any means . . . , as they could have but little prospect of advancing to offices. (LJ 226)

Similarly, in WN, Smith tells us that in economically primitive societies "[e]very man . . . is in some measure a statesman, and can form a tolerable judgment concerning the interest of the society, and the conduct of those who govern it" while the expansion of the division of labor makes that increasingly impossible (WN 782–3). He thinks the modern loss of a capacity to judge well politically, among the laboring masses, is a serious problem, and he urges some level of public education to help correct for it, but he does not suggest that it is fully overcomeable. The participatory democracies of ancient times were dependent on slave economies (LJ 226), and are in any case gone forever. As Smith's admirer, Benjamin Constant, noted in 1819, it is impossible for the citizens of a large modern nation to participate in the running of their affairs with anything like the equality with which ancient Athenian citizens helped run their city:

> The share which in antiquity everyone held in national sovereignty was by no means an abstract presumption as it is in our own day. The will of each individual had real influence. . . . Consequently the ancients were ready to make many a sacrifice to preserve . . . their share in the administration of the state. Everybody, feeling with pride all that his suffrage was worth, found in this awareness of his personal importance a great compensation.
>
>   This compensation no longer exists for us today. Lost in the multitude, the individual can almost never perceive the influence he exercises. Never does his will impress itself upon the whole; nothing confirms in his eyes his own cooperation.[21]

But Smith's disinclination to see republicanism as the cure for political ills is not rooted simply in this contrast between ancient and modern conditions. He also has an interesting argument to the effect that *no* association, of any kind, can ever reflect the voices of all its members equally. The point is made several times in LJ that even in a small club, "there is generally some person whose counsil is more followed than any others, and who has generally a considerable influence in all debates" (LJ 202; see also 226; TMS 336). Smith was a member of a number of Scottish clubs and may be drawing on his own experience. It is of the nature of human conversation that some people dominate, that some voices "lead" others, guide them, even where the people participating are equal in wealth, power, and the opportunity to speak. And those who are most capable of doing this, and who know their own interest best, may thereby lead others to give up their own interests. "In the publick deliberations," Smith says, the voice of the worker "is little heard and less regarded, except upon some particular occasions, when his clamour is animated, set on, and supported by his employers, not for his, but their own particular purpose." Workers are of course weaker than their employers, but by their "superior knowledge of their own interest," merchants also succeed in imposing upon their political superiors in the rentier class, persuading them "to give up both [their] own interest and that of the publick" (WN 266–7). Thus the hope expressed in Jürgen Habermas's recent political theory, that we might eventually determine conditions for an "ideal speech situation," and anticipated in Smith's time by Rousseau's vision of the social contract, is for Smith a chimera. People will never be equal in debating power, and the better debaters will use their skill to impose upon the weaker ones.

Smith's weak enthusiasm for republicanism in general is further evident in his lukewarm support for the current of thought in his time that has been retrospectively dubbed "civic humanism" or "civic republicanism." As we have seen, he emphatically does not share the Aristotelian view that politics is the arena of virtue par excellence, that the political life is the crown of the moral one. Virtue is paradigmatically a private matter, for him, dependent on a strong inner-directedness and exercised best in relations among family members, friends, and immediate neighbors. Richard Teichgraeber captures well Smith's attitude toward the political life:

> [Hutcheson, Hume, and Smith] no longer looked upon human virtue in terms of a person's conscious pursuit of a larger public good. Virtue was now the result of the proper orchestration of private passions. . . . [W]e more fully grasp their economic doctrines if we understand how they were founded in a de-politicized view of individual morality and de-moralized view of politics.[22]

Smith does not believe that one's status as a citizen is much relevant to one's moral decency, and, aside from his nod toward the political importance of public education, is not concerned, as Rousseau was, that the state should "make" virtuous citizens.[23] In addition to education, the civic republicans tended to see equal participation in the military and a rough equality of property-ownership as essential to equal citizenship, and Smith was fairly unconcerned about both of these issues. He does remark in LJ (196–8) that great inequality in property can be politically harmful, and Donald Winch has I think rightly suggested that Smith's call for the abolition of primogeniture and entail is meant in part to help meet civic republican goals (ASP 66–7). Smith wanted to break up long-standing accumulations of landed property both because that would lead to more efficient uses of land and because these gluts of economic power had a baleful effect on the polity. As Winch says, Smith's call for militia training to nurture the courage and loyalty of citizens is likewise a nod to civic republican goals. Yet some of the most bitter criticisms WN received had to do with its claim that standing armies are superior to militias and sometimes even helpful to liberty,[24] and his civic republican critics understood rightly, I believe, that Smith's commitment to their principles was a tepid one.

60. National Glory; War

If Smith is lackluster about civic republicanism, a good part of the reason is probably that he dislikes its tendency to glorify the state. People should not see their highest or final end in their *res publica*, he believes, should not identify their worth with their nation's glory, both because that has nothing to do with their individual worth and because such identification is the source of one of the greatest of human evils: war.

Here Winch misses the forest for the trees. As against those who ally Smith with radically individualist *laissez-faire* doctrines of nineteenth-century liberals and their tendency toward "pacific sympathies" (ASP 104), Winch brings out elements of WN that would seem to fit, respectively, a "classical-renaissance view of communal 'magnificence'" (ASP 135), and a glorification of "the patriotic and heroic military virtues" (ASP 105). These are linked themes: If the magnificence of our nation is a great good, if it is something we ought to promote, then we have to be willing to fight for it. National glory is a positional good, a good one nation can have only at the expense of other nations, and the competition for it therefore always raises the possibility of war. The ability of a state to wield a vigorous and effective military force is itself an important component of its magnificence. In addition, the public treasures and grand pageants of a magnificent state can be enhanced by pilfering from other nations, while the fact that a state displays such signs of glory can make it a tempting target for other nations' ambitions of conquest. So it is no wonder that those who see an individual's *telos* as lying in his or her political community tend also to see war among nations as something inevitable, even desirable. If Smith were a descendant of the Renaissance civic republicans, therefore, he would also be an ancestor of modern nationalism. I think the tendency to read Smith, instead, as prefiguring nineteenth-century economic liberalism, with its "pacific sympathies" and hostility to nationalism, is in this respect exactly right.

This is not to say that the passages Winch finds to support his view are not in Smith. What he misses is their context, the overall picture into which they fit. Thus, for instance, Smith does believe that "a certain expence is requisite for the support of [the sovereign's] dignity" (WN 814), as Winch reports (ASP 132), and he does also say that that expense naturally increases as societies become more opulent. But one would never imagine, from Winch's account of this chapter (WN V.i.h), that it consists of three short paragraphs, that it is in all less than half a page long, far and away the shortest part of Smith's consideration of the legitimate expenses of the sovereign and indeed quite the shortest chapter in WN. The attention Smith gives to this subject is dismissive, implying that the dignity of the sovereign does not deserve much attention.[25]

Similarly, although Smith is happy to grant that "Versailles is an ornament and a honour to France, Stowe and Wilton to England" (WN 347, quoted in ASP 133), this comes as a *concession*, at the end of a long chapter attacking the wastefulness of public expenditure in general. It comes in fact but three paragraphs after the remark that kings and ministers are "always, and without any exception, the greatest spendthrifts in the society." The chapter stresses throughout that the "profusion" of government is a far greater threat to the wealth of a nation than the prodigality of individuals could ever be (WN 342). Against a standard argument criticizing private luxury spending, Smith makes the case that criticism of this kind is more appropriately directed at public officials. "Let [kings and ministers] look well after their own expence," he says, "and they may safely trust private people with theirs. If their own extravagance does not ruin the state, that of their subjects never will." The mere comparison implies that public officials, even kings, do not inherently deserve a more luxurious way of living than their subjects, and Smith drives home the indignity of the comparison by repeatedly lumping kings and other government officials in the category of "unproductive laborers" (WN 330–31, 342). He also tells us that the maintenance of "a numerous and splendid court" is the sort of "publick prodigality" that can ruin a nation. And when at the end of the chapter he does concede that some of the luxuries on which rulers spend money benefit the nation as a whole, he picks out buildings and book and art collections, not the pageants, feasts, and royal finery that directly symbolize national power. One reason he gives for favoring the former over the latter is that they lead to the employment of productive laborers ("masons, carpenters, upholsters," etc.)—that they provide opportunities for independent, dignified labor to common people. Smith's interest in communal glory for its own sake is slender. The concession he makes to the value of a Versailles, a Stowe, or Wilton is far too little and comes far too late to override the *critique* of "communal magnificence" that has preceded it.

More generally, Smith opposes the glorification of nations throughout both TMS and WN. The final edition of TMS includes a highly sceptical account of the love of one's nation. What Smith considers true love of country has nothing much to do with one's country's collective achievements, much less its "glory" vis-à-vis other nations. It consists instead in love for the laws and institutions that preserve peace and promote the well-being of one's fellow citizens (TMS 231). This kind of love of country is not in principle, and only rarely in practice, in conflict with love of mankind in general, and the kind of love that is directed to one's country as *opposed* to mankind in general, the kind that is most often called "love of our own country," is something of which Smith is profoundly suspicious. He begins his account of this feeling by saying that we are disposed to view the warriors, statesmen, poets, and the like of our own nation "with the most partial admiration" (TMS 227–8), and the word "partial" already signals that this is not a morally admirable admiration. In the next paragraph, he associates love of our own country with "the most malignant jealousy and envy" of other nations, "the mean principle of national prejudice" that is responsible for injustice and a mark of "savage" and "coarse" dispositions. Against this ugly disposition, he sets up Scipio Nascia's reputed call for Rome to refrain from war against Carthage, as "the liberal expression of [an] . . . enlarged and enlightened mind." He then turns to the rivalry, in his own day, between England and France, saying that this jealousy "is surely beneath the dignity of two such great nations" and that each should really view the other's prosperity as benefiting it as well. He concludes the paragraph by calling on every nation "to promote, instead of obstructing the excellence of its neighbours."

All this fits beautifully with a central theme of WN. In WN, Smith condemns "national prejudice and animosity" as a particularly egregious source of bad economic policy (WN 474–5), and directs practically his entire economic doctrine against the maxims by which "nations have been taught that their interest consist[s] in beggaring their neighbours" (WN 493). At the very opening of the book—in the discussion of exchange in chapter ii, and even, implicitly, in the first chapter's tracing of wealth to the division of labor rather than to natural resources, over which one might need to compete—we learn that the pursuit of wealth is not a zero-sum game, not a competition in which the success of some must come at the cost of the failure of others, and we are taught throughout that the wealth of one nation, by providing a market for other nations' goods, promotes, rather than obstructs, the wealth of all other nations. Indeed, we learn eventually to understand "the wealth of nations" as referring to something that nations can hold, and promote, collectively. "Commerce," says Smith, ". . . ought naturally to be, among nations, as among individuals, a bond of union and friendship" (WN 493). This is one explanation of John Millar's remark that Smith was the Newton to Montesquieu's Lord Bacon:[26] Smith developed the argument to support Montesquieu's famous claim that commerce promotes international peace. Smith associates mercantilism with specious arguments for setting one nation against another, and with unnecessary, costly, and violent attempts to achieve national "vainglory." He lists the establishment of colonies among the baleful effects of mercantilist policies, and concludes WN by calling for the end of government support for the East India Company, a withdrawal of the British military and civil presence in the American colonies, and a general shift in the political climate such that Britain might come "to accommodate her future views and designs to the real mediocrity of her circumstances" (WN 947). From the very first sentence to the very last sentence of the book, Smith is implicitly or explicitly combating economic views that set nation against nation. It is indeed not much of an exaggeration to say that puncturing the fantasies that lead people to seek national glory is the primary aim of WN.

And what most repulses Smith about the search for national glory is the violence it breeds. Winch misses the forest for the trees again when he says that "Smith always regarded the art of war as the noblest of arts" (ASP 105).[27] To support such a claim, Winch adduces three passages from the revised sixth edition of TMS, published in 1790. These three passages, he maintains, "portray [. . .] the patriotic and heroic military virtues in glowing terms" (ibid.). In context, the passages are far more equivocal than that. The first comes from a chapter in which Smith notes that we are "by nature recommended" more to the care of our own country than to universal beneficence, the second from a chapter in which he shows us how we might try to reach beyond that natural recommendation to have concern for other peoples, and the third from his praise of self-command as the foundation of all other virtues. The gist of the chapters in which these citations appear is to show that even though national loyalty is *in fact* more natural to us than care for all "sensible beings," the latter *should* be our ultimate goal (TMS 235 ¶1), and the second passage uses the cheerful willingness of soldiers to sacrifice their own personal interests to urge us to sacrifice our limited interests, including national ones, when they conflict with a more universal good:

> Good soldiers . . . frequently march with more gaiety and alacrity to the forlorn station, from which they never expect to return, than they would to one where there was neither difficulty nor danger. . . . In the greatest public as well as private disasters, a wise man ought to consider that he himself, his friends and countrymen, have only been ordered upon the forlorn station of the universe; that had it not been necessary for the good of the whole, they would not have been so ordered . . . A wise man should surely be capable of doing what a good soldier holds himself at all times in readiness to do. (TMS 236)

Smith thus turns military virtues against themselves, against the national animosities that a true citizen of the universe should learn to overcome: we are to see ourselves and our countrymen as serving "the good of the whole." He uses the glory traditionally attaching to military accomplishments as a metaphor for facing difficulties stoically in any circumstance, urging us to see our entire lives as a sort of military posting to "the forlorn station of the universe."

In the third of Winch's passages, although Smith does call war "the great school both for acquiring and exercising . . . magnanimity," he notes that we admire magnanimity in "the greatest criminals"—in robbers and highwaymen, whose punishments we endorse even as we admire their fortitude—and reminds us that "[g]reat warlike exploit" may appeal to us "though undertaken contrary to every principle of justice, and carried on without any regard to humanity" (TMS 239). Unequivocal praise for the art of war this is most assuredly not, and Smith's warning that the martial virtues may indifferently be used to pursue justice or injustice sounds through the whole of TMS VI (see, e.g., 241–2, 254, 264). The overall recommendation seems to be that we try to steer the noble virtue of self-command into humble, private uses rather than cultivate it in the morally hazardous arena of war. The closest Smith comes to a paradigm of self-command is the strength to pursue what one sees as the truth, regardless of audience or other external reward: Parmenides lecturing to a room emptied of all but Plato, or the Duke of Marlborough, not in his actual military achievements, but in the strength by which he resisted ever taking rash actions or uttering a rash word (251–3). Courage and self-mastery are indeed great virtues, for Smith, but their greatest achievement comes in a stoic fulfillment of our moral duties, not on the battlefields where nations destroy themselves to serve the vanity of foolish rulers.

Winch's interpretation is a good example of what happens when one cites passages in Smith's writings without attending to their placement in the exposition of his full view (see §1 of this book). In TMS VI.ii the military virtues come off as aesthetically admirable, but used, more often than not, for vile and horrific ends. A passage added to Book III describes the experience of war and faction as especially well-suited to the development of self-command (TMS 153). The "boisterous and stormy sky" of military exploit helps us attain the "awful and respectable" if not the "amiable and gentle" virtues. Yet Smith frames this discussion of the usefulness of war within a broader comparison between the amiable and the awful virtues, in which he explicitly declares that the *former*, and not the latter, provide the proper and deepest foundation for self-command:

> Our sensibility to the feelings of others, so far from being inconsistent with the manhood of self-command, is the very principle upon which that manhood is founded. The very same principle or instinct which, in the misfortune of our neighbour, prompts us to compassionate his sorrow; in our own misfortune, prompts us to restrain the abject and miserable lamentations of our own sorrow. (TMS 152)

He goes on to say that the person "best fitted by nature" for acquiring the soft and gentle virtues will also be best fitted for acquiring austere and respectable ones. The catch is that being well "fitted" by nature to acquire a virtue does not mean one will actually acquire it, and the passage about the "boisterous and stormy sky" occurs within Smith's concession that gentle people, even if well-*suited* to be also strong, un–self-pitying people, will often not develop that side of themselves unless they are exposed to hardships and dangers. After making that concession, he warns us that the soldiers who do acquire courage and self-command are all too likely to become callous and inhumane. For "his own ease," Smith says, a soldier tends to "make light" of the harm he causes, and to refrain from developing a proper regard for other people's rights.[28] So Smith's overall attitude is exactly the opposite of the one usually attributed to him. Under the right conditions, he believes, the gentle virtues lead, by way of self-command, to the awful and respectable ones, while the latter do not necessarily lead to the former. Humane concern for other people's misery is the best road to self-command, while war is a dangerous one.

In any case, whatever regard Smith may have had for the virtues one can acquire in wartime, he clearly detested actual war. He calls Britain's wars "expensive and unnecessary" (WN 344), describes the crusades as a "destructive frenzy" (406), and characterizes the constant state of war in feudal times as "a scene of violence, rapine, and disorder" (418). He says soldiers are given to "idleness and dissipation" and often to "rapine and plunder" (WN 470; see also 100). He never misses an opportunity to stress the "waste of stock" caused by wars, the enormous expense that goes into waging them (344–5, 406, 427, 440–45, 613–15, 661, 906, 925–6, 929, 944–6)—an important point in his debate with mercantilists who saw war as a *source* of wealth. Indeed, Smith treats war as the worst kind of government "waste and extravagance" (343–5, 925, 929), the worst enemy of "the natural progress of things towards improvement," the great "disease" that only "the uniform . . . effort of every man to better his condition" can combat (343). His emphasis on the unending quiet effort by which capital grows in spite of war expresses his wonder not at how stubbornly selfish everyone is, but at how doggedly successful masses of ordinary people are in improving their world despite the huge obstacles thrown in their way by their vainglorious leaders.

This connection between war and waste is developed most fully in WN II.iii. Smith lists three sources of "publick prodigality" when he embarks on his direct critique of wasteful government spending: "a numerous and splendid court, a great ecclesiastical establishment, [and] great fleets and armies . . ." (¶31 on p. 343). To the last of these, alone of the three, he feels compelled to add: ". . . who in time of peace produce nothing, and in time of war acquire nothing which can compensate the expence of maintaining them, even while the war lasts." Mercantilist dogma held that wars could bring economic gain well beyond the expence of the army. Smith builds up a slow attack on this dogma. In ¶32 he says that almost all nations manage to build up stock in spite of the profusion of governments *as long as* the times they live in are "tolerably quiet and peaceable." Paragraphs 33 and 34 strategically pick the seventeenth-century civil wars, the Wars of the Roses, the Norman Conquest, and the invasion of Julius Caesar, as points at which one might have expected English capital accumulation to be severely disrupted: all wars, unlike the successful campaigns against the Dutch in the seventeenth century, or against the French in the eighteenth century, at which the most nationalist of Britons would recoil. Finally, ¶35 neatly brings these scenes of "civil discord," the fire and plague of London, and the Jacobite rebellions together with the supposedly glorious military adventures Britain had lately fought against the Dutch and the French. Just as the confusion of the fire, the plague, the invasions, and the civil wars brought "absolute waste and destruction of stock," that "not only retard[ed] . . . the natural accumulation of riches, but . . . left the country, at the end of the period, poorer than at the beginning," so, Smith insists, did the wars fought to satisfy mercantilist adventurism. Smith blurs the lines among civil war, response to invasion, and foreign expeditions; he refuses to see any significant difference between the wars lamented as national tragedies and the wars acclaimed as national triumphs, refuses to see wars in which only the poor got killed as more acceptable than wars affecting the whole country. The mercantilist wars with the Dutch and the French had wrought destruction of capital—to put their cost in the crude terms for which they had been fought—perhaps less visibly, but no less certainly, than the Jacobite rebellions or the fire and the plague of London. Had they not been fought,

> [m]ore houses would have been built, more lands would have been improved, and those which had been improved before would have been better cultivated, more manufactures would have been established, and those which had been established before would have been more extended; and to what height the real wealth . . . of the country might, by this time, have been raised, it is not perhaps very easy to imagine.

But if war is so obviously destructive of national wealth, why would a government ever start a war? Smith suggests that Britain's aggressive wars in the past century had been egged on by a class of people who stood to gain from their fellow citizens' losses. He notes that manufactures "may flourish amidst the ruin of their country, and begin to decay upon the return of its prosperity" (445), and suggests that Britain's "shopkeepers" had been willing to employ the "blood and treasure of their fellow citizens" to acquire an empire of customers for themselves (613). A none-too-subtle imputation of treason can be heard in these last remarks. Smith inverts the standard association of patriotism with willingness to go to war here, such that it is the *supporters* of war who are unpatriotic. This caustic denunciation of those who support wars in which other people suffer comes to a head in the following passage:

> In great empires the people who live in the capital, and in the provinces remote from the scene of action, feel, many of them scarce any inconveniency from the war; but enjoy, at their ease, the amusement of reading in the newspapers the exploits of their own fleets and armies. To them this amusement compensates the small difference between the taxes which they pay on account of the war, and those which they had been accustomed to pay in time of peace. They are commonly dissatisfied with the return of peace, which puts an end to their amusement, and to a thousand visionary hopes of conquest and national glory from a longer continuance of the war. (WN 920)[29]

People "remote from the scene of action" are happy to put up with the death of hundreds or thousands of their less well-off fellow citizens for "the amusement of reading in the newspapers the exploits of their own fleets and armies." In the case of Britain at least, those who felt this way were not only callous but foolish, in Smith's opinion, since the "thousand visionary hopes of conquest and national glory" they entertained were merely that: *merely* "visionary," *merely* "hopes," as we will be told at the very end of WN. Anyone made aware that this is what his war taxes, however small, are paying for could hardly want to go on paying for it, whatever he may have wanted while caught up in the illusion giving him amusement. Supporting a war because one believes one is achieving glory is one thing; supporting a war in order to participate in a *fantasy* of such glory is quite another. And those who participate in the fantasy while living in a situation of comfort and safety are under a sort of double illusion. That wars of "great empires" are fought by one set of people and cheered on by quite another, that the people "dissatisfied with the return of peace" live in places "remote from the scene of action," suggests a cognitive dissonance in those who promote such wars, an illusion that one is achieving martial glory when one is really sitting safely at home. As making stage machinery visible can disrupt one's suspension of disbelief in the theater, so Smith's stating the purpose of the taxes this way can destroy the illusion on which their acceptability depends. Any decent merchant or landowner, if he comes to see the "national glory" he has been enjoying in the light in which Smith presents it here, should feel ashamed of his support for war. Without the sinking fund that keeps war taxes low, says Smith a few lines earlier, people "would soon be disgusted with the war": disgust is, clearly, what he wants to bring us to. Of course, we get there, at least in the first instance, by considering our pocketbooks rather than the lives of our fellow citizens, but, as we have seen many times, throughout WN Smith both reveals his hatred of oppression and argues for measures to alleviate it on grounds of material self-interest. The heartlessness in this passage belongs not to Smith, but to those stupid or cruel enough to want others to die for their own illusions of glory.

61. Conclusion

In all the respects this chapter has considered—in Smith's concerns about the virtue and limited knowledge of politicians; in his tendency, in that light, to steer political energies away from day-to-day policy and toward the mainte- nance and slow change of long-term laws and institutions; in his relative uncon- cern with the difference between republics and monarchies; and in his great concern to try to turn people away from an obsession with their nation's "glory," or standing vis-à-vis other nations—Smith challenges the centrality that earlier philosophers had given to the political realm. Joseph Cropsey and Richard Teichgraeber have pointed this out, saying that Smith wants to move from "pol- ity" to "economy," from a focus on communal governance to a focus on com- mercial affairs. Vivienne Brown, more accurately I think, argues that "the eclipse of polity was effected not by economy but by ethics," that Smith gave an in- tensely private conception of morality pride of place over *both* political *and* commercial affairs (ASD 211–12). Both the flourishing of commerce and a gov- ernment that guarantees justice and liberty for all are for Smith important inso- far as they help individuals to pursue rich and decent private lives. Neither derives its importance from the good of the nation as a single unit. The gover- nance of nations, like the wealth of nations, is but ancillary to the development of individual moral sentiments.

Epilogue

CHAPTER TWELVE

Learning from Smith Today

Item. Three years after Smith died, in 1793, Henry Dundas rose in Parliament to defend the rechartering of the East India Company. Dundas was a Scot who had known Smith well. In 1787, he had invited Smith to stay with him in his Wimbledon villa. He had also solicited Smith's advice about free trade with Ireland in 1779, and a year later had helped Smith become a Commissioner of Customs. By 1793, moreover, WN had become very famous. In 1791 it had received a fulsome eulogy from William Pitt himself, the Prime Minister under whom Dundas served.[1]

Now the disapproval with which Smith regarded the British East India Company could not well be missed by anyone at all familiar with WN or Smith's views in general. And Dundas himself had been active, a decade earlier, in promoting the reform of British practices in India. So we might reasonably assume that Dundas was not only familiar with but sympathetic to Smith's criticisms of those practices. But when he rose to speak on April 23, 1793, he simply shoved those criticisms out of his way. Acknowledging that what he was about to propose stood "in opposition to established theories in government and in commerce," he said that, while these theories "were just and applicable in other cases, . . . yet he found it dangerous to listen to them, when he was devising a plan of government and a system of trade for British India." He continued:

> No writer upon political economy has as yet supposed that an extensive empire can be administered by a commercial association; and no writer on commercial economy has thought, that trade ought to be shackled by an exclusive privilege. In deviating from these principles, which have been admitted and admired, I am sensible, that my opinions have popular prejudices against them, but I am supported by successful experience; and when the House adverts to the peculiarities of the subject before them, they will at once see, that I am not attempting to overturn theories, though I am unwilling to recede from old and established practice. I wish . . . to arrest the attention of the House, and to fix it on the advantages which Great Britain actually possesses, and then to ask, whether it would be wise or politic to forego them in search of greater advantages which may exist only in imagination?[2]

Et tu, Dundas. It is hardly too much to say that this speech represents the true funeral for Smith's ideas, the laying to rest of the last ghost of a chance that Smith might influence actual politics as he had, albeit pessimistically, aspired to do. If even Dundas, who knew Smith so well, addressing a policy that Smith had so thoroughly undermined, could dismiss his views in this shallow and nasty way, what chance did they ever have of being properly understood and used later on? And Dundas's dismissal is remarkably nasty. Smith goes un-named,[3] lumped together with all other "writers upon political economy," and then associated with the "popular prejudices" that he had worked so hard to enlighten. Dundas implies also that Smith knew nothing of how the East India Company functioned in "experience," certainly nothing of the "peculiarities" or details of that experience, that he was writing mere "theories" and that the advantages he claimed for ending the government's support for the Company existed "only in [his] imagination." One might never suspect, from this speech, that Smith's work was as rich in empirical detail as in theory, much less that the book was devoted to trying to wake Britain up from her disastrous attempts to possess empires that properly exist "in imagination only."[4] Dundas reveals in-deed how very well he knows Smith, in his ability to use Smith's own modes of arguing against Smith's teachings. That, ironically, may be the only way in which Smith had a lasting impact on him.[5]

There is a second irony here. The episode teaches a deeply Smithian doctrine to a degree that Smith himself may not have anticipated: that people will adopt just those elements of a writer they respect that fit their own projects and preconceptions, while ignoring anything that might challenge them to change their mind. Smith could not have been clearer about the evils of the British East India Company, and his analysis of it is one of the least "theoretical," most historically informed, sections of WN. It is, moreover, hard to believe that one could really accept any part of his critique of mercantilism, and demonstration of the value of the system of natural liberty, while still approving of the East India Company; no policy position of Smith's follows more readily from his general views than that one. Yet, without bothering to engage with his specific objections to the Company, a man who considered himself and was considered one of Smith's closest disciples was ready to toss Smith's views aside as if Smith had done nothing but pontificate without evidence, as if he were a theoretical philosopher who never attended to facts.

The appropriate moral to be drawn from the episode could of course be just that Dundas was a shallow scoundrel, but there is no particular reason to sup-pose that of Dundas. A more general and more depressing moral is plausible: that even people who greatly respect a moral or political thinker will claim that he is "impractical," "doesn't understand the facts," or something of the sort, as soon as he asks something of them that would call for a personal or political sacrifice. If so, the hope that any moral or political writer, even one as judicious and hard-headed as Smith, can ever effect real change in other human beings begins to look feeble. The barriers to serious political reform are tremendous—people who occupy or seek political office are almost always, in all regimes, too beholden to those who already have wealth and power to risk challenging them in any significant way—and the barriers to individual moral reform are, if any-thing, worse: Nobody likes to strip off "the mysterious veil of self-delusion" and face "the deformities of his own conduct" (TMS 158). Self-deceit runs deep in human beings, as Smith stressed as much as anyone ever has, and perhaps it runs even deeper than he allowed for. Perhaps almost all people, and people involved with politics particularly, are virtually *incapable* of reforming themselves in any substantial way, or at least incapable of doing so deliberately, in response to rational argument. Perhaps only historical accident and nonrational forces, like the accidents and forces that overturned feudalism, can effect substantial, constructive social change.

If we take this dark message away from our study of Smith, it applies equally to "left-wing" attempts to eradicate poverty, racism, and the like as to "right-wing" attempts to conserve religious values, or to foster national wealth and glory. Left-wingers boast of their openness to reform, as of their high moral standards in general, but rarely want to listen to proposals that they reform their own views or manner or strategy; many left-wing activists are in fact notorious for their difficulties in accepting criticism. Right-wingers boast of their humility, before God and before tradition, but tend to be anything but humble in promoting their policies. The inability to listen to criticism, to admit error, and to change one's views significantly, crosses party lines—which suggests, not that we should opt for a particular style of politics, but that it is foolish to expect much from politics in general.

I don't want to leave our study of Smith with quite such a quietistic view, and will later draw some constructive political advice from his work. But the warning that Smith's comprehensive political vision is unlikely ever to be established, because people in politics hardly ever have the courage and fairness to do anything that might cost them their careers, is a useful one, and should be borne in mind even when we arrive at political teachings one might take away from Smith.

Before we try to take anything constructive away from Smith, however, there are some further barriers in the way of any attempt to use him for policy disputes today. As Charles Griswold has written, "[It is] impossible to see Smith as either 'conservative' or 'liberal,' 'right' or 'left,' in the contemporary American sense of these terms" (AVE 295n 64). This is partly because of changes in the political issues since Smith's day. But it is partly because of features intrinsic to Smith's way of writing on politics. Griswold stresses the degree to which Smith's writings are not ideological: "If we expect social philosophy to have a . . . rigorous structure, then all of [Smith's recommendations] will seem hopelessly unsystematic and ad hoc" (AVE 296). This unsystematic, ad hoc quality is a testimony to Smith's realism, but it makes it hard to tell where Smith might stand on issues that have arisen since his day. Indeed, the difficulty of claiming Smith's legacy is not a recent one; it goes back to the period immediately after his death.

Item. About a decade after Smith died, in 1799–1800, the Combination Acts were passed in Britain. These Acts strengthened existing laws against attempts of workers to unite in order to bargain collectively for better wages. One might argue that such combinations interfere with the natural workings of the free market in labor, and thereby invoke Smith's authority in favor of these Acts. Or one might cite Smith's declaration that masters always combine and get away with it, while workers get condemned for the same activity (WN 84–5), along with his remark that laws in favor of workers are "always just and equitable" (158), and use Smith to oppose such Acts. In any case, William Pitt, a man who had admired Smith since his college days,[6] got the Combination Acts passed, but Sir Francis Burdett and Benjamin Hobhouse, who opposed the Acts, quoted Smith in support of their opposition.[7] And two devoted Smithians—Joseph Hume and Francis Place—were crucial, twenty-four years later, to the movement that repealed the Combination Acts and made trade unions legal in Britain.[8]

Item. Emma Rothschild has pointed out that "there is something of Smith on both sides of the parliamentary debate" over a minimum wage at the end of the eighteenth century (ES 62). Pitt, who opposed the regulation of wages, could draw on Smith's claim that the poor already had good wages and reasonably invoke Smith's free trading principles against the regulations. Samuel Whitbread, who promoted the regulation, used language more like Smith's own, was seen, like Smith, as a friend of the poor, and could reasonably appeal to the exceptions Smith allowed to free trading policies. Who better represents Smith's own views, Pitt or Whitbread? Pitt's own views on workers and poverty are by themselves a curious motley. Gertrude Himmelfarb notes that in 1796 he proposed a remarkably far-reaching poverty program: one that included "rates in aid of wages, family allowances, money for the purchase of a cow or some other worthy purpose, schools of industry for the children of the poor, wastelands to be reclaimed and reserved for the poor [and] insurance against sickness and old age."[9] Yet he persecuted advocates of universal suffrage, opposed the minimum wage, and passed the Combination Acts. Which of Pitt's views best reflects his Smithian commitments? We might say that the Pitt of the poverty legislation is the truly Smithian Pitt, and that only the French Revolution made Pitt suspicious of worker agitations. Or we might see Pitt as coming to his Smithian senses only when he opposed all government interference with economic relationships, and recognized the dangers of worker combinations. We might also try to reconcile the two Pitts, toning down both the apparent "leftist" pitch of his poverty program and the apparent "rightist" tone of his other policies.

The problems about Whitbread and Pitt, and about the two Pitts, are just special cases of a more general difficulty in determining Smith's proper legacy. As Himmelfarb, Rothschild, and Donald Winch have all brought out in detail, those invoking Smith at the end of the eighteenth century included liberal and radical reformers like John Millar (Smith's student), Richard Price, Thomas Paine, Jeremy Bentham, Condorcet, the Abbé Sièyes, and Mary Wollstonecraft,[10] but also included Pitt, Frederick Eden, Thomas Malthus, and the increasingly conservative Edmund Burke. Which of these streams of reception represent what Smith himself believed? Which properly extrapolated, from WN, what

Smith would have said about the issues, especially regarding the poor, that came to dominate political debate after he died?

The fairest, most reasonable thing to say is that both streams represent an authentic piece of Smith's legacy, and that neither one can claim that legacy definitively. The "leftist" stream picks up on Smith's strong and consistent sympathy for the poor, and the many indications in his work that government favoritism for this section of society is just and equitable. The "rightist" stream picks up on Smith's suspicion of radical change of any kind, and of government intervention in society, especially when that intervention requires a large bureaucracy. I am inclined to think Smith's strong moral concern for the poor, and view of them as equal in decency and desert to everyone else in society, would have led him more toward the left than the right of the later political spectrum, but this is speculation. What matters is that *both* attempts to claim Smith must be speculation. There are arguments supporting both, but Smith died too soon for us to know what he would actually have said about post–French Revolutionary political economy. The assumption, which came to be unquestioned by the early nineteenth century, that *of course* Smith would have supported strict laissez-faire policies and opposed government programs on behalf of the poor is entirely unjustified. There were, initially, both "left Smithians" and "right Smithians," just as there were later to be both "left Hegelians" and "right Hegelians." This initial reception appropriately reflects the fact that Smith lived before the modern divisions between left and right arose—before the French Revolution—as well as the fact that his thought is both subtle and complex, and does not readily lend itself to dogmatic views on any political matter.

To elaborate the historical differences between Smith's time and ours: I argued in part IV, chapter 10 that the French Revolution ushered in the modern notion of distributive justice, and the corresponding concern, among many political agents, that government policy be directed toward alleviating or eradicating poverty, and perhaps even to altering or abolishing the property arrangements in society with that end in mind. But if this concern was not on the horizon in Smith's lifetime, then there is no reason to think we should be able to determine his views on it.

In addition, the large corporations that have dominated capitalist economies since the beginning of the twentieth century did not exist in Smith's time, nor were there many large factories, of the sort that became central to the nineteenth-century British economy and to the complaints of economic reformers from that time on. The pin factory in the beginning of WN is misleading: It is not the kind of workplace Smith usually has in mind. C. K. Kindleberger has indeed noted that Smith seems not to have anticipated the Industrial Revolution.[11] But the Industrial Revolution has increasingly made large firms the most efficient way of doing business in many sectors of the economy (when industry depends on expensive machines, startup and energy costs alone make for enormous economies of scale, and thereby make it difficult for small firms to compete with large ones). Smith's failure to anticipate the Industrial Revolution therefore goes along with a failure to anticipate the degree to which large corporations would come to dominate free market economies. It is very hard to know what Smith would have said about these corporations, although it is unlikely that he would have welcomed them. Smith treats the British East India Company and its ilk as aberrations from the free-flowing capital formations he thinks markets will naturally produce,[12] but of course the East India Company, unlike modern corporations, was explicitly granted a trading monopoly, and was in addition given quasi-governmental powers, including the power to make war and peace. One might use these features to keep Smith's critique of the East India Companies from having any implications for modern corporations, which are at least nominally restrained from monopoly power by antitrust legislation, and which result from limited liability laws and from the economies of scale to which modern technologies give rise. But much of Smith's critique of the East India Company has nothing to do with either its monopolistic status or its quasi-political powers; its scale, and consequent need for middle managers who are insulated from the direct consequences of many of their actions, alone raised large problems. One needs, besides, to wonder whether the man who said that the law "ought to do nothing to facilitate . . . assemblies" among people of the same trade would have approved of limited liability, let alone the myriad other ways in which governments have favored corporations over small businesses.

Now some of these ways of favoring large corporations come straight out of the mercantilist playbook against which Smith directs his polemical energy in WN. When the U.S. government decides to "save" the American steel industry by hampering the import of foreign steel, or when it slaps large tariffs on Japanese cars to try to force American consumers to buy the more poorly made models coming out of Ford, GM, and Chrysler, it helps private interests against the good of the people as a whole in precisely the way that Smith abhorred. When Senators slip subsidies to large agricultural interests into the national budget—in the name of support for "small family farms" who receive a tiny fraction of the total amount—they are granting what Smith called "bounties" that have, if anything, even less justification than did any bounty in Smith's own time. When a mayor of a city—as the mayor of Chicago recently did—claps himself on the back for offering favors to Boeing for relocating to his area (a move that was expected to bring in a whopping 500 new jobs . . .), he favors one sector of the economy over another in a way that he has no reason to think will be good for his city as a whole, let alone his country as a whole, over the long term. Both Republicans and Democrats do this sort of thing constantly, even while professing strong "free-trading" principles; the most pro–free market Republicans in the Senate brazenly violate their principles to help large business interests among their constituents.

Yet it will not do simply to decry these throwbacks to mercantilist protectionism. The political realities today are such that it is hard for governments to disentangle themselves from large businesses even if they sincerely want to do so. To mention just a few of the least controversial reasons for this:

First, the fact that large corporations have become the most efficient way of organizing much economic activity means that there simply *will* be many large conglomerations of stock in every nation. These conglomerations will in turn employ large numbers of workers, which means that a small number of directors and major shareholders will inevitably wield vast power over other people's economic lives. Neither cities nor nations can afford to overlook this fact. Even if corporations never contributed to political campaigns, they would still exercise enormous power over the governments in their areas by virtue of the many people, which in a democracy means the many voters, whose lives they shape. If GM or GE shuts down or severely cuts back its business in a particular town, the entire economy can go sour, and no politician can or should ignore that possibility. Hence politicians need to listen disproportionately to the demands of corporate leaders, even if they personally oppose those demands, and even if their campaigns avoid corporate contributions.

Second, even if they were to avoid both corporate and personal welfare programs, modern governments would necessarily be far larger, and more heavily involved in their citizens' lives, than Smith could have anticipated. There are many reasons for this. One is that defense expenditure, and the role of defense in national economies, has become far larger than Smith would have expected. The rise of nationalism in the nineteenth century, and its dominance over world politics, through two huge wars in the twentieth century, into the bloody struggles of Asian and African nations in the 1970s and 1980s, and on into the wars that continue to dominate the Balkans, the Middle East, and much of Asia, has shown that bad economic policies are not the only cause of war and that world peace will not necessarily come along with free trade. Both liberals and socialists have played down the importance of nationalism, explaining it away in materialist terms that do not begin to account for the cultural issues that have made it so difficult for, say, Berbers and Arabs, Serbs and Croatians, or Turks and Kurds to share a single political unit. Liberal as well as socialist governments have, moreover, often tacitly governed by way of an ethnic power base, even while denying that ethnic divisions matter (think of the cultural politics that continue to determine insider and outsider status in Britain, France, and Germany; of Stalin's reliance on his home state of Georgia for a power base; or of the Assad family's reliance on their native Alawite minority in Syria). The weapons of war have also gotten both far more dangerous and far more expensive. Smith can hardly be expected to have anticipated a war in which tanks, smart bombs, and extremely complicated aircraft would take the place of rifles and battleships. Unlike even the British navy of his time, moreover, which depended upon a great deal of governmental investment,[13] modern-day military technology requires many firms to produce goods that can *only* be used for military purposes. Thus the eighteenth-century British navy might have requisitioned a huge amount of dried or cured food, but if the government should, in a given year, not need that food, it could normally be sold to private consumers. The same is not true of an F-16, or most of its components. Not only are defense budgets large, therefore, but governments are the sole source of demand for a very large number of companies, and can exert significant influence over the economy by the contracts they offer for everything from fighter planes to certain kinds of software. The loophole Smith allowed for government to intervene in the economy, insofar as defense trumps opulence, has become a gap large enough to fit many a protectionist truck.

In addition, transportation and communication, which Smith himself thought would often need government oversight, have come to take forms that endanger their users in ways Smith could not have imagined. Trains, planes, and automobiles need far more regulation, to be used safely, than horse-drawn carriages ever did. Phone lines and email systems allow for invasions of privacy far more subtle than those to which postal systems were prone. Smith himself considered the repair of roads and the running of post offices to be appropriate jobs for government (WN 724, 726). *A fortiori*, it may be reasonable for governments to run or regulate everything from rail systems to email traffic. Yet the placement of airports alone gives governments great influence over which geographical areas will flourish and which will flounder. The hiring of firms to run and maintain communication and transportation systems, moreover, gives governments an economic role by which they can very often favor one company over another in subtle and inappropriate ways.

Finally, the complexity of modern technology, along with the greatly speeded-up rate at which it changes, makes it more important than it has ever been before for everyone in society to be well-educated in their early years, and to have access to good, impartial sources of information throughout their lives. Workers need more specialized knowledge than they ever needed before to produce goods effectively, and consumers need more specialized knowledge than they ever needed before to *buy* goods wisely. It is far easier today than in Smith's day for people to be misled, both by those who employ them and by those who sell goods to them. The complexity of modern products makes it hard even for very well-educated people to know whether a particular product is harmful, or harmful in certain circumstances, or even whether it is well-made. In the eighteenth century, one needed just to have lived in the world a while, or at most to know someone who worked on carriages, to tell whether a particular carriage was well and safely made; the basic technology had been around for centuries, and was in any case fairly simply constructed. To know the equivalent amount about a modern car—to know, say, whether Ford's SUVs are balanced poorly—one practically needs a degree in engineering. Similarly, finding out whether a particular workplace is dangerous might be something for which word of mouth would suffice in the eighteenth century, but today it easily can be, and often is, concealed. And this is just to speak of safety. It is extremely easy for appliance and software companies to persuade the public, untruthfully, that they "need" an upgrade on a product, that it is pointless to continue to service that product,[14] or that a product cannot possibly be built for lifetime use. It is equally easy for firms to conceal the full truth about the nature of the benefits they offer, about subtly oppressive practices in their workplace, or about whether their workers can count on job security. In these circumstances, education and information are necessary for people to make even moderately well-informed choices, and for a free market, therefore, to reflect even roughly what individuals freely will. Hence it is more necessary than ever before that governments ensure good education and information to those who lack the means to do so for themselves. What Smith valued in the free market requires, far more than it did in his own day, that education costs for the poor be borne by the public, and that the government take great efforts to protect consumers and workers against unobvious hazards. In European countries, these factors contribute to a very large government indeed; in the United States, the government role in consumer and worker protection has been fairly small, but that is then compensated for by laws allowing for individuals to recover huge damages in suits.[15]

The dream of a true free trade is thus today even more of an "Oceana or Utopia" than it seemed in Smith's time (WN 471). No sensible person does or could advocate a fully free trade in Smith's sense. Those who call themselves "libertarians" generally complain about unions but not about corporations, make all sorts of excuses for government activity taken in the name of defense, and suggest, without apparent concern for the justice and safety issues that Smith recognized, that education and transportation be put entirely in private hands. It is hard to imagine the immensely realistic Smith himself advocating the abolition of either unions or corporations, or urging governments to refrain from the defense, education, transportation, and communication expenditures that modern conditions require of them. A more Smithian response to these conditions is to recognize that both economic structures and government roles change with changes in historical circumstances, and that what Smith had to say to eighteenth-century Europe need not be much like what he would say to the global economic and political arena of the twenty-first century.

What we can more confidently learn from Smith is a model for the integration of philosophy and social science. There are people today, in both philosophy and the social sciences, who want to integrate the two, but in what I would take to be the wrong direction: They want philosophers to tailor their accounts of the human mind, or human society, to what psychologists and sociologists have to say, such that moral theories, for instance, will follow the account that psychologists give us of when and how people can take responsibility for their decisions. Smith provides a model of a relationship that goes in the other direction, of how a philosophical understanding of knowledge, human nature, and such moral concepts as liberty and justice can inform a study of history or society. When Smith uses his account of common-sense knowledge both to validate people's ordinary economic decisions and to criticize popular prejudices like those against corn merchants or apothecaries (see §4 above), or when he recognizes the role of strict laws of justice in giving people the security that makes them willing to accumulate capital, or when he employs his theory of imaginative projection to get us to sympathize with the poor, then he provides a wonderful model of how a deep and thorough philosophical understanding can guide a project in the social sciences. At the same time, he provides a model of how a moral philosopher might most effectively encourage morally necessary change: by turning to social science, where the details of human life can come out, rather than relying on the abstractions of philosophy alone. Today moral and political philosophy have become extremely abstract, concerned far more with the correct formation of principles than with how those principles might sensibly apply to the concrete situations we face. Smith's turn from philosophy to history and the analysis of social structures represents a wise and morally admirable acceptance of the fact that what philosophers do is too far removed from the details of everyday life to provide, on its own, much of an answer to real political questions. Philosophy and social science need to work together; they are not identical or even continuous with each other, but philosophy can guide social science, while social science can give content to philosophical principles. WN is a model of this kind of symbiosis, and some of the greatest other works to exemplify the model were intended to be successors to WN: John Stuart Mill's *Principles of Political Economy*, for instance, or Alfred Marshall's *Economics*.

Smith also offers us some more specific guidance to how social science ought to be conducted. As I have stressed throughout, Smith's economics is couched in highly literate narrative form, making use of the imagination to help develop many points and reaching for a way to develop technical discussions out of notions that he expects the reader to have already, as part of common sense. The idea that writing clearly and imaginatively is intrinsically important to what social scientists have to teach is a valuable one, and a corrective to those who consider abstract mathematical models the best way to gain insight into how human beings behave. It is, among other things, of supreme importance that social scientists not be misled by their specialized languages into supposing they have a key to behavior that ordinary folk lack. The history of prediction in the social sciences is a poor one, and economists, supposedly the most rigorous of social scientists, have not generally had a better track record than ordinary businesspeople in guessing where inflation and employment, for instance, will go in any particular time period. It behooves all social scientists to be extremely humble about how much their sciences can accomplish, and seeing their work as grounded in common sense and common language should help them achieve that.

The grounding in common sense and common language can also help economists to recognize that what they study is part of a vast, shared body of human thought and practice and that their work is, therefore, intimately connected with that of political scientists, psychologists, sociologists, and anthropologists. What Smith draws on above all for evidence in economics, and what can unite all these different ways of studying human beings, is history, and Smith is an excellent model for how the social sciences could properly be called, as once they were, the "historical sciences." The advantage of rooting social science in history is that claims can be made over a much larger range of human experience—a much larger and richer "data set"—and can be made more sensitive to differences in outlook and practice across cultures and time periods. A school of economists that returned to Smith might begin to train its graduate students significantly in history, and not just economic history (many graduate programs lack even a requirement in that), which would surely improve the wisdom to be found in economic analyses and predictions, particularly in matters that have political import. When we are told that minimum wage laws reduce employment, it would be nice to see evidence for this—if that is indeed the way the evidence goes—drawn from at least a century of human experience, and not just from microstudies of current cases. Smith's study of gold and silver prices over four centuries is a good model for what this can look like.

We can also learn a thoughtful, moderately Stoic attitude toward history from Smith. There is an important moral question about how much individuals who occupy positions of power, or influence those who do, should hope and expect to *change* history. The quietist attitude that no one should, since no one can, aim to change history is one response to this question, as is the activist alternative by which we each have a duty to try to make this world a better place for future generations. Smith stands between these two attitudes, although he leans more toward the first than the second. For Smith, significant historical change tends to occur over a period considerably longer than that of any individual life, and to result mostly from factors independent of the actions of even the cleverest and most powerful individuals. The detailed effects of any historical change can also not be well predicted, although they can be explained in retrospect. Consequently, individuals should be modest about what they can expect to do to improve the world, seeking primarily to carry out their moral duties as those are defined in the society and historical period they inhabit, and to nudge their society toward change in at most a few, very carefully thought-through respects. Above all, the individual needs to expect that he or she *will not live to see* the results of the changes he or she hopes for. A good social or political change is one that takes time, and slowly builds a place for itself within the ongoing life of a community. Precisely those changes that can be fully instituted within a short time-span are the changes that are most likely to be disruptive rather than helpful, and eventually either to be rolled back or to have unexpected, unfortunate consequences. A Smithian attitude toward history is thus not exactly a quietist one, but it is one resigned to slow, small change.

There is a related Smithian attitude toward empirical facts, whether current or historical, from which social scientists as well as political activists can learn. As we have seen, Smith gives strong priority to particular facts over general theories, stressing repeatedly that human knowledge is most reliable when it is highly contextual. Smith is, for this reason, perhaps the most empirical of all the empiricists, pursuing his version of "the science of man" in a particularly messy, fact-laden rather than theory-laden way. He is also kept from firm ideological commitments by this respect for the particular. Ideologies depend on generalizations, on theories about human nature, economics, politics, and so on from which general policy prescriptions can be drawn. A thinker who emphasizes the unique features of each human situation will constantly find exceptions to the generalizations, and therefore make exceptions to the prescriptions. Those who try to push every feature of human life into the Procrustean bed of "rational choice" or libertarian theory are therefore no more Smith's true heirs than those who are willing to explain everything with some Marxist category. Smith's intellectual progeny in this regard can be found far more among novelists and essayists like E. M. Forster or George Orwell, with a dispassionate eye out for the telling detail, the quirky particulars that give texture to human life. One can easily imagine the author of the *Wealth of Nations* delighting in *A Passage to India* or *Down and Out in Paris and London*, not so easily imagine him nodding enthusiastically along with the latest intemperate screed by George Gilder or Robert Bork.

Finally, political activists, as well as social scientists, can take away from Smith some general lessons about the nature of law and politics that are useful whatever one's point of view. Both left- and right-wingers can learn, first, to be patient and modest in their advocacy of change, and to attend to the many ways in which their proposals might run aground or drift off course due to contingencies or to the embeddedness of certain interests and prejudices. They can learn, that is, to try hard to look forward to possible consequences of their proposed actions that may at the moment look unlikely, and to tailor their proposals such as to win over their opponents, rather than impatiently brushing opponents away as stupid or biased. They may also learn in general to distrust politicians, and political action, and to direct their avowed desire to improve people's lives, wherever possible, to the problems of friends, families, and neighbors. When their goals do seem to need large-scale social change, they may recognize that governments, to be just, need to work through very general, clearly comprehensible laws, rather than through offices with a lot of discretionary power, and through simple, transparent, readily accountable institutions. Smith contributed a clear account of how general laws, applied by an independent judiciary, prevent government power from being used arbitrarily, or to favor one individual over another. He contributed even more to our understanding of the importance of good institutional design, bringing out the need for institutions to have carefully framed incentive structures, to address basic and ongoing needs rather than single, immediate problems, and to fit in with their society's history and traditions. What Smith says about the laziness and ineffectiveness of Oxford professors, Catholic clergymen, and middle managers in the British East India Company should provide a powerful object lesson for anyone who thinks a major social problem is likely to be well addressed by a large and complex bureaucracy, whether privately or publicly run. Far better to institute simple changes in law, like Smith's recommendation that paper money no longer be issued for amounts smaller than £5, or to promote small-scale institutions, strongly accountable to those they serve, like Smith's little public schools (funded partly by those they serve).

These various lessons—about the advantages of an economics grounded in history and common sense, and expressed in narrative more than in mathematical formulae; about the wisdom of expecting significant social change to come in the long-term rather than in the short; and about the greater justice, and effectiveness, of proposals for political change that are imbued with a respect for the rule of law and are willing to work through simple, small-scale institutions—are valuable to social scientists and political activists of all stripes. One can, indeed, find true heirs to Smith among both left- and right-wing thinkers and activists. Social scientists who, like Smith, have used imaginative narrative and historical example to bring out the nature of the human condition include Friedrich Hayek and Amartya Sen, T. H. Marshall and Daniel Bell, Colin Turnbull and Clifford Geertz, Hannah Arendt and Michael Walzer. Among political activists, we can find a Smithian modesty, realism, and respect for tradition and slow change in Hayek again as well as John Stuart Mill, in the Fabian socialists as well as the British Conservative Party. I do not mean to say that these people consciously turned to Smith, although in some cases they did, just that they share a tone and an attitude toward human affairs that Smith, as much as anyone, helped to promote.

I'd like to conclude with something a bit more specific than this. I said earlier that there is a "left Smithian" legacy at least as true to Smith's teachings as that of the better known "right Smithians." I am sympathetic to the former, as is probably clear by now, and in any case they have not received the attention of their right-wing counterparts. So what, concretely, might a left Smithian have to say about some of today's major socioeconomic issues?

A proper answer to this question would require another book, and one by someone expert in economics or political science, which I am not. I can only sketch what directions I think such an answer should take. I will consider one contemporary socioeconomic issue in some detail, as an example of the approach I recommend, and then turn more briefly to other areas in which "left Smithian" proposals might usefully be made.

Consider the damage a large company can do to a local environment by dumping hazardous waste in an important natural resource, or to a local economy by picking up and moving its operation elsewhere, after having dominated the labor market for many years. Both of these charges were made about General Electric in the town of Pittsfield, Massachusetts, near which I used to live. For decades, GE dumped large amounts of PCBs and other hazardous materials in the Housatonic River, but refused to do anything to clean up the river after this came to light in 1977 (it came to an agreement with Pittsfield to do some cleanup in 1999). And after having long been the main employer in town—75 percent of the town's workers were employed by GE in the 1950s—it shifted most of its operation to the South in the 1970s, leaving behind a local economy that has remained depressed and underemployed for two decades.[16]

What can governments do about a case like this? Anticapitalists will say that such cases show why capital ought to be owned, or at least tightly controlled, by the state, and will decry the "greed" that large firms demonstrate when they inflict harms of this magnitude. Dogmatic defenders of laissez-faire will say that the free market will eventually iron all such problems out, or that they are due

to too *much* government regulation rather than too little, and they will sometimes add praise for the civic virtues of the people who run GE and similar
firms.

A Smithian of any kind will begin by getting both the moral insults hurled at
company directors by the left, and the compliments bestowed on them by the
right, out of the picture. Directors and major stockholders are not particularly
greedy, no more so than most of their workers and the people who complain
about their practices, nor are they particularly virtuous. One should not expect
of them either more or less self-interest than we do of other economic agents.
Nor should one expect the politicians who would pass laws controlling the uses
of capital to be any less "greedy," or otherwise ambitious, than the owners of
stock. That alone should give pause to those who imagine that putting capital
under political control will solve the problems of capitalism. (And one look at
the environmental devastation suffered by nations under Communist regimes
will confirm that *that* problem, at least, tends to be exacerbated rather than
solved when politicians direct the uses of capital.) We may expect benevolence
and other high virtues of other human beings in small social spheres, not
among the large anonymous groups that constitute the economic and political
realms. Widespread or persistent social problems, moreover, like the local environmental and economic damage that large firms can inflict, normally reflect
deeply rooted structural features of a society, not the virtues or vices of individuals.

Both left and right Smithians should also be willing to engage in a full-
fledged sympathetic projection into the plight of those affected by environmental damage and firm relocations. Smith would have been repulsed by the right's
tendency to blame the poor's problems on themselves. Smith himself, as we
have seen (§51), went to great lengths to get his readers to imagine in detail
how poor workers are driven to desperation when their pay is inadequate (WN
85) or why poor workers tend to suffer more than the rich from the anonymity
of cities (795). It is difficult to imagine him being anything but angered by the
insensitivity displayed when a writer like George Gilder, himself prominent and
well-off, proclaims that "in order to succeed, the poor need most of all the spur
of poverty";[17] certainly, no one who had really tried to imagine himself into the
situation of poor people would ever write something like that. Casual invoca-
tions of "tough love," by which one means that in a free market poor people can
work their own way out of any suffering, are alien to Smith's writings about the
poor. In both LJ and WN, Smith was forthright about the harm that commercial
society can inflict on its weakest members, and although he believed that there
were compensations for those harms, he engaged in careful analysis of how
poor people are put at a relatively greater educational disadvantage in an advanced than in a more primitive society, he proposed some redistributions of
wealth from rich to poor, and he never claimed that one cares most for the poor
by setting them adrift and seeing how they fare on their own. So all followers of
Smith should agree that modern problems that particularly affect the poor, like
environmental damage and frequent job relocations, require one to understand

the degree to which poor people cannot solve all their problems by themselves, and to seek resources, elsewhere in society, that can help them without compromising their dignity and independence.

Next, Smithians of any kind will agree that social problems need not always be solved by way of government. Associations of private individuals can also be of help, and will sometimes be more effective. Labor unions were preceded in Britain by worker groups called "Friendly Societies," which provided health and life insurance of a sort to their members, and were in addition pleasant, well-loved sources of community. As late as 1874, these societies enrolled 2,250,000 members—as compared with the 60,000 who bought health insurance from private companies.[18] It's not at all clear that unions, focused as they are exclusively on winning wages and benefits from employers, are in all ways an improvement on these massive self-help efforts. Modern-day unions might do well to offer good unemployment insurance and job retraining programs on their own (perhaps good health and life insurance policies as well). Workers anchored in such unions would be protected somewhat against firm relocations, and might even be able to cope with a job market geared, as it often is these days, toward temporary rather than permanent employment. If there had been unions of this sort in Pittsfield, GE's departure would have caused far less harm. And unions with such programs might attract more workers, and thereby increase their bargaining power and political clout.

Aside from unions, associations formed for benevolent purposes can sometimes be useful. Smith himself does not give private benevolent associations much of a role in solving social problems. He was suspicious of the benevolence shown in the medieval world by both the church and wealthy landowners, pointing out how both used their good works to establish relationships of dependency with those they aided, the one ensuring that poor people came under the thrall of its religious teachings and the other using their poor dependents as soldiers in their private armies. But Smith knew of no major nongovernmental sources of benevolent aid other than the church and private individuals. Today we have large, secular foundations, supported, to be sure, by the gifts of wealthy individuals, but not run by them or directed toward their personal glorification. Some of these organizations—Doctors Without Borders, Habitat for Humanity—already do help solve social problems, and more could do so. Leftists often do not want private organizations to take on this role, believing that government ought to offer aid as a *right* to the poor and oppressed, and fearing that if private groups help these groups instead, government will abdicate that proper role. Leftist foundations, like the Ford Foundation, therefore tend more to fund research into public problems than programs for solving the problems. But this sticking to principle is counterproductive, and therefore counter to the realism that makes Smith such an attractive figure. Why not simply use whatever means are available to solve a problem? And if that means that the Ford Foundation must put some of its resources into building its own low-income housing, its own schools, or offering its own health or unemployment plans, then so be it. Perhaps the privately run programs will serve as a model for what government programs could do, or perhaps, in some cases, they will serve as a model for what not to do. Even the latter would be useful, since failed private experiments are less costly, and easier to dismantle, than programs established by the state.

The final point of agreement we are likely to find between left and right Smithians is that where government does need to act, it should operate as much as possible through markets. Pollution credits—costs per hazardous product emitted, which can then be traded or sold among different companies—will be preferable to a law against emitting more than x amount of a given substance, which then must be enforced by a complex and slow-moving bureaucracy. If something similar ("layoff credits"?) could be worked out for the damage firms do when they lay off large numbers of workers—if a cost could be imposed on each firm per worker laid off and that cost could then be traded among firms— that would also be desirable.

From here on in, right Smithians and left Smithians are likely to diverge. A right Smithian will expect the free market, left alone, to solve both the environmental and the employment problems, and may hold that the problems are made worse by existing government regulations. Laws offering excessive protection to workers, they might say, drive firms like GE from Pittsfield to less onerous political climates.[19] The more governments remove such regulations, the more likely it is that the invisible hand of the market will take care of everyone.

A left Smithian will reject this as overly complacent, as placing too much faith in the invisible hand as a way of solving all problems, and as overlooking features of the particular situation, including the legal and social circumstances that make large firms like GE possible, that already defy the basic principles of free exchange. GE is too well protected against the vicissitudes of the market, a left Smithian will say, to worry as much about its workers as it would have to do if it were but one of a thousand small firms. The left Smithian might also draw on the ways in which Smith himself recognized the structural imbalances in power between employers and employees, and between large stock-owners and other members of society. At the same time, the left Smithian, unlike the anticapitalist leftist, will want to (a) respect the cognitive and moral limits on political agents, and therefore avoid trusting the government to succeed where business leaders fail, (b) work through general laws rather than bureaucrats with discretionary powers, (c) try to base those laws on structures that already exist, and (d) try to address the underlying factors leading to the current problems rather than just those problems themselves. What then might a left Smithian propose, as a way of dealing with the sort of damage that GE inflicted on Pittsfield?

Here are three possibilities, in ascending order of radicalism:

(1) The left Smithian might propose a general plant-closing law, modeled on but extending existing legislation, to try to minimize the sort of shock to a local economy that can result from the move of a large firm like GE. There exists now

a minimal plant-closing law (WARN) that requires sixty days' prior notification before a closing takes place; one might add to this a requirement that all workers laid off be paid a certain amount, as unemployment coverage, to help tide them over until they can find new work. (Indeed, Smithians of all sorts should probably like to see the burden of unemployment insurance shifted from the state to the private sector: far better to give those who immediately cause layoffs an incentive to avoid them.[20]) Alternatively, the payment could be reduced if a firm put in place a good retraining program. The simplest way to deal with the problem, and therefore probably the best, would be to institute a law requiring all firms, in all circumstances, to pay a certain proportion of their workers' salaries in unemployment coverage whenever a worker was laid off without cause. If every worker fired without cause was paid, say, 5 percent of the total salary she had accumulated over the period she worked for her firm, the coverage would both reward loyalty appropriately and reflect the fact that someone who has worked for the same firm for thirty years may find it harder to find a new job than another person who has been with the firm for just two years. Perhaps one might add that the payments could cease once the worker accepted another job, which would provide an incentive for firms to develop good retraining programs.

Note that a response like this to the problem of relocation (a) imposes a predictable cost on relocation rather than trying to prevent it, and thereby recognizes the fact that such mobility is a deeply rooted feature of the current economic landscape; (b) works through a simple, general, and easily enforceable law; and (c) builds on laws and practices that are already present in our society. The same will be true of the other two solutions.

(2) To prevent companies from *becoming* quite as large as they sometimes are, a left Smithian might promote an amendment to existing antitrust legislation: that it consider the potential monopsony a firm may hold over labor markets as well as the potential monopoly it may hold over the market for its product.[21] Currently, when the FTC examines a proposed merger for possible antitrust violations, it considers only the effect of the merger on product markets. Monopolies can charge prices far above the market rate, and antitrust law is concerned with whether a large company has the ability to impose monopoly prices on the consuming public. American antitrust law is fairly scrupulous about what counts as a monopoly, holding firms in violation if they are able to prevent lower-priced goods from competing with theirs just in some local markets, or just for some of the products they sell. But it is concerned solely with the possibility that a firm might exercise excessive control over the market for *goods*, not with its power over the market for labor.

Large firms do not, however, have baleful effects solely on the market for goods. They also often constitute a monopsony over the market for labor, especially in local regions, and it is from this danger that the problems surrounding relocation arise. When one firm offers, say, 800 of the 900 positions for trained welders in a given area, it can both dictate working conditions for welders in that area, and exert power over the entire local labor market: attracting many people, over a course of years or decades, either to train as welders, or, if they are already welders, to move to the area. If, then, it abruptly picks up and leaves, it can devastate the entire local economy. Laborers who have spent many years in one kind of work often cannot easily change over to another line of work, nor can they move from place to place with anything like the fluidity of capital. As Smith observed, "a man is of all sorts of luggage the most difficult to be transported" (WN 92–3). So a firm that constitutes a monopsony over a local labor market can inflict a variety of direct and indirect harms on a class of people who are in general not able to fend well for themselves in the free market.

Thus one way to cut down on the dangers posed by large firms is to guard by law against their coming into existence, where they form monopsonies over labor, or require that such potential monopsonies make room for local competition for themselves, just as large media outlets are required to make room in various ways for competing outlets for their product in local markets. Not only would a requirement that the FTC look out for potential monopsonies as well as monopolies help protect workers, moreover, it would indirectly do something to alleviate the environmental issues we raised. For one important way by which firms are able to get local governments to waive, or fail to enact, environmental legislation is by the threat they hold over the labor market. All a large firm needs to do is say that it will leave a region for mayors, town councils, state legislatures and the like to cave in where the firm opposes some law or regulation.

On the other hand, this proposal is not as "clean" as the preceding one. While an extension of antitrust law to include potential monopsonies over labor might be fairly easy to write into a general law, it would have to be administered by the less than fully transparent, less than easily predictable FTC. A Smithian should beware of any legal enactment that needs to rely on a large bureaucracy and its discretionary powers. It is all too easy for caprice or corruption to creep into an institution endowed with discretionary powers, and the members of such institutions do not receive the degree of public scrutiny that would give them a strong incentive to stay fair and impartial. So getting the FTC to look out for excessive control over the labor market is Smithian in the sense that it builds on existing practice, and in that it aids the weak against the strong, but it does not entirely live up to Smith's standards for good law. In addition, it may on occasion be the case that only a firm large enough to be a monopsony will have the capital to risk investing in certain areas at all (just as only a monopoly will risk making certain products—for which reason Smith himself was willing to grant some temporary monopoly powers). A Smithian, even a left Smithian, will therefore want to be careful about exactly what form this proposal takes. Perhaps it could be combined with the first proposal, such that only or especially firms that constitute labor monopsonies would be subject to the requirement of unemployment coverage for their workers, or that such firms would be subject to higher coverage than other firms.

(3) A third possibility, which reaches now to issues beyond relocation, is that

firms above a certain size, in stock holdings or number of employees, would be required by law to set up a bicameral form of governance for themselves, in which one chamber would consist of employee representatives along with representatives of the communities in which the firms are located, while the other chamber continued to consist of stockholders. The first chamber could ensure fair treatment of workers within the firm, and could do so in a way more respectful of the firm's internal culture and need for growth than outside regulators are likely to be, but it would have to include representatives of the community outside the firm as well as worker representatives so that (a) the worker representatives would not just act as a "closed shop" toward other potential employees in the area, and (b) issues where both the workers and the stockholders of a firm may have interests opposed to those of the neighborhood—issues like the firm's production of air and water pollution—could be taken up. Community representatives to a particular firm's chamber might be elected directly to their position, or chosen, randomly or by each firm, out of a pool of people elected to be community representatives to all firms in the area.

An enactment mandating this sort of corporate structure would explicitly recognize a fact that Smith seems well aware of but his followers have often found it convenient to ignore: that large firms are really political entities, in their relationship to their workers and to the communities around them, and not merely "private" players. The proposal does not, however, go in the direction that socialists might prefer. By maintaining a chamber of stockholders, it retains the capitalist basis for structuring industry, retains the notion that stock should be in private hands, and traded in free markets, not in the hands of governments. The chamber of workers and citizens will just put a *check* on socially irresponsible uses of capital, just cut down on some of the worst externalities that can go with capitalism. Note that this is a liberal rather than a civic republican use of democracy—democracy is here not a good in itself, but a check on the abuses of unelected power—and that that liberal, instrumentalist attitude toward democracy is also very Smithian (see §59, above).

Making large firms democratically accountable, even in this limited way, would of course be a significant change from current practice, but I think it is the sort of significant change that fits in well with Smith's notion of good institutional design. Bicameral legislatures exist in many American political systems, so the proposal borrows from an old, traditional structure. And instead of mandating how, precisely, firms should act, as regards their workers and neighbors, the proposal provides an open-ended structure for the workers, community members, and stockholders to work that out for themselves, on a case-by-case basis. The proposal thus respects the particularist nature of human decision-making, and the useful role of market forces (represented here by the incentives driving the stockholders) in guiding economic decisions. Even with a bicameral structure of governance, different firms will make very different decisions about employee benefits, working hours, neighborhood blight, and the like, in response to their different economic circumstances. It is just that electoral recall, as well as a decrease in profits, will constrain those decisions.

This proposal too could be combined with one or both of the previous ones—only firms that threaten to become a monopsony over labor, say, would have to institute bicameral governance for themselves, or a firm that did so might be permitted to have less generous unemployment coverage.

These three proposals are but samples of policies a left Smithian might advocate. I have elsewhere proposed some secular institutions that might alleviate the anonymity of modern urban society—a problem that Smith himself acknowledged—and advocated the return of the lot, in local politics at least, as a way of both fostering political judgment among the citizenry and counteracting the tendency of political power to gravitate to the wealthy, even in democracies.[22] I would add to these suggestions that, in this day of the World Wide Web especially, governments could do some simple, very Smithian things to increase both the amount consumers know about products and the amount workers know about potential workplaces. Systems for gathering, by computer, both praise and criticism of firms and products from consumers, and both praise and criticism of workplaces from workers, could be easily set up, more or less on the model of the systems that already exist for firms to get feedback from their customers. Firms never have an interest in spreading the results of this feedback to the public at large, however, whereas a government office that did so could significantly add to the incentives for firms to provide high-quality products and good working conditions, and the disincentives against shoddy workmanship, dishonesty, and oppression of workers. A regular mechanism like this would be far less cumbersome than fighting bad behavior by lawsuits, moreover, and is more necessary today than ever before given the anonymity and size of modern societies, both of which provide cover against the word of mouth that once punished bad employers and dishonest merchants. And although it is possible that private entities like *Consumer Reports* might help out in this area here and there—very patchily, as *Consumer Reports* itself does—and although it might be a good idea if even a government agency of this kind operated in part on a fee-for-service basis, it is hard to imagine that the private sector alone would ever carry out this job adequately (the information cannot be paid for by advertising, after all). We truly have an area here "which it can never be the interest of any individual, or small number of individuals, to erect and maintain" but which can more than repay its cost to a great society (WN 688)—an area where government intervention, on Smith's terms, is fully legitimate.

But in the end my interest in providing the reader with a menu of possible left Smithian social programs is less to promote any particular item on this menu than to give content to the notion of a "left-Smithian" attitude toward politics, to show how Smith lends himself to uses by the left as well as the right. And the point of that demonstration is, in part, to urge leftists to learn from the political and moral wisdom of Smith, but in part also to urge all Smith's readers, of whatever political persuasion, to recognize that what he has to teach crosses political boundaries, is quite separate from any specific vision of the ideal polity.

A grounding in common sense, a respect for the importance of imagination and sympathy to understanding our fellow human beings, a resignation to the dominance of self-interest in large public arenas, an understanding of the importance of general laws and of slow change, and an overall humility before the unpredictability of history—all these are lessons from which anyone interested in politics can profit, and that will be useful likewise to social scientists, and to those simply fascinated with the workings of human nature. A purely philosophical interest in human beings is indeed what Smith's work, with its scepticism about the success of political change, most encourages. The best way to read Adam Smith the social scientist is by way of Adam Smith the philosopher: Social science is for him, as it should be for all of us, but one part of the love of wisdom.

NOTES

Introduction

1. Griswold, *Adam Smith and the Virtues of Enlightenment* (Cambridge: Cambridge University Press, 1999); Haakonssen, *The Science of the Legislator* (Cambridge: Cambridge University Press, 1981) and *Natural Law and Moral Philosophy* (Cambridge: Cambridge University Press, 1996).

2. For instance, David Raphael, *Adam Smith* (Oxford: Oxford University Press, 1985) and Jack Weinstein, *On Adam Smith* (Belmont: Wadsworth, 2001).

3. Vivienne Brown, however, takes up many philosophical issues in her *Adam Smith's Discourse* (London: Routledge, 1994), as does Jeffrey Young, in *Economics as a Moral Science* (Cheltenham: Edward Elgar, 1997).

Part I: *Methodology*
Chapter One: Literary Method

1. For abbreviations, see pp. xiii–xiv.

2. Søren Kierkegaard, *Concluding Unscientific Postscript*, trans. D. Swenson and W. Lowrie (Princeton: Princeton University Press, 1941), pp. 447–8, 464–5, 491. Haakonssen speaks of a "Socratic element" in Smith in SL 56, 66. See also AVE 201, 207.

3. As the editors of TMS say, Smith probably has Hume in mind here.

4. Again, he has Hume in mind (T 316–17).

5. Joseph Cropsey, for instance: "The man who observes the joy of another will himself experience joy, and the spectator of grief or of fear will himself feel some measure of grief or fear" (PE 14; see also 17–19).

6. By, for instance, W. R. Taylor in *Francis Hutcheson and David Hume as Predecessors of Adam Smith* (Durham: Duke University Press, 1965), pp. 109, 113, 116.

7. Smith complained in a 1780 letter that when a critic of his on defense "Wrote his book, he had not read mine to the end"—noting, rightly, that WN does not "disapprove of Militias altogether" (Corr 251). Stephen Macedo describes the advantages Smith saw in churches, while overlooking the disadvantages Smith also notes, in "Community, Diversity, and Civic Education: Toward a Liberal Political Science of Group Life," *Social Philosophy and Policy* 13, no. 1 (1996), 242–52.

8. Smith extends his criticisms of the act of navigation, suggesting that even its defense value has been exaggerated, at WN 595–614 (see esp. 597–8).

One commentator who has recognized the structure of the argument in WN IV.ii is Peter McNamara: "Smith's arguments are a response, rather than a concession, to the mercantilists' twin preoccupations of power and plenty. . . . It is . . . significant that he posed the defense-versus-opulence trade-off so sharply. . . . The mercantilists regarded the two concerns as so interconnected that they were seldom in conflict." McNamara, *Political Economy and Statesmanship: Smith, Hamilton, and the Foundation of the Commercial Republic* (Dekalb: Northern Illinois University Press, 1998), pp. 88–9.

9. Franklin Court, "Adam Smith and the Teaching of English Literature," *History of Education Quarterly*, Fall 1985, p. 326.

10. Jerry Muller, *Adam Smith in His Time and Ours* (Princeton: Princeton University Press, 1993), 55, 147, 150.

11. Marshall, *The Figure of Theater: Shaftesbury, Defoe, Adam Smith, and George Eliot* (New York: Columbia University Press, 1986), chap. 7, and Griswold, AVE, 48–58, 63–70.

12. Marshall, pp. 169, 174. The whole of 171–77, especially, offers a wonderful account of the degree to which Smith understands the notion of the self as growing out of a movement between "actor" and "spectator" positions.

13. Deirdre McCloskey (*The Rhetoric of Economics*, second edition [University of Wisconsin, 1998]) has argued that *all* economists use rhetorical techniques to some degree, and need to be read accordingly. I suppose I want to say that Smith uses these techniques more self-consciously, incorporates them more fully into his method, than most of the writers McCloskey discusses. Above all, Smith does not *aim at* the erasure of rhetoric, or use rhetoric to try to erase rhetoric, in the way that, on McCloskey's persuasive account, modern economists do. He is closer to a social scientist like Clifford Geertz, embracing and sometimes making explicit the role of narrative in his work.

14. Rothschild, ES 55, and Thompson, *Customs in Common* (London: Merlin, 1991), 201 n5, citing Anon, *Thoughts of an Old Man of Independent Mind though Dependent Fortune on the Present High Prices of Corn* (1800), p. 4.

15. Simmons, *The Lockean Theory of Rights* (Princeton: Princeton University Press, 1992), p. 9 and n 4 on that page. The internal quotation is from Andrei Rapaczynski, *Nature and Politics* (Ithaca: Cornell University Press, 1987), p. 15.

16. Fleischacker, *A Third Concept of Liberty: Judgment and Freedom in Kant and Adam Smith* (Princeton: Princeton University Press, 1999), pp. 210–12, 191–203.

17. See ASP 146–7.

18. But sometimes, Smith thinks, they themselves fell prey to the confusion they exploited:

> Money in common language . . . frequently signifies wealth; and this ambiguity of expression has rendered this popular notion so familiar to us, that even they, who are convinced of its absurdity, are very apt to forget their own principles . . . Some of the best English writers upon commerce set out with observing, that the wealth of a country consists, not in its gold and silver only, but in its lands, houses, and consumable goods of all different kinds. In the course of their reasonings, however, the lands, houses, and consumable goods seem to slip out of their memory, and the strain of their argument frequently supposes that all wealth consists in gold and silver. (WN 449–50)

19. If anything, Smith says (WN 193), the real price of precious metals should *rise* slightly over time, since they have a small use value in addition to their exchange value (for jewelry, cutlery, and the like) and these uses will increase, along with the increase in the use of all sorts of luxury goods, as a nation gets wealthier.

20. For Gibbon, see Frances Hirst, *Adam Smith* (New York: Macmillan, 1904), p. 165. For Blair, see his letter to Smith of April 3, 1776 (Corr 187–8).

21. Lord Shelburne, quoted in Kirk Willis, "Ideas of Smith in Parliament," *History of Political Economy* 11 (1979), 529.

22. Joseph Schumpeter, *History of Economic Analysis*, ed. E. B. Schumpeter (New York: Oxford University Press, 1954), pp. 184–5.

23. Muller, *Adam Smith*, 27.

24. Thus the increased "dexterity" that the division of labor brings to workers is made

to look, in its initial appearance, almost machine-like; on each of the two subsequent occasions, later in the book, on which he explicitly compares industrial workers to machines, the word "dexterity" is again used to designate the machine-like quality about them (see WN 18–19 and 118–19). Similarly, "toil and trouble" are given an almost technical sense distinguishing them from such more positive aspects of labor as "skill," "dexterity" or "industry" (47).

25. Quoted in Stewart R. Sutherland, "The Presbyterian Inheritance of Hume and Reid," in R. H. Campbell and Andrew Skinner, *The Origins and Nature of the Scottish Enlightenment* (Edinburgh: John Donald, 1982), p. 132.

26. "Philosophy . . . has no other root but the principles of Common Sense; it grows out of them, and draws its nourishment from them" (*Thomas Reid's Inquiry and Essays*, R. Beanblossom and K. Lehrer, eds., Indianapolis: Hackett, 1983, p. 6)

27. The most thorough and forceful case for reading Smith as a sceptic is to be found in Griswold, AVE 155–78. Griswold admits, however, that "Smith nowhere denominates his position 'skeptical'" (170; see also 160 n 18), and I find his case for Smith's scepticism—in any sense, at least, that would conflict with a full-throated endorsement of common-life beliefs—very strained. I criticize this aspect of Griswold's account in "The Philosopher of Common Life," *Mind*, 109, no. 436 (October 2000), 916–23.

28. If philosophy cannot dispel the doubts it raises, says Reid, then "I despise Philosophy, and renounce its guidance—let my soul dwell with Common Sense" (ibid., p. 6). There is one place where Smith expresses similar sentiments: "Gross sophistry has scarce ever had any influence upon the opinions of mankind, except in matters of philosophy and speculation; and in these it has frequently had the greatest" (WN 769).

29. I am indebted to ASD 195–6 for the last three citations. Brown makes a similar point to mine, but sees the appeal to common sense as a matter of rhetorical strategy rather than epistemological commitment.

30. See also WN 109, 286, 290, 316, 347.

31. See, in addition to the citations below, 361, 396, 440, 488, 523, 555, 563, 631, 637, 640, 755, 865, 902.

32. Smith described WN as his "very violent attack . . . upon the whole commercial system of Great Britain" (Corr 251).

33. Stanley Cavell, *The Claim of Reason* (Oxford: Oxford University Press, 1979), p. 125.

34. A similar explanation is supposed to dispel prejudices against apothecaries: 128–9.

Chapter Two: Epistemology and Philosophy of Science

1. In an interesting and elegant reading of these essays, together with the "History of Astronomy" and the "Considerations Concerning the First Formation of Languages," Ralph Lindgren has claimed to find a "predominantly conventionalist epistemological position" and a tendency to antirealist, if not outright idealist, metaphysics in Smith (Lindgren, "Adam Smith's Theory of Inquiry," *Journal of Political Economy* 1969, pp. 900–901). Although Lindgren has a number of very astute insights, and I agree with his emphasis on the importance of language to Smith's conception of all human activity, from theory-building to trade, his case for Smith's conventionalism and antirealism requires him to ignore (1) the firm assumption that there is an external world underlying the entirety of the "External Senses" essay (see especially EPS 140), (2) the importance of observation, which Smith, *pace* Lindgren, construes in a realist way, to the arguments of both "External Senses" and the "History of Astronomy," and (3) the realism implicit in the

distinction Smith draws in "Formation of Languages" between "the . . . matter of fact" and the artificial way in which we *describe* that matter of fact (LRBL 216). Indeed, Lindgren badly distorts one passage in "Ancient Logics" to make his point: He has Smith claiming that "the structure of our ideas 'seems to have arisen more from the nature of language, than from the nature of things'" (Lindgren, 908), but what "arise[s] . . . from the nature of language" in Smith's own text are certain doctrines of *Plato's*, and of other practitioners of "abstract Philosophy" (EPS 125), not the ideas of human beings in general.

2. AVE 168–9. See also footnote 27 to chapter 1 above, and text thereto.

3. TMS 9, ¶3. Hume announces the novelty of his use of the term "impressions" at T 2n and E 18.

4. T 183. Smith says that "to approve of another man's opinions is to adopt those opinions, and to adopt them is to approve of them" (TMS 17), which not only makes believing a matter of "approval" but, in context, makes shared belief exactly like shared sentiments.

5. Smith's account of language is permeated by this assumption: see especially LRBL 204–5, 214, 215–16, 218, 224. It is in this respect that I think Lindgren was right to point to Smith's theory of language as a model for his entire account of inquiry (see note 1 above).

6. "For [Aristotle] the mark of practical thinking is that it is concerned with particulars, and that some of the premises in practical reasoning are premises about particulars. . . . It is as animals endowed with needs, desires, and the power of voluntary locomotion that we are alive to particular facts through sense perception. By nature animals perceive or otherwise apprehend pretty much what they need to in order to act so as to live and propagate. Thus, to be one who takes in the particulars of one's circumstances is already to be an agent or an incipient agent." Sarah Broadie, "The Problem of Practical Intellect in Aristotle's Ethics," in *Proceedings of the Boston Area Colloquium in Classical Philosophy*, vol. 3 (1987). See also Terence Irwin, *Aristotle's First Principles* (Oxford: Clarendon Press, 1988), pp. 118–20, 261–3. For further examples of the linkage between interest and attention to detail in Smith, see WN 833, 836, 838–9, 844, 885.

7. See chapter 6 of my *Third Concept of Liberty.*

8. I am indebted to David Hilbert for pointing out to me that the fact that Smith accepted Hume's psychology does not by itself show that he accepted Hume's metaphysics. Once one accepts associationism as a full account of the psychology of causation, it becomes a bit difficult to find grounds for believing in causal realism as a metaphysical view. But certainly the psychological and the metaphysical claims are not identical.

9. See also WN 313 where, in words that echo the book's title, Smith claims that the Scottish bankers who were led into disaster by the practice of "drawing and re-drawing" were confused because they failed to grasp the underlying source ("nature and causes") of their troubles. The echo of the title suggests that when Smith set out to explain the "nature and causes of the wealth of nations," he meant to clear up confusions that depended precisely on the difference between accidentally linked phenomena and true causal regularities.

10. "Nothing requires greater nicety, in our enquiries concerning human affairs, than to distinguish exactly what is owing to *chance*, and what proceeds from *causes* . . . [I]f I were to assign any general rule to help us in applying this distinction, it would be the following: *What depends upon a few persons is, in a great measure, to be ascribed to chance, or secret and unknown causes: What arises from a great number, may often be accounted for by*

determinate and known causes" ("Of the Rise and Progress of the Arts and Sciences," *Political Essays*, ed. Knud Haakonssen, Cambridge: Cambridge University Press, 1994], p. 58). The same notion may be implied in Hume's third rule for judging of causes at effects, at T 173, which insists on a "constant union betwixt the cause and effect."

11. E 92–3. It is perhaps not irrelevant, if this chapter influenced Smith, as I think it did, that Hume illustrates his point by way of an example of causal regularities in economic exchanges: E 89.

12. Hume gives a wonderfully nuanced account of these levels of regularity in his chapter on miracles in the *Enquiry,* which immediately follows the one on causality in human affairs.

13. See Anthony Waterman, "Economics as Theology: Adam Smith's *Wealth of Nations,*" *Southern Economic Journal* 68, no. 4.

14. Skinner, *A System of Social Science*, second edition (Oxford: Clarendon Press), p. 41n.

15. See, for instance, Charles Taylor, "Rationality," *Philosophy and the Human Sciences* (Cambridge: Cambridge University Press, 1985).

16. EPS 75 adds "novelty and unexpectedness," but not predictive ability, to beauty and simplicity. See also Deborah Redman, *The Rise of Political Economy as a Science* (Cambridge: MIT Press, 1997), p. 85: "A failure to appreciate prediction as a goal of science is one of [Dugald Stewart's] criticisms of Smith." But Eric Schliesser sees prediction as very important to Smith and cites EPS 103 in support: *Indispensable Hume: From Isaac Newton's Natural Philosophy to Adam Smith's "Science of Man"* (Ph.D. dissertation, University of Chicago, 2002), chap. 3.

17. Compare McCloskey's discussion of prediction as a scientific criterion, and argument that it is not a good criterion for the scientific status of economics (*Rhetoric*, 150–51). Here and elsewhere, I find McCloskey's account of what economics *should* be—a humanistic, historical, and rhetorically self-aware science—very close to what Smith hoped it would be.

18. Compare Martin Heidegger on the type of empiricism that insists on beginning from sense-data rather than ordinary objects: "We never really first perceive a throng of sensations, e.g., tones and noises . . . ; rather we hear the storm whistling in the chimney, we hear the three-motored plane, we hear the Mercedes in immediate distinction from the Volkswagen. Much closer to us than all sensations are the things themselves. We hear the door shut in the house and never hear . . . mere sounds. In order to hear a bare sound we have to listen away from things, divert our attention from them, i.e., listen abstractly" ("Origin of the Work of Art," in Albert Hofstadter (trans.), *Poetry, Language, Thought*, New York: Harper & Row, 1971, p. 26).

19. For a very helpful account of the history of political arithmetic, and Smith's relationship to it, see Redman, *Rise*, pp. 142–51, 215–18, and 250–53. I disagree with Redman, however, that in declaring his lack of faith in political arithmetic Smith was concerned only about "the irresponsible use of unreliable statistics" (Redman 251). Redman seems to me closer to the mark when she says that Smith felt that mathematical systems "embodied a greatly oversimplified explanation for [social] phenomena," that he thought the social scientist "was obliged to hold more closely to the messy facts and resist giving in to coherence and elegance" (Redman 217). My account of Smith's reservations about political arithmetic has much to do with "holding closely to the messy facts."

20. Nothing I say in this section is intended to suggest that Smith's version of empiricism is unique. We can find similar ways of using classical texts in Hume, and a similar concern to give the credentials of authoritative sources in many other earlier writers.

There are, however, ways in which Smith differs from his peers, at least in what he emphasizes and what he plays down. He is, for instance, considerably more skeptical of the uses of statistical evidence than other writers on political economy in his day, and he relies more on his own observations than Hutcheson or Hume did in their writings on society.

21. Similarly, a Mr. Meggens gets called "judicious" on 226, another unnamed author is called "eloquent and, sometimes, well-informed" on the same page, and M. Messance is complimented, again, for his "great diligence and fidelity" on 257. Certain manuscript accounts are described as "well authenticated" on 227. Smith constantly evaluates his sources even while using them: for other examples, see 169, 317, 320, 426, 506, 739, 755, 899, 905, 918, 922.

22. The practice of describing the reliability of one's sources was widespread among prior empiricists, going back at least as far as Bacon: see Steven Shapin, *A Social History of Truth* (Chicago: University of Chicago Press, 1994), chap. five.

23. For instance: 89, 173, 186–8, 191, 205, 240, 247, 568, 571, 574, 576, 680, 730.

24. This last remark brings to mind Hume's warning, in "On Miracles," that travelers are inclined to pack their tales with "miraculous" events: E 117.

25. Other citations from classical sources: 235–6, 241, 587, 685–6. The last of these draws an economic inference from classical statuary.

26. See editors' comment on WN 152, n50.

27. Nathan Rosenberg, "Some Institutional Aspects of the *Wealth of Nations*," *Journal of Political Economy* 68 (1960).

28. Unsurprisingly, much of what Smith tells us on the basis of his own experience and conversations has to do with Scotland: see, for example, 69, 92–3, 97, 99, 107, 121, 133.

29. Of course, he had few written sources he could turn to for information on this subject. Frederick Eden's 1797 *The State of the Poor* is often considered the first serious attempt to survey the condition of the poor. Arguably that honor belongs to the *Wealth of Nations* itself.

30. Shapin traces this list of criteria back to the seventeenth century, pointing out anticipations of Hume in Locke, especially: *Social History*, pp. 228–38.

31. Elsewhere, he treats his oral informants much as he does written texts, expressing doubts about the truth of some of what he has heard on the basis either of his own observations or of the disputability inherent to the subject on which his informant was testifying (177, 261).

32. I discuss the relationship between these two in *Third Concept*, chap. two. The importance of judgment in WN is the subject of *Third Concept*, chap. six.

33. Athol Fitzgibbons, *Adam Smith's System of Liberty, Wealth and Virtue* (Oxford: Oxford University Press, 1995), p. 194. A helpful corrective to Fitzgibbons' view can be found in Emma Rothschild, ES 131–6. See also below, §37.

34. See also TMS 87, 128, 165, 166, 185. Smith also often seems to personify nature, describing it as if it had conscious intentions and as if those intentions were wise and benevolent: "Nature . . . exhorts mankind to acts of beneficence" (86). "Nature, when she formed man for society, endowed him with an original desire to please" (116)

Chapter Three: Moral Philosophy

1. Note the wonderful use of "savage," here, to describe the *Europeans* in America! Compare 636, where a Dutch policy in Indonesia is described as "savage" ("barbarous," in the first edition).

2. Editors' introduction, p. *40*, my emphasis.

3. As, once again, Kierkegaard was to say: *Concluding Unscientific Postscript*, 68–74, 246–7, 320–22. Haakonssen makes an intriguing comparison between Smith and Kierkegaard on SL 77.

4. Sometimes Smith drops proto-Kantian hints that a concern for the equal worth of each and every human being lies at the basis of all moral sentiments (TMS 90, 107, 137. See Stephen Darwall, "Sympathetic Liberalism: Recent Work on Adam Smith," *Philosophy and Public Affairs*, 1999, pp. 153–4). This point, if it could be justified, might point the way toward an account of how the impartial spectator can correct for local biases and maintain universalist aspirations. But Smith says very little to justify the point.

5. A standard solution to the "Adam Smith Problem": see the editors' introduction to TMS, *20–21*.

6. See §22 below and *Third Concept*, 154–6, 170.

Part II: *Human Nature*

Chapter Four: Overview

1. In his *Religion Within the Limits of Reason Alone* especially, but also in Book I, Part I, chap. 3 of the *Critique of Practical Reason*.

2. Taylor, "Interpretation and the Sciences of Man," *Philosophy and the Human Sciences* (Cambridge: Cambridge University Press, 1985).

3. Ronald Meek, *Smith, Marx, and After* (London: Chapman & Hall, 1977), chap. 2.

4. Donald Davidson, *Inquiries into Truth and Interpretation* (Oxford: Oxford University Press, 1984).

5. Pufendorf comments wrily on More's and Campanella's utopias: "I suppose . . . perfect men are more easily imagined than found" (LNN IV.iv.7; 541).

6. Ryan Hanley has carried out a deep investigation of these different kinds of self-love in Smith in "Magnanimity and Modernity: Self-Love in the Scottish Enlightenment," Ph.D. dissertation, University of Chicago, June 2002.

7. The most important recent discussion of this topic is *For Love of Country*, eds. M. Nussbaum and J. Cohen (Boston: Beacon Press, 1996). See also Nussbaum, *The Cosmopolitan Tradition* (New Haven: Yale University Press, forthcoming).

8. TMS 335–6. Nicholas Phillipson discusses the importance of conversation to Smith's moral theory in "Adam Smith as civic moralist," *Wealth and Virtue*, I. Hont and M. Ignatieff (eds.) (Cambridge: Cambridge University Press, 1983), pp. 188–9.

9. Ibid., 198–200.

10. TMS 19. On theater, see TMS 107, 123, 143, 176–7; on poetry, see LRBL, *passim*, TMS 123–5, 143, and EPS 194, 243; on music, see EPS 187–207, esp. 194 and 204–5.

11. This "conduciveness to utility without actual utility" is I think a direct ancestor of Immanuel Kant's "purposiveness without purpose" in his writings on aesthetics (Fleischacker, *Third Concept*, 147, 190–91). TMS was employed in aesthetic theory by several Germans before Kant: the editors' introduction mentions its influence, in this regard, on Lessing and Herder (*30–31*).

12. Hutcheson had located beauty in a balance between uniformity and variety (OB, chapter II).

13. Jean-Jacques Rousseau, *Discourse on the Moral Effects of the Arts and Sciences* (the so-called "First Discourse"), translated in *The First and Second Discourses*, R. Masters and J. Masters (ed. and trans.), (New York: St. Martin's Press, 1964).

14. By Peter Minowitz, in *Profits, Priests and Princes* (Stanford: Stanford University Press, 1993).

15. Indeed, he famously said that he considered David Hume, an avowed agnostic (and possibly an atheist), to "approach [. . .] as nearly to the idea of a perfectly wise and virtuous man as perhaps the nature of human frailty will permit" (Corr 221).

16. The more standard reading of this verse sees the image of God in our intellect, not our emotions, but since Smith has shifted the emphasis in morality from intellect to sentiment, it makes sense for him, correspondingly, to see God's image in our sentiments.

17. Similarly, he uses the phrase "demigod within the breast" to describe the impartial spectator within us, saying that it is "partly of immortal, . . . partly . . . of mortal extraction" (131). Insofar as we judge of one another impartially, we take up something of a "God's-eye view" of the universe, a view beyond both our own interests and the interests of the people we are judging.

18. Note that all the citations in the last two sentences come from the final, 1790 edition of TMS. I agree with the TMS editors' judgment that Smith retained a commitment to natural religion throughout his life, even if he increasingly dropped any commitment to Christianity (*19–20*, 383–401). The editors note, in this context, Smith's contemptuous sneer at "whining Christian[s]" in a letter to Alexander Wedderburn shortly before Hume's death. Anthony Waterman ("Economics as Theology") argues for a more Christian Smith.

19. In the middle of this discussion, Smith puts three paragraphs on the terrible unfairness of nature, stressing the degree to which "violence and artifice prevail over sincerity and justice," and quoting the bishop of Clermont to the effect that our world is in universal disorder, and that "the wicked prevail almost always over the just" (TMS 169). No less careful a scholar than Charles Griswold takes these lines to be a moment at which Smith despairs of there being a God (AVE 325–6). Griswold says that "Smith neither prepares us for [the bishop's] outburst nor has a word to say in response to it. . . . The bishop's . . . words disrupt rather than confirm Smith's narrative about natural religion." But in fact the sentences that immediately precede and succeed the quotation make clear that for Smith the lines simply help show why those who believe in a providential God also need to believe in an afterlife. If one has been following the general flow of argument, which is designed to show that "the noblest and best principles" in human nature—our moral sentiments—and not merely our personal fears, urge us to believe that this is not the only world, that God will establish justice for all "in a life to come," one will find the quotation from the bishop not at all disruptive of Smith's point.

20. Throughout that chapter, he is concerned about the ability of churches and clerics to foster moral virtues, by example and by creating communities that provide the mechanisms of social approval and disapproval he had emphasized in TMS.

21. WN 944–5: he here also uses the phrase "impartial spectator."

22. Vivienne Brown's intriguing reading of justice as a lesser virtue therefore goes too far, in my opinion, in that she fails to see the degree to which it expresses the impartial stance that Smith takes to be basic to all virtue; this suggests some questions about her reading of WN as an "amoral" book.

23. See Darwall, "Sympathetic Liberalism."

24. This is but one of many connections between Smith and Kant: see Darwall, "Sympathetic Liberalism" and my essays, "Philosophy and Moral Practice: Kant and Adam Smith," *Kant-Studien* 1991 and "Values Behind the Market: Kant's Response to the *Wealth of Nations*," *History of Political Thought*, Autumn 1996.

25. The distinction between these two sets of issues is not a sharp one, since one

important way in which human rewards differ is that some people receive, from childhood onward, better *means for developing* intelligence and virtue than others do. Smith was neither unaware of nor unworried about this fact, but I think we can stick with the distinction in types of issues for the purpose of organizing his arguments.

26. Polanyi, *The Great Transformation* (Boston: Beacon, 1944), p. 44.

27. See also 104 ("[the owner of stock] endeavours to supply [his workers] with the best machinery which either he *or they* can think of"—my emphasis) and LJ 346, 351.

28. The word he uses is "musick," which for the Greeks included all the arts: "music" is that over which the Muses watch.

29. There are passages in which Smith seems to be much less egalitarian than this. The most important of these is TMS 161–3, which Brown relies upon to make her case that "only a refined few" can achieve true virtue for Smith, while the rest of humankind can at best live at a second-order level of morality (ASD 83, 208). On 161–3, Smith does say that "the coarse clay of which the bulk of mankind are formed cannot be wrought up to" true moral perfection, that they can be expected to act only "with tolerable decency." Practically everyone can be "impressed with a regard to general rules," he says, and that will be sufficient to keep them acting with tolerable decency, but true moral greatness, being "the very first of [our] kind" rather than just the second, lies in heeding the "nice and delicate" guidance of the impartial spectator at all times, not in merely following established rules.

What I am inclined to do with this passage is what I shall suggest, later on, that we do with the famous TMS IV.i passage on vanity. Both passages come from the first edition of the book (an editor's note on 164 argues that one paragraph of III.5 must date from an early version of Smith's lectures and is inconsistent with other elements of TMS: I am suggesting that the same may be true of the whole chapter), and both express the strongly Stoic views that Smith seems to have held at that point in his career. In the last edition of TMS, Smith submerges or rejects much of his earlier Stoicism, and simultaneously—not, I think, coincidentally—evinces a more pronounced commitment to egalitarianism. It may be that as he came to work more on political economy and less on moral principles, he also thought more about the lives of laboring people and his earlier, elitist attitudes came to seem to him less and less tenable.

At any rate, the elitism of the "coarse clay" passage is in severe tension with the strong egalitarianism implicit in Smith's impartial spectator device, as well as with many explicit passages in TMS. To take one example, in addition to those discussed in the text: The opening chapters of Books I (i–iv) and III (1–3) describe every human being as naturally coming to internalize the attitudes of the spectators he or she encounters, as naturally coming to set up an impartial spectator within him- or herself, and as naturally recognizing the superiority of praiseworthiness to mere praise. *Everyone*, that is, not just a refined few, is normally subjected to the influences that make one capable of the highest moral achievement. This account of moral development is in clear tension with III.5.1, where most people are described as learning propriety merely by absorbing "established rules of behavior."

30. Justice is not, however, the *only* virtue that expresses equality: TMS 137 makes proper generosity also follow from seeing "the real littleness of ourselves."

31. Much of Smith's opposition to policies that help one sort of trade over another is based on the notion that such policies violate the sovereign's duty to show "equality of treatment" to every order of citizen (see, for instance, 825, 877, 905).

32. Quoted in Muller, *Adam Smith*, 163.

33. See Fleischacker, *The Ethics of Culture* (Ithaca: Cornell University Press, 1994), chap. 5.

34. Ross, *Life*, 166.

35. Bentham, *Works* (Edinburgh: Tait, 1843), vol. 2, pp. 253–4.

Chapter Five: Self-Interest

1. George Stigler, "Smith's Travels on the Ship of State," in *Essays on Adam Smith*, eds. Andrew Skinner and Thomas Wilson (Oxford: Clarendon, 1975), p. 237.

2. Internal quotation from Bernard Bailyn, *The Origins of American Politics* (New York: Vintage, 1968), p. 41.

3. See Locke, *Essay Concerning Human Understanding*, II.xxi38, 43–4, 62, II.xxviii.5–8; Jerome Schneewind, *The Invention of Autonomy* (Cambridge: Cambridge University Press, 1998), 142–55; and Stephen Darwall, *The British Moralists and the Internal 'Ought'* (Cambridge: Cambridge University Press, 1995), pp. 149–71.

4. On Shaftesbury and his relation to Locke, see Darwall, *British Moralists*, pp. 176–8.

5. The desire for self-approval may lead one, after all, to sacrifice everything one has, including one's life.

6. The worst of these policies, the ones leading to the greatest destruction of resources, are "expensive and unnecessary wars" (344–5; see also 925 and 929, which repeat a number of the points from II.iii). When we bear in mind, in addition, that Smith repeatedly tells us that soldiers, unlike productive laborers, are given to "idleness and dissipation" (470), it becomes clear that one purpose of Smith's polemic on behalf of the desire for social status is to invite a comparison with the desire for martial glory. The "uniform, constant, and uninterrupted" desire to improve ourselves socially works "silently and gradually" (345), in contrast with the noisy suddenness of war; it requires, and hence leads to, lifetime patterns of "frugality and good conduct" (341, 342, 345, 929), in contrast with the flamboyant devil-may-care behavior of soldiers; and it is no more vainglorious, no more aimed at praise rather than praiseworthiness, than is the desire that motivates military exploits. So the commercial disposition, "base and selfish" as it may be (349), comes off fairly well in comparison with the violent, impetuous, imprudent, and ultimately little more noble impulse that leads nations to destroy themselves on the battlefield. See also §60 below, for Smith's attitude toward war.

7. See TMS 63–4 and WN 794 on the likelihood that the poor will be more ascetic than the rich.

8. "When a Man acts in behalf of Nephews or Neices, and says they are my Brother's Children, I do it out of Charity; he deceives you: for if he is capable, it is expected from him, and he does it partly for his own Sake: If he values the Esteem of the world, and is nice as to Honour and Reputation, he is obliged to have a greater Regard to them than for Strangers. . . ." Mandeville, "An Essay on Charity, and Charity Schools," in *The Fable of the Bees,* ed. F. B. Kaye (Oxford: Clarendon, 1924), p. 253. (See also the whole of this chapter.)

9. Nor would a self-respecting butcher give away his meat to customers with the means to pay for it. Gloria Vivenza is right to "doubt whether the impartial spectator would . . . sympathize with a butcher who gave away his meat, or even sold it at a lower price than he should." Vivenza, *Adam Smith and the Classics* (Oxford: Oxford University Press, 2001), p. 63.

10. Compare Patricia Werhane, *Adam Smith and His Legacy for Modern Capitalism* (New York: Oxford University Press, 1991), p. 94: "Smith notices that economic exchanges cannot operate in the 'vacuum' of self-interest but require co-operation and co-ordination. . . . [F]ree trade requires the co-operation of two parties or two countries. Tradespeople often work together, sometimes even in collusion, despite their competitive

relationships. This co-operation is also seen in the relationships between townspeople and farmers . . . In all these cases, co-operation is both natural and required for the advantage of our self-interests."

11. I don't want to override Smith's disclaimer altogether; the fact that he added it in WN, and removed the extended comparisons between exchange and speech that had appeared in LJ, suggests that he came to have doubts about its legitimacy. But I don't think the doubts were very significant. Presumably, he came to recognize that economic exchanges are neither in fact always accompanied by talk nor even carried out between two people in direct contact with one another. Furthermore, in most circumstances offering a shilling to one's butcher is not really an attempt at persuasion: it is a move in a conventional game, which both parties need no persuasion to play. Any talk, and certainly any persuasion, needed to set up the game has been done long ago, and elsewhere. But the ability to speak and persuade was certainly necessary to *establish* systems of exchange, and exchange itself is, like speech, one form of the basic tendency of human beings to take actions in conjunction with other human beings, to pursue projects jointly. Exchange and speech may then be merely analogous to one another, or they may both spring from the same root impulse, or perhaps exchange follows from speech. In WN, Smith doesn't want to commit himself to one of these possibilities over the others (although he does say that the derivation of exchange from speech seems the most "probable" to him). That hardly matters. Market interactions are virtually impossible without conversation; they may not quite *be* speech, but they depend crucially upon it.

12. Aristotle, *Politics* I.2, 1253a7–18, as translated in Jonathan Barnes (ed.), *The Complete Works of Aristotle* (Princeton: Princeton University Press, 1984).

13. Continental philosophy of language, from Saussure onward, stresses the first of these conditions; Anglo-American philosophy of language, especially as developed by Donald Davidson, emphasizes the second.

14. But even here the word "only" in the second sentence qualifies the extent to which benevolence is being written out of the picture. No such qualification appears in a similar argument in Mandeville, cited by the editors at the bottom of the page: and Smith will similarly, toward the end of the paragraph, say that beggars do not depend upon charity "entirely," where Mandeville had reduced "charity" itself to the self-interest of the donors.

15. James Steuart, *Inquiry into Political Economy* (London: Cadell & Davies, 1805), p. 212, my emphasis.

16. Translated as "Nature's Domain," in *French Utopias*, ed. and trans. Frank E. Manuel and Fritzie P. Manuel (New York: The Free Press, 1966), pp. 93–4.

17. Tommasso Campanella, "City of the Sun" (1623), trans. Thomas W. Halliday, in Henry Morley (ed.), *Ideal Commonwealths* (New York: The Co-operative Publication Society, 1901), p. 148.

18. The lawyer Guy-Jean Target, at the beginning of the French Revolution, quoted in Simon Schama, *Citizens* (New York: Alfred A. Knopf, 1989), p. 291.

19. Gordon Wood, *Creation of the American Republic* (Chapel Hill: University of North Carolina Press), p. 69. As Rothschild says, for Smith politics "requires very little in the way of civic virtue" (ES 233).

20. "The important aspect of Adam Smith's emphasis on self-love, as he calls it, is non-tuism of the person with whom he bargains. He doesn't interest himself—he may, but he doesn't necessarily, interest himself—in what the person with whom he's bargaining is doing with his family. He may be interested in all sorts of things with which he favours his family and wider circles in society." Lionel Robbins, *A History of Economic Thought*, ed. S. G. Medema and Warren Samuels (Princeton: Princeton University Press,

1998), p. 132. Stigler would have been much closer to the truth had he described WN as "a stupendous palace erected upon the granite of non-tuism."

21. TMS 317: the language here echoes his dismissal of Mandeville, on 313.

22. The same slip between "polity" and "society" occurs several times on PE 110–11 and 113.

23. See above §12, Muller, *Adam Smith*, 133, and AVE 294, 296–300.

24. See my "Insignificant Communities," in Amy Gutmann (ed.), *Freedom of Association* (Princeton: Princeton University Press, 1998), pp. 275–8.

Chapter Six: Vanity

1. See, for instance, AVE 225, 263, 326.

2. ASP 91–2 very much presents WN as "painted within the framework" of TMS IV.i.10, as do Fitzgibbons (168–9), Cropsey (PE 133–4), and Muller (134).

3. Griswold himself stresses, against more Stoic interpretations, that Smith does not entirely disapprove of the pursuit of wealth: see, especially, AVE 226–7 (including note 56 on 226) and 265. Nevertheless, the degree to which, on Griswold's view, Smith regards the pursuit of wealth as a corruption is sufficient to warrant an expectation that he would have engaged in far more moral criticism of commercial society than he did.

4. Nussbaum, "Duties of Justice, Duties of Material Aid: Cicero's Problematic Legacy," *Journal of Political Philosophy* 8, no. 2, 2000, 199–200. But see now "'Mutilated and Deformed': Adam Smith on the Material Basis of Human Dignity," in Nussbaum, *Cosmopolitan Tradition*, which argues forcefully that Smith is considerably less willing in WN than in TMS to regard poverty as "external" to the quality of a human being's life. Even here, however, Nussbaum does not think, as I do, that Smith rejects his earlier stoicism in the later editions of TMS.

On Smith and stoicism, see also Vivenza, *Smith and the Classics*, chap. 2 (esp. 61–4) and Postscript (esp. 202–12).

5. "The Market and the Republic," in Ignatieff, *The Needs of Strangers* (New York: Viking, 1984). See also Ryan Hanley's brilliant comparison of Smith to Rousseau, in TMS IV.i and elsewhere: "Rousseau's Diagnosis and Adam Smith's Cure," presented at APSA, Boston, 2002.

6. Readers unpersuaded that Smith simply overlooked the problems in this passage when reworking TMS should note that *any* interpretation of the relationship between TMS IV.i and Smith's other economic writings will have to make some move along the lines I am recommending. If TMS IV.i is to be taken, as Griswold urges, as "the frame" of all Smith's economic thought, then we need to account for why Smith, as Griswold admits, "does not . . . stress that betterment . . . is founded on a deception" in WN (AVE 263). Either Smith disguised his real views in WN or he expressed himself inadequately in TMS IV.i. Both interpretations, and any other that recognizes the tension between TMS IV.i and the other writings, must find one or another strand in Smith unrepresentative of his settled views. My reading has the advantage of stressing later over earlier writings.

7. Howard Caygill rightly understands this last phrase to refer to "the political direction of wealth in the interest of the common welfare," and maintains that Smith moved gradually from this position to the free trade doctrine of WN: Caygill, *Art of Judgment* (Oxford: Basil Blackwell, 1989), p. 91. See also Brown (ASD 155 n35): the celebration of "police" in this passage, she says, "is at odds with the argument of WN," and the passage "could not have occurred in WN."

8. Smith does remark in WN that premiums given to honor excellent artisans "are not liable to the same objections as bounties" (WN 523), but he also goes on to make clear

that these are *not* "encouragements to advance" any kind of manufacture, noting explicitly that the latter are wrongly assimilated to premiums (524).

Smith's opposition to bounties seems to have been the last piece of his free trade doctrine to develop. In both LJ and ED Smith had held that the bounty on corn-exportation at least kept England well supplied with cheap corn (see editor's note 7 to WN 506). In WN, he argues vigorously against that view (506–17). But even WN, in its first edition, was willing to justify some bounties under the "defence is more important than opulence" principle; by the third edition, in 1784, Smith reversed even this concession (note p-p to 518–19 and text thereto). His careful reworking of the WN chapter on bounties contrasts starkly with a complete absence of alterations to the remark I have just considered in TMS, in subsequent editions. I take that to be evidence that he did not look closely at this whole chapter of TMS.

9. See W. L. Taylor, *Francis Hutcheson and David Hume as Predecessors of Adam Smith* (Durham: Duke University Press, 1965), chapter IV.

10. WN 337, 342–3, 345, 405, 513, 540, 674, 925, 929. See also Taylor, *Hutcheson and Hume,* pp. 109–17.

11. See note k on TMS 275 and pp. 292–3.

12. See paragraph 14 on pp. 142–3 and the sentence marked r-r by the editors in paragraph 8 on p. 139. Nussbaum notes, in " 'Mutilated and Deformed' . . . ," that Smith continues to urge a stoic apathy toward our own misfortunes, even while inveighing against taking such an attitude to the sufferings of our relatives and friends. She suggests that this asymmetry is incoherent: ". . . if calamities are bad when they affect others, why are they not really bad when they affect the self?" But I think Smith is not suggesting that calamities are bad only when they affect other people: just that our attitude *toward* such calamities should be stoic in our own case and compassionate in the case of others. This fits with his general belief that morality, correcting for our natural strong partiality toward ourselves, urges us to moderate self-concern and to expand concern for others (TMS 23, 25).

13. Nussbaum (ibid.) argues that Smith himself displays a callousness toward the poor, even in the sixth edition revisions, when he writes that "mere poverty excites little compassion," that "[w]e despise a beggar" (TMS 144). I take it that Smith is *reporting* a natural attitude here, not *endorsing* it, and that the criticisms he offers of that attitude in I.iii are supposed to be borne in mind as we read this passage. But Smith's tone is hard to figure out, in the lines Nussbaum quotes, and I do not offer my reading of them over Nussbaum's with great confidence. (On the difficulties in gauging Smith's tone in general, see §1 of this book.)

14. On the subject of "preferred indifferents" in Stoic thought, see Glenn Lesses, "Virtue and Fortune in Stoic Moral Theory," *Oxford Studies in Ancient Philosophy,* ed. Julia Annas (Oxford: Clarendon Press, 1989). I am indebted to Rachana Kamtekar for clarification of this point.

15. "Virtue is open to everyone, admits everyone, invites everyone—freeborn, freedman and slave, king and exile" (Seneca, *De Beneficiis* III.18, translated by J. Cooper and J. F. Procopé in Seneca, *Moral and Political Essays* (Cambridge: Cambridge University Press, 1995), p. 256. Similarly, Epictetus, who was himself born a slave, makes light of the difference between freedom and slavery in *Discourses* IV.i.

16. See the part of TMS IV.i.10 quoted above and TMS 50–51.

17. See Fred Hirsch, *Social Limits to Growth* (Cambridge: Harvard University Press, 1976).

18. Vivenza uses, as proof of Smith's distance from the Stoics, the fact that he was

interested in "guarantee[ing] a minimum of well-being, education and consideration even to the less fortunate classes: something the Stoics would not have been concerned with" (212, n 91).

19. The former is "taste" proper, for him, while the latter is our "empirical interest in the beautiful" (*Critique of Judgment*, §41).

20. Cavell, *Claim of Reason*, p. 120.

21. Ibid., 123.

22. For this terminology, see Christine Korsgaard, *Sources of Normativity* (Cambridge: Cambridge University Press, 1996), pp. 19, 49–89.

23. We are competing here for positional goods: see Hirsch, *Social Limits of Growth*.

24. TMS 50, 186; LJ 334–5, 337, 377–9, 487; WN 96, 178, 338, 340.

25. For a contemporary economist's defense of this point, see Deirdre McCloskey, "Christian Economics?" *Eastern Economic Journal* 25 (4, Fall 1999): 477–80.

Part III: *Foundations of Econonics*
Chapter Seven: Foundations of Economics

1. For economic guides to WN, see Vincent Bladen, *From Adam Smith to Maynard Keynes* (Toronto: University of Toronto Press, 1974) Samuel Hollander's *The Economics of Adam Smith* (Toronto: University of Toronto Press, 1973), or Mark Blaug's chapter on Smith in *Economic Theory in Retrospect*, fifth edition (New York: Cambridge University Press, 1997). A lively introduction can be found in Robbins, *History of Economic Analysis*. For a fascinating but controversial view, see ASD, chapters 6 and 7.

2. Jack Weinstein, *On Adam Smith* (Belmont: Wadsworth, 2001), p. 72. There is a reason for the many ellipses in this quotation: The medieval view can be attributed to Smith only if one ignores much of his actual language. I will restore the missing words shortly, and it will then become clear that the attribution is misguided.

3. Weinstein, p. 74. Weinstein wants to align Smith strongly with medieval just price theory, saying that Smith does not include profit in natural price and that one is therefore "forced to wonder whether profit is somehow 'unnatural,' and whether or not this is implicitly one of Smith's many criticisms of greed." It is, however, not true that Smith leaves profit out of natural price: "When the price of any commodity is neither more nor less than what is sufficient to pay the rent of the land, the wages of the labour, and the profits of the stock employed in raising, preparing and *bringing it to market*, . . . the commodity is then sold for what may be called its natural price" (WN 72, my emphasis). The profits involved in bringing something to market, as the next paragraph makes clear, include the profit "of the person who is to sell [the finished product] again"—the profit of the merchant, who "buys" the good from the workers and sells it "again" in the market—which Smith calls "the proper fund of [the merchant's] subsistence." Smith's point in these paragraphs is indeed precisely the opposite of the one Weinstein attributes to him: He aims to show that "common language" makes a *mistake* when it excludes profit from the proper cost of a commodity. Only commodities that someone is willing to trade regularly will anyone else be willing to produce, so the profit of merchants is essential to the long-term production of commodities, and thus very much part of their natural price. The importance of commerce to production is a central teaching of WN, and one of the ways in which it is most concerned to overcome long-standing popular prejudices.

4. But see Schliesser, *Indispensable Hume*, who argues trenchantly that the analogy to gravitation would really only hold if market and natural prices gravitated toward *one*

another. I think Smith explains himself badly but does want to use an analogy with gravitation. A better way to put the analogy might be as follows: Market prices will gravitate toward one another—buyer's prices and seller's prices will attract one another toward an equilibrium point—and natural price expresses, not the source of gravitation, but the point at which the two types of prices meet.

In his chapter 4, Schliesser provides a brilliant account of how "natural price" provides a theoretically useful gap between ideal conditions and empirical reality.

5. See Richard Teichgraeber, *'Free Trade' and Moral Philosophy* (Durham: Duke University Press, 1986), 182n12.

6. There is something a bit circular in this argument. Smith uses a common language definition of "cheap" as "easy to come at" and "dear" as "hard to come at," while acknowledging himself that "easy to come at" is just a synonym for "costs little labor" and "hard to come at" is a synonym for "costs much labour" (50–51). The argument does not primarily depend on this equation, however—the point about the proper order of empirical explanation does most of the work—and I think Smith would say that common language generally reflects the facts about our natural and social worlds, and that the common meaning of words like "cheap" and "dear" reflects our common understanding that when we exchange goods we are simply "coming at" them, indirectly, through our labor, as we might once have "come at" them directly by making them ourselves.

7. On the importance of sectoral analysis to the argument of WN, see ASD 164–82, 196–206.

8. "Or whatever else is the common and favourite vegetable food of the people": WN 95–6, 206, 258–9.

9. This is not entirely true: It might add to *your* value, and if you are off to a job interview, that might be of real significance. But Smith is presumably thinking of aristocrats who do not seek or take jobs, and for them it is probably true that the service of their valets has no economic value.

10. But see Bladen, *From Adam Smith*, pp. 65–7, who provides an interesting reinterpretation of the distinction between productive and unproductive labor that sheds light on why menial labor is so prevalent in underdeveloped economies, and why such labor is both rarer and better recompensed in better developed ones.

11. In connection with this section, see Emma Rothschild's chapter on the invisible hand in ES (116–56). Not only is Rothschild's own reading of the nature and role of the invisible hand metaphor an extremely intriguing one, but her footnotes contain the most complete survey of literature on this topic I have ever seen.

12. Passages that express the same view, but without the vivid phrase, include WN 374, 524–5, 530, 630.

13. Fitzgibbons maintains that "Smith's invisible hand was the hand of divine Providence" (Fitzgibbons, *Adam Smith's System*, p. 89; see also 193–4). I disagree with this, as will be clear. Rothschild shows that this view was held by nineteenth-century *opponents* of Smith (ES 118), and argues that Smith himself was strongly opposed to the Stoic notion of "providential order" that Fitzgibbons attributes to him (131–6). I would modify this latter point a little. As I argued in §9, I think it is clear that Smith did hold out the possibility of a providential order as a reasonable element of a *moral* faith, but that he never relied on such a possibility in his *scientific* accounts—in his descriptions of how our sentiments, or society, or markets, work. As Rothschild says, "the existence of order does not imply the existence of design" for Smith (ES 135).

Smith's Stoic faith also seems to have declined as he got older: see §§25–27 above.

14. "Nothing but exemplary morals can give dignity to a man of small fortune," he

says (WN 810), so an institution that needs to be served by morally exemplary people will do well to discourage the profit-motive in its employees.

15. Waterman, "Economics as Theology," 16. See also Rosenberg, "Institutional Aspects," and Werhane, *Adam Smith's Legacy*, chap. 4. Werhane offers a partial critique of Rosenberg.

16. Fitzgibbons, *Adam Smith's System*: see note 13 above.

17. If this is news, it is news primarily to Hobbesians, to those who picture human beings as so inevitably in conflict with one another that the result of their unregulated individual activities should hardly *ever* yield good results for society as a whole. On such a picture, the idea that an invisible hand of society might often guide individual activities toward a good for all would seem absurd. Like Hutcheson and Hume, Smith rejects Hobbes's unsociable conception of human beings, and we may take his invisible hand accounts to be part of this anti-Hobbesian polemic.

18. Implicitly, this argument depends upon Smith's analysis of sympathy in TMS. We build trust and understanding of other people's "character[s] and situation[s]" through sympathy, but sympathy is a highly particularized mechanism, which works most effectively between people who see each other often. As a consequence, people will always tend to trust those they know more than those they don't know—their neighbors more than unfamiliar fellow countrymen and unfamiliar countrymen more than unfamiliar people from foreign countries.

19. The man of virtue "really adopts" the sentiments of the impartial spectator (TMS 147), which, as we have seen earlier, essentially reflect moral sentiments widespread in his society; the man of lesser virtue adopts less lofty sentiments that his society also, tacitly, approves of (62).

Part IV: *Justice*
Chapter Eight: A Theory of Justice?

1. See, for instance SL 1, 83, 89, RP 97, Werhane, *Adam Smith and His Legacy*, 44 and 78; or Fitzgibbons, *Adam Smith's System*, 140.

2. John Rawls, relying on Sidgwick, places Smith in "the utilitarian tradition" in *Theory of Justice* (Cambridge: Harvard University Press, 1971), p. 22n, and again in *Political Liberalism* (New York: Columbia University Press, 1993), p. xiv.

3. There are implicit references. The phrase "impartial spectators" appears on 945, the phrase "bettering one's condition" appears throughout II.iii (echoing TMS 50), WN 180–81 looks like a rewrite of TMS 184, the notion that there is an upper-class (loose) and a lower-class (strict) standard of morals appears both at TMS 63–4 and at WN 794, and the phrase "invisible hand" of course appears in both books. None of these echoes requires a reader of WN to look back at TMS, however.

4. And when they do appear, they almost always refer to legal rather than natural rights. Smith speaks, for instance, of the "right of primogeniture" (WN 574) or the "right" of the British Parliament to tax the colonies (621) or the "right" a diocese had to elect its bishop (804), meaning by "right," in all these cases, a privilege granted by some legal system, not something that the agent has by virtue of natural justice. He talks of "sacred rights of mankind" just once (582), although one or two other passages are ambiguous, and may be talking of natural rather than legal rights (e.g., 188 and 626).

5. I do not, however, agree with Griswold's claim on the same page that "nothing we have in [Smith's] published or unpublished works (including the student lecture notes) comes anywhere close to articulating 'general principles which are always the same,'" or

the related implication, on 35–7, that the "sort of theory and History of Law and Government" that Smith said he was working on, late in his life, was likely to be very different from what we now have, in LJ, as Smith's lecture notes on jurisprudence. On the first point: LJ does attempt to provide a "general principle which is always the same" for each of the legal topics it takes up (see, e.g., 8–9, 16–17, 63–5, 87, 92–3, 104), even if it doesn't do so in a very satisfying way. On the second: Smith's mode of composing works for publication, from what we know of both TMS and WN, always began from and relied heavily upon his lecture notes. Finally, "a sort of theory and History" is an excellent description of the fluid movement between abstract principle and historical illustration that we find throughout both LJ and WN. So I think it is extremely likely that Smith's manuscript on jurisprudence would have been a neatened-up, and somewhat more elaborate, version of LJ.

6. The early fragment is printed in the back of the standard Glasgow edition of TMS: see pp. 389–90.

7. If we look closely at the opening passage, which seemed to proclaim the unequivocal immunity of beneficence from enforcement, we also find one line hinting at the more complicated view: where a beneficiary fails to show gratitude to a benefactor, Smith says, "it would be impertinent for any third person, *who was not the superior of either*, to intermeddle" (79).

8. Smith here follows Locke's description of the enforcement of the law of reason in the state of nature: see ST §§8–13 (esp. §10).

9. For the need to moderate resentment, see TMS 38, 40, 68–9, 73–4, 160–61, 172. The plethora of references reflects the great importance of this to Smith: "There is no passion, of which the human mind is capable, concerning whose justness we ought to be so doubtful," no passion more in need of being filtered through "the sentiments of the cool and impartial spectator" (38). Smith describes both the unjust person and the person too filled with resentment as like "wild beasts" that threaten the very possibility of society (40, 86).

10. Haakonssen notes this at SL 106.

11. The editors of TMS take this author to be Kames, but Haakonssen argues, plausibly I think, that it is probably Hume: SL 203n20. See, however, D. D. Raphael, *Concepts of Justice* (Oxford: Clarendon Press, 2001), p. 117.

12. *Summa* I-II, Q90, A4.

13. He regards it, however, as an *enforceable* failure of beneficence. For Pufendorf it was a straightforward injustice: "But it is our feeling that perfect obligation rests upon parents to maintain their children so long as they cannot maintain themselves . . . For surely they would do a great injury to their offspring, if they begot them only to die" LNN IV.xi.4 (627–8). So Smith and Pufendorf agree that parents should be punished for neglecting their children, but disagree about what justifies that punishment. Why they disagree about this is unclear.

14. TMS 331; but see the whole discussion on 330–34 and 339–40.

15. One can of course abolish a systematic injustice while grandfathering in the generation that grew up with expectations shaped by the system. But such grandfathering-in may be politically impossible in many cases. Reform is often time-sensitive—a moment arises in which normally powerful aristocrats, clerics, or businesspeople are suddenly politically weak, and can be stripped of an unjust privilege they have long enjoyed—and if the present generation of people who benefit from an injustice are allowed to keep their privileges, they may in future use the power they gain from those privileges to roll back the reform.

16. I draw here on Rawls's useful distinction between "summary rules" and "practice rules" in "Two Concepts of Rules" (Rawls, *Collected Papers*, ed. S. Freeman, Cambridge: Harvard University Press, 1999). See also Alasdair MacIntyre, *After Virtue*, second edition (Notre Dame: University of Notre Dame Press, 1984), pp. 187–90.

17. Indeed, it might even be a boon for liberty if the rules of justice did vary across societies. Then individuals unwilling to "submit to the regulations" made in any one society might find regulations more to their liking elsewhere.

18. Martha Nussbaum traces the idea that the duties of justice alone are owed across national borders to Cicero, and criticizes that idea, in "Duties of Justice, Duties of Material Aid."

19. The one major exception to this method occurs in Smith's remarks on punishment, where he does directly compare what governments do with what "reason and nature," by way of the resentment of the impartial spectator, would require (LJ 126). He calls the death penalty often inflicted on theft, for instance, much too severe because it goes beyond what "the resentment of the injured person" would require (128), and describes other punishments, both in other societies and in his own society, as too strict or too mild for the same reason. As I suggested above, it is not clear that this mode of argument actually works so well, since it is not clear what a "natural," as opposed to a socialized, impartial spectator would feel. And Smith's pronouncements about what this spectator will feel—such that theft is "contemptible and despicable [rather] than fit to excite our resentment" (128) while rape and some kinds of fraud can only be properly punished by death (120–21, 132)—do seem uncharacteristically arbitrary. None of this material re-appears in WN, or in the later editions of TMS, which is some indication that Smith did not have a lot of confidence in it. So I'm not inclined to take this one piece of transcendent criticism of legal systems too seriously. And those who want to lay more stress on it than I do should remember that it is unique, that Smith's criticisms of slavery, polygamy, primogeniture, and the like, are all couched in different terms.

20. Smith expressed a stronger abhorrence of slavery than practically any of his contemporaries. In case one is tempted to suppose that Smith's muted moral response to slavery in WN was in any way based on the sort of racism to be found in Hume and Kant (see Charles Mills, *The Racial Contract*, Ithaca: Cornell University Press, 1997), it is worth bearing in mind this remarkable passage from TMS:

> There is not a negro from the coast of Africa who does not . . . possess a degree of magnanimity which the soul of his sordid master is too often scarce capable of conceiving. Fortune never exerted more cruelly her empire over mankind, than when she subjected those nations of heroes to the refuse of the jails of Europe, to wretches who possess the virtues neither of the countries which they come from, nor of those which they go to, and whose levity, brutality, and baseness, so justly expose them to the contempt of the vanquished. (TMS 206–7)

21. But, again, he does say that the laws required to *support* monopoly control over a sector of trade tend to be "cruel" and "oppressive" (WN 648–9).

22. They may have approved of the colonial enterprise nevertheless, but then they would be likely either (a) to deny that there had been as much injustice as Smith avows, (b) to say that a bit of injustice was a reasonable price to pay for the good that the colonies brought to the natives, or (c) to deny that any nation could or should worry about justice in the Hobbesian *bellum omnium contra omnium* that constitutes the international order.

23. I hope it is obvious that what I am saying does not give comfort to anyone who would like to return to the old misunderstanding of Smith as a utilitarian. If justice goes along with utility, throughout WN, then we have no basis on which to place utility over justice, any more than we do to place justice over utility.

Chapter Nine: Property Rights

1. Property is, we might say, doubly conventional. When justice is violated by killing or grievous bodily injury, we can expect all human beings to agree that at least a prima facie evil has occurred, to feel some sort of shock or horror at the event. Where people will disagree, and where even the impartial spectator may not deliver an unequivocal verdict, is over what circumstances can excuse or justify the killing or bodily injury, or over what precise punishment should be meted out in response to inexcusable murder and battery. But when we come to infringements of property, we cannot expect all human beings to recognize the same events as even prima facie wrongs, to be able to determine, on the basis of their natural reactions, so much as where the relevant injury might lie. Only where a particular regime of property is already in place will it be clear when someone has been injured by another's removal of material goods he or she claims.

2. Hume does believe in private property, and opposes egalitarian redistributivist schemes, but he gives reasons of utility for this opposition, not reasons of justice. A regime that tried to equalize property would be oppressive and would likely make its people poor, but it would not necessarily be unjust. Of course, systems of justice are themselves justified by their utility, for Hume, but a distinction can nevertheless be drawn between the basic utility of minimizing disputes, with which, Hume thinks, justice is directly concerned, and something that harms society without leading it into endless civil strife. The rules of a particular system of justice can be bad in the latter sense without threatening a society with the possibility of civil war. Such rules may deserve rethinking, for Hume, but they will not be unjust.

3. Aristotle, *Politics* II.v and Aquinas, *Summa Theologica*, II-II, Q66, A2, as translated in *The Political Ideas of St. Thomas Aquinas*, ed. Dino Bigongiari (New York: Hafner Press, 1953).

4. See also WN 335: "Our ancestors were idle for want of a sufficient encouragement to industry." Smith tells us that a world of equality would be a world of poverty at LJ 195.

5. "[W]e find in Locke a variety of styles of argument for moral conclusions, sitting side by side and without any explanation of their differences" (Simmons, *Lockean Theory of Rights*, p. 45). See Simmons's rich account of Locke on property in chapter 5 of this book.

6. Note that this is a *moral* justification for the right to property—as much so as any other moral justification Hutcheson provides. It is not correct to say, as Richard Teichgraeber does ('*Free Trade*,' 52), that Hutcheson regards political matters as outside the realm of morality, as a realm in which utility matters *instead of* morality. Teichgraeber says that "Hutcheson does not show exactly how perfect rights derive from the moral sense" (51), but Hutcheson in fact does exactly that, in this passage.

7. Contrast Hutcheson, SMP II.4.ii, 283: "'Tis no fictitious state."

8. Hutcheson had already granted that "The accident of first occupation may be a trifling difference," but he said that "a trifle may determine the right to one side, when there is no consideration to weigh against it on the other" (SMP II.6.v, 318). So for Hutcheson "first occupation" is a trifle but it nevertheless determines "the right." For

Hume, it seems to be *just* a trifle, useful for settling disputes where no other mark of ownership will do so, but something that can easily be overruled if we can find another basis on which to establish stable possession.

9. Consider especially Book III of TMS, where the entire argument is devoted to the importance of self-perception, self-judgment, and self-approbation, but where we also get an elaborate account of how we come to a notion of selfhood by way of the "looking-glass" of society (110–13).

10. Smith even continues the section I have quoted with a little imagined colloquy between the picker and his would-be injurer: "You may ask indeed, as this apple is as fit for your use as it is for mine, what title have I to detain it from you. You may go to the forest (says one to me) and pull another. You may go as well as I, replied I. And besides it is more reasonable that you should, as I have gone already and bestowed my time and pains in procuring the fruit." It is hard to imagine Locke's characters, in the property chapter, engaging in such a discussion. Why would they? Social interaction, like conversation, plays no role in establishing the foundations of morals, for Locke. The foundations of morals *consists* in the shaping of sentiments by social interaction, for Smith, and conversation is a great fund of our moral attitudes and rules (see TMS 159).

11. The point in the passage is that the attribution of property rights is a matter of propriety rather than of utility, and that may be true. But it still is not obvious where propriety lies in this case. When, say, one man has tamed a sheep but his friend and two neighbors have also often taken care of it, how do we settle disputes among these people about who, in propriety, deserves the milk?

12. Pufendorf, whose work Smith knew well, had described objections of precisely this sort: "Imagine two men, one swift of foot and the other slow; it is obvious that in such a case the pair is ill-matched in the race to secure property. Therefore, the right whereby what is seized belongs to the first one to occupy it, is [not] founded . . . upon nature" (LNN IV.iv.5, p. 539).

13. Again, Pufendorf describes Velthuysen as having argued that "There is no natural reason for one receiving a right by first occupancy any more than by first laying eyes upon a thing" (ibid., p. 538).

14. LJ 17; note also the appeal to "expectations" in the hunting discussion on 19.

15. Compare Turgot: "[the] most sacred of all property [is] . . . the property of man in the fruit of his labor" ("Lettre sur le commerce des grains," cited in ES 85).

16. As Haakonssen points out: SL 106–7. Haakonssen is wrong, however, to say that WN 138 is "the only passage . . . in Smith's work" giving the appearance that Smith subscribed to Locke's account of property. The four other citations from WN in this paragraph also give that appearance, as do WN 710 ("It is only under the shelter of the civil magistrate that the owner of . . . valuable property, *which is acquired by the labour of many years* . . . can sleep a single night in security"), and LJ 177. Haakonssen's explanation of how Smith differs from Locke on property can explain these passages, I think, but that does not gainsay the fact that Smith gives the *impression* of being an uncritical Lockean whenever he says things like this, and does nothing in his published work to correct for that impression.

17. SL 107, my emphasis. Haakonssen does not spell out what the other circumstances might be, and, as I have indicated previously, I don't think this can be done in a precise and comprehensive way. Haakonssen also says that Smith gives "a very lucid exposition of the spectator theory of property" at LJ 17, and seems to think that Smith has shown how any impartial spectator, independent of conventions and social history,

might come to see certain expectations of property as "reasonable" ones. I do not think Smith has shown this.

18. This line occurs in the middle of a paragraph about poll-taxes, and I have seen people maintain that *only* poll-taxes, for Smith, are supposed to be "badges of liberty." This is a seriously confused reading of the passage. The paragraph sets out to refute the charge that poll-taxes, in particular, are "badges of slavery." Smith's refutation turns on the claim that *all* taxes (thus *even* the poll-tax) are badges of liberty, since they show that the payer, "as he has some property, . . . cannot himself be the property of a master." Being subject to taxation is a mark of property-ownership, and property-ownership is a mark of a being a free citizen rather than a slave: someone "subject to government, indeed" but not subject to any other citizen's personal rule. Therefore being subject to taxation—*all* taxation—is a mark of liberty.

19. In particular, Haakonssen cites the famous "four maxims" on taxation in WN (825–7), but these principles in no way suggest that taxes pose a challenge to property rights.

20. The passage continues: "It is not very unreasonable that the rich should contribute to the publick expence, not only in proportion to their revenue, but something more than in that proportion." In terms of today's debates, these remarks put Smith firmly on the side of progressive taxation!

21. Dugald Stewart, "Life of Adam Smith," EPS 321–2.

22. The governmental activities Smith himself condemns as "wasteful" tend to be unnecessary wars, and the ceremonies of royal pomp and circumstance (see WN II.iii and §60 of this book). He never calls any expenditure designed to help the poor wasteful or unnecessary.

23. See D. W. Haslett, "Is Inheritance Justified?" *Philosophy and Public Affairs* Spring, 1986; and J. D. Trout and S. A. Buttar, "Resurrecting 'Death Taxes': Inheritance, Redistribution, and the Science of Happiness," *Journal of Law & Politics* 16.

24. The phrase "bourgeois radicalism" is Isaac Kramnick's: see his introduction to Tom Paine's *Common Sense* (Harmondsworth: Penguin, 1976), pp. 46–55.

25. Letter to Thomas Mann Randolph, 05/30/1790.

26. Letter to Madison, 09/06/89. The line about the earth belonging to the living could have come straight from Smith: Smith says it is absurd to deny "that every successive generation of men have . . . an equal right to the earth, and to all that it possesses" (WN 384; see also LJ 69 and especially LJ 468: "the earth and the fulness of it belongs to every generation").

27. Paine, *Rights of Man*, in *The Writings of Thomas Paine*, Moncure Daniel Conway (ed.) (New York: GP Putnam, 1894), vol. II, 496–7. The tax moved by steps of 3 pence per pound, such that estates of less than £5000 would be taxed at a rate below 10%, while everything above £23,000, in an estate, would go to the government. This proposal is preceded by a Smithian analysis of luxury taxes, and critique of duties on the necessary goods of the poor (495–6).

28. Haakonssen, NL 172. Haakonssen says on 169 that Millar took over Smith's natural jurisprudence "in all its essentials," and the quotations he brings from Millar on 161–4 bear this out.

29. Smith's account of intestate succession does allow family members a natural right to inherit if they were dependent on the deceased at the time of death. But he says explicitly that "forisfamiliated" children (emancipated or independent children) have no natural right to their parents' goods. Given that Smith considers the support of children,

even during the parents' lifetime, to be a matter of beneficence rather than justice, he is of course not in much of a position to argue that children have a claim of justice on their parents' goods after the latters' death.

It is interesting to compare Smith on this subject with John Simmons's account of inheritance rights in Locke: Simmons, *Lockean Theory of Rights*, pp. 204–12. Simmons argues that Locke's general theory leads naturally to significant limitations on the right to inherit, but acknowledges that "Locke nowhere suggests this" (211). Smith does suggest this (at WN 859, quoted below), has a theory of property that puts the legitimacy of inheritance into doubt at least as much as Locke's does, and is much more inclined explicitly to raise those doubts than was Locke. The somewhat radical implications Simmons draws from Locke should therefore follow, a fortiori, from Smith.

30. The only commentator who recognizes that "distributive justice" in the jurisprudential tradition Smith inherited is very different from the notion that goes by that name today is Vivenza (*Smith and the Classics*, 198–202). The account of Smith on distributive justice in Young, *Economics as a Moral Science*, chapter 6, is also quite good, although Young shares the misconception that reads modern distributive justice into what he calls "the Aristotelian-Scholastic" version of the natural law tradition (p. 131).

31. RP 219. See also 168 and 228 on Condorcet's commitment to the translation and popularization of WN. Winch nevertheless sees the redistributivism of Paine and Condorcet as differentiating them from Smith (218–19); as I shall argue in the next chapter, I think this is based on a misunderstanding of Smith's attitude toward distributive justice.

ES carries out a full-scale comparison between Smith and Condorcet, with which I am very sympathetic.

32. Gertrude Himmelfarb, *The Idea of Poverty* (New York: Alfred A. Knopf, 1984), 78–83.

33. Ibid., 67–73.

Chapter Ten: Distributive Justice

1. The material in this chapter is elaborated in Fleischacker, *A Short History of Distributive Justice* (Cambridge: Harvard University Press, 2004).

2. As Vivenza writes, "Classical distributive justice aimed to *maintain* inequality, while . . . distributive justice [in modern economics] aims to correct it" (*Smith and the Classics,* 202).

3. He also provided indirect support for 4. Smith evinced a deep suspicion of aid to the poor from sources other than the state. He emphasized the fact that the generosity of the great feudal lords had as a consequence the "servile dependency" of their tenants (WN 412, 414–17), and that a similar political price came with the medieval church's aid to the poor:

> The hospitality and charity of the clergy too, not only gave them the command of a great temporal force, but increased very much the weight of their spiritual weapons. Those virtues procured them the highest respect and veneration among all the inferior ranks of people, of whom many were constantly, and almost all occasionally, fed by them. Every thing belonging or related to so popular an order, its possessions, its privileges, its doctrines, necessarily appeared sacred in the eyes of the common people, and every violation of them, whether real or pretended, the highest act of sacrilegious wickedness and profaneness. (WN 802)

The consequence, says Smith, was "the most formidable combination that ever was formed against the authority and security of civil government, as well as against the liberty, reason, and happiness of mankind." The church managed, by way of its generosity to the poor, to preserve "the grossest delusions of superstition" against "all danger from any assault of human reason" (802–3).

Smith thus considers the aid offered by both of the major institutions that helped the poor in medieval and early modern times to have bolstered power structures that had very baleful effects on human liberty. His remarks point strongly in the direction of the view that it is the state, not private individuals or institutions, that ought to take on the burden of helping the poor.

4. *Idea*, 61. Himmelfarb notes that commentators often confuse Smith's attack on the laws of settlement with an attack on the Poor Law. I made that mistake myself in my previous book (*Third Concept*, 167).

5. For instance by Joseph Townsend in his 1786 *Dissertation on the Poor Laws*.

6. *Idea*, 62, 46. See also Daniel A. Baugh, "Poverty, Protestantism and Political Economy: English Attitudes Toward the Poor, 1660–1800," in *England's Rise to Greatness*, ed. Stephen Baxter (Berkeley: University of California Press, 1983), p. 86). Knud Haakonssen has called WN "the greatest working-man's tract ever written" (cited in AVE 261).

7. Walter Trattner, *From Poor Law to Welfare State*, fifth edition (New York: Free Press, 1994), p. 18.

8. Bronislaw Geremek, *Poverty: A History*, trans. Agnieszka Kolakowska (Oxford: Blackwell, 1994), p. 20.

9. Baugh, "Poverty, Protestantism . . . ," p. 80.

10. Baugh, p. 83.

11. Ibid., p. 85.

12. Note that Smith here identifies *himself* with a person widely regarded as the lowest of the low. See §16, above.

13. The lower sort, said Mandeville, "have nothing to stir them up to be serviceable but their Wants, which it is Prudence to relieve but Folly to cure" (quoted in Baugh, note 53). Want is necessary to motivate the poor: "if nobody did Want no body would work." Mandeville here echoes William Petty, who thought the poor should be kept busy even if they merely moved "stones at Stonehenge to Tower-Hill, or the like; for at worst this would keep their mindes to discipline and obedience, and their bodies to a patience of more profitable labours when need shall require it" (Baugh, 77) and anticipates Arthur Young, who declared in 1771 that "every one but an ideot knows, that the lower classes must be kept poor, or they will never be industrious." So wages must be capped, and leisure hours restricted. The poor should work long hours, for low wages, else they would lose the habit of working altogether. The common practice of "work[ing] for four days in order to drink for three, Saturday, Sunday and good St Monday being devoted to pleasure" was an evil one (Neil McKendrick, "Home Demand and Economic Growth," in McKendrick (ed.), *Historical Perspectives: Studies in English Thought and Society*, London: Europa Publications, 1974, p. 183).

Smith says, about this last practice specifically and about the notion, generally, that the poor are idle: "Excessive application during four days of the week is frequently the real cause of the idleness of the other three, so much and so loudly complained of. Great labour, either of mind or body, continued for several days together, is in most men naturally followed by a great desire of relaxation, which . . . is almost irresistible. . . . If it is not complied with, the consequences are often dangerous, and sometimes fatal . . . If masters would always listen to the dictates of reason and humanity, they have frequently occasion rather to moderate, than to animate, the application of many of their workmen" (WN 100).

14. At LJ 540 he suggests that good education can reduce drunkenness by giving poor children "ideas with which [they] can amuse [themselves]."

15. Henry Fielding was but one of many writers who worried about the blurring of ranks consequent on the lower order's consuming luxury goods: "the very Dregs of the People," he wrote in 1750, "aspire . . . to a degree beyond that which belongs to them." Neil McKendrick says that Smith's contemporaries "complained that those becoming marks of distinction between the classes were being obliterated by the extravagance of the lower ranks; that working girls wore inappropriate finery, even silk dresses" (McKendrick, "Home Demand," p. 168)

Others, nominally at least, worried about the effect of luxury on the poor's own well-being. Here is Daniel Defoe:

[I]f such Acts of Parliament may be made as may effectually cure the Sloth and Luxury of our Poor, that shall make Drunkards take care of Wife and Children, spendthrifts, lay up for a wet Day; Idle, Lazy Fellows Diligent; and Thoughtless Sottish Men, Careful and Provident . . . there will soon be less Poverty among us. ("Giving Alms no Charity," in *The Shortest Way with the Dissenters and Other Pamphlets*, Oxford, 1927, pp. 186–8)

Similarly, Sir Frederick Eden's famous 1797 report "constantly complained of the misspending of the poor on unnecessary luxuries and inessential fripperies." Even Elizabeth Gaskell, writing in the mid-nineteenth century, felt compelled "to offer some explanation of the extravagance of . . . working class wives" who indulged in ham, eggs, butter, and cream. (McKendrick, pp. 167–8, 191–2).

16. Strictly speaking, he identifies it with "all the social virtues" (270), but he treats beneficence as prominent among those virtues.

17. *Politics* III.9–11 and VI.2–3.

18. There is also a tradition, in the Christian as in the Hindu and Buddhist worlds, of people *voluntarily* taking on poverty, and of course these poor monks were held to be especially virtuous, not vicious. But it was essential to their virtue that they had renounced material goods, so there was no suggestion that they ought to be given the means to live comfortably.

19. George Clarke (ed.), *John Bellers: His Life, Times and Writings* (London: Routlege and Kegan Paul, 1987), 55. See also 52.

20. Schneewind, *Invention*, 79–80.

21. Grotius gives the bestowing of legacies as an example of an act expressing attributive justice (LWP I.I.viii.3; 37), and giving full information to prospective business partners (II.XII.ix.2; 347–8), sacrificing your life for your country (II.XXV.iii.3; 579), troubling innocent civilians as little as possible in times of war (III.XIII.iv.2–3; 759), and being merciful to needy debtors (III.XIII.iv.1; 759) as examples of acts demanded of us by "the law of love." Only the last of these examples has anything to do with helping the needy.

22. Schneewind (*Invention*, 78–80) and Haakonssen (NL 26–30) both claim that Grotius introduced the distinction between "perfect" and "imperfect" rights. Grotius does lay out the basis for this distinction (LWP 35–6), but without ever quite using the terms "perfect right" and "imperfect right." See further discussion in Fleischacker, *Short History*.

23. There has been much speculation that TMS 232–4 is a comment on the French Revolution. Given that we have no letters by Smith mentioning the Revolution, nor so much as a comment reported in his name, and given also that the revisions to TMS were completed by November 18, 1789—a month before the Jacobin Club was formed, and

only two weeks after the sermon by Richard Price that so enraged Edmund Burke—I see little reason to believe this.

Rothschild (ES 54–5, and notes thereto) suggests several alternative political events as background to TMS 232–4.

24. David Thomson, *The Babeuf Plot* (London: K. Paul, Trench, Trubner, 1947), p. 33. The summary was not written by Babeuf, although he endorsed it at his trial.

25. One cannot find it even in Rousseau. In the *Discourse on Inequality* Rousseau presents the establishment of property as the source of most of the horrors of human life: of the suffering of the poor, and of oppression, crime, and war. He does not, however, say that the establishment of property, or the inequality that comes with it, is *unjust*. Rather, he accepts the view that "justice" is a term for certain kinds of offenses against property, so that it makes no sense to describe the institution of property itself as either "just" or as "unjust." "[A]ccording to the axiom of the wise Locke," he says, "where there is no property, there is no injury" (*First and Second Discourses*, p. 150). The paradise Rousseau imagines is one that lies beyond both property and justice.

26. See Aquinas, *Summa*, II-II Q61 A1, A3, Q62A1, as translated in *Summa Theologiae*, Latin text and English translation (New York: McGraw Hill, 1964–81). Hont and Ignatieff wrongly associate the right of necessity with distributive justice at the bottom of NJ 29.

27. MacIntyre, *Whose Justice? Which Rationality?* (Notre Dame: University of Notre Dame Press, 1988), p. 307.

28. *Summa* II-II, Q66, A2.

29. The first case concerns homicide in the case of a shipwreck, and the third the requisitioning of goods, and other harm caused to innocent citizens, in the course of war. As we have seen, these are standard cases in which the right of necessity was held to apply, in the writings of Grotius and his followers. There is also a moment in WN where Smith is probably evoking Grotius's account of the right of necessity. One of Grotius's examples is that "if fire has broken out, in order to protect a building belonging to me I can destroy a building of my neighbour" (LWP II.ii. 6.3; 193). At WN 324, Smith argues for some limitations on the freedom of the banking industry by way of a comparison with laws to prevent the spread of fire: "The obligation of building party walls, in order to prevent the communication of fire, is a violation of natural liberty, exactly of the same kind with the regulations of the banking trade which are here proposed." Clearly Smith both knew and accepted the right of necessity in the jurisprudential tradition.

30. Hont and Ignatieff say, several times, that for post-Grotian thinkers the right of necessity was an exception to the rules of property rather than an ongoing, structural feature of those rules (NJ 25–6, 29), while it constituted a permanent, structural feature of justice for Aquinas. This is simply not true. Necessity constituted an exception to property rules for Aquinas as well.

31. NJ 14. Hont and Ignatieff cite Thomas Pownall's 1776 letter to Smith and James Anderson's 1777 *Observations on National Industry* in support of this claim. But the passage in Pownall says nothing about Smith's views on the market in foodstuffs, focusing rather on Smith's analysis of money, while the passage in Anderson says nothing about the inappropriateness of using long-term economic models to deal with short-term crises (Anderson defends the corn bounty against Smith as a general policy: He is not interested in the freezing of prices, or opening of granaries, in times of crisis).

It is true that many writers in the eighteenth century—everyone who believed in a "police" of the economy—took Smith to be too focused on the long term to the exclusion of the short; it is not true, as far as I can tell, that that complaint was particularly directed against Smith's view of the corn trade. The claim that "[b]y 1776, Smith remained the only standard-bearer for 'natural liberty' in grain" (NJ 18) is certainly false: see ES 74–81, which demonstrates that Turgot too held that position in 1776 and that Condorcet held it as late as 1792.

32. Richard Tuck, *Natural Rights Theories* (Cambridge: Cambridge University Press, 1979), p. 20.

33. This reverses the implicit claim, at NJ 37, that concern for the poor was integral to the justification of property until Locke, and only became "a side-constraint, rather than a structuring condition" on property from Locke onward.

Part V: *Politics*
Chapter Eleven: Politics

1. "As the end of all laws should be the general good and happiness of a people, which chiefly depends on their virtue: it must be the business of legislators to promote . . . true principles of virtue, such as shall lead men to piety to God, and all just, peaceable, and kind dispositions towards their fellows; . . . As pious dispositions toward God, a firm persuasion of his goodness, and of his providence governing the world, and administering justice in a future state . . . are the sources of the most sublime happiness, so they are the strongest incitements to all social, friendly, and heroic offices. The civil power should take care that the people be well instructed in these points, and have all arguments presented to their understandings, and all rational inducements proposed which can raise these persuasions, and confirm these dispositions" (SMP III.ix.1, vol. II, 310–11).

2. In general, Smith says, those in the top echelons in society—whether they get there by birth, by money, or by political power—are prone to be *less* virtuous than those lower down: Smith argues that people in "the middling and inferior stations of life" are more likely to achieve virtue than their social superiors at TMS 54–6 and 63–4, and that poor workers are drawn to particularly strict moral systems at WN 794–6.

3. Compare ASD 137: "given the cynicism evident in TMS concerning the standards of probity in public life, there is a presumption that it is unlikely that a sage would ever become a national hero."

4. TMS 134. The passage first lists those who actively help mankind in three broad categories—"statesmen and legislators," "poets and philosophers," and those who have improved our material standard of living—and then describes these paragons of the *vita activa* as, respectively, the "protectors," "instructors," and "benefactors" of mankind. Since the latter two terms nicely characterize the latter two divisions in the first list, I presume the first term is meant to correspond to the first division. So statesmen and legislators, at their best, protect us (from violence, presumably); they do not improve our characters or material conditions.

5. See, for instance, the paragraph just preceding the one from which my quotation comes: 687, ¶50.

6. Himmelfarb, *Idea*, 59.

7. Ibid., 60.

8. Charles Griswold describes Smith's call for the state to require basic education as an "imposition on the liberties of the people for reasons of public utility" (AVE 294). But Smith disclaims a purely utilitarian defense of this measure: "Though the state was to derive no advantage from the instruction of the inferior ranks of people, it would still

deserve its attention that they should not be altogether uninstructed" (WN 788). The sentences leading up to this line make clear, moreover, that instruction deserves the state's attention because mentally mutilated people lose an "essential part of the character of human nature." It is for the sake of the common people's own liberty that the state needs to ensure that they are instructed.

9. In *Third Concept*, I develop the notion that Smith's view of freedom should be seen as lying between the standard "negative" and "positive" concepts of liberty, rather than as simply a version of the "negative" one. Freedom has conditions, for Smith, and the government needs to provide those conditions where the market does not.

10. Jeff Weintraub makes clear that there are actually several different "public/private" distinctions, on some but not all of which a business or church would count as "private": see "The Theory and Politics of the Public/Private Distinction," in Weintraub and Kumar (eds.), *Public and Private in Thought and Practice* (Chicago: University of Chicago Press, 1997).

11. Chaudhuri, *The Trading World of Asia and the English East India Company, 1660–1760* (Cambridge: Cambridge University Press, 1978), p. 21.

12. Nicholas Phillipson characterizes the whole of Smith's moral and political writings as "a discourse on the social and ethical significance of face-to-face relationships between independently-minded individuals" (Phillipson, "Adam Smith as civic moralist," in I. Hont and M. Ignatieff (eds.), *Wealth and Virtue*, Cambridge: Cambridge University Press, 1983, p. 198).

13. Moreover, since the sovereign collects taxes from all the produce of the nation, his material interest is directly tied to that produce being as great as possible (637–8, 730). The sovereign is also the only agent whose "pride and dignity" is connected to the power of the nation (739–40), and "the permanent grandeur" of whose family is tied to the prosperity of the people (903).

14. On the importance of good institutional design to Smith, see also Rosenberg, "Institutional Aspects" and Muller, *Adam Smith, passim,* but especially chapters 9, 11, and 12.

15. See also the alternative proposal he made for resolving this conflict to Alexander Wedderburn in 1778 (Corr 377–85).

16. Millar, *Origin and Distinction of Ranks*, 1771 [from a 1960 edition, pp. 177–8; cited in ASD 125]. The phrase "projecting spirit," and the negative accent on "projecting," have direct parallels in Smith: see WN II, chapters ii–iv.

17. The First Amendment may have been influenced by Smith's case for religious disestablishment: see Fleischacker, "Adam's Smith Reception Among the American Founders, 1776–1790" *William and Mary Quarterly,* October 2002.

18. Stanley Cavell offers a similar account of radical change (although he calls it "revolution"):

> The internal tyranny of convention is that only a slave of it can know how it may be changed for the better, or know why it should be eradicated. Only masters of a game, perfect slaves to that project, are in a position to establish conventions which better serve its essence. This is why deep revolutionary changes can result from attempts to conserve a project, to take it back to its idea, keep it in touch with its history. . . . Only a priest could have confronted his set of practices with its origins so deeply as to set the terms of Reformation. (*Claim of Reason*, 121)

19. Winch describes Smith as expressing "a mild and ambivalent hint of a preference for the Whigs" (ASP 52), on the basis of the passage from LJ 320, quoted below. He says nothing about the passage at LJ 319, or the material in WN I discuss below.

20. Frances Hirst has suggested this: "As a politician Smith was doubtless attracted by the prospect of introducing a strong democratic and republican strain into Parliament." Hirst, *Adam Smith* (New York: Macmillan, 1904), 177–8. Joseph Cropsey argues brilliantly that Smith's pervasive praise for Holland in WN may also express a preference for republicanism (PE 75–6).

21. Constant, "The liberty of the ancients compared with that of the moderns," in Biancamaria Fontana (ed.), *Benjamin Constant: Political Writings* (Cambridge: Cambridge University Press, 1988), p. 16.

22. Teichgraeber, 'Free Trade,' 10.

23. Rousseau, "Discourse on Political Economy," in *The Social Contract and Discourses*, trans. G.D.H. Cole (London: JM Dent, 1973), 139.

24. See discussion in ASP 106–12.

25. Smith treats court "pageantry" in a similarly dismissive fashion at WN 908–9.

26. "The great Montesquieu pointed out the road. He was the Lord Bacon in this branch of philosophy. Dr Smith is the Newton" (quoted in EPS 275n, from Millar, *Historical View of English Government,* 1812 edition, vol II, 429–30n).

27. Smith does at one point say that the "art of war . . . is . . . the noblest of all arts" (WN 697). To get Smith's full view of war, however, we need to put this passage together with the much more critical ones I cite below. And the passage itself deserves a suspicious eye. Smith is in the middle of arguing that war ought in advanced societies to be the province of a professional, standing army—one of the most controversial positions in the entirety of WN—so he has a rhetorical reason to concede the nobility of martial skills. Indeed the quoted phrase comes as part of a comparative sentence that provides a premise for his controversial overall argument: "The art of war, *as* it is certainly the noblest of all arts, *so* in the progress of improvement it necessarily becomes one of the most complicated" (my emphasis). Smith then uses the fact that it becomes so complicated to argue that modern states ought not to rely on militias. He differed here with his friends Hume and William Robertson, and with practically everyone else in his cultural milieu. His more civic republican friends, for whom the nobility of martial virtues meant that every citizen should participate in the defense of their country, were harshly critical of his apparent abandonment of the militia cause (ASP 105–6, and Lois Schwoerer, *"No Standing Armies!" The Antiarmy Ideology in 17th Century England*, Baltimore: Johns Hopkins University Press, 1974, esp. 192–5). So the polemical point of Smith's argument works exactly against the view he seems to uphold in the tag on which Winch relies. Note also that Smith says here only that the "art" of war, not war itself, is noble.

28. Smith warns that war is often carried out "contrary to every principle of justice, and . . . without any regard to humanity" (TMS 239).

29. Winch, puzzlingly, entirely overlooks the tone of this passage (ASP 135–6), reading it as though it were a straight-faced comment on the advantages of funding wars by debt rather than by taxes.

Epilogue
Chapter Twelve: Learning from Smith Today

1. Ross (*Life*, 305, 374), discusses Smith's friendship with Dundas. Pitt's eloquent tribute can be found in Salim Rashid, "Adam Smith's Rise to Fame: A Reexamination of the Evidence," *Eighteenth Century: Theory and Interpretation* 23, no. 1 (1982), 82. I agree with Rashid that WN was actually not very well known in Britain until around the time of this speech by Pitt. On this point, see also Willis, "Ideas in Parliament," and Richard

Teichgraeber, "'Less Abused than I had Reason to Expect': The Reception of *The Wealth of Nations* in Britain, 1776–90," *The Historical Journal* 30, 2 (1987). For a dissenting view, see Richard Sher, "New Light on the Publication and Reception of the *The Wealth of Nations*," *Adam Smith Review*, forthcoming.

2. *The Parliamentary History of England, From the Earliest Period to the Year 1803* (London: TC Hansard, 1817), vol. XXX (1792–4), pp. 659–60.

3. He gets invoked against Dundas by Philip Francis, later in the discussion, also without being named: "[I]s it an airy speculation to affirm that a trading company is unqualified for sovereignty, is unfit to be trusted with the government of a great kingdom; that their interests in one character are incompatible with their duties in the other; that such an interest should never be united with such a power, or that the subjects of the sovereign will certainly be sacrificed to the profits of the merchant? . . . [T]hey were qualified to be merchants, and utterly unqualified to be sovereigns" (ibid., 687). With which, compare WN 637–8: "[A] company of merchants are . . . incapable of considering themselves as sovereigns, even after they have become such. Trade, or buying in order to sell again, they still consider as their principal business, and by a strange absurdity, regard the character of the sovereign as but an appendix to that of the merchant . . . As sovereigns, their interest is exactly the same with that of the country which they govern. As merchants their interest is directly opposite to that interest." See also 752, 819.

4. WN 947: Smith here is talking about the British Empire in the Americas, not about British India—which was not formally an empire yet—but his point generalizes, I think, to the empire that was beginning to develop under the auspices of the East India Company.

5. Kirk Willis writes: "Neither Pitt nor Dundas, despite their obvious respect for Smith and familiarity with his doctrines, could escape traditionalist thinking on how to deal with the abuses of the East India Company." ("Ideas of Smith in Parliament," 535. Willis goes on to say that they never even "mentioned Smith or his principles" in Parliamentary debates on this issue. I think the quotation I have given shows that that is not true.)

6. Willis, 533–4, esp. note 106.

7. Ibid., 516.

8. On Hume and Place, see E. P. Thompson, *The Making of the English Working Class* (Harmondsworth: Penguin, 1980), pp. 563–7. Thompson notes that Hume and Place had earlier voted against certain protections for workers "on Dr. A. Smith's grounds of letting Trade alone." He also notes that Place believed that trade unions would naturally disappear once they were legal.

9. Himmelfarb, *Idea*, 75.

10. See RP chap. 5; Himmelfarb, *Idea*, chap. 3; and ES chap. 2, esp. 53.

11. C. K. Kindleberger, "The Historical Background: Adam Smith and the Industrial Revolution," in T. Wilson and A.S. Skinner (eds.), *The Market and the State* (Oxford: Oxford University Press, 1976).

12. "In a free trade an effectual combination cannot be established but by the unanimous consent of every single trader, and it cannot last longer than every single trader continues of the same mind" (WN 145).

13. On the navy and its expenses see John Brewer, *The Sinews of Power* (Cambridge: Harvard University Press, 1988).

14. It is an important, and disturbing, fact about the modern world that many products can only be serviced by those who make them. This gives firms a control over the market for their products that they never would have had in Smith's day.

15. It was said of the Roman Empire that it was a tyranny tempered by assassination; we might say, of the contemporary United States, that it is a corporate despotism tempered by lawsuits. And where the left praises these lawsuits as putting a check on corporate abuse, and the right complains that they are often frivolous and excessively costly, a true follower of Smith would recognize that the explosion of huge lawsuits represents an unintended, inefficient, but natural outgrowth of our society's technological and political history.

16. See Sarah Wildman, "City Limits," in *The New Republic*, 03/06/00.

17. Quoted in Trattner, *op. cit.*, p. 363.

18. Barry Supple, "Working-class Self-help and the State," in McKendrick (ed.), *Historical Perspectives*, 216–17.

19. And in fact "When the EPA proposed designating Pittsfield a 'Super Fund' cleanup site, the company threatened to close its one remaining local office" (Wildman, "City Limits").

20. Among the other advantages of such a change would be that the state's bureaucracy would shrink somewhat, and that those who administer unemployment compensation would be more likely to know their clients.

21. The FTC does look out for potential monopsonies over products (e.g., a film distributor can in many circumstances be practically the only buyer for other firms' films), but not, as far as I know, for monopsony over labor.

22. The first of these proposals appears in "Insignificant Communities," and the second in *Third Concept*, 274 (see also 236–40).

INDEX LOCORUM

GENERAL INDEX

impartiality, 1, 9, 72–83, 187, 230, 235, 241–
43, 247, 268, 278, 270n.17, 290n.22
imperfect rights. *See* rights
imperialism. *See* colonialism
indirect ethics, 52, 208
inequality of wealth, 73–75, 78–79, 91, 101,
110–11, 139–41, 196–97, 201, 204–5,
214, 223, 225, 249, 274–75, 304n.2,
307n.25
independence, 47, 56, 91, 94, 99, 110, 114,
137–39, 142, 146, 153, 160–61, 207, 230,
240, 243, 247, 251, 272, 275, 284n.14,
303n.29, 309n.12
inheritance, 151, 163, 176–77, 189, 197–201,
303n.23, 303n.29, 304n.29
inheritance tax. *See* taxes
intentions, 44–45, 47, 96–97, 108, 126, 138–
140, 142, 152, 164, 167, 181–83, 185,
187, 191, 288n.34, 312n.15
interest, 9, 14, 17, 26–28, 35, 37, 41–42, 52,
55–57, 61, 63, 67, 72–73, 76, 79, 85–86,
88–92, 94–101, 108, 115, 118–20, 133,
138–42, 151–52, 170, 172, 181, 183–85,
192, 194, 201, 207, 230, 233–34, 236–44,
246–49, 252–53, 266, 272, 279–81,
283n.20, 284n.7, 286n.6, 286n.19,
290n.17, 309n.13, 311n.3. *See also*
self-interest
inventions (inventor), 13, 21, 23, 31–32, 34–
35, 76, 107, 176, 185, 192, 244–45,
292n.3, 306n.20, 306n.22
invisible hand, 5, 10, 44–45, 96, 108, 111,
148–42, 239–40, 276, 297n.11, 297n.13,
298n.17, 298n.3
Irwin, Terrence, 286n.6

Jefferson, Thomas, 198
judgment, 1, 7, 12–13, 16, 23–24, 26, 28,
32–33, 36, 40, 43–46, 49–54, 63, 65–66,
72–73, 81, 97, 105, 129, 132, 147, 153,
162, 166, 168, 187, 189–90, 205, 216, 231,
233, 235, 238–39, 241, 243, 247–48, 280,
284n.16, 287n.10, 288n.32, 290nn.17–18,
294n.7, 296n.19, 302n.9
judiciary, 243, 272
Julius Caesar, 255
jurisprudence, 16, 31, 39, 48, 64, 80, 119,
145–48, 153, 155, 157–61, 164–65, 169–
78, 188–189, 192, 198–201, 209, 212–13,
217–18, 299n.5, 303n.28, 304n.30,
307n.29; "natural" jurisprudence, 145–47,
155, 161, 164–65, 169–71, 173–74, 188,
200, 303n.28

justice, 1, 5–6, 8–9, 44–49, 51, 54–55, 66–
67, 70–74, 79, 82, 88, 92–94, 98, 102,
107, 112, 118–20, 123, 139, 145–226,
229–30, 233–35, 241, 251, 253, 257, 264–
65, 269, 272–73, 290n.19, 290n.22,
291n.30, 294n.4, 298n.2, 298n.4, 299n.9,
299n.11, 299n.13, 299n.15, 300nn.17–28,
300nn.22–23, 301n.1, 304n.29, 307n.25,
307n.27, 307n.30, 308n.1, 310n.28; as a
moral virtue, 9, 45, 47, 49, 72–73, 145,
149, 151, 154, 158, 164, 168; attributive
justice, 211–12, 306n.21; commutative justice, 149, 157, 200, 212–13, 215; corrective
justice, 209–10; distributive justice, 1, 19,
57, 75, 80, 86, 99–100, 108, 110, 113,
132–34, 137, 145, 149, 179, 196–98, 200–
26, 234, 265, 274, 301n.2, 303n.23,
304nn.1–2, 304n.30, 304n.31, 307n.26,
312n.21; enforceability of, 45, 79, 148–50,
153–57, 165, 168–69, 200, 203, 211–13,
215–20; expletive justice, 211; "natural" justice, 146–47, 153, 159, 161, 165–69,
298n.4; precision of, 145, 149–58, 161–68,
173, 198, 301n.1; universal justice, 159,
209
just price. *See* price

Kames, Henry Home, Lord, 299n.11
Kamtekar, Rachana, 2, 295n.14
Kant, Immanuel, 3, 26, 34, 61, 71, 74, 76,
102, 116, 164–65, 168, 190, 284n.16,
289n.4, 289n.11, 290n.24, 300n.20
Kaye, F. B., 292n.8
Keynes, Maynard, 296n.1
Kierkegaard, Søren, 5, 283n.2, 289n.3
Kindleberger, C. K., 265, 311n.11
Kolakowska, Agnieszka, 305n.8
Korsgaard, Christine, 296n.22
Kramnick, Isaac, 303n.24
Kuhn, Thomas, 32

Labor Theory of Value, 124–31
laissez-faire, 204, 250, 265, 273
language, speech, 3, 20, 23, 25, 29, 45, 52–
53, 71, 73, 78, 89, 91–94, 132, 148, 153,
167, 170–71, 182, 184, 188, 193, 199, 211,
264, 270, 284n.18, 285–6n.1, 286n.5,
287n.18, 293n.13, 294n.11, 294n.21,
296nn.2–3, 297n.6
Law, John, 16
law, 7–8, 10, 15, 18, 20–21, 25–26, 28–30,
32, 38–39, 45, 55, 64, 70–71, 79–80, 87,
89, 94, 96, 99, 139, 145–49, 151–55, 157,

308n.2, 309n.10, 309n.12, 310n.21, 312n.15
Pollock, Jackson, 117
pollution. *See* Environmental Protection
positivism, 49, 54, 63
poverty, 10, 12, 14, 39, 40, 42, 54, 56, 68, 76, 79–80, 89, 97, 104–12, 114, 118–20, 128, 130, 132–33, 137–38, 140–41, 145–46, 151, 157, 160–61, 171, 173, 192, 194, 196–97, 201–2, 205–9, 211–26, 236, 229, 234, 237, 239, 241–42, 247–48, 255, 263–66, 269, 274–75, 288n.29, 292n.7, 294n.4, 295n.13, 301n.2, 301n.4, 303n.22, 303n.27, 304n.3, 304n.32, 305n.6, 305nn.4–9, 305n.13, 306n.15, 306n.18, 306nn.14–15, 307n.25, 308n.33, 308n.2
Pownall, Thomas, 307n.31
price: equilibrium price, 124, 254, 297; just price, 54, 123–24, 296n.3; market price, 38, 54, 123–24, 132, 297n.4; natural price, 18, 123–24, 130, 132, 296n.3, 296n.4, 297n.4; nominal price, 18, 124–31; real price, 18, 123, 124–31, 284n.19
Price, Richard, 201, 264, 307n.23
Priestley, Joseph, 35
primogeniture, 7–8, 25, 54, 79, 147, 159, 170–71, 198, 249, 298n.4, 300n.19
private sector, 236–42, 277, 280
productive labor, 110, 134–38, 251, 292n.6, 297n.10
property rights. *See* rights
prostitutes, 40, 159
Providence, Providentialism, 44–45, 71, 108, 100–11, 137–40, 206, 290n.19, 297n.13, 306n.15, 308n.1
Ptolemy, 32
public good (versus particular good), 47, 63, 96–97, 99, 142, 230, 237, 240–41, 249
public spirit, 66, 96, 98–99. *See also* Love of Country
Pufendorf, Samuel, 16, 65, 96, 150, 211–14, 298n.3, 299n.13, 302nn.12–13
punishment, 9, 15, 45, 73, 84, 148–49, 151, 154–55, 158, 160, 166, 169, 171, 240, 253, 280, 299n.13, 300n.19, 301n.1

Quesnay, François, 2, 37

Racine, 12
Rand, Ayn, 91, 229
Randolph, Thomas Mann, 303n.25
Rapaczynski, Andrei, 284n.15

Raphael, David, 283n.2, 299n.11
Rashid, Salim, 310n.1
Rational Choice Theory, 64, 272
Rawls, John, 225, 298n.2, 300n.16
real price. *See* price
Redman, Deborah, 287n.16, 287n.19
Reid, Thomas, 1, 22–23, 200, 285nn.25–26, 285n. 28
relativism, 52–53, 64, 119, 169
religion, 10, 53, 70–72, 163, 165, 204, 206, 229, 289n.1, 290nn.18–19. *See also* Christianity
religious freedom. *See* freedom
republicanism, 96, 232, 246–49, 250, 266, 279, 310n.20, 310n.27
resentment, 45, 67, 71–74, 82, 98, 149, 151–52, 155–57, 160–65, 175, 181, 191, 299n.9, 300n.19
Revolution, American, 197, 247
Revolution, French, 198, 201, 204, 213–14, 245, 264–65, 293n.18, 306n.23
Riccoboni, Marie Jeanne de Heurles Laboras de Mezieres, 12
Richardson, Samuel, 12
right of necessity, 209, 213, 215–20, 307n.26, 307n.29, 307n.30. *See also* rights
rights, 96, 102, 145–46, 151, 153, 157, 175–76, 178–82, 186–88, 191–93, 195, 197–98, 200–1, 203, 207–8, 212, 214–17, 219, 221–22, 225–26, 247, 254, 275, 284n.15, 298n.4, 301n.5, 301n.8, 302nn.12–13, 303n.27, 304n.29; imperfect rights, 153, 200, 211–12, 306n.22; perfect rights, 150, 153, 211–12, 214, 301n.6, 306n.22; property rights, 145, 152–53, 163, 165, 171–72, 174–202, 209, 211, 213, 215–17, 220–26, 301n.1, 301n.6, 302n.11, 303n.18, 303n.19, 307n.30
Robbins, Lionel, 293n.20, 296n.1
Rosenberg, Nathan, 39, 288n.27, 298n.15, 309n.14
Ross, Ian, 2, 292n.34, 310n.1
Rothko, Mark, 117
Rothschild, Emma, 236, 238, 264, 284n.14, 288n.33, 293n.19, 297n.11, 297n.13, 307n.23
Rousseau, Jean-Jacques, 69, 96, 107, 109, 114, 210, 213, 224, 246, 248–49, 289n.13, 294n.5, 307n.25, 310n.23

Samuels, Warren, 293n.20
Saussure, Ferdinand de, 293
"savages," 80, 133, 251, 288n.1

Townsend, Joseph, 305n.5

tradition, 35, 54, 100, 106, 117, 141, 151,
157, 165, 172, 174, 176–77, 179, 200–1,
204, 206, 209, 211–14, 218, 221, 226, 229,
243, 246, 253, 263, 272–73, 279, 289n.7,
294n.4, 298n.2, 304n.30, 306n.18,
307n.29, 311n.5

tranquility, 5, 65, 68, 78, 81, 105–6, 113–14.
See also happiness

Trattner, Walter, 305n.7, 312n.17

Trout, J. D., 303n.23

Tuck, Richard, 222, 308n.32

Turgot, Anne-Robert-Jacques, baron de l'Aulne,
302n.15, 308n.31

Turnbull, Colin, 273

Twombly, Cy, 117

unemployment, 111, 126, 137–38, 140, 156,
201, 205, 208, 224, 235, 248, 270–71,
275–78, 280, 312n.20

United States, 16, 49, 53, 80–81, 86, 131,
170, 193, 197, 231–32, 244–45, 247, 252,
263, 266, 269, 277, 279, 288n.1, 292n.2,
293n.13, 293n.19, 309n.17, 311n.4

universal justice. *See* justice

unproductive labor, 110, 134–38, 251,
297n.10

utilitarianism, 47, 178–79, 52, 54, 57, 69,
145, 172, 178–80, 190, 246, 298n.2,
301n.23, 308n.8

utility, 9, 52–53, 69, 145, 172–73, 178–79,
192, 197, 199–200, 218, 225, 245–46,
289n.11, 301n.1, 301n.6, 301n.11,
301n.23, 308n.8

Utopia, Utopians, 65–66, 96, 245, 269,
289n.5, 293n.16

Value: absolute value, 123; in exchange (exchange value), 15, 92–93, 124–25, 128–30,
133, 135–36, 176, 178, 284n.19, 297n.6; in
use, 1, 128

Van Doesburg, Theo, 117

vanity, 75, 80, 104–20, 205, 207, 223, 229–
30, 252–53, 255, 291n.29, 292n.6

Velthuysen, Lambert van, 302n.13

vice, 48, 111, 206, 207, 229–33, 233–36, 274

virtue, 1, 4–5, 7, 9, 41, 46, 48–49, 52, 55–
56, 63, 66, 68, 70, 72–82, 84, 86, 88, 94,
96, 100, 102–3, 112–13, 115, 118, 120,
145–51, 153–56, 158, 164–66, 168, 176,
179, 190–91, 194, 200–1, 203, 209, 211,

213, 223, 225, 229, 231–33, 235–36, 240,
249–50, 252–54, 257, 267, 274, 283n.1,
288n.33, 289n.8, 290n.20, 290n.22,
290n.25, 291nn.29–30, 293n.19,
295nn.14–15, 298n.4, 298n.19, 300n.16,
300n.20, 304n.3, 306n.16, 306n.18,
308nn.1–2, 309n.12, 310n.27; amiable virtues, 44, 66, 86, 254; awful virtues, 44, 66,
86, 254

Voltaire, 12, 15, 70

Walzer, Michael, 273

war, 17, 55–56, 67, 101, 109, 147, 150, 152,
157, 198, 206, 222, 226, 229–31, 245,
250–57, 267, 292n.6, 301n.2, 303n.22,
306n.21, 307n.25, 307n.27, 307n.29,
310n.29

Waterman, Anthony, 139, 287n.13, 290n.18,
298n.15

Watt, James, 35, 245

Watts, Isaac, 206

wealth, 1, 3, 10, 17–19, 24, 29, 48, 56, 67,
73–74, 79, 84, 87, 91, 101, 104–15, 117–
18, 120, 137, 139–41, 145–46, 159, 161,
163, 197–98, 201, 204–7, 209, 214, 224,
235, 248, 251–52, 254–55, 257, 262–63,
272, 274–75, 280, 284nn.18–19, 286n.9,
287n.13, 288n.27, 288n.29, 288n.33,
289n.8, 290n.24, 294n.3, 294n.7, 309n.12,
311n.1

Wedderburn, Alexander, 290n.18, 309n.15

Wedgwood, Josiah, 97

Weinstien, Jack, 283n.2, 296n.2, 296n.3

Weintraub, Jeff, 2, 309n.10

Werhane, Patricia, 292n.10, 298n.1, 298n.15

Whigs, 246, 309n.19

Whitbread, Samuel, 264

Wildman, Sarah, 312n.16, 312n.19

Wilkes, John, 15

Willis, Kirk, 284n.21, 311nn.5–7, 310n.1

Wilson, Thomas, 292n.1, 311n.11

Winch, Donald, 200–1, 232, 249–50, 252–53,
264, 304n.31, 309n.19, 310n.27, 310n.29

Wittgenstein, Ludwig, 23, 27

Wollstonecraft, Mary, 264

Wood, Gordon, 293n.19

Xenophon, 4

Young, Arthur, 305n.13

Young, Jeffrey, 283n.3, 304n.30